Architectural
Formulas
Pocket
Reference

Architectural
Formulas
Pocket
Reference

Robert Brown Butler

McGraw-Hill

New York   Chicago   San Francisco   Lisbon   London
Madrid   Mexico City   Milan   New Delhi   San Juan
Seoul   Singapore   Sydney   Toronto

Copyright 2002 by The McGraw-Hill Companies, Inc. All rights re-
served. Printed in Canada. Except as permitted under the United
States Copyright Act of 1976, no part of this publication may be
reproduced or distributed in any form or by any means, or stored
in a data base or retrieval system, without the prior written per-
mission of the publisher.

1 2 3 4 5 6 7 8 9 0   1WBC/1WBC   6 5 4 3 2 1 0

Library of Congress Cataloging-in-Publication Data

Butler, Robert Brown
Architectural Formulas Pocket Reference
ISBN 0-07-137036-6

*This book's sponsoring editor was first, Wendy Lochner, sec-
ond, Larry Hager, and third, Cary Sullivan. The editing supervisor was Steven Melvin, and the production supervisor was
Sherri Souffrance. The book's text and headers were set in
BuQuet, BuHB, BuMonde, and BuLwark, all typefaces designed
by Robert Brown Butler, and the book itself was designed and
formatted by Robert Brown Butler. The book was printed and
bound by Webcom Ltd.*

McGraw-Hill books are available at quantity discounts to use
as premiums and sales promotions, or for use in educational
and corporate training programs. For more information write
to the Director of Special Sales, McGraw-Hill, Two Penn Plaza,
New York, NY 10121-2298. Or contact your local bookstore.

This book was printed on recycled acid-free paper containing
a minimum of 50% recycled de-inked fiber.

Studies in algebra, in geometry, in mechanics characterize teaching directed towards the essential and the functional in contrast to the apparent. One learns to look behind the facade, to grasp the root of things, to recognize the undercurrents, the antecedents of the visible.

Paul Klee
Dessau
1929

About the Author

Robert Brown Butler is a registered architect
and a widely respected author. He has more
than forty years' experience in architecture,
which includes a B. Arch from Cornell in 1964,
12 years' experience in construction,
and many years' work in architectural
offices in Georgia, California,
Colorado, and New York.
This is Mr. Butler's sixth
book on architecture.

CONTENTS

2. WOOD 55

CONTENTS

CONTENTS

5. MASONRY   271

6.   OTHER STRUCTURE   285

7.   CLIMATE CONTROL   301

CONTENTS

CONTENTS

9. ELECTRICAL   423

10. ILLUMINATION   441

11. ACOUSTICS   469

12. DESIGN   485

A. USEFUL FORMULAS 503

PREFACE

In this age of computers no larger than the palm of your hand, and telephones hardly larger than your thumb, an architectural engineering designer could make good use of a pocket-sized volume of this profession's "formulas and nothing but the formulas." A little volume stripped of all but the barest text required to utilize its algebra —which one could take anywhere, and use at any time, in any place, in any kind of architectural scenario, with any kind of person who may need your counsel. This book, no bigger than the inside of a jacket pocket, easily satisfies this need.

However, this little collection of formulas, so streamlined in its brevity, was distilled from a reserve of knowledge that was far more vast. For its origin was a two-volume compendium of architectural engineering knowledge, written by this author, that encompasses nearly 1,600 pages, with each page being more than twice the size of this one. However, a thin thread of simplicity runs through those larger volumes that not only makes this volume possible but obvious: the earlier volumes' then-newly-devised format for sizing virtually any functional component in a building: the "recipe" approach, wherein each formula is followed by a brief menu of its unknowns in a manner that is as simple and easy to follow as the recipes in a cookbook. And in this book those earlier recipes, which themselves were distillations of much larger reserves of knowledge, have been further refined, perhaps to their ultimate degree of conciseness and accessibility. Indeed, the more a work of this kind sweeps aside all other information and hones in on the simple, unique nature of each unknown, the more quickly comprehensible each such variable becomes —which for the experienced professional can be the most precious kind of knowledge.

It is also relevant to mention this book's two parents for another reason. Since it would take many more of these small pages to cite all the sources and describe all the derivations of the more than 1,300 formulas found herein, it is wiser merely to redirect one's efforts to locate the sources and derivations of this volume's algebra to those two larger volumes, *Mechanical Systems: Architectural Engineering Design*, and *Structural Systems, Architectural Engineering Design*, each of which lists in detail its great variety of sources and contains a lengthy appendix of its formulas' derivations. For in fact, no new knowledge has entered between the covers of this book that wasn't already long at rest between the covers of those two parent volumes.

However, even those ancestral volumes have a parent —of which this book is a mere grandchild: *The Standard Handbook of Architectural Engineering*, written by this author and published by McGraw-Hill in 1998. It is relevant to mention this progenitor because the very first paragraph of its preface so concisely defines the scope of all its later issue that it should be recited here *in toto*:

Beneath a building's aura of aesthetics and stylized motifs lies an assembly of functional parts. And each part must have the proper size. If too small, it may fail under stress; if too large, money is wasted. This is true for every functional conponent —beam, post, base, pipe, wire, light, duct, batt, hinge, or nail— in every building, from shed to skyscraper, anywhere in the world.

So there you have it. A subject as universally vast as all the functional components of all the buildings in the world —distilled, first, to a thick volume for general designers, then further distilled to a pair of thick volumes for engineering specialists; and now distilled to the smallest, most symbolic representation of the hundreds of physical forces that shape buildings that may house thousands of people; so that anyone owning such knowledge —or yearning to own it— may access it quickly and concisely in the most evanescantly mobile manner.

So for you, your colleagues and your clients, may your use of this little book be a foretaste of the joy of its results.

The author takes extreme pleasure in acknowledging those who assisted him in preparing this volume. First are the book's three sponsoring editors at McGraw-Hill, Wendy Lochner, Larry Hager, and Cary Sullivan; then Steven Melvin, the book's Senior Editing Supervisor. Deserving acknowledgees who reside closer to the author's refuge are Harry Wirtz, computer graphics consultant; Duane Degutis, computer technician; and the author's wife, Janis Y. Butler.

TABLE 1-1: WEIGHTS OF CONSTRUCTION MATERIALS

CONSTRUCTION	Weight, psf of surface area

Wood joists 16" o.c. w/ ½" sheath'g: 2×10s , 8; 2×12s   10
Metal joists 16" o.c.: JW-10×14, 5; JWE 12×12 .... 8.5
Reinf. concrete slab, unfinished, per in. t 12.5
Concrete slab on metal deck, 2½" t, 40; 4"t 50
Flexicore, 6", unfin. floor, 42; lightweight conc. 35
Stairways: wood, 20–25; steel, 40–50; conc. 80–95
Floor finishes: ½" plywood, linoleum, cork, vinyl tile 1.5
   ⁵⁄₈" plywood + W/W carpet w/ underlayment 3
   1¹⁄₈" plywood, 3.4; 1" nom. hardwood, 4; 1" slate .. 15
   2" nom. T & G, 4; ceramic or terra cotta tile 12
   Underfloor raceways, 4–7; metal raised floors   6–14
Stud walls, wood: 2×4s 16" o.c., 3; 2×4s 16" o.c. 6
  Metal 2×4s 16" o.c., 2; 2×6s 16" o.c. 4
  Above w/ ½" sheath'g, +1.5; w/ drywall per side ..... +3
  w/ double drywall 2S, 10.5; w/ plaster per side ..... +8
Conc. block wall (cav. void): 4", 30; 8", 55; 12" 85
Above w/ cavities grouted: 8", 90; 10", 115; 12" 140
Brick walls: NW: 4", 34; 8", 72; 12" 108
  MW: 4", 39; 8", 81; 12", 125; SW: 4", 46; 8" 96
Masonry veneers/facings: 2", 32; 4" 50–55
Wood paneling, 2.5; wood siding, 5.5; wood shingles .. 3
4" glass blk, 18; ¼" pl. glass, 3.3; gl. curtain wall 10–15
Plaster on metal lath, per surface 8.5
Ceramic tile veneer, per surface 18
Insulation: batts, per 4" t, 1.0; foam boards, per " t 0.2
Wood rafters 16" o.c. w/ ½" sheath'g: 2×10s, 10; 2×12s 12
Lightwt. wood trusses, 3–5; open web steel joists 4–15
Sprinkler systems (per lf): 1" dry, 2; 1" wet 2.5
  2" dry, 4; 2" wet, 6; 3" dry, 8; 3" wet, 12; 4" dry 12
  4" wet, 18; 6" dry, 21, 6" wet 33
Ceiling fin.: acoustic fiber, 1; ½" drywall 2.2; ⁵⁄₈" dw 2.8
Suspended ceiling, metal w/ acoustic tile 1.8
Ceiling raceways, incl. header, laterals, whips, fixt. 5–6
Roof finishes: corrug. galv. steel, 12 ga, 4.9; 18 ga, 2.4
Shingles: wood 1" thick, 3; asphalt 2; copper or tin .. 2

1. STRUCTURAL BASICS

Dead Loads: $W_D = A_1\omega_1 + A_2\omega_2 + ... + A_Z\omega_Z$

W_D = total dead load supported by structure, lb
A_1 = surface area of const. supported by structure, sf
ω_1 = unit weight of const. supported by structure, psf

Live Load Reduction, Floors:

Step 1. Find the live load reduction from

    a. $R = 0.08\,A$ **b.** $R = 40\%$
    c. $R = 23.1\left(1 + \omega_D/\omega_L\right)$

R = allowable live load reduction, %. Min. value governs. Reductions are not allowed for public assembly areas or where live loads ≥ 100 psf.
A = area of floor supporting live load, sf
ω_D = uniform unit dead load on floor area, psf
ω_L = uniform unit live load on floor area, psf

Step 2. Compute the structure's total safe unit load.

$$\omega_T = \omega_D + 0.01\,\omega_L(100 - R)$$

ω_T = total safe unit load on floor area, psf
ω_D = uniform unit live load on floor area, psf

ω_L = uniform unit dead load on floor area, psf
R = minimum live load reduction, from Step 1, %

Live Load Reduction, Roofs:

	Roof area (horiz. proj.), ft²		
Roof slope	0-200	201-600	600+
Flat up to 4 in/ft	20	16	12
4 to 12 in/ft	16	14	12
More than 12 in/ft	12	12	12
Greenhouse or lath roofs	10	10	10

Live Load Reduction, Snow:

$$\omega_{RS} = \kappa_G \, \omega_S + 35 \, H - 0.025 \, (\Delta - 20) \, (\omega_S - 20)$$

ω_{RS} = reduced allowable unit snow load for roof, psf
κ_G = gable roof factor. If roof is gable or other pyramidal profile, $\kappa_G = 1.2$. If roof is shed, inclined, or flat, $\kappa_G = 1.0$.

TABLE 1-2: ALLOWABLE LIVE LOADS

OCCUPANCY	Uniform Load, psf
Uninhabitable attics	20
Catwalks, upper floors and attics in dwellings	30
Residences, classrooms, hotel/motel rms, rest rms ...	40
Conference rooms, offices, private car garages	50
Dorms, school labs, libraries, assembly w/ fixed seats	60
Bowling alleys, retail upper floor, light mfg.	75
Public corridors, storage attics, telephone closets ..	80
Entrance lobbies, ballrooms, gyms, stairs, retail ...	100
Light industrial, office files, stage areas, platforms	125
Armories, bakeries, comm'l kitchens, library stacks	150
Heavy storage, service docks, walks	250
Floors w/ movable wall partitions .... add 20 psf	
Swimming pools .... 65 lb per ft of depth/ft²	

ω_S = safe snow load for flat roofs, psf. $\omega_S \geq 20$ psf.
H = potential height of any snow buildup at valleys, parapets, offsets, and roof steps, etc., ft. This is a partial load on the roof span.
$\varDelta$ = slope of roof, °. Roof must slope at least 20°.

Impact Loads, Equivalent Weight:

$$P_I \kappa_e = P(1 + v_I)$$

P_I = equiv. weight of impact load as normal load, lb
κ_e = elastic factor depending on structural material. $\kappa_e = 1.50$ for steel, 1.65 for wood, 1.10 for concrete or masonry if slab on grade, 1.05 for concrete or masonry if not slab on grade.
P = actual weight of impact load, lb
v_I = velocity of moving load at impact, fps. If v of load is in mph, v_I fps = $1.47 \times v$ mph; if load is a falling object, $v_I = 8 H^{0.5}$ fps.

Impact Loads, Structural Design:

Step 1. Find the minimum section modulus for each structural member below.

$$(1 + v_I) L P_I = \kappa f_y S$$

v_I = velocity of load at impact, fps.
  $v_{I\text{-}fps} = 1.47 \ v_{I\text{-}mph} = 8 H^{0.5}$ ft.
L = length of span, in.
P_I = actual weight of impact load, lb
κ = span factor, 8 for simple spans with rigid supports, 4 for simple spans with nonrigid supports, 1 for cantilevers
f_y = yield stress of structural material, psi
S = section modulus of structural section, in³

Step 2. From reference data, select a structural member whose section modulus ≥ the value found above.

Inertial Loads: $P_i = \kappa_m P$

P_i = equivalent weight of inertial load against support, horizontal or vertical, lb

κ_m = moving load capacity increase factor, based on type of Inertial load as described below:

Load	Capacity increase factor
Pendant-operated craneways, similar supports	1.10
Motor-driven machinery & supports	1.20
Cab-operated craneways, overhead runways ...	1.25
Hangers that support floors & balconies	1.33
Reciprocating machinery	1.50
Elevator supports & cables	2.00
Impact loads	see page 29

P = actual weight of moving load, lb

Torque or Torsion Loads:

$$T = 0.0284 f_o \delta^3$$

T = maximum torque force allowed to turn bolt, ft-lb
f_o = maximum unit torsion stress for bolt steel, psi
δ = bolt diameter, in.

Wind Velocity vs. Pressure:

$$P = 0.0033 \, v^2 \cos \angle$$

P = wind pressure, psf
v = wind velocity, mph. 1 mph = 1.47 fps.
$\angle$ = angle from vertical, if any, of wind load area, °

Wind Velocity vs. Glazing Thickness:

$$90,000 \, t \geq A^{0.8} \, (\upsilon \, \kappa_g)^{1.6}$$

t = minimum thickness of glazing, in.
A = surface area of glazing, vertical projection, sf.
   L/W ratio of glazing area must be ≤ 3.
υ = maximum local wind velocity, mph.
κ_g = glazing coefficient, based on type of glazing:

Type of glazing	κ_g
Tempered glass	0.25
Heat-strengthened glass	0.50
Double glazing, $A \geq 30$ sf	0.56
Double glazing (t = total pane thickness)	0.67
Float, sheet, or plate glass	1.00
Laminated glass, total t	2.00
Sandblasted or etched glass	2.50

Wind Load Amplification: Wind is a pulsing force
that can "push" and "pull" on an exposed architectural
detail until the fatigued material fails. Thus a wind moment amplification factor should be added to any structure that may support a wind load according to

$$\kappa_a = \frac{250 \, W}{(250 \, W - L)}$$

κ_a = wind moment amplification factor added to normal
   structural load.
W = wind load against building facade: unit wind load
   (psf) × height of load against each column (ft) ×
   width of load against each column (ft), lb or kips
L = length of beam connecting to top of column in direction opposing wind load W, in.

Wind Height Adjustment: Wind velocities are typically measured 30 ft above the ground. Thus if a building is more than about 50 ft high its design wind load should be increased. A building's height is measured from the lowest exposed portion of its base.

$$300\,P \geq v^2\,(0.033\,h)^{0.143}$$

P = effective pressure of wind due to height above ground, psf.

v = max. wind velocity, from local climatic data, mph

h = height of building, measured from lowest elevation of base to peak of roof, ft

Note: In above formula multiply P by 1.15 for each of the following onsite conditions that may exist:

1. Importance factor if the building is a hospital, fire or police station, disaster center, etc. to be used as a haven during a major wind event.
2. If the shape's height-to-width ratio exceeds 5 (i.e. tanks, solid towers, large chimneys, etc.)
3. If the building faces winds blowing across lakes, oceans, rivers, or other large bodies of water.
4. If the building is more than 60 ft high and is near where winds funnel into narrow areas.

Wind Facade Force: A strong wind can push a building's windward facade as if it were the leaf of a huge hinge whose pin lays horizontally along the facade's base. Every building must resist this primary wind load from any direction. As the building's strength depends on the material its structure is made of, this force is covered in Wood, Wood Bracing Design, page 88; Steel, Bracing, page 138; and Concrete, Bracing Design, page 247.

Wind Seam Shear: A strong wind blowing against the long wall of a narrow building can push the top of the long wall against the tops of its end walls which can shear the end walls from the roof above. This shear is resisted by the building's connections between the tops of its end walls and the roof above as designed below.

Step 1. Find the wind load against the building.

$$W = A\,P$$

W = maximum wind force against exposed facade (vertical projection), lb

A = area of exposed facade, vertical projection, (ignore minor areas as chimneys, etc.), sf

P = maximum local wind pressure, psf

Step 2. Determine the seam shear along seam $A\,B$.

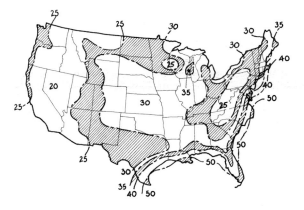

Fig. 1-1. Wind load map.

$$W = L\,\eta\,b\,V$$

W = total wind force acting on seam (horiz. proj.), lb
L = length of seam, in.
η = number of seams in building
b = width of seam stress area, in.
V = maximum seam shear along line AB, psi

Step 3. Check the construction at seam AB for safety.

Wind Pier Rigidity: A strong wind blowing against a building facade with large openings can topple the piers between the openings. This force is resisted by each pier's rigidity as designed below.

Step 1. Compute the rigidity of each pier in the facade.

$$\nabla = 20/[3\,h/_w + (h/_w)^3]$$

∇ = relative rigidity of each pier
h = unbraced height of each pier, in.
w = width of each pier in direction of load, in.

Step 2. Determine the safe horizontal force that can be resisted by each pier due to its rigidity. Each part of the structure must independently resist this load to avoid progressive collapse of the building.

$$F = W\nabla/(\nabla_a + \ldots + \nabla_z)$$

F = safe horizontal force against top of each pier, lb
W = total wind force acting at tops of all piers, lb
∇ = relative rigidity of each pier, from Step 1

Step 3. Investigate the pier cross-sections for shear.

$$W = v\,A$$

W = total wind force against tops of all piers, lb

v = actual unit shear in all piers, psi. Compute this value, then compare it with the safe shear for the type of construction material used.

A = total section area of all piers, in^2

Step 4. Check each pier for deflection, the reciprocal of rigidity as found in Step 1. The least value governs.

$$\Delta_{allow} = {}^1/_\nabla \leq 0.00417\,h$$

Δ = allowable deflection of each pier. In multi-pier walls, if half the piers are safe in deflection the whole wall is safe.

∇ = relative rigidity of each pier

h = unbraced height of each pier, in.

Wind Uplift Force:
When a wind blows over a building it creates a partial vacuum above which pulls the roof upward. This can destroy light buildings with large roofs with low pitches. Common loci of failure are roof-to-wall seams and wall-to-foundation seams.

Step 1. Compute the uplift load on the structural seam.

$$W_\blacklozenge = 1.25\,\kappa_u\,A\,P$$

$W_\blacklozenge$ = wind uplift load due to horizontal wind force at base of structural seam, lb

κ_u = wind load uplift factor. κ_u = 1.0 if bldg. is on level terrain, 1.25 if on a rise, 1.5 if bldg. ht. $\geq$ 80 ft.

P = maximum local unit wind pressure, psf.

Step 2. Find the structural seam's resisting strength.

$$R = W + C$$

R = total resisting strength of structural seam, lb

W = total weight of construction above seam, lb

C = strength of each connector in seam, lb

Step 3. Compare the structural seam's uplift load with its resisting strength.

Step 4. Design a stronger seam connection if necessary.

Wind Overturning Force:

A strong wind blowing against a tall, thin, or light building can turn the building over. This rotational force is resisted by the building's weight plus the withdrawal resistance of anchor bolts, tie-downs, or other connectors that hold the building to its foundation on its windward side.

Step 1. Find the facade force against the building's maximum exposure.

$$W = 0.0033 \, A \, v^2$$

W = total wind load against facade (vert. proj.), lb
A = total area of exposed facade, sf. Ignore minor projections but include roof.
v = maximum local wind velocity, mph. If surrounding terrain is rugged, multiply v by 1.3.

Step 2. Find the withdrawal force on the anchor bolts along the bottom of the windward facade, usually by taking moments about a pivot point P.

$$F_{cc1} M_{cc1} + \ldots + F_{ccZ} M_{ccZ} = F_{c1} M_{c1} + \ldots + F_{cZ} M_{cZ}$$

F_{cc1} = 1st force acting counterclockwise around ₵ of moments at P, lb.
M_{cc1} = moment arm of F_{cc1}, ft
F_{c1} = 1st force acting clockwise around ₵ of moments at P, lb
M_{c1} = moment arm of F_{c1}, ft
F_{c2} = 2nd force acting clockwise around P, lb

M_{c2} = moment arm of F_{c2}, ft

Step 3. Size the connectors along the foundation of the facade with the most exposure.

$$V_\bullet \leq v_\bullet \, (|L/S| + 1)$$

$V_\bullet$ = safe withdrawal strength of all connectors located in a row along ₵ of moments, lb. If anchor bolts are used, each must be at least $\frac{1}{2}$ in. diameter and extend at least 7 in. into reinforced concrete and 15 in. into unreinforced masonry.
$v_\bullet$ = safe withdrawal strength of each connector, psi
L = length of row of connectors, ft
S = safe spacing of connectors along row, ft

Structural Systems: Every structural member must satisfy three physical laws:

1. The sum of all vertical loads and reactions in a member or system equals zero; or $\Sigma V = 0$.
2. The sum of all horizontal loads and reactions in a member or system equals zero; or $\Sigma H = 0$.
3. The sum of all moments, clockwise and counter-clockwise, about any point equals zero; or $\Sigma M = 0$.

   Structural members with slopes $\leq 45°$ are treated as horizontal structure while those whose slope $\geq 45°$ are treated as vertical structure. Isolated forces acting obliquely to horizontal or vertical are *vectors*.

Beam Vertical and Horizontal Shear:

$$V_{max} = \boxed{V?}$$

V_{max} = maximum vertical shear of span due to load, lb
$\boxed{V?}$ = applicable vertical shear formula

VERTICAL SHEAR FORMULAS:

Rectangular sections:	$V_v = 0.67 f_v b d$
Steel W, M, or C sections:	$V_v = 0.91 f_v t_w d$
Steel Tee sections:	$V_v = 0.71 f_v b d$
Circular sections:	$V_v = 0.59 f_v d$

HORIZONTAL SHEAR FORMULAS:

Rectangular sections:	$V_h = 0.5 f_h b L_h$
Steel W, M, or C sections:	$V_h = 0.5 f_h t_w L_h$
Steel Tee sections:	$V_h = 0.5 f_h b L_h$
Circular sections:	$V_h = 0.5 f_h d L_h$
Connections:	$V_h = f_h b L_h$

V_v = maximum vertical shear, lb
f_v = safe unit stress in vertical shear, psi
V_h = maximum horizontal shear, lb
f_h = safe unit stress in horizontal shear, psi
b = width of vertical or horizontal shear plane, in.
t_w = web thickness of W, M, or C steel shape, in.
d = depth or diameter of vertical shear plane, in.
L_h = length of horizontal shear plane, in.

Beam Bending Moment: M_{max} = 🅜❓

M_{max} = max. moment of span due to applied load, in-lb
🅜❓ = applicable beam bending moment formula

Maximum Beam Moment, Multiple Loads:

$$M_{max} = 🅜❓_1 + 🅜❓_2 + ... + 🅜❓_Z$$

M_{max} = maximum moment due to total applied load, in/lb
🅜❓ $_1$, 🅜❓ $_2$, etc. = applicable beam bending moment formulas for each partial load

Beam Deflection: $\Delta_{max} = \boxed{D?} \leq \kappa_\Delta L$

Δ_{max} = maximum deflection of beam span due to load, in.
$\boxed{D?}$ = applicable deflection formula for beam load
κ_Δ = coeff. of allowable deflection, in/in. of span
L = total length of span, in.

Beam Camber Design: $\Delta_c = 0.0104\,L$

Δ_c = min. camber of beam (crown ht. above ends), in.
L = total length of span, in.

Moment of Inertia: $I = \boxed{I?}$

I = moment of inertia of geometric section
$\boxed{I?}$ = applicable moment of inertia formula.

Moment of Inertia of Built-up Sections:

$$I = (\boxed{I?}_1 + ... + \boxed{I?}_y) - (\boxed{I?}_2 - ... - \boxed{I?}_z)$$

$\boxed{I?}_1$, $\boxed{I?}_y$, etc. = moment of inertia formula for each
built-up partial section area in total section

TABLE 1-3: ALLOWABLE BEAM DEFLECTIONS

TYPE OF LOAD	Coeff. of allow. deflection, in/in.
Industrial or utilitarian roof beams	1/180 = 0.00556
Concrete beams: initial Δ due to live load	1/180 = 0.00556
Initial Δ due to dead load	1/360 = 0.00278
Long-term Δ due to live & dead load	1/240 = 0.00416
Wood I-joists	1/480 = 0.00208
Live load plus impact load	1/640 = 0.00156
Other beams w/ plaster/drywall on underside	1/360 = 0.00278
No plaster/drywall on underside	1/240 = 0.00416
If beam often supports large irreg. loads	multiply above by 1.18
If ponding could occur on roofs	multiply above by 2.0

TABLE 1-4: PROPERTIES OF GEOMETRIC SECTIONS

SECTION	C-S area, A	Section Modulus, S	Moment of Inertia, I
	b = width of section; d = depth of section		
SQUARE: Axis of moments thro' center	d^2	$0.17\,d^3$	$0.083\,d^4$
SQUARE: Axis of moments thro' base	d^2	$0.33\,d^3$	$0.33\,d^4$
RECTANGLE: Axis of mom. thro' center	bd	$0.17\,bd^2$	$0.083\,bd^3$
RECTANGLE: Axis of mom. thro' base	bd	$0.33\,bd^2$	$0.33\,bd^3$
CIRCLE: Axis of moments thro' center	$0.785\,d^2$	$0.0982\,d^3$	$0.0491\,d^4$
RECTANGLE: Axis of mom. thro' diagonal	bd	$\dfrac{0.17\,b^2 d^2}{(b^2 + h^2)^{0.5}}$	$\dfrac{0.17\,b^3 d^3}{(b^2 + h^2)}$
EQUIL. CROSS: Axis of mom. thro' center	$Bh + bH - bh$	$\dfrac{BH^3 + bh^3}{6H}$	$\dfrac{BH^4 + bh^4}{12H}$
REG. HEXAGON: Axis of mom. thro' center	$2.60\,b^2$	$0.683\,b^3$	$0.619\,b^4$
REG. OCTAGON: Axis of mom. thro' center	$2.41\,b^2$	$1.33\,b^3$	$1.38\,b^4$

$\blacksquare_z$, $\blacksquare_z$, etc. = moment of inertia formula for any removed areas in total section

Beam Bearing Area, Allowable Load:

$$P = a_a \, b_b \, f_c \sin \angle$$

P = maximum load reaction of beam resting on bearing area of its support, lb
a_a = length of beam resting on bearing area, in.
b_b = width of beam resting on bearing area, in.
f_c = safe compressive stress of material above or below seam, whichever stress is less, psi
$\angle$ = angle between beam and support, °

Columns: A column derives its strength from its section area, the ratio of its height to its least thickness
(*slenderness ratio*), and the rigidity of its connections
(*end condition factors*) to the structure above and below.
A column has four end condition factors as described below, and their various combinations have several values
known as *K Factors* which are listed in Table 1-5.

1. **Rotation fixed.** Structure-to-column connection
    is rigid so no hinging action of one against the
    other can occur.
2. **Rotation free.** Structure-to-column connection
    is flexible so a hinging action of one against the
    other can occur.
3. **Translation fixed.** The column's top is kept from
    moving laterally by the structure bearing against
    its side.
4. **Translation free.** The column's top can move later-
    ally because no structure bears against its sides.

Column Eccentric Loads:

$$V_a \, S_y = V_x \, e_x \, A$$

V_a = equivalent axial load on column in X axis, lb
S_y = section modulus of column about Y axis, in³
V_x = eccentric load on column in X axis, lb
e_x = eccentricity of load on column in X axis, in.
A = section area of column, in²

P-Delta Effect:
The total effect of all loads on a column or straight wall may cause its top to translate, which may convert a concentric load into an eccentric load, which may cause the structure's top to translate even further until it fails. This second-order translation force is the *P-Delta Effect*.

Individual members: $P_\Delta \approx 2.35 \, \kappa_i \, Z^{0.33}$
Structural systems: $b \, P_\Delta \approx 141 \, \kappa_i \, Z^{0.33}$

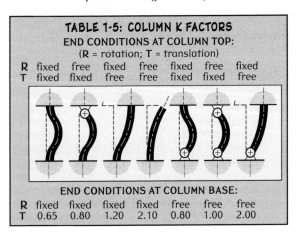

TABLE 1-5: COLUMN K FACTORS
END CONDITIONS AT COLUMN TOP:
(R = rotation; T = translation)

R	fixed	free	fixed	free	fixed	free	fixed
T	fixed	fixed	free	free	fixed	fixed	free

END CONDITIONS AT COLUMN BASE:

R	fixed	fixed	fixed	fixed	free	free	free
T	0.65	0.80	1.20	2.10	0.80	1.00	2.00

b = least plan dimension of total building, ft

P_Δ = P-Delta effect, a secondary load factor for vertical structure and bracing in a building. The higher the floor, the greater its P_Δ.

κ_i = wall frame instability coefficient, based on height of floor in building from the bar graph below:

```
◄──────── Building Height: Number of Floors ────────►
 2   4   6   8  10  15  20  25  30  35  40  45  50  55  60  65
├───┼───┼───┼──┼──┤┴┴┴┴┴┴┴┴┴┴┴┴┴┴┴┴┴┴┴┴┴┴┴┴┴┴┴┴┴┴┴┴┴┴┤
1.08 1.09 1.10 1.15  1.20    1.30 1.40 1.50 1.60  1.80   2.00
◄──────── Wall Frame Instability Coefficient, κᵢ ────────►
```

Z = seismic zone factor

Structural Bracing:

Bracing for vertical structure rigidifies connections between beams and columns and reduces their unbraced spans, thereby enabling them to be lighter, stiffer, and stronger. The most common vertical bracing unit is the *frame*, a usually rectangular area one story high and one bay wide that is bordered by a ceiling beam above, a floor beam below, and a column on each side. A *single-bay frame* has no columns within its module, a *multi-bay frame* has one or more columns within its module, and a *multi-story frame* is two or more floors high. A building is usually braced horizontally by its floors, whose rigid planes absorb lateral and torsion loads against the facades and distribute them evenly throughout the plans. The most common horizontal bracing is plywood sheathing on wood joists and reinforced concrete slabs.

All structural bracing connections must be designed to carry the full axial and shear forces carried by the connected members.

Structural Bracing Design, Braced Frames:

A braced frame is a single- or multi-bay frame made rigid by diagonal braces that typically form triangles with the frame's connected beams and columns.

Step 1. Compute the total lateral load acting on each frame in each story of the building. Half of each story load acts on the top of the frame and half on its bottom, then the load acting on the bottom frame is transferred to any frame below.

For each story: $W = 0.0033\ H_s\ L\ S^2$

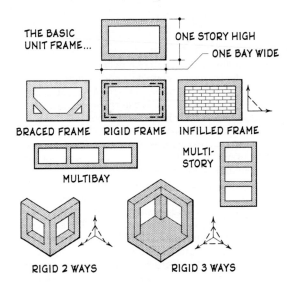

THE BASIC
UNIT FRAME...

ONE STORY HIGH

ONE BAY WIDE

BRACED FRAME   RIGID FRAME   INFILLED FRAME

MULTIBAY

MULTI-
STORY

RIGID 2 WAYS   RIGID 3 WAYS

Fig. 1-2. Types of structural bracing.

W = lateral wind load against frame, lb. This load creates two external forces against each frame in each story: an external *moment* (approximately half acting on the top of the frame and half acting on its bottom), and an external *shear* acting on the base of the frame of each story. As wind loads are reversible, these forces must be similarly resisted on both sides of the building.

H_s = height of frame in each story, ft

L = length of lateral wind load area $\perp$ to windstream, ft

S = maximum wind speed, mph.

Step 2. Sum the cumulative external shears for each story. This is done by adding the story shears downward through the building.

    a. Story T: $V_T = W$

    b. Story $T-1$: $V_{T-1} = W + W_{T-1}$

    ... ↓

    c. Story 1: $V_1 = W + W_{T-1} + ... + W_1$

V_T = cumulative external shear in top story, lb

V_{T-1} = cumulative external shear in story below, lb

W_{T-1} = lateral wind load in story below top story, from Step 1, lb

V_1 = cumulative external shear in story 1

    W and W_1 are as previously defined

Step 3. Find the lateral load due to moment on each brace at the top of the frame in each story by taking moments at the base of the upwind facade.

    a. Story T: $W_T L_T + W_{T-1} L_{T-1} = H_T B_T$

    b. Story $T-1$: $W_{T-1} L_{T-1} + W_{T-2} L_{T-2} = H_{T-1} B_{T-1}$

    ... ↑

    c. Story 1: $W_1 L_1 = H_1 B_1$

W_T = lateral wind load against frame of top story (vert. proj.), lb. If top story has a parapet above ceiling line, W_T includes force against parapet.

L_T = length of moment arm from ₵ of moments to ₵ of wind load, ft.

W_1, W_{T-1}, W_{T-2}, etc. = lateral wind load against frame of story 1 (vertical projection), lb.

L_1 = length of moment arm from ₵ of moments to ₵ of wind load W_1, ft

H_T = height from base of bldg to top of story 2, ft

B_T = lateral brace load at top of frame in story 2, lb

H_1 = height from base of bldg to top of story 1, ft

B_1 = lateral brace load at top of frame in story 1, lb

Step 4. Find the cumulative load due to moment on each brace in each story by adding the lateral brace loads up through the building's height to the floor being braced.

    a. Story T: $M_T = B_T + B_{T-1} + \cdots + B_1$
    b. Story T−1: $M_T = B_{T-1} + \cdots + B_1$
    ... ↓
    c. Story 1: $M_1 = B_1$

M_T = cumulative force due to moment on brace in story 2, lb

M_1 = cum. force due to moment on brace in story 1, lb

    B_T and B_1 are as previously defined

Step 5. Compute the total axial load on each brace in each story.

    a, b, c ... for each story: $P_s \cos \angle = P_\Delta (V_s + M_{bs})$

P_s = total axial load on each brace in each story, lb

$\angle$ = angle between intersecting braces and beams or frames, °

P_Δ = P-Delta effect for each story
$\qquad V_s = M_1$ and $M_{bs} = M_T$, all of which are
$\qquad$ previously defined

Step 6. Design each brace in each story.

$\qquad$ **For each story:** $\quad P_s = f_t A_s$

P_s = total axial load on brace in each story, lb
f_t = safe unit stress in tension for each brace, psi
A_2 = minimum cross-section area of each brace, in^2

Structural Bracing Design, Rigid Frames:

A rigid frame is a vertical rectangle with a beam along its top and bottom, a column on each end, and four corners that are rigid so the beams and columns cannot rotate about each other.

Step 1. Find the beam's net moment at the connection.

$$M_n = \boxed{M?}_{neg} - \boxed{M?}_{pos}$$

M_n $\quad$ = net beam moment due to rigid connection, in-lb
$\boxed{M?}_{neg}$ = max. neg. mom. above fixed ends of beam, in-lb
$\boxed{M?}_{pos}$ = max. pos. mom. of beam, usually at midspan, in-lb

Step 2. Find each column's added equivalent load due to its moment resulting from the rigid connection.

$$0.5 \, L \, M_n = h \, M_c$$

L $\quad$ = length of span, in.
M_n = net beam moment at rigid connection, in-lb
h $\quad$ = height of column, in.
M_c = added column moment at rigid connection, in-lb

Step 3. Design the column based on the material of which it is made.

48

Structural Bracing Design, Infilled Frames:

An infilled frame is usually a vertical rectangle whose inner wall is filled with masonry or other solid construction that gives the frame a stiffness that resists any inplane load. Two such frames at right angles to each other with an end-in-common brace each other against side thrusts; and such a frame combined with a rigid floor or roof slab resists wind and torsion loads in every direction.

Step 1. Compute the wind shear at the base of the building's lowest floor.

$$V_w = 0.0033\, A\, v^2$$

V_w = total wind shear against base of frames, lb
A = area of wind load surface (vert. projection), sf
v = maximum windspeed against building, mph

Step 2. Compute the cracking shear strength of the frame's infill, then compare this value with the wind shear found in Step 1.

$$V_s = \eta\, f_i\, t\, L^2 / (1.37\, L - 0.16\, h) \le V_w$$

V_s = cracking shear strength of infill, lb
f_i = rated shear strength of infill material, psi
η = number of bays in infill frame. If bays are of different size, compute V_s for each bay then add the partial values to obtain total V_s.
t = thickness of infill, in.
L = length of infill, in. This includes half the thickness of the columns or frame at each end.
h = height of infill, in.
V_w = total wind shear load from Step 1, lb

Step 3. Compute the infill's compression strength, then compare this value with the wind shear found in Step 1.

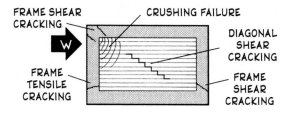

Fig. 1-3. Types of infilled frame failure.

c. Conc.: $V_c = 2 \eta f_m (I h t^3)^{0.25} \cos^2 (\tan^{-1} h/_L) \geq V_w$
s. Steel: $V_c = 3 \eta f_m (I h t^3)^{0.25} \cos^2 (\tan^{-1} h/_L) \geq V_w$

V_c = compression shear strength of infill, lb
f_m = safe compression stress of infill material, psi
I = moment of inertia of column in frame, in⁴
$\quad \eta$, h, L, t, and V_w are as previously defined

Step 4. Design the columns to resist shear and moment due to the infill load according to the formulas below:

  a. $V_c = V_w + E_x$
  b. $M_c = 0.05 \, h V_w + M_d$

V_c = total compression shear strength of columns, lb
E_x = existing lateral shear loads on the column, lb
M_c = total moment resisted by column, ft-lb
M_d = moments due to existing loads, ft-lb
$\quad V_w$ and h are as previously defined

Step 5. Design the beam connections above and below the infill to carry the following infill shear forces:

  a. $V_u = (V_w \, h/_L) - S_d$
  b. $V_d = (V_w \, h/_L) + S_{dl}$

V_u = total upward shear force on end of frame, lb

V_w = wind shear load against base of lowest floor, lb, from Step 1

h = height of infill, 120 in.

L = length of infill, 320 in.

S_d = existing shear force due to dead load, lb

V_d = total downward shear force on column, lb

S_{dl} = existing shear force due to dead & live load, lb

    V_w, h, and L are as previously defined

Step 6. If the beam above each infill is not restrained by an infill above (typical of top floors), it should be designed according to equation **a** below. If the beam below the infill is not restrained by an infill or other solid material below (typical of bottom floors), it should be designed according to equation **b** below.

    a. $M_u = 0.05\, V_w\, h - M_d$

    b. $M_b = V_w\, h + M_{dl}$

M_u = total negative moment in upper beam, ft-lb

M_b = total positive moment in lower beam, ft-lb

M_{dl} = existing moment due to dead and live load, ft-lb

    V_w, h, and M_d are as previously defined

Horizontal Thrust of Oblique Load:

$$W_v\, A = W_r \sin\left(\tan^{-1} {}^{V}\!/_{h}\right)$$

W_v = total gravity load on arch, opposing rafters, or other opposing sloping structural members, lb

A = horiz. area of load on sloping members, sf

W_r = resultant outward or horizontal thrust of sloping members on their bases, lb

v = vertical component of load, in.

h = horizontal component of load, in.

Vectors: $V_a = W_r \sin (\tan^{-1} v/h)$

V_a = vertical component of vector A, lb
W_r = magnitude of resultant load, lb
v = vertical component of load
h = horizontal component of load

Tie Rod Design:

Step 1. Find the total load supported by the tie rod.

$$W_T = s L (\omega_L + \omega_D) + 0.0033 \, s \, H \, v^2$$

W_T = total load on each tie rod or other structural member, lb
s = unit spacing between tie rods or other structure, ft
L = length (horizontal projection) of each tie rod or other structural member, ft
ω_L = maximum unit live load on member, psf
ω_D = maximum unit dead load on member, psf
H = height (vertical projection) of each member, ft
v = maximum local wind velocity, mph

Step 2. Find the load reaction at each roof support. This is done by taking Σ moments about one support, then subtracting the load at one support from the roof's total load to find the load at the other support.

Step 3. Draw a free body diagram around one side of the roof (e.g. the left side), then take moments about peak of roof P and solve for required tie rod tensile strength T as sketched below.

$$\Sigma M_P: \quad (\circlearrowleft \text{ or } +) \text{ loads} - (\circlearrowright \text{ or } -) \text{ loads} = 0$$

Step 4. Check that actual force $T \le$ required T when the wind is calm (then the only roof load is its total load).

Flat Plate Design: The formulas below are used to design metal plates, plywood panels, glass panes, or other planar materials whose safe tensile stress and modulus of elasticity are known.

Square flat plate that is flexibly or semirigidly supported by continuous adhesive or closely-spaced connectors along all four edges:

Tension: $\quad f_{t\text{-}max} = 0.28\ W/t^2$

Deflection: $\quad \Delta_{max} = 0.044\ W L^2/E\,t^2$

Square flat plate that is rigidly supported by continuous adhesive or closely-spaced connectors along all four edges:

Tension: $\quad f_t = 0.31\ W/t^2$

Deflection: $\quad \Delta_{max} = 0.014\ W L^2/E\,t^2$

Rectangular flat plate that is flexibly or semirigidly supported by continuous adhesive or closely-spaced connectors along the underside of all four edges:

Tension: $\quad f_t = \dfrac{0.75\ W}{t^2\ (L/S + 1.61\ S^2/L^2)}$

Deflection: $\quad \Delta_{max} = \dfrac{0.14\ W}{E\,t^3\ (L/S^3 + 2.21/L^2)}$

Rectangular flat plate that is firmly and fixedly supported by continuous adhesive or closely-spaced connectors along the underside of all four edges.

Tension: $\quad f_t = \dfrac{0.50\ W}{t^2\ (L/S + 0.62\ S^5/L^5)}$

Deflection: $\quad \Delta_{max} = \dfrac{0.028\ W}{E\ t^3\ (L/S^3 + 1.06\ S^2/L^4)}$

Circular flat plate that is flexibly or semi-rigidly supported by continuous adhesive or closely-spaced connectors along the underside of all four edges:

Tension: $\quad f_t = 0.39\ W/t^2$

Deflection: $\quad \Delta_{max} = 0.22\ W r^2/E\ t^2$

Circular flat plate that is firmly and fixedly supported by continuous adhesive or closely-spaced connectors along the underside of all four edges:

Tension: $\quad f_t = 0.24\ W/t^2$

Deflection: $\quad \Delta_{max} = 0.054\ W r^2/E\ t^2$

For all the flat plate design formulas above,

f_t = safe unit tensile stress for plate material, psi

W = total uniform load acting perpendicularly on plate, lb.

t = thickness of plate, in.

Δ_{max} = maximum deflection of plate, in. In most scenarios, $\Delta_{max} \leq 1/180$ the plate's maximum span.

L = distance between supports, in. If plate is square, L = length of one side; if rectangular, L = length of long side.

E = modulus of elasticity of plate material, psi

S = length of shorter side of plate if it is rectangular, in.

r = radius of plate if it is circular, in.

TABLE 2-1: ALLOWABLE LUMBER UNIT STRESSES

SPECIES, const. grade	f_b, psi	f_v, psi	f_h, psi	f_t, psi	$f_{c/\!/}$, psi	$f_{c\perp}$, psi	E, psi
Cedar: Northern white	675	450	65	350	625	205	600,000
Western	875	600	75	450	850	265	900,000
Douglas Fir, Larch	1,200	900	95	625	1,150	385	1,500,000
Hemlock, Eastern; Tamar'k	1,050	600	85	525	975	365	1,000,000
Western	1,050	600	90	550	1,050	280	1,300,000
Oak, white or red; Hickory	1,450	1,000	200	700	900	500	1,500,000
Pine, Eastern White	800	500	65	400	750	220	1,000,000
Northern	950	650	70	475	875	280	1,100,000
Southern	1,250	925	105	650	1,300	405	1,500,000
Redwood	950	850	80	475	925	270	900,000
Spruce, Eastern	875	750	65	450	800	255	1,100,000
Engelman	800	700	70	400	675	195	1,000,000
Gluelams: Douglas fir, dry	100F	1,000	165	900	1,500	385	1,700,000
Plywood, Douglas Fir	750	800	690	690	350		

Woods treated with preservatives or fire retardants: multiply above stresses × 0.90
Other than construction lumber grades: multiply factors below × stresses for species above:

Select Structural	2.00	1.30	1.00	1.95	1.40	1.00	1.22
No. 1	1.70	1.20	1.00	1.68	1.09	1.00	1.22
No. 2	1.38	1.10	1.00	1.38	0.88	1.00	1.11
Standard	0.56	0.80	1.00	0.56	0.81	1.00	1.00

2. WOOD

Wood Moisture Content vs. Dimensions:

$$\frac{D_f}{D_i} = \Delta_S = \frac{100 - \kappa\,(30 - M_f)}{100 - \kappa\,(30 - M_i)}$$

D_f = final dimension of wood member. D_f = in. if tangential or radial, in³ if volumetric.

D_i = initial dimension of wood member. D_i = in. if tangential or radial, in³ if volumetric.

Δ_S = rate of wood shrinkage or swellage, in/in.

κ = coeff. of swellage/shrinkage for species of wood. $\kappa = \kappa_R$ for radial change, κ_T for tangential change, and κ_V for volumetric change.

M_f = final moisture content of wood member, %. $30\% \geq M_f \geq 0\%$.

M_i = initial moisture content of wood member, %. $30\% \geq M_i \geq 0\%$.

Vertical Shear:

Rectangular sections: $\qquad V_v = 0.67\,f_v\,b\,d$

Circular sections: $\qquad\quad V_v = 0.59\,f_v\,d$

V_v = end reaction (total vertical shear), lb

f_v = max. unit vertical shear stress for wood used, psi

TABLE 2-2: SECTION PROPERTIES OF LUMBER
Contemporary Lumberyard Dimensions

NOM. SIZE, in.	Dress'd size in.	C-S area, in^2	Sec. Mod. S_x, in^3	Mom. of In. I_x, in^4
LIGHT FRAMING (2 to 4 in. thick, 2 to 4 in. wide):				
2 × 2	1.5 × 1.5	2.25	0.56	0.42
2 × 3	1.5 × 2.5	3.75	1.56	1.95
2 × 4	1.5 × 3.5	5.25	3.06	5.34
4 × 4	3.5 × 3.5	12.3	7.15	12.5
JOISTS & PLANKS (2 to 4 in. thick, 6 in. and wider):				
2 × 6	1.5 × 5.5	8.25	7.56	20.8
2 × 8	1.5 × 7.25	10.9	13.1	47.6
2 × 10	1.5 × 9.25	13.9	21.4	98.9
2 × 12	1.5 × 11.3	16.9	31.6	178
3 × 6	2.5 × 5.5	13.8	12.6	34.7
3 × 8	2.5 × 7.25	18.1	21.9	79.4
3 × 10	2.5 × 9.25	23.1	35.7	165
3 × 12	2.5 × 11.3	28.1	52.7	297
4 × 6	3.5 × 5.5	19.3	17.6	48.5
4 × 8	3.5 × 7.25	25.4	30.7	111
4 × 10	3.5 × 9.25	32.4	50.0	231
4 × 12	3.5 × 11.3	39.4	73.8	415
POSTS & TIMBERS (at least 5 in. thick, no more than 2 in. wider than thick):				
6 × 6	5.5 × 5.5	30.3	27.7	76.3
6 × 8	5.5 × 7.25	41.3	51.6	194
8 × 8	7.5 × 7.5	56.3	70.3	264
8 × 10	7.5 × 9.5	71.3	113	536
10 × 10	9.5 × 9.5	90.3	143	679
10 × 12	9.5 × 11.5	109	209	1,204
12 × 12	11.5 × 11.5	132	253	1,460
BEAMS & STRINGERS (at least 5 in. thick, more than 2 in. wider than thick):				
6 × 10	5.5 × 9.25	52.3	82.7	393
6 × 12	5.5 × 11.5	63.3	121	697
8 × 12	7.5 × 11.5	86.3	165	951

b = min. width or diameter of vertical shear plane, in.
d = minimum depth of vertical shear plane, in.

Horizontal Shear:

Rectangular sections: $\quad V_h = 0.5\, f_h\, b\, L_h$
Circular sections: $\qquad V_h = 0.5\, f_h\, d\, L_h$
Connections: $\qquad\qquad V_h = f_h\, b\, L_h$

V_h = horizontal shear end reaction, lb
f_h = maximum unit stress in horizontal shear for
species & grade of wood, psi
b = width or diameter of horizontal shear plane, in.
L_h = length of horizontal shear plane, in.

Notched Beam Design:

Notch at bottom of beam: $\quad d\, V = 0.67\, f_v\, b\, d_{eb}^{\,2}$
Notch at top: $\quad V = 0.67\, f_v\, b\, [d - e\,(d - d_{et}\, {}^t\!/_{d_{et}\, t})]$

V = vertical reaction of beam at end support, lb
f_v = safe unit shear stress of wood used for beam, psi
b = breadth or width of beam, in.
d = full depth of beam, in.
d_e = notched depth of beam, in. $d_e = d_{et}$ if notch is at
top of beam, d_{eb} if notch is at bottom.
e = horizontal extension of notch from support, in.

Bending Moment Design, Single Loads:

Step 1. Find the beam's maximum moment and section
modulus from

$$\boxed{M?} = M_{max} = f_b\, S_x$$
Two equations, two unknowns

$\boxed{M?}$ = applicable moment formula

M_{max} = maximum moment of applied load, in-lb
f_b = safe unit bending stress of wood used, psi
S_x = section modulus of beam section, in^3

Step 2. Select the section moduli of standard lumber sizes that is ≥ S_x, then list their section areas. The beam with the smallest area is the economic section.

Bending Moment Design, Multiple Loads:

Step 1. Divide the total load into parts which can be quantified by common beam load formulas as follows:

TABLE 2-3: SWELLAGE/SHRINKAGE RATES OF WOOD			
	Coefficient of Swellage/Shrinkage		
SPECIES	Radial (κ_R)	Tangential (κ_T)	Volumetric (κ_V)
Softwoods: Cypress	0.13	0.21	0.35
Cedar	0.09	0.18	0.28
Douglas Fir	0.15	0.24	0.38
Balsam Fir	0.10	0.23	0.38
Hemlock	0.13	0.24	0.37
Larch	0.15	0.30	0.47
Pine, Eastern white	0.07	0.20	0.27
Sugar	0.10	0.19	0.26
Southern	0.17	0.25	0.41
All others	0.13	0.24	0.37
Redwood	0.90	0.15	0.23
Spruce	0.13	0.24	0.38
Tamarack	0.12	0.25	0.45
Hardwoods: Ash	0.15	0.24	0.43
Beech	0.18	0.40	0.57
Elm	0.15	0.32	0.49
Hickory	0.24	0.37	0.60
Maple	0.13	0.28	0.43
Oak, all species	0.17	0.36	0.48
Walnut	0.18	0.26	0.43

$$M_{max} = M_1 + M_2 + \dots M_Z$$

M_1, M_2, etc. = applicable moment formula for each partial load

M_{max} = maximum moment of beam due to total load, in/lb

Step 2. Find the beam's maximum unit stress.

$$M_{max} = f_b S_x$$

M_{max} = maximum moment of beam due to total load, in/lb
f_b = maximum unit bending stress for wood used, psi
S = section modulus of beam section, in^3

Depth Reduction Factor: $f_{rd}\, d^{0.11} = 1.31\, f_b$

f_{rd} = reduced safe unit bending stress of wood member whose depth exceeds 12 in, psi
d = depth of beam, 12 or more in.
f_b = safe unit bending stress of species and grade of wood used, psi

Curvature Reduction Factor:

$$f_{rc} = f_b\, [1 - 2{,}000\, (t/r)^2]$$

f_{rc} = reduced safe unit bending stress of curved wood member, psi
f_b = safe unit bending stress of species and grade of wood used, psi
t = min. thickness of laminations, in. For nonlaminated beams, $t = 1.5$ in.
r = beam's max. radius of curvature from inside face of curve, in. $t/r \le 1/100$ for hardwoods and Southern pine, 1/125 for other softwoods.

Deflection Design, Beams & Girders:

Step 1. Compute the beam's maximum deflection from

$$\boxed{\text{D?}} = \Delta_{max} = \; \leq \; \kappa_{\Delta} \, L$$

$\boxed{\text{D?}}$ = applicable deflection formula

Δ_{max} = maximum deflection due to applied load, in.

κ_{Δ} = coeff. of allowable deflection

L = length of span from ₵ of supports, in.

Deflection Design, Decking:

$$24 \, \kappa_{sp} \, W \, L^3 = E \, t^3$$

κ_{sp} = span pattern coefficient, as described below. In this equation, $\Delta_{max} \leq \frac{1}{240} L$.

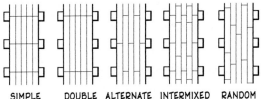

SIMPLE SPANS:	DOUBLE SPANS:	ALTERNATE SPANS:	INTERMIXED SPANS:	RANDOM SPANS:
$\kappa_{sp} = 0.13$	$\kappa_{sp} = 0.054$	$\kappa_{sp} = 0.092$	$\kappa_{sp} = 0.095$	$\kappa_{sp} = 0.10$

Fig. 2-1. Span patterns for timber decking.

W = total weight of load, psf

L = maximum length of decking span, in.

E = mod. of elasticity of wood used for decking, psi

t = thickness of decking, in.

Bearing Area: $P = b_a \, b_b \, f_c \sin \angle$

P = total end reaction on bearing area, lb

b_a = width of beam above bearing area, in.
b_b = width of support below bearing area, in.
f_c = safe unit compression stress in compression par-
      allel to grain for wood used, psi
$\angle$ = intersection angle between beam and support, °

Lateral Support: $r = d/t$

r = ratio of beam depth to thickness. Find r from ac-
     tual measurements or Fig. 2-2, then determine
     adequate lateral support of the beam.
d = depth of beam, in. nom.
t = thickness or width of beam, in. nom.

Lateral Bracing Design:

Step 1. Find the beam's safe unit bending stress from

$$f_{bs} = f_b \left[1 - 0.92 \left(f_b \kappa_e L_u d / b^2 E\right)^2\right]$$

RATIO OF DEPTH TO THICKNESS
(NOMINAL DIMENSIONS)

LOCATION OF LATERAL SUPPORTS:

— 0 — NO LATERAL SUPPORT REQUIRED

2:1 AT ENDS OF BEAM, OVER SUP-
4:1 PORTS, & UNDER POINT LOADS
ABOVE + ALL COMPRESSIVE EDGES
5:1 HELD IN PLACE FOR ENTIRE LENGTH
ABOVE + BRIDGING OR
BLOCKING AT MAX. 8'-0"
6:1 TOP & BOTTOM EDGES HELD IN
7:1 PLACE FOR ENTIRE LENGTH

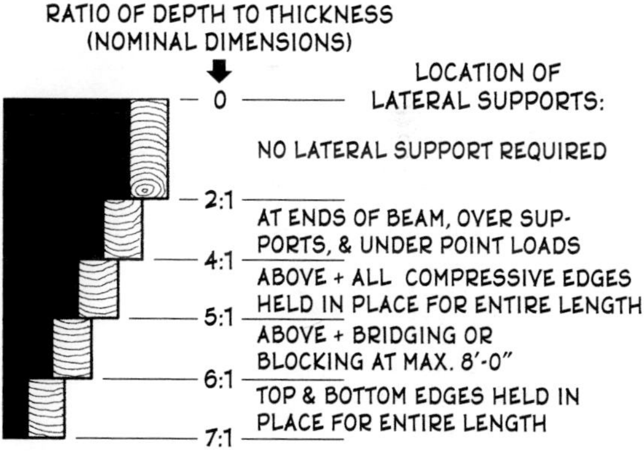

Fig. 2-2. Lateral support specifications.

f_{bs} = safe unit bending stress of beam, psi
f_b = design unit bending stress of wood used, psi
κ_e = effective length coefficient, as follows:

Type of span	κ_e
Single span, point load at center of span ..	1.61
Single span, uniform load	1.84
Cantilever span, pt. load on unsup'd end ...	1.69
Cantilever span, uniform load	1.06
Any other single or cantilever span	1.92

L_u = length of span between lateral bracing, in. Try a L_u above and solve for f_{bs}, then use f_{bs} in Step 2 and solve for L_u. If $L_{u2} > L_{u1}$, try a lower L_u.
d = depth of beam, in.
b = breadth or width of beam, in.
E = modulus of elasticity for wood used, psi.

Step 2. Use f_{bs} above and solve for L_u below.

$$\kappa_e \; \boxed{M?} = 0.167 \, f_{bs} \, b \, d^2$$

$\boxed{M?}$ = applicable moment formula for beam load.
All other values are as previously defined.

Single-Tapered Beam Design,
Uniform loads, uniform widths, free supports:

Step 1. Find the beam's minimum depth at its shallow end from

$$V = 0.67 \, f_v \, b \, d_{min}$$

V = maximum shear reaction at bearing end, lb
f_v = safe unit shear stress of wood used, psi
b = breadth or width of beam, in.
d_{min} = minimum depth of beam, in.

Step 2. Determine the beam's maximum depth at its deep

end. The beam's underside may be horizontal or also taper upward, and the beam may be notched at its upper end at the top or bottom as long as net $d_{max} > d_{min}$.

Step 3. Find the beam's critical depth d_c, where the beam's moment and deflection are maximum, from below.

$$d_c \, d_{max} = d_{min} \, (2 \, d_{max} - d_{min})$$

d_c = critical depth of beam, in.
d_{max} = maximum depth of beam, in.
d_{min} = minimum depth of beam, in.

Step 4. Verify that the beam's moment at its critical depth ≤ maximum moment created by the beam's design load from

$$M_{max} \leq \frac{1.5 \, w \, L^2 \, d_{max}^2}{d_{min} \, (2 \, d_{max} - d_{min})}$$

M_{max} = maximum moment due to beam load, in-lb
w = unit uniform load on span, pLF
L = length of beam span, in.
d_{min} and d_{max} are as previously defined

Step 5. Investigate the beam for safe deflection at its critical depth d_c. (If a tapered beam is adequately designed at its shallow end, this is rarely necessary).

Single-Tapered Beam Design, One or more point loads, uniform widths, free supports:

Step 1. Find the beam's minimum depth d_{min} and maximum depth d_{max} similarly as in Steps 1 and 2 above.

Step 2. Find the beam's maximum moment at its critical depth from formula or by drawing its moment diagram, then note the point of maximum moment on the span.

Step 3. Verify that the beam's moment at its critical depth ≤ the maximum moment created by the beam's shear load at its critical depth from

$$M_c \leq \frac{1.5 \, V d_c^2}{2 \, d_{min} \tan \angle}$$

M_c = bending moment at span's critical depth, in-lb
V = maximum shear load at critical depth, lb
d_c = critical depth of beam, in.
d_{min} = minimum depth of beam at shallow end, in.
$\angle$ = angle of taper of single-tapered beam span, °

Double-Tapered Beam Design,
Uniform loads, uniform width, free supports:

Step 1. Find the beam's minimum depth at its ends from

$$V = 0.67 \, f_v \, b \, d_{min}$$

V = maximum shear reaction at bearing end, lb
f_v = safe unit shear stress of wood used, psi
b = breadth or width of beam, in.
d = depth of beam, in.

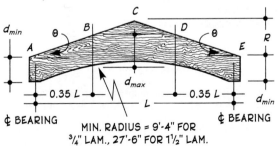

Fig. 2-3. Double-tapered beam specifications.

Step 2. Knowing the beam's width b and its maximum bending moment M_{max}, find its maximum depth d_{max} from the formula below. Once d_{max} is found, it may be increased to satisfy other design criteria regarding the beam's upper and lower edges.

$$4.57\ M_{max} = f_b\ b\ d_{max}^{1.89}$$

M_{max} = max. moment of double-tapered beam span, in-lb
f_b = safe unit bending stress of wood used, psi
b = breadth or width of beam, in.
d_{max} = maximum depth of beam at or near center of span, in.

Step 3. If the beam is pitched or curved, draw its ends and underside in elevation, then locate d_{max} at 0.35 L in from the ₵ of the beam's end supports. Then extend the tops of the beam up from points A and E through points B and D to the beam's peak at C. The line $A\ B\ C\ D\ E$ profiles the minimum height of the the beam's upper edge.

Step 4. Find the beam's bending moment and section modulus at its midspan and quarterspans, then check the beam's stresses at these span points as follows:

$$M^2/f_b^2\ S_x^2 + M^2 \tan^2 \angle/f_v^2\ S_x^2 + M^2 \tan^4 \angle/f_c^2\ S_x^2 \le 1.00$$

M = bending moment of beam section at midspan or quarterspan, in-lb
f_b = safe unit stress in bending for species and grade of wood, psi
S_x = section modulus of beam section at midspan or quarterspan, in³
$\angle$ = net angle of taper on each side of beam span, °
f_v = safe unit shear stress of wood used, psi
f_c = safe unit compression stress of species and grade of wood used, psi

Step 5. Check the beam for maximum deflection from

$$\Delta_{max} = 0.013 \, WL^3/E \, I + 2.5 \, WL/E \, b \, d_{min}$$

W = total uniform load on beam, lb
L = length of beam span, in.
E = modulus of elasticity of wood used, psi
I = moment of inertia of beam section, in^4
b = breadth or width of beam, in.
d_{min} = minimum depth of beam, in.

Step 6. Determine the beam's horizontal deflection at its supports from the formula below. If Δ_{hor} exceeds the end supports' ability to move laterally as the span deflects and contracts, a slotted or roller connection must be installed under one support.

$$\Delta_{hor} \, L = 2 \, R \, \Delta_{max}$$

Δ_{hor} = max. horiz. deflection of beam at supports, in.
R = rise of beam: vertical distance from top of beam above end supports to peak at center of span, as shown in Fig. 2-3, in.
    L and Δ_{max} are as previously described

Two-hinged Timber Arch Design:

Step 1. Tentatively assume a feasible size for the arch, then mechanically draw one-half of it in elevation and divide it into a number of equal segments.

Step 2. Find the horizontal and vertical lengths X and Y for each segment point along the half arch.

Step 3. Knowing the arch's allowable loads, determine the arch's reactions and lateral thrusts at its two pin supports as sketched in Fig. 2-4.

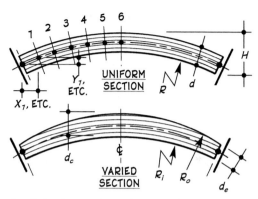

Fig. 2-4. Types of two-hinged timber arches.

Step 4. Considering the arch as a beam with a simple span and free supports, sum the moments at one support then compute the bending moments and axial thrusts at each segmental point along the arch.

Step 5. Tentatively assuming adequate lateral support of the arch, size its rectangular section at each segmental point along the arch as follows:

$$P/f_b\, b\, d + M/0.167\, f_b\, b\, d^2 \leq 1.00$$

P = maximum point load at each section segment, lb
f_b = safe unit bending stress for species and grade of wood, psi
b = breadth or width of arch, in.
d = depth of arch, in.
M = maximum moment at each section segment, in-lb

Step 6. Investigate the arch for safe shear stress at its base and at its point of maximum shear according to

$$V_{max} = 0.67 f_v b d_b$$

V_{max} = maximum shear at base of arch, lb
f_v = safe unit shear stress of wood used, psi
b = breadth or width of arch, in.
d_b = depth of arch at its base, in.

Step 7. Investigate the arch's lateral stability. The arch is laterally stable if d/b at any point along the span is 5 or less and if lateral bracing is installed at intervals of 6 d or less along the span.

Step 8. Investigate the arch for safe radial stress. A safe radial stress is virtually assured if $r \geq 2.0$ (horiz. length of arch ÷ height of arch).

$$M_{max} = 0.67 r f_c b d_b$$

M_{max} = maximum moment in arch, in-lb
r = minimum radius of curvature of arch, from ₵ of curve to inner face of arch, in.
f_c = safe unit stress in compression perpendicular to grain for species and grade of wood, psi
        b and d_b are as previously defined

Step 9. Investigate the arch for safe deflection. Here $\Delta \leq$ the length of the arch's outer edge ÷ 180. Again, safe deflection is virtually assured if $r \geq 2.0$ (horiz. length of arch ÷ height of arch).

$$\Delta_{max} \leq 0.013 \, W L^3 / E I$$

Δ_{max} = maximum moment in arch, in-lb
W = total weight of uniform load on arch, lb
L = length of arch's outer edge, in.
E = modulus of elasticity of wood used, psi
I = moment of inertia of arch section, in⁴

Three-Hinged Arch Design:

Step 1. Determine the arch's allowable stresses, then find the maximum load reactions at the base and crown of each half-arch. Each arch has three kinds of loads: *gravity load on span of full arch, gravity load on span of half-arch,* and *wind load on height of arch.* Then fill out the schedule below by computing the horizontal and vertical reactions for each of the eight listed load combinations:

	V_L	V_R	H_L	H_R
1. Dead load on full arch	—	—	—	—
2. Snow load on full arch	—	—	—	—
3. 1 + 2 above on full arch	—*	—*	—*	—
4. Dead load on half arch	—	—	—	—
5. Snow load on half arch	—	—	—	—
6. 4 + 5 on half arch	—	—	—	—
7. Wind load on height of arch	—	—	—	—
8. 7 + dead load on ht. of arch	—	—	—	—

* These are usually the maximum load reactions

Step 2. Knowing the above reactions, find each half-arch's maximum section at its base according to the formulas below. Select the maximum values for V_V and V_H from the the schedule in Step 1, solve for A in both equations, then use the larger A for subsequent design.

    a. $V_V \leq 0.67 f_c b d_b = 0.67 f_c A$
    b. $V_H \leq 0.67 f_v b d_b = 0.67 f_v A$

V_V = maximum vertical reaction at base of arch, lb
V_H = maximum horiz. reaction at base of arch, lb
f_c = safe unit comp. stress ‖ grain of wood used, psi
f_v = safe unit shear stress of wood used, psi
b = uniform breadth or width of arch, in.
d_b = depth of arch at base (in-to-out dimension), in.

A = area of arch section at base, in². Solve for A in both equations, then select the higher A, then pick a standard gluelam section width b and depth d_b whose product ≥ A.

Step 3. Tentatively estimate the arch's depth at its crown and tangents.

Step 4. Locate lateral bracing along each half-span's tangent points and possibly elsewhere so L/b ≤ 50 and L ≤ 72 in. Although this is the minimum spacing required by Code, an often simpler and safer criterion is $L ≈ 14\,b$.

Step 5. Locate the arch's three pins at the midpoints of its crown and bases, then readjust its horizontal and vertical dimensions if necessary. Theoretically any dimension changes require recomputing every force noted in Step 1, but usually the differences are negligible.

Step 6. Check the arch for safe design at several points on its span including each point of lateral support. At each point along the arch's span d_c/b should ≤ 5.00, d_{t1} should ≥ $d_c + b$, and d_{t2} ≥ $d_b + b$ (see Fig. 2-5).

$$P/f_c\,A + M/f_b\,S_x \leq 1.00$$

P = maximum load at arch's crown, lb
f_c = safe unit compression stress parallel to grain for species and grade of wood, psi
A = section area of arch at selected point on span, in²
M = maximum bending moment of arch section at selected point along its span, in-lb
f_b = safe unit bending stress of wood used, psi
S_x = section modulus of arch section at selected points along span, in³
    f_c and A are as previously defined

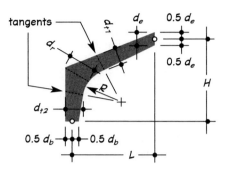

Fig. 2-5. Half-arch analysis of three-hinged arch.

Step 7. Check the arch for safe radial stress as described below. [A safe radial stress is virtually assured if $r \geq 2.0$ (horiz. length of half-arch ÷ height of arch)].

$$M_R \leq 0.67 \, r f_c \, b \, d_r$$

M_R = maximum radial moment of arch, in-lb.
r = radius of curvature of half-arch, from ₵ of curve to inner face of arch, in.
f_c = safe unit comp. stress ‖ grain of wood used, psi
b = uniform breadth or width of arch, in.
d_r = thickness of half-arch at its corner, in.
     f_c and b are as previously defined

Step 8. Check the arch for safe deflection (≤ length of outer edge/180). Safe deflection is virtually assured if $r \geq 2.0$ (horiz. length of half-arch ÷ height of arch).

$$\Delta_{max} \leq 0.013 \, W L^3 / E I$$

Δ_{max} = maximum moment in arch, in-lb
W = total weight of uniform load on arch, lb

L = length of arch's outer edge, in.
E = modulus of elasticity of wood used, psi
I = moment of inertia of arch section, in⁴

Lightweight Wood I-Joist Design:

Step 1. Find each joist's maximum bending moment.

$$M_{max} = \boxed{M?}$$

M_{max} = maximum moment of span due to load, in/lb
$\boxed{M?}$ = applicable moment formula for load: this is usually *uniform load, single span, supports free*
L = length of span, in.

Step 2. Select a trial section based on the member's maximum moment.

$$M_{max} = f_b S_x$$

M_{max} = maximum moment of span due to load, in/lb
f_b = safe unit stress, psi. This equals actual f_b – lateral load stress allowance f_n. Tentatively let f_n = 100 psi, then verify in Step 3.
S_x = section modulus, in³. Solve for this value, then select a truss with the next highest S_x.

Step 3. Check the trial member for safe lateral load.

$$f_n A \geq s h P$$

f_n = lateral load unit stress allowance, psi. Solve for actual f_n then compare with allow. f_n from above.
A = section area of I-joist, in²
s = lateral spacing of I-joist, ft.
h = height of wind load area, if any, ft
P = unit wind load, if any, psf

Step 4. Check the trial member for safe vertical shear.

$$V \geq 0.67 \, f_v \, A$$

V = I-joist end reaction, lb
f_v = safe unit stress in vert. shear, normally 800 psi
A = section area of I-joist, in²

Step 5. Check the trial member for maximum deflection.

$$\Delta_{max} = 0.0130 \, WL^3/EI \leq 0.00208 \, L$$

Δ_{max} = maximum deflection of trial member, in.
W = total load on beam, lb
L = length of span (horizontal projection), in.
E = modulus of elasticity, normally 1,500,000 psi
I = moment of inertia of section, from Table 1-4, in⁴

Gluelam Design:

Step 1. Find the beam's minimum depth from

$$M_{max} = \boxed{M?} = 0.167 \, f_b \, b \, |d^2 \blacktriangleright|_t$$

$\boxed{M?}$ = applicable moment formula
f_b = safe unit bending stress of wood used, psi
b = width of beam section, in.
d = depth of beam section, in.
t = thickness of lamination, in.

Step 2. If the gluelam is a rectangular section, check for vertical shear as follows:

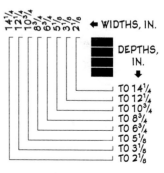

← WIDTHS, IN.

14¼
12¼
10¾
8¾
6¾
5⅛
3⅛
2⅛

DEPTHS, IN.
↓

TO 14¼
TO 12¼
TO 10¾
TO 8¾
TO 6¾
TO 5⅛
TO 3⅛
TO 2⅛

Fig. 2-6. Typical gluelam dimensions.

$$V_v = 0.67 f_v b d$$

V_v = total load, lb
f_v = actual unit stress in vertical shear for wood used,
  psi. Solve for f_v, then compare with safe f_v.
  b and d are as previously defined

Step 3. Investigate the beam section for deflection.

$$\Delta_{max} = \boxed{D?} \leq \kappa_\Delta L$$

Δ_{max} = maximum deflection of span due to load, in.
$\boxed{D?}$ = applicable deflection formula; unknowns are:
  W = total weight of load, lb
  L = length of span, in.
  E = modulus of elasticity of wood used, psi
  I = moment of inertia of beam section, in⁴
  κ_Δ = coeff. of allowable deflection for span

Timber Dome Design:

Step 1. Determine the allowable stresses in each rib, especially f_b, $f_{c\parallel}$, $f_{c\perp}$, and E for the species and grade of wood used.

Step 2. Knowing each rib's horizontal length, angle of incline from base to crown, and radius of curvature, draw the rib in elevation, measure the arc's angle and radius, then find its curved length by trigonometry.

Step 3. If each rib is continuous from base to crown (excepting the central ring), find each rib's total segmental load W_1, W_2, W_3, etc. at each lateral support, then design the ribs' sections according to the formulas below. Each segmental load area is a trapezoid whose wider base is toward the perimeter of the dome and whose center is at the intersection of each rib and each lateral support.

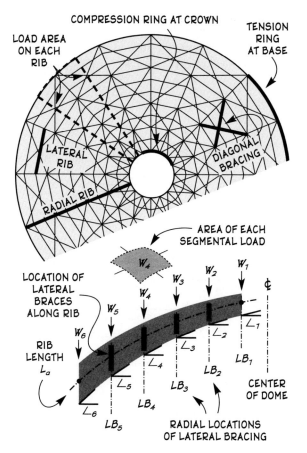

Fig. 2-7. Timber dome details.

    a. $P_1 = W_1/\cos \angle_1$
    b. $P_2 = W_1 + W_2/\cos \angle_2$
    c. $P_n = W_1 + ... + W_n/\cos \angle_n$ ... etc.

Then size each section at its point of lateral support from

    a. $P_1 = b\,d_1\,f_{c//}$
    b. $P_2 = b\,d_2\,f_{c//}$
    c. $P_n = b\,d_n\,f_{c//}$ ... etc.

Step 4. Find the lateral load for each ring of lateral bracing, including the halo ring at the crown, from

a. Lateral load 1: $P_{L1} = \dfrac{W_1 \cot \angle_1}{2 \sin (180/n)}$

b. Lateral load 2: $P_{L2} = \dfrac{W_1 \cot \angle_1 - (W_1 + W_2) \cot \angle_2}{2 \sin (180/n)}$

c. Lateral load 3:
$$P_{L3} = \dfrac{(W_1 + W_2) \cot \angle_2 - (W_1 + W_2 + W_2) \cot \angle_3}{2 \sin (180/n)}$$

d. Lateral load n:
$$P_{Ln} = \dfrac{(W_1 + ... \ W_{n-1}) \cot \angle_{n-1} - (W_1 + ... + W_n) \cot \angle_n}{2 \sin (180/n)}$$

In the above formulas, n = the number of ribs in the dome. If each lateral brace also supports the roof load between adjacent braces and ribs, its section must resist this load's maximum moment; i.e. $M_{max} \le 0.125 \ W L_r$.

Step 5. Size the section (if rectangular) of each lateral brace according to the formula below:

$$P/f_c\,A + M/f_b\,S_x \le 1.00$$

Step 6. Design the dome's base tension ring from

a. Rectangular section: $\quad b\,d \le \dfrac{W_a \cot \angle_\eta}{2\,f_t \sin (180/\eta)}$

b. Round section: $\qquad \delta^2 \le \dfrac{W_a \cot \angle_\eta}{1.57\,f_t \sin (180/\eta)}$

Step 7. Design the dome's diagonal bracing. These are usually turnbuckled tensile rods between the ribs and lateral braces; then their diameters are sized as follows:

$$\delta_1{}^2 \le \frac{W_1}{1.57\,f_t \sin \angle_1 \cos \alpha_1}$$

$$\delta_2{}^2 \le \frac{W_1 + W_2}{1.57\,f_t \sin \angle_1 \cos \alpha_1}$$

$$\dots \text{etc.}$$

$$\delta_\eta{}^2 \le \frac{W_1 + W_2 + \dots + W_\eta}{1.57\,f_t \sin \angle_1 \cos \alpha_1}$$

Step 8. Design the lateral brace-to-rib connectors. These are usually bolted steel angles and thus are designed as described on page 146.

Step 9. Design the diagonal bracing-to-rib connectors. These are typically steel angles and thus are designed as steel truss chords as described on page 116.

Wood Hypar Design:

Step 1. Knowing the membrane's horizontal area and height, and assuming double 1 in. nom. construction for the membrane, determine the membrane's maximum unit dead load and live load. Then find the membrane's edge loads and base loads (each = 0.25 total load) from the following two formulas:

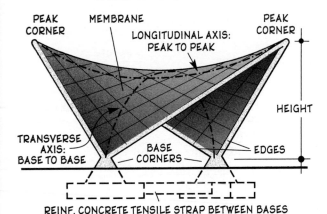

Fig. 2-8. Anatomy of a hypar.

    a. Total Edge Load: $P_e = 0.29 \, A \, (W_D + W_L)$
    b. Total Base Load: $P_b = 0.58 \, A \, (W_D + W_L)$

P_e = hypar load supported by each edge, lb
A = area of hypar membrane, horiz. projection, sf
W_D = total dead load of hypar membrane, lb
W_L = total live load supported by hypar membrane, lb
P_b = total hypar membrane load on each base, lb

Step 2. Find the membrane's boundary shear stress from

$$P_b \, L_L = 2 \, v_{sb} \, H \, L_S$$

P_b = total hypar membrane load on each base, lb
L_L = length of hypar's longest side, ft
v_{sb} = actual unit shear stress at membrane edge, plf
H = ht. of hypar membrane from base ¢ to peak ¢, ft
L_S = length of hypar's shortest side, ft

Step 3. Investigate the wood laminae for safety in tension and compression as described below. Compare maximum f_c with allow. f_c for the wood used. If the hypar is square and both laminae are the same species and grade of wood, only one equation needs to be solved.

    a. Compression: $v_{sb} L_a = A_{lf} f_c (L_L + L_S)$

    b. Tension: $\quad\quad\ \ v_{sb} L_t = A_{lf} f_c (L_L + L_S)$

L_a = length of hypar's longitudinal axis: distance btwn. its two farthest corners, ft. If hypar is a square or rectangle, $L_a = (L_L^2 + L_S^2)^{0.5}$ and $L_a = L_t$ below.

L_t = length of hypar's transverse axis: distance between hypar's two nearest opposite corners, ft

A_{lf} = section area of hypar membrane per LF of edge, in^2. This equals the thickness of one layer of lumber in the membrane × 12 in.

f_c = unit stress in comp. ⊥ grain of wood used, psi

    v_{sb}, L_L, and L_S are as previously defined

Step 4. If any boards are not long enough to span the membrane's width, design a connector to transfer the gathered load of one abutting board to the next. If this is done with nailed pieces of galvanized sheet steel, they must satisfy the formulas below:

    a. $f_c b t \le 0.9 f_t g w$

    b. $f_c b t \le f_v \eta$

f_c = actual unit compression stress perpendicular to grain of wood used, psi

b = breadth or width of abutting boards, in.

t = thickness of abutting boards, in.

f_t = safe unit tensile stress for galv. sheet steel, usually 15,000 psi

g = thickness of sheet steel, in. 16 ga. = 0.0625 in,

18 ga. = 0.0495 in, 20 ga. = 0.0392 in, 22 ga. = 0.0313 in, 24 ga. = 0.0248 in, 26 ga. = 0.0196 in, and 28 ga. = 0.0156 in.

w = minimum width of metal connection, in.

f_v = safe shear strength of each nail transferring load from one abutting board to the next, lb

η = number of nails driven through each half of the connector into each abutting board

Step 5. Find the force in each membrane edge according to the four edge design formulas below. If the hypar is square, one equation serves for all sides.

a. Edge AB: $F_{c\text{-}ab} = \dfrac{f_c L_{ab}}{\cos(\tan^{-1} H/L_{ab})}$

b. Edge BC: $F_{c\text{-}bc} = \dfrac{f_c L_{bc}}{\cos(\tan^{-1} H/L_{bc})}$

c. Edge CD: $F_{c\text{-}cd} = \dfrac{f_c L_{cd}}{\cos(\tan^{-1} H/L_{cd})}$

d. Edge DA: $F_{c\text{-}da} = \dfrac{f_c L_{da}}{\cos(\tan^{-1} H/L_{da})}$

$F_{c\text{-}ab}$ $F_{c\text{-}bc}$ $F_{c\text{-}cd}$ $F_{c\text{-}da}$ = compressive force at each edge AB, BC, CD, and DA from side of membrane to base of hypar, lb

L_{ab} L_{bc} L_{cd} L_{da} = length of each membrane edge AB, BC, CD, and DA, ft

f_c = actual unit compression stress at each edge, psi

H = height or rise of hypar membrane (vertical distance between ¢ of base and ¢ of peak), ft

Step 6. After finding the above forces F, use them to design each edge's section as described below. In these equations find section area A, then select b and $d \leq A$.

If the hypar is square, one formula serves for all sides.

    a. Edge *AB*: $F_{c\text{-}ab}/f_c = A_{ab} \leq b_{ab}\, d_{ab}$
    b. Edge *BC*: $F_{c\text{-}bc}/f_c = A_{bc} \leq b_{bc}\, d_{bc}$
    c. Edge *CD*: $F_{c\text{-}cd}/f_c = A_{cd} \leq b_{cd}\, d_{cd}$
    d. Edge *DA*: $F_{c\text{-}da}/f_c = A_{da} \leq b_{da}\, d_{da}$

Step 7. Design the hypar's base and footing.

Wood Column Design:

Step 1. Tentatively estimate the column's size.

$$V \approx \kappa_t f_c b^2$$

V = total vertical load on column, lb or kips
κ_t = trial complication factor. Try between 0.20 (simple) and 0.60 (complicated), depending on eccentric loads, lateral loads, column K factors, etc.
f_c = safe unit stress in compression parallel to grain for species & grade of wood, from Table 2-1, psi
b = trial width of square section, in.

Step 2. Determine the column K factors.

Step 3. Investigate the column's slenderness ratio.

$$L/b \leq 50$$

L = clear unbraced length or height of column, in.
b = minimum width of column section, in.

Step 4. Find the trial section's design load.

$$V_d = V_a + K_y V_x + K_x V_y + K_y V_{ex}\,(e_x A/S_y) + K_x V_{ey}\,(e_y A/S_x)$$

V_d = total design load on column, lb or kips
V_a = axial load from above column, lb or kips

V_x = column load in X axis, lb or kips
V_y = column load in Y axis, lb or kips
V_{ex} = eccentric load on column in X axis, lb or kips
e_x = eccentricity of load in X axis, in. $e_x = 1 + 0.5 \; b_x$.
　　　For round wood columns, $e = 1 + $ radius, in.
A　= area of trial column section, in^2
S_y = section modulus of trial section about Y axis, in^3
V_{ey} = eccentric load on column in X axis, lb or kips
e_y = eccentricity of load in Y axis, in. If column is
　　　square, $e_y = e_x$.
S_x = section modulus of trial section about X axis, in^3
　　　K_x and K_y are as previously defined

Step 5. Find the moment due to any wind load against the column.

　　a. Load acts on top of column:　$M = PL$
　　b. Load acts on length of column:　$M = 0.50 \; WL$

M = column bending moment due to lateral load, in-kips
P = concentrated load against top of column, kips.
　　　Wind load acts through any one beam against the
　　　column's top.
W = uniform load against length of column (i.e.
　　　floor/floor height of facade area, vertical projec-
　　　tion × width of facade area between 2 columns ×
　　　unit wind load), kips
L = clear unbraced length of column, in.

Step 6. Investigate the trial section regarding combined compression and bending in both axes:

$$(V_d/A \, f_c) + (M_x/S_y \, f_c) + (M_y/S_x \, f_c) \; \leq \; 1.00$$

M_x = moment of column side load in X axis, in-kips. As moment M computed in Step 5 acts against only one side of column at one time, set $M = M_x$ or M_y,

whichever has highest S; then other moment = 0.
M_y = moment of side load in Y axis, in-kips
$\qquad V_d$, A, f_c, S_y, and S_x are as previously defined

Use the following formula to find a wood column's safe unit compression stress based on its slenderness ratio.

$$f_c L^2 \approx 0.3 E d^2$$

f_c = safe unit comp. stress ‖ grain for wood post, psi.
$\qquad$ Find actual f_c, then compare with safe f_c.
L = unbraced length of post or column, in.
E = modulus of elasticity of wood used, psi
d = minimum thickness of column along its unbraced length, in.

Tapered Wood Column Design:

$\qquad X$ axis: $\quad d_{ex} = d_{x\text{-}min} + 0.33\,(d_{x\text{-}max} - d_{x\text{-}min})$
$\qquad Y$ axis: $\quad d_{ey} = d_{y\text{-}min} + 0.33\,(d_{y\text{-}max} - d_{y\text{-}min})$

d_{ex}, d_{ey} = equivalent dimension of tapered column in X or Y axis, in. For square and round columns, $d_{ex} = d_{ey}$.
$d_{x\text{-}min}$, $d_{y\text{-}min}$ = minimum dimension of tapered column in X or Y axis, in.
$d_{x\text{-}max}$, $d_{y\text{-}max}$ = maximum dimension of tapered column in X or Y axis, in.

Spaced Wood Column Design:

Step 1. Determine the column's K factors.

Step 2. Verify that the column's dimensions satisfy all five formulas below. If the column has more than two vertical members or three spacers, each added piece is designed as the initial ones.

If $m/e < 20$, $f_c' \le \dfrac{0.75\,E}{(L/d)^2}$

If $m/e < 10$, $f_c' \le \dfrac{0.90\,E}{(L/d)^2}$

$f_c' \le \dfrac{0.50\,E}{(m/d)^2}$

$f_c' \le \dfrac{0.30\,E}{(L/D)^2}$ $L/d \le 50$

The smallest f_c' above must $\le$ f_c = allow. unit compression stress parallel to grain for the column's wood, psi

Step 3. Design the member-to-spacer connectors as follows:

a. Find m/d.
b. Knowing m/d and the column wood, go to the bar graph below and find end block coefficient κ_e at m/d in line A and the wood species lines.

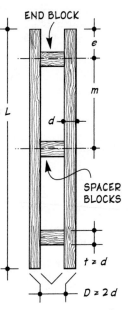

Fig. 2-9. Anatomy of a spaced column.

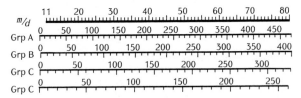

For wood species in each Group, see Table 2-5 on p. 92.

Step 4. Knowing κ_e, the section area A of one vertical member, and the spacer bolt's safe unit stress in tension f_t, find the bolt's diameter as described below.

$$\kappa_e A = 0.71 f_t \delta^2$$

Bracketed Column Design: $P_e S_c = a A_c P_b$

P_e = equivalent axial load of bracket load, lb
S_c = section modulus of column, in³
a = lateral length from bracket ₵ to column ₵, in.
A_c = section area of column, in²
P_b = total bracket load on column, lb

Pole Frame Structure Design:

Step 1. List each pole's loads, safe stresses, and subsoil values. This includes W_D, W_L, W_{snow}, W_{wind}, f_v, f_b, $f_{c\|}$, E, and any related values.

Step 2. Determine the pole's total vertical and horizontal loads. Lateral wind loads are considered to act at a point 2'-0" from the pole's top.

Step 3. Knowing the pole's full axial load P (lb), its effective lateral load W_L (lb), and the pole material's allowable compression stress $f_{c\|}$ (psi), find the pole's minimum diameter δ_{min} (in.) at its top from the formula

$$0.785\, \delta_{min}^2 \geq P/f_{c\|} + (0.024\, W_L^{0.62} + 3.10)^2$$

Step 4. Knowing the pole's top diameter δ_{min} (in.), its above-ground height H (ft), and its tentatively assumed depth of imbedment d_e (6 ft is usually a good dimension to start with), find the pole's maximum diameter δ_{max} (in.) at its base or butt from

→ß▊☰▯▦♀❋⚒☞💡☊▯◖

$$\delta_{max} \geq \delta_{min} + 0.080 \, (H + d_e)$$

δ_{max} = maximum diameter of pole at butt or base, in.
δ_{min} = minimum diameter of pole at top or peak, in.
H = length of pole from peak to groundline, ft
d_e = embedment depth of pole from groundline to butt, ft

Step 5. Depending on whether each pole is *restrained at base* (rigid surface surrounds pole at groundline) or *unrestrained at base* (no rigid surface surrounds pole at groundline), solve for L_u in formula **a** or **b** below. If solved L_u < actual L_u, adjust the pole's depth of imbedment d_e until solved $L_u \geq$ actual L_u.

a. Pole is restrained at base:
$$s_p \, \delta_{max} \, d_e^{\,2} = 4.25 \, P_h \, (L_u - 2)$$

b. Pole is unrestrained at base:
$$s_p \, \delta_{max} \, d_e^{\,2} = 3.54 \, P_h + 2.78 \, [P_h \, s_p \, \delta_{max} \, d_e \, (L_u - 2)]^{0.5}$$

P_h = horiz. load against pole (2.0 ft below top), lb
s_p = allowable passive pressure of soil per LF below groundline, psi. s_p = 400 psi for compact well-graded soil, sand, or gravel; 200 psi for average soils or sands; 100 psi for poor soils.
  d_e, δ_{max}, and L_u are as previously defined

Step 6. Check the pole for safe bending moment according to the formula below. Solve for f_b, then compare this value with allowable f_b.

$$M_{max} = 122 \, P_h \, (L_u - 2 + 0.25 \, d_e) \leq f_b \left[\delta_{max} + \frac{(L_u + 0.25 \, d_e)]^3}{L_u + d_e} \right]$$

M_{max} = maximum safe bending moment in pole, in-lb
f_b = safe unit bending stress of wood used, psi
  P_h, L_u, d_e, and δ_{max} are previously defined

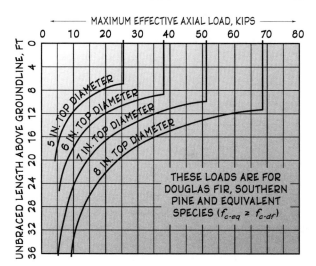

MAXIMUM EFFECTIVE AXIAL LOAD, KIPS

THESE LOADS ARE FOR DOUGLAS FIR, SOUTHERN PINE AND EQUIVALENT SPECIES ($f_{c\text{-}eq} \geq f_{c\text{-}df}$)

Fig. 2-10. Pole-frame load graph.

Step 7. Knowing the pole's L_u (ft) and δ_{max} (in), check L_u for maximum effective axial load from Fig. 2-10.

Step 8. Knowing L_u (ft) and δ_{max} (in), check that $L_u/\delta_{max} \leq 3.67$, then investigate the pole for safe bearing stress from the formula below. Solve for actual $f_{c\parallel}$, then compare with safe $f_{c\parallel}$.

$$E = 26.6 \, f_{c\parallel} \left(\frac{L_u}{\delta_{max} + 2\,\delta_{min}} \right)^2$$

E = modulus of elasticity of wood used, psi
$f_{c\parallel}$ = safe unit stress in compression parallel to grain for species and grade of wood, psi
L_u, δ_{min}, and δ_{max} are as previously defined

Step 9. Design the pole's footing. If the pole base is backfilled with soil, its footing area = 3.14 δ_{max}^2 unless a 1'-0" reinforced concrete pad is beneath the pole's butt; then the footing area = pad area. If the pole's base is imbedded in concrete, the footing area = pad area. In each case the footing's area must be investigated for safe bearing as described on page 243.

Wood Bracing Design:

Step 1. Determine the location and number of braces to resist the load in each floor from each side of the building.

Step 2. Compute the wind load resisted by each brace on each floor. Here this load is calculated only for the upper floor braces. The equation below includes forces due to wind moment and wind shear.

$$V_w h = v_w w_w (h + h_p) (1.5 h + 0.5 h_p)$$

V_w = lateral wind load resisted by each brace, lb
h = height of floor in which brace is installed, ft
v_w = maximum unit wind load for local area, psf
w_w = width of wind load area resisted by brace, ft
h_p = height of any major building area (parapet, roof, etc.) projecting above upper end of brace, ft

Step 3. Size each brace as described below.

$$V_w = f_c A \cos \angle$$

V_w = lateral wind load resisted by brace, lb
f_c = safe compression stress of brace according to species and grade of wood, psf
A = minimum section area of brace, in^2
$\angle$ = angle of diagonal brace to horiz. member above, °

Wood Shear Wall Design:

Step 1. Compute the maximum wind load against each shear wall.

$$V_w = 0.0033 \, A \, v^2$$

V_w = maximum wind load against end of shear wall, lb
A = vertical area of wind load surface, sf. A usually
     = shear wall spacing × maximum story height.
v = maximum wind speed against shear wall, mph.

Step 2. Compute the shear wall's compressive strength, then compare this with V_w found in Step 1.

$$V_c = 2 \, f_{ct} \, (I \, h \, t^3)^{0.25} \cos^2 (\tan^{-1} h/L)$$

V_c = compressive strength of shear wall, lb
f_{ct} = safe compressive/tensile strength of plywood, from Table 2-1, psi
I = moment of inertia of boundary framing based on its actual section area, in^4
h = maximum clear story height of shear wall, in.
t = thickness of shear wall sheathing, in.
L = length of shear wall, in.

Step 3. Install required braces at each corner of the boundary framing. A good design is flat A36 steel angles located on each side of each corner, at least two equal-diameter bolts through each leg plus one at the corner, and all bolts and legs centered on the intersecting members' axes.

Step 4. Find the force resisted by each bolt in each leg. Locate the bolts equally apart and in from fulcrum A.

$$V_c = \eta \, V_b$$

V_c = lateral load resisted by each brace, lb

η = number of braces in wall
V_b = lateral load resisted by each bolt in each leg, lb

Step 5. Size the bolt diameters in terms of type of shear and direction of the wood's grain.

Step 6. Size the angles. Try an angle thickness, then find its width from

$$V_b L_1 + V_b L_2 + \ldots + V_b L_z = 0.167 f_b b d^2$$

V_b = lateral load resisted by each bolt, lb
L_1 = length of angle leg from fulcrum to bolt 1, in.
L_2 = length of angle leg from fulcrum to bolt 2, in.
f_b = safe unit stress in bending for type of steel, psi
b = thickness of angle leg, in.
d = minimum width of angle leg, in.

TABLE 2-4: STRENGTH OF COMMON NAILS

WOOD SPECIES, Const. grade	Nail designation, in/penetration, lb					
	8d	10d	12d	16d	20d	30d
Cedar: N. white	25	29	30	34	44	49
Western red	35	41	43	48	63	69
Douglas fir	78	92	95	107	139	154
Oak, white	154	181	187	211	274	303
N. Pine, E. Hemlock ..	59	70	72	81	106	117
Southern Pine	78	92	95	107	139	154
Redwood	44	52	53	60	78	86
Spruce: Eastern	49	58	60	67	87	97
Engelman	33	39	40	45	58	65
Select structural grade .... multiply above values × 1.30						
No. 1 grade .. mult. × 1.20; No. 2 grade, mult. × 1.10						
Std. grade ... mult. × 0.80; Utility grade, mult. × 0.60						
Nails clinched mult. × 1.50; Nails at angles, mult. × 0.83						
Nails in end grain .... multiply above values × 0.67						
Nails in metal fasteners ... multiply above values × 1.25						
Safe withdrawal loads .... mult. above × 0.33/in. penetr.						

Safe Spacing of Nails in Wood Framing:

$$12\, f_v \;=\; V\, S$$

f_v = safe strength of each nail carrying load, lb
V = load transmitted from member to support, plf
S = maximum spacing btwn nails carrying load, in. o.c.

Withdrawal Strength of Nails in Framing:

$$V \;=\; \eta\, f_v$$

V = total withdrawal nail load transmitted from member to support, plf
η = number of nails carrying withdrawal load
f_v = safe strength of each nail carrying load, lb

Screw & Lag Bolt Design:

Step 1. About a fulcrum point A in the structural section take Σ moments that compares the applied load with the resisting action of the bolt(s):

$$H\, a_1 \;=\; R\, a_2$$

H = horizontal force against held member, lb.
a_1 = length of moment arm from ¢ of held member to point A, in.
R = resisting force of lag bolt(s) in parent member, lb
a_2 = length of moment arm from each lag bolt to A, in.

Step 2. Find each bolt's minimum diameter and length.

$$R\, \eta \;=\; 1{,}800\, L\, \sigma^{1.5}\, d^{\,0.75}$$

R = resisting force of lag bolt in parent member, lb
η = number of connectors in structural assembly
L = penetration length of each connector, in.

TABLE 2-5: STRENGTH OF THREADED CONNECTORS

WOOD SCREWS: Size	Min. embedment ⊥ grain, in.	Withdrawal strength, lb per in. penetration [1, 2]			
		Grp A	Grp B	Grp C	Grp D [3]
no. 6	1	45	68	90	139
7 [4]	$1\frac{1}{16}$	50	76	98	153
8	$1\frac{1}{8}$	55	82	108	167
9	$1\frac{1}{4}$	59	89	115	178
10	$1\frac{5}{16}$	63	96	125	194
12	$1\frac{1}{2}$	72	109	141	220
14	$1\frac{11}{16}$	81	124	160	248
16	$1\frac{7}{8}$	90	137	178	277
18	2	96	146	190	297
20	$2\frac{1}{4}$	105	160	208	324
24	$2\frac{5}{8}$	122	186	242	377

LAG BOLTS Dia., in.	↓	Grp A	Grp B	Grp C	Grp D
$\frac{1}{4}$	$1\frac{3}{4}$	126	172	210	295
$\frac{5}{16}$	$2\frac{3}{16}$	150	206	251	350
$\frac{3}{8}$	$2\frac{5}{8}$	173	238	289	400
$\frac{7}{16}$	3	193	265	325	450
$\frac{1}{2}$	$3\frac{1}{2}$	215	295	360	500
$\frac{9}{16}$	4	235	320	390	545
$\frac{5}{8}$	$4\frac{3}{8}$	252	345	420	587
$\frac{3}{4}$	$5\frac{1}{4}$	287	394	482	670
$\frac{7}{8}$	6	328	450	550	768
1	7	359	492	603	840

1. If heads are exposed to weather, use 0.75 × above.
2. For shear strength, multiply above values by 1.40.
3. Wood species under each group are as follows:
   Group A: balsam fir, cedar, redwood, spruce, white pine.
   Group B: cypress, hemlock, hem-fir, poplar.
   Group C: sweetgum, Douglas fir, South. pine, tupelo.
   Group D: ash, beech, birch, hickory, maple, oak.
4. Drywall screws are the same as no. 7 wood screws.

σ = specific gravity of parent wood structure
d = minimum diameter of connector, in.

Screw Holding or Tensile Strength:

$$A_t = 0.785 (\delta - 0.974/\eta)^2$$

A_t = tensile stress section area of screw thread, in^2.
Find A_t, then multiply $A_t \times$ screw steel f_t to find
the screw's actual tensile strength. For coarse-
threaded screws, the relation between screw diameter and A_t is:

Dia., in.	A_t, in^2	Dia., in.	A_t, in^2	Dia., in.	A_t, in^2
$3/8$	0.078	$7/16$	0.107	$1/2$	0.142
$9/16$	0.182	$5/8$	0.226	$3/4$	0.334
$7/8$	0.462	1	0.606	$1^1/8$	0.763

δ = diameter of screw, in.
η = number of threads per in. in screw shaft. For
coarse-threaded screws the relation between
screw diameters and η is:

Dia., in.	A_t, in^2	Dia., in.	A_t, in^2	Dia., in.	A_t, in^2
$3/8$	16	$7/16$	14	$1/2$	13
$9/16$	12	$5/8$	11	$3/4$	10
$7/8$	9	1	8	$1^1/8$	7

Corbel Design:

Step 1. Find the load on each bolt in the corbel.

$$V = \eta \, v$$

V = total shear load on connection, lb
η = number of bolts in connection
v = shear load carried by each bolt, lb

Step 2. Determine the type of connection (single or
double shear), bolt length, and direction of load (paral-

TABLE 2-6: ALLOWABLE BOLT LOADS

FOR MED-GRAIN DOUGLAS FIR, LARCH, SOUTH. PINE

BOLT LENGTH [1]	Stress	3/8	1/2	5/8	3/4	7/8	1	1 1/8
		←——— Bolt diameter, in. ———→						
1 1/2	Sgl shr ⊥ gr.	330	430	480	520	560	600	—
"	" ‖ gr.	370	470	590	710	830	950	—
	Dbl shr ⊥ gr.	370	430	490	540	590	650	—
"	" ‖ gr.	670	960	1210	1460	1700	1940	—
2 1/2	Sgl shr ⊥ gr.	330	480	610	720	800	880	—
"	" ‖ gr.	370	650	1020	1470	1720	2000	—
	Dbl shr ⊥ gr.	620	720	810	900	990	1080	—
"	" ‖ gr.	730	1290	1870	2370	2810	3220	—
3 1/2	Sgl shr ⊥ gr.	330	480	660	930	1220	1470	—
"	" ‖ gr.	370	650	1020	1470	1920	2200	—
	Dbl shr ⊥ gr.	640	980	1130	1260	1390	1520	—
"	" ‖ gr.	730	1300	2050	2860	3660	4380	—
5 1/2	Sgl shr ⊥ gr.	330	480	800	1000	1260	1410	1800
"	" ‖ gr.	370	650	1020	1470	1990	2610	3300
	Dbl shr ⊥ gr.	640	930	1410	1880	2180	2380	2600
"	" ‖ gr.	730	1300	2050	2940	4000	5250	6540

Bolt dia., in. >		5/8	3/4	7/8	1	1 1/8	1 1/4	1 1/2
7 1/2	Sgl shr ⊥ gr.	660	930	1300	1610	1800	1980	2300
"	" ‖ gr.	1020	1470	1990	2610	3300	4080	5870
	Dbl shr ⊥ gr.	1260	1820	2420	3040	3500	3800	4370
"	" ‖ gr.	2050	2940	4000	5250	6600	8150	11650
9 1/2	Sgl shr ⊥ gr.	—	930	1060	1430	1800	2280	2940
"	" ‖ gr.	—	1470	1990	2620	3300	4080	5870
	Dbl shr ⊥ gr.	—	1640	2270	2950	3710	4460	5500
"	" ‖ gr.	—	2940	4000	5250	6600	8150	11750

Spruce, hemlock, hem-fir, rdwd   mult. above values × 0.71
Oak and similar hardwoods ... mult. above values × 1.41
Wet conditions of use .... mult. above values × 0.67
Densely grained lumber .... mult. above values × 1.06
Open-grained lumber .... mult. above values × 0.95

1. Specified lengths are for bolts imbedded in main members of joints in double shear (dbl shr) and thinner members of joints in single shear (sgl shr).

lel or perpendicular to grain), then find the bolt's minimum diameter from Table 2-6.

Step 3. Compute the length of the vertical shear planes through which the bolt loads are transmitted from the corbel to the post.

$$V_c = \eta\, f_h\, t\, L_h$$

V_c = total load on each corbel connection, lb
η = number of shear planes in corbel connection
f_h = safe unit horiz. shear ∥ grain of wood used, psi
t = thickness of corbel (width of horizontal shear planes in corbel), in.
L_h = minimum length of horizontal shear planes in corbel, in. This includes only the shear plane and not the area of the bolt holes in it.

Step 4. Compute the total length of the corbel.

$$L = L_h + \eta\,(d + 0.125) + 4\,d$$

L = minimum total length of connection, in.
η = number of bolts in shear plane
      L_h and d are as previously defined

Sheet Metal Fastener Design: $\quad V = \kappa_f + \eta\, f_v$

V = joist end reaction on stamped metal hanger, lb
κ_f = flange factor, lb. If fastener has flanges that fit over top of support, κ_f for 18 ga. steel = 580 lb, 16 ga. = 840 lb, 14 ga. = 1,230 lb, 12 ga. = 2,020 lb.
η = number of nail holes in part of fastener attached to member or parent support, whichever is less
f_v = safe shear strength of each nail or screw, lb. f_v for N10 nail ($2\frac{1}{2}$ in. × 9 ga. dia.) = 92 lb; N16 nail ($2\frac{1}{2}$ in. × 8 ga. dia.) = 134 lb; N20 nail ($2\frac{1}{2}$ in. × 6 ga. dia.) = 145 lb; #8 × $1\frac{1}{4}$ in. screw = 76 lb.

Hinge Design:

    a. Hollow core doors: $L \approx 0.04\,(h\,w\,t)^{0.63}$
    b. Solid core doors: $L \approx 0.06\,(h\,w\,t)^{0.63}$

L = total pin length of hinges, whether 2 or 3 per
    door, in. If $L \le 7$ in. ➤ 2 hinges; if $L = 7{-}10$ in. ➤
    2 or 3 hinges; if $L \ge 10$ in. ➤ 3 hinges.
h = height of door, in.
w = width of door, in.
t = thickness of door, in.

Oblique Loads:

Step 1. Find the oblique load's H and V components.

    Horizontal: $H = \dfrac{h\,P}{(h^2 + v^2)^{0.5}}$

    Vertical: $V = \dfrac{v\,P}{(h^2 + v^2)^{0.5}}$

H = horizontal weight component of oblique load, lb
h = horizontal dimension (run) of oblique load $\angle$
P = oblique load, lb
v = vertical dimension (rise) of oblique load $\angle$
V = vertical weight component of oblique load, lb

Step 2. Compute the allowable stress at the face of the
meeting between the oblique load and the parent member. The equation below is Hankinson's formula.

$$f_c\,f_p = f_a\,(f_c \sin^2 \angle + f_p \cos^2 \angle)$$

f_c = safe unit stress in compression ∥ grain for
    species and grade of wood, psi
f_p = safe unit stress in compression ⊥ grain of wood
    used, psi. Face of meeting should be perpendi-
    cular to axis of parent member.

WOOD

$\angle$ = angle between axis of oblique load and axis of parent member, °

Step 3. If the minor member fits into a notch in the parent member, find the notch's minimum depth.

$$P^2 = f_a \, b \, d_n \, (P + V)$$

b = width of notch in parent member, in.
d_n = minimum depth of notch, in.
   P, f_a, and V are as previously defined

Step 4. Compute the parent member's minimum depth.

$$P \, a \, \eta \, (L - a) = 0.167 \, f_c \, b \, L \, (d_r - d_n)^2$$

P = axial gravity load of the minor member on the parent member, lb
a = distance of load center from near end of parent member, in.
η = number of load conditions on the parent member
L = total length of parent member, in.
d_r = minimum total depth of parent member, in.
   f_c, b, and d_n are as previously defined

Step 5. Connect the minor member to the parent member. If the members are no wider than 4 in, one method is to glue-and-screw plywood gussets onto each side of the intersecting members. The optimal relation between thickness of structure, thickness of plywood on each side, and length of screws is listed below.

Structure t	Plywood t	Screw length
2 in. nom.	$\frac{1}{2}$ in.	$1\frac{5}{8}$ in.
3 in. nom.	$\frac{5}{8}$ in.	2 in.
4 in. nom.	$\frac{3}{4}$ in.	$2\frac{1}{2}$ in.

COMMON TYPES OF STRUCTURAL STEEL

A36	A529	Carbon. A36 is widely used.
A441	A572	High-strength low-alloy.
A242	A588	Corrosion-resistant high-strength alloy.
A325	A449	High extra-strength (bolts and rivets).

Structural steel working stresses are proportional to yield stresses as follows:

$$f_v \leq 0.40\, f_y \qquad f_c \leq 0.60\, f_y$$
$$f_t \leq 0.60\, f_y \text{ except for pinned members,}$$
$$\text{then } f_v \leq 0.45\, f_y$$
$$f_b \leq 0.66\, f_y \text{ if } b/t \text{ ratio} \leq 65/f_y^{0.5}$$
$$f_b \leq 0.66\, f_y \text{ if } b/t \text{ ratio} > 65/f_y^{0.5}$$
$$f_{bearing} \leq 0.90\, f_y$$

TABLE 3-1: ALLOWABLE STEEL STRESSES

STEEL TYPE	SHAPES, PLATES, BARS						BOLTS, RIVETS		
		Std.		Compact					
	f_y	f_t	f_c	f_b	f_t	f_c	f_b	f_v f_h	f_t f_c	f_v
A36	36.0	22.0		24.0			14.5	19.1	9.9
A529	42.0	25.2		27.5			17.0	20.0	13.2
A441	40.0	24.0		26.4			16.0	—	—
	46.0	27.6		30.4			18.4	—	—
A572	42.0	25.2		27.5			17.0	19.8	13.2
	50.0	30.0		33.0			20.0	21.5	11.1
A242, A588	50.0	30.0		33.0			20.0	23.1	154
A307	36.0 (used for bolts & studs)							20.0	10.0
A325	73.0 (used for bolts & studs)							44.0	21.0
A449	81.0 (used for bolts & studs)							34.7	23.1
A490	90.0 (used for bolts & studs)							54.0	28.0
A502-1	38.3 (used mostly for rivets)							23.0	17.5
A402-2,3	65.0 (used mostly for rivets)							39.0	22.0

All stresses are in kips per square in (ksi)

3. STEEL

Beam Shear:

Vertical shear:	$V_v = 0.91 f_v t_w d$
Horizontal shear:	$V_h = 0.5 f_v t_w L_h$

V_v = vertical shear end reaction of steel section, kips.
V_h = total horizontal shear load, kips. Usually $V_h = V_v$.
f_v = safe unit shear stress for type of steel, ksi.
      Solve for this, then compare with safe f_v.
t_w = web thickness of W, M, or C steel section, in.
d = depth of W, M, or C steel section, in.
L_h = length of horizontal shear plane, in.

Bending Moment:

Step 1. Find the beam's moment, then section modulus.

$$\boxed{\text{M?}} = M_{max} = f_b S_x$$

$\boxed{\text{M?}}$ = applicable moment formula
M_{max} = maximum moment of total load, in-lb or in/kips
f_b = safe unit stress in bending for type of steel, ksi
S_x = section modulus of beam section, in³

Step 2. Find the beam's economic section, then its maximum unbraced length L_u, from Table 3-2.

TABLE 3-2: ECONOMIC SECTIONS, STEEL BEAMS

A36 steel   **MAXIMUM UNBRACED LENGTH, ft**

Compact design

ECONOMIC SECTION	S_x	f_y = 36.0 ksi		f_y = 50.0 ksi	
		L_u 0.60 f_y	L_c 0.66 f_y	L_u 0.60 f_y	L_c 0.66 f_y
W 36 × 300	1,110	35.3	17.6	25.4	14.9
W 36 × 280	1,030	33.1	17.5	23.8	14.9
W 36 × 260	953	30.5	17.5	21.9	14.8
W 36 × 245	895	28.6	17.4	20.6	14.8
W 36 × 230	837	26.8	17.4	19.3	14.8
W 33 × 221	757	27.6	16.7	19.8	14.2
W 36 × 210	719	27.6	16.7	19.8	14.2
W 33 × 201	684	24.9	16.6	17.9	14.1
W 36 × 194	664	19.4	12.8	13.9	10.9
W 36 × 182	623	18.2	12.7	13.1	10.8
W 36 × 170	580	17.0	12.7	12.2	10.8
W 36 × 160	542	15.7	12.7	11.4	10.7
W 36 × 150	504	14.6	12.6	11.3	10.5
W 33 × 141	448	15.4	12.2	11.1	10.3
W 36 × 135	439	13.0	12.3	11.0	8.8
W 33 × 130	406	13.8	12.1	10.8	9.9
W 33 × 118	359	12.6	12.0	10.7	8.6
W 30 × 116	329	13.8	11.1	9.9	9.4
W 30 × 108	299	12.3	11.1	9.8	8.9
W 30 × 99	269	11.4	10.9	9.7	7.9
W 27 × 94	243	12.8	10.5	9.5	8.9
W 24 × 94	222	15.1	9.6	10.9	8.1
W 27 × 84	213	11.0	10.5	9.4	8.0
W 24 × 84	196	13.3	9.5	9.6	8.1
W 24 × 76	176	11.8	9.5	8.6	8.1
W 24 × 68	154	10.2	9.5	8.5	7.4
W 21 × 68	140	12.4	8.7	8.9	7.4
W 24 × 62	131	8.1	7.4	6.4	5.8

TABLE 3-2: ECONOMIC SECTIONS, STEEL BEAMS

A36 steel
Compact design

ECONOMIC SECTION		MAXIMUM UNBRACED LENGTH, ft			
		f_y = 36.0 ksi		f_y = 50.0 ksi	
		L_u	L_c	L_u	L_c
	S_x	0.60 f_y	0.66 f_y	0.60 f_y	0.66 f_y
W 21 × 62	127	11.2	8.7	8.1	7.4
W 24 × 55	114	7.5	7.0	6.3	5.0
W 18 × 55	98.3	12.1	7.9	8.7	6.7
W 21 × 50	94.5	7.8	6.9	6.0	5.6
W 18 × 50	88.9	11.0	7.9	7.9	6.7
W 21 × 44	81.6	7.0	6.6	5.9	4.7
W 18 × 40	68.4	8.2	6.3	5.9	5.4
W 16 × 40	64.7	10.2	7.4	7.4	6.3
W 18 × 35	57.6	6.7	6.3	5.6	4.8
W 14 × 34	48.6	10.2	7.1	7.3	6.0
W 16 × 31	47.2	7.1	5.8	5.2	4.9
W 14 × 30	42.0	8.7	7.1	6.5	6.0
W 12 × 30	38.6	10.8	6.9	7.8	5.8
W 16 × 26	38.4	6.0	5.6	5.1	4.0
W 12 × 26	35.3	7.0	5.3	5.1	4.5
W 12 × 26	33.4	9.4	6.9	6.7	5.8
W 14 × 22	29.0	5.6	5.3	4.7	4.1
W 12 × 22	25.4	6.4	4.3	4.6	3.6
W 10 × 22	23.2	9.4	6.1	6.8	5.2
W 12 × 19	21.3	5.3	4.2	3.8	3.6
M 14 × 18	21.1	4.0	3.6	3.4	2.9
W 12 × 16	17.1	4.3	4.1	3.6	2.9
W 12 × 14	14.9	4.2	3.5	3.6	2.5
M 12 × 11.8	12.0	3.0	2.7	2.6	1.9
W 8 × 10	7.81	4.7	4.2	3.7	3.4
M 19 × 9	7.76	2.7	2.6	2.3	1.9
W 6 × 9	5.56	6.7	4.2	4.8	3.5
M 8 × 6.5	4.62	2.5	2.4	2.0	1.8

Deflection: $\Delta_{max} = \boxed{D?} \le L\kappa_\Delta$

Δ_{max} = maximum deflection due to load, in.
$\boxed{D?}$ = applicable deflection formula:

    L = length of span, in.
    E = modulus of elasticity for structural steel,
        usually 29,000,000 psi
    I = moment of inertia of beam section, in^4
κ_Δ = coefficient of allowable deflection

A steel roof beam or girder may also be sized by the formula below to support ponding water on it.

$$1.11\, L_S\, L_P{}^4/I_P + s\, L_S{}^4/I_S \le 86{,}800$$

L_S = column spacing parallel to beams supporting roof (length of secondary members), ft
L_P = column spacing perpendicular to beams supporting roof (length of primary members), ft
I_P = moment of inertia of primary members, in^4. Multiply I_P by 0.85 if members are trusses or open-web steel joists.
s = spacing of secondary members, ft
I_S = moment of inertia of secondary members, in^4. Multiply I_P by 0.85 if members are trusses or open-web steel joists.

Lateral Bracing Design:

Step 1. Investigate the beam for adequate bracing for compact or standard design by finding L_c and L_u.

    a. **Compact design:** $L_b \le L_c$
    b. **Standard design:** $L_b \le L_u$
    c. **Slender design:** $L_b \ge L_s$

L_b = actual unbraced length of beam, ft

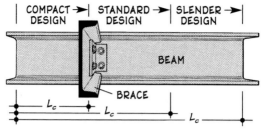

Fig. 3-1. Lateral bracing details.

L_c = maximum unbraced span for compact design, ft
L_u = maximum unbraced span for standard design, ft
L_s = maximum unbraced span for slender design, ft. If
      compact design and standard design are **NG**, use
      L_u to find f_{rb} in Step 2 below.

Step 2. If the beam is inadequately braced for compact
or standard design, compute its reduced safe stress for
bending from

$$0.60\, f_y\, L_u = f_{rb}\, L_b$$

f_y = safe yield stress for type of steel, ksi
f_{rb} = reduced safe stress in bending, ksi
      L_u and L_b are as previously defined

Step 3. Size the beam's lateral bracing. The member selected for bracing must satisfy both equations below.

    a. Minimum d_{lat}: $d_{lat} \leq 0.61\, d$
    b. Minimum S_{lat}: $S_{lat} \leq 0.25\, S_x$

d_{lat} = minimum depth of lateral bracing, in.
d = depth of parent beam, from steel tables, in.
S_{lat} = section modulus of lateral bracing, in^3
S_x = section modulus of parent beam, in^3

➔ℬ▓Ⅰ▢▦♀✳✂⛿🔔🔎🕮🕲

Width-Thickness Ratios of Steel Members:

$$b/t \le \kappa_{bt}/f_y^{0.5}$$

b = maximum depth, width, or diameter of major dimension of structural steel member, in.

t = minimum thickness of minor dimension of structural steel member, in.

TABLE 3-3: WIDTH/THICKNESS COEFFICIENTS
STRUCTURAL STEEL MEMBERS, w/t or $b/t \le \kappa_{bt}/f_y^{0.5}$

Structural member, submember, or element	κ_{bt}
Unstiffened compression members:	
Single-angle struts, double angles w/ spacers	76
Single angles in contact, plate girder stiffeners, angles projecting from compression members, beam compression flanges	95
Tee stems	127
Stiffened compression members:	
Flanges of rect. sections of uniform thickness ..	238
Perforated cover plates	317
All other uniformly compressed elements	253
Web plates, 6,000; Cover plates	7,500
Angle legs, beam or tee flanges	2,700
Plates, 2,300; Tee stems	3,000
Distance btwn plate fasteners in built-up members:	
Nonstaggered fasteners, 127; Staggered fast.	190
Compact sections:	
Unstiffened elements of any compression flange ..	65
Stiffened elements of any compression flange ...	190
Circular tubular sections	45
Webs in flexural compression	640
Noncompact sections:	
Unstiffened elements of any compression flange..	95
Stiffened elements of any compression flange ...	253
Circular tubes, 95; Webs in flexural compr.	970

κ_{bt} = required width/thickness ratio of steel member to ensure lateral stability

f_y = specified yield strength of steel member, ksi

Lateral Bracing Design for Eccentric Loads:

Step 1. Find the lateral support's resistant axial load P_r by taking moments at the meeting of the beam's vertical axis ₵ and its bottom flange ₵ (see Fig. 3-2).

$$P_e \, d_e = P_r \, d_r$$

P_e = eccentric load on beam, lb or kips

d_e = length of moment arm between vertical axis of moments and axis of eccentric load, in.

P_r = lateral load required to resist eccentric load, lb or kips. Compare the supporting member's f_c and f_t, then use the smaller f in the equation $P_r = f A$ to find the support's minimum section area.

d_r = length of moment arm between horizontal ₵s of beam's upper and lower flanges, in. The moment arm's top usually acts at the top of the lateral support and at the bottom of the fillet on the underside of the upper flange. Thus $d_r = d - k - 0.5$ bottom flange thickness, in.

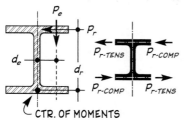

Step 2. Knowing the lateral support's resistant load P_r and safe compression stress f_c, find the member's least section area from $P_r = f_c A$.

Fig. 3-2. Eccentric load analysis.

Bearing Plate Design:

Step 1. Compute the bearing plate's minimum area.

$$W = f_c A$$

W = weight of load on bearing plate, lb or kips
f_c = maximum unit stress in compression for supporting material beneath plate, psi or ksi
A = minimum area of bearing plate, in^2

Step 2. Design the bearing plate's length and width. **c**
below may be used to design the supporting wall's width.

  a. Minimum area = $b\,d$
  b. Optimal length $d \approx 2 \times$ width b.
  c. Min. 2 in. support beyond plate on all sides.

Step 3. Compute the bearing plate's thickness.

$$t = 1.73\,(0.5\,d - k)\,(W\!/\!A f_b)^{0.5}$$

t = minimum thickness of plate, in.
d = length of bearing plate $\perp$ to beam axis, in.
k = distance from bottom of steel section up to web
toe fillet, from steel tables, in.
f_b = safe unit stress in bending for type of steel, ksi
W and A are as previously defined

Beam Web Stiffener Design:

Step 1. Investigate the beam for web stiffness.

$$P_w = 0.75\,f_y\,t\,(b + \kappa_L\,k)$$

P_w = maximum web load on beam flange, kips
f_y = safe yield stress for type of steel, ksi
t = minimum thickness of beam web, in. Solve for t,
then compare with actual t of steel shape.

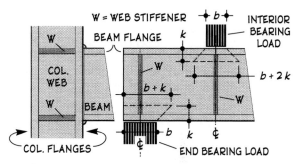

Fig. 3-3. Beam & column web stiffening details.

b = length of bearing load on top of flange or length of bottom flange on bearing surface below, in.

κ_L = load location factor. $\kappa_L = 1$ for end loads, 2 for interior loads.

k = length from outer face of flange to web toe of fillet, from steel tables, in.

Step 2. Design the beam web stiffeners if required.

$$P_w = 2 f_y t b$$

t = thickness of web stiffener, in. t must $\geq$ beam web thickness and should preferably be 1.5 more.

b = width of web stiffener on each side of beam web, in. $b \leq 0.5$ (0.8 beam flange width – beam web t).

Column Web Stiffener Design:

Step 1. Check the column for web stiffness. Stiffeners are required if $t_{cw} \leq$ the smaller of the two values below.

    a. $t_{cw} \leq 0.0056 (d_c + 2 k) (f_{yc})^{0.5}$

    b. $t_{cw} \leq f_{yb} b_{bf} t_{bf}/f_{yc} (t_{bf} + 5 k)$

t_{cw} = thickness of column web, in.
d_c = depth of column, in.
k = length from outer face of column to web toe of fillet, from steel tables, in.
f_{yc} = safe yield stress of column steel, ksi
f_{yb} = safe yield stress of beam steel, ksi
b_{bf} = breadth or width of beam flange, in.
t_{bf} = thickness of beam flange, in.

Step 2. Size the column web stiffeners if required.

$$b\,t = 0.5\,t\,(0.8\,b_{cf} - t_{cw})$$

b = minimum width of column web stiffener, in.
t = thickness of column web stiffener, in. This ≈ thickness of beam flange.
b_{cf} = width of column flange, from steel tables, in.
t_{cw} = thickness of column web, in.

Built-Up Beam Design:

Step 1. Draw the beam's shear and moment diagrams and find V_{max} and M_{max}.

$$V_{max} = 0.50\,W_{UNIF.\ LOAD} + P_{EACH\ PT.\ LOAD}\,(a\,b/L)$$
$$M_{max} = 0.125\,W_{UNIF.\ LOAD}\,L + \eta\,P_{EACH\ PT.\ LOAD}\,(a\,b/L)$$

η = number of point loads on span
All other terms are obvious from the text

Step 2. Tentatively size the beam's web. Consider trying a web depth $d_w \approx 0.08$ span and web thickness $t_w \approx 0.006\,d_w$, then check the section's slenderness ratio d_w/t_w.

$d_w/t_w \le 322$. **OK** $d_w/t_w \le 200$; best $d_w/t_w \le 162$
$t_w \le \frac{1}{4}$ in. (indoors) or $\le \frac{5}{16}$ in. (outdoors)

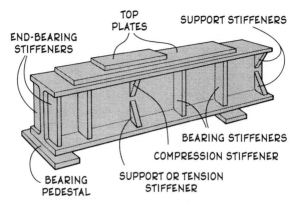

Fig. 3-4. Anatomy of a built-up beam.

Step 3. Knowing M_{max}, f_b, d_w, and t_w, tentatively size the beam's top and bottom flanges according to

$$A_f \approx M_{max}/f_b \, d_w - 0.167 \, d_w \, t_w$$

A_f = section area of each flange (usually plates, double angles, or built-up plates), in². $A_{top \, fl} = A_{bot \, fl}$.

Also check each flange for local buckling according to

$$b_{flange}/t_{flange} \leq 95/f_y^{\,0.5}$$

Step 4. Investigate the tentative flange section for safe shear and moment as follows:

$$V_{max} \geq f_v \, (A_{web} + A_{fl})$$

Plate flanges: $\quad V_{max} \geq f_v \, (d_w \, t_w + 2 \, b_{fl} \, t_{fl})$

Double angles: $\quad V_{max} \geq f_v \, (d_w \, t_w + 4 \, A_{angle})$

Built-up plates: $\quad V_{max} \geq f_v \, (d_w \, t_w + 2 \times A_{ea. \, pl})$

$$M_{max} \geq 2\,f_b/d_w\,(I_{web} + I_{flange})$$

Plate flanges: $M_{max} \geq 24\,f_b/d_w\,(t_w\,d_w^3 + 24\,b_{fl}\,t_{fl}\,d_w)$

Double angles: $M_{max} \geq 24\,f_b/d_w\,(t_w\,d_w^3 + 48\,A_a\,d_\phi^3)$

Built-up plates: $M_{max} \geq 24\,f_b/d_w\,(t_w\,d_w^3$
$$+ 24 \times A_{ea.\,pl} \times d_\phi^3)$$

d_ϕ = distance from each angle or plate to horizontal ϕ
of built-up beam, in.
    All other unknowns are as previously defined.

Step 5. Locate the stiffeners that should be between the upper and lower flanges on each side of the web. Stiffeners should be above each support, under heavy point loads, and at the ends of any cantilevers; and intermediate stiffeners may be required along the span.

Step 6. Knowing t_w, t_{flange}, f_y, the weight P of any point loads, and the bearing length l_b of any base plate under each such load, investigate the possibility of required stiffeners below each point load according to

If $P \geq 0.75\,f_y/t_w\,(L_b + 0.25\,t_{flange})$
point-load-bearing stiffeners are required

Step 7. Knowing f_v, d_w, and t_w, locate each end-panel stiffener at span length a from its supports according to

$$a^2\,(f_v\,d_w - 62{,}000\,t_w^2) = 83{,}000\,d_w^2\,t_w^2$$
For a, select a practical dimension $\leq a_{max}$
(e.g. if $a_{max} = 38.8$ in, try $a = 36$ in.)

Step 8. Locate any required intermediate stiffeners along the span. These must be equally spaced along any part of the span where they are required.

Step 9. Knowing the shears $f_{v\text{-}is}$ at each end-panel or

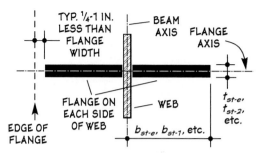

Fig. 3-5. Plan of built-up beam stiffener details.

point-load stiffener as well as the values for d_w and t_w, find $a_{i\text{-}max}$ in each subspan a_i according to

$$a_{i\text{-}max}^2 \, (f_{v\text{-}is} \, d_w - 62{,}000 \, t_w^2) = 83{,}000 \, d_w^2 \, t_w^2$$

If any $a_{i\text{-}max}$ ≥ its corresponding a_i, no intermediate stiffeners are required along that part of the span. If any $a_{i\text{-}max}$ ≤ its corresponding a_i, stiffeners are required. Then perform the following math:

$a_{i\text{-}max}/a_{i\text{-}max}$ = no of panels ➡ round off to next highest number

No. of panels/a_i = uniform spacing of intermediate stiffeners at each a_i

∴ no. of panels = no. of interm. stiffeners at each a_i

Step 10. Check for combined tension and shear stress in each panel as follows:

a. View the beam's moment diagram and note the maximum moment $M_{p\text{-}max}$ in each panel.
b. Compute S_x for the beam section in each panel.
c. Find the actual $f_{b\text{-}max} = M_{p\text{-}max}/S_x$ in each panel.

d. If actual $f_{b\text{-}max} \leq 0.75\,f_b$, allow. v must $\leq 0.4\,f_y$.

e. If actual $f_{b\text{-}max} \leq 0.60\,f_b$, allow. f_b must $\leq 0.4\,f_y$.

If **d** and **e** are not satisfied, fatten the beam section, usually by thickening t_w or widening b_{flange}.

Step 11. Investigate that the compression flange is restrained against rotation.

$$\frac{w}{12\,t_w} = \text{actual } f_c \leq \text{allow. } f_c = \frac{10{,}000}{(h/t)^2}\left[5.5 + \frac{4.0}{(a/h)^2}\right]$$

If actual f_c not $\leq$ allow. f_c, fatten the beam section

Step 12. Knowing maximum shear V_{max} at each support, design the end-bearing stiffeners at each support from

$$0.95\,V_{max} \geq 2\,f_v\,b_{st\text{-}e}\,t_{st\text{-}e}$$

Usually set $b_{st\text{-}e}$ slightly less than the flange's projection, solve for $t_{st\text{-}e}$, then select a slightly thicker practical plate size. Then check the stiffener's width-thickness ratio from

$$b_{st\text{-}e}/t_{st\text{-}e} \leq 95/f_y^{0.5}$$

The above assumes each stiffener is a plate. Each can also be an angle whose shorter leg lies against the web (better if the beam's parts are bolted or riveted and not welded); then disregard the angle leg that is parallel to the web when computing its width-thickness ratio.

Step 13. Size the other stiffeners. In the interest of simplicity and overall economy it is often wiser to size the stiffener at the largest net shear reaction (usually the end support), then make all others the same size.

Step 14. Design the beam's web-to-flange connections. Knowing the length of span L (in.), maximum horizontal shear V (kips), flange dimensions b_f and t_f, and the moment arm $d_{\textcent}$ from flange $\textcent$ to girder $\textcent$, first find the connector's required unit strength $f_{u\text{-}c}$ (kips/linear in) from

$$f_{uc}^{\ 2} \geq 0.027 \left(\frac{V_{hor}}{L} \right)^2 + \left(\frac{V\, b_f\, t_f\, d_{\textcent}}{0.083\, b_w\, t_w^{\ 3} + b_f\, t_w\, d_{\textcent}^{\ 3}} \right)^2$$

Step 15. If the web-to-flange connectors are welds, then, knowing a weld is on each side of the web ($\eta = 2$ welds), the strength E of the welding electrode, and the required weld's thickness, find each weld's safe unit strength f_{uw} (kips/linear in) from

$$f_{uw} = 0.21\, \eta\, t_w\, E \qquad \dots \text{then compare } f_{uc} \leq f_{uw}$$

Step 16. Continuing the welded connector possibility: knowing each weld's unit strength $f_{uw\text{-}a}$, f_v, and f_y, find the weld's minimum length L_{uw} from

$$127\, f_{uw} \geq L_{uw}\, f_v\, f_y^{\ 0.5}$$

Step 17. Continuing the welded connector possibility: knowing t_w and f_y, find the connection's maximum spacing of contiguous welds s_{uw} from

$$127\, t_w \geq s_{uw}\, f_y^{\ 0.5}$$

Knowing each weld's minimum length L_{uw} and maximum spacing s_{uw}, the weld can now be specified.

Step 18. Knowing the stiffener-to-web connector's height h, f_y, and the actual and maximum unit shears f_{va} and f_v, find the connector's unit strength $f_{u\text{-}c}$ from

$$h\, f_{u\text{-}c}\, f_y^{\ 1.5} \geq 6{,}270\, f_{va}\, f_v$$

Step 19. If the stiffener-to-web connectors are welds, then, knowing E, the number of welds on both sides of both stiffeners, and the weld's required thickness t_w, find its safe unit strength $f_{u\text{-}w}$ (kips/linear in.) from

$$f_{u\text{-}w} = 0.21 \, \eta \, t_w \, E$$
... compare with $f_{u\text{-}c}$, which is now $f_{uwa} \leq f_{uw}$

Step 20. Continuing the welded stiffener-to-web possibility: knowing the beam's unit load w, web thickness t_w, and each weld's actual and maximum unit stresses f_{uwa} and f_{uw}, find the weld's minimum length from

$$L_w \, (f_{uw} - f_{uwa}) \geq w \, t_w \, f_{uwa}$$

Step 21. Continuing the welded stiffener-to-web possibility: knowing the beam's total unit load ω and web thickness t_w, find each weld's safe spacing s_{uw} from

$$s_{uw} \geq \omega \, t_w$$

Flange Stiffener Design:

Step 1. Determine the beam flange load acting on each stiffener. Typically each flange load is divided in half, then each half acts on one stiffener as a point load located directly above the stiffener's ₵ of gravity.

Step 2. Draw a vector diagram of the load on one side of the web. Here half the flange load componentizes into vertical, horizontal, and resultant vectors wherein W_{hor} is a seam shear that acts between the stiffener's top and the flange's underside, W_{ver} is a seam shear that acts between the stiffener's side and the web's side, and W_{diag} is a resultant force that is used to compute W_{hor} given W_{ver}. W_{hor} is also a compression force that acts against the face of the web; so theoretically the web between the two opposing W_{hor} forces should be checked for crushing strength, but this deficiency doesn't occur if beam web $t \geq$ stiffener stem t. If the stiffeners are tensile members that connect to the bottom flange, W_{hor} becomes a tensile force pulling away from the web; then the web-to-

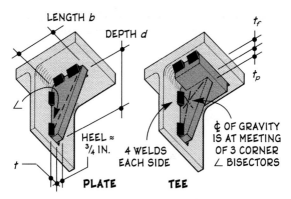

Fig. 3-6. Two types of flange stiffeners.

stiffener seam must resist this tensile stress on both
sides of the web. Finally, find the stiffener's vector components as follows:

$$W = W_{ver} \qquad\qquad W_{hor} = W_{ver} \sin \angle$$
$$W_{hor} = W_{diag} \sin \angle \qquad W_{ver} = W_{diag} \cos \angle$$

Step 3. Design the welds. Knowing stiffener loads W_{hor}
and W_{vert}, size the welds as described on page 160.

Pratt or Warren Truss Design:

Step 1. Find the reactions at the truss supports.

> **Symmetrical loads:** $V_\bullet = R_\bullet + L_\bullet$
> **Unsymmetrical loads:** See pages 37–38

$V_\bullet$ = total load on truss, lb or kips
$R_\bullet$ = vertical reaction at right end of truss, lb or kips
$L_\bullet$ = vertical reaction at left end of truss, lb or kips

Step 2. Isolate one end of the truss with a free body diagram, then find the diagonal chord's axial load as follows:

$$R_\spadesuit = A_\spadesuit \sin \angle_a \qquad R_\spadesuit = A_\spadesuit \cos \angle_a$$

$R_\spadesuit$ = vertical reaction at right end of truss, lb or kips
$A_\spadesuit$ = axial load of diagonal chord A, lb or kips
$\angle_a$ = angle between diagonal chord A and horiz., °

Step 3. Find the axial forces in struts A through I alphabetically by taking ΣV forces and ΣH forces about each successive panel point.

Subsequent steps. Isolate the panel point that includes the strut to be sized with a free body diagram, then compute the strut's axial load as follows:

$$\Sigma \text{ vertical: } A_\spadesuit = B_\spadesuit \sin \angle_{b\text{-}v}$$

$A_\spadesuit$ = axial load of chord A, from analysis of previous panel points, lb or kips
$B_\spadesuit$ = axial load of chord B, lb or kips
$\angle_{b\text{-}v}$= angle between chord B and vertical, °

$$\Sigma \text{ horizontal: } J_\spadesuit = F_\spadesuit + I_\spadesuit \cos \angle_{i\text{-}h}$$

$C_\spadesuit$ = horizontal resultant of chord C, kips
$D_\spadesuit$ = axial load of chord D, lb or kips
$B_\spadesuit$ = axial load of chord B, lb or kips
$\angle_{b\text{-}h}$= angle between chord B and horizontal, °

Truss Chord Design:

Step 1. Determine whether the chord(s) are in compression or tension.

Step 2. Select a trial section for the chord(s).

$$P = \kappa f A$$

P = equivalent axial load on chord(s), lb or kips

κ = trial and error coefficient for chord design. $\kappa \le$ 1.00. For short struts that carry large loads, try $\kappa = 0.5-0.6$; for long struts that carry small loads, try $\kappa = 0.8-0.9$.

f = safe stress in compression (f_c) or tension (f_t) for type of truss chord steel, psi.

A = net area of least section through strut, in^2

Step 3. Select a steel section whose area exceeds the chord's minimum area. Try to select an angle with one leg at least 1.5 times longer than the other, or else the angle's radius of gyration r_x will likely be too small.

Step 4. If the chord(s) are in tension, find their minimum A, then select a section whose area $\ge A$. If the chord(s) are in compression, find their slenderness ratios R_x and R_y, then find the member's safe unit stress in both axes.

Tension: $\qquad\qquad P = f_t A$

Compression, X axis: $\quad R_x = {}^{L}/_{r_x} \rightarrow f_{srx}$

Compression, Y axis: $\quad R_y = {}^{L}/_{r_y} \rightarrow f_{sry}$

P = effective eccentric load on each chord, lb or kips

f_t = safe unit tensile stress for chords, psi or ksi

A = least section area of each chord, in^2

R_x = slenderness ratio about X axis of chord(s)

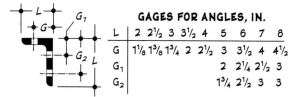

	GAGES FOR ANGLES, IN.							
L	2	2½	3	3½	4	5	6	7	8
G	1⅛	1⅜	1¾	2	2½	3	3½	4	4½
G₁						2	2¼	2½	3
G₂						1¾	2½	3	3

Fig. 3-7. Steel truss gage data.

L = unbraced length of chord, in.
r_x = radius of gyration of chord section in X axis, in.
f_{srx} = safe unit stress in X axis at R_x, ksi
R_y = slenderness ratio about Y axis of strut(s)
r_y = radius of gyration of chord section in Y axis, in.
f_{sry} = safe unit stress in X axis at R_y, ksi

Step 5. If the chord(s) are in compression, find if they are safe in each axis. If **NG** in either axis, try a larger section or locate stitch bracing along its length.

$$X \text{ axis: } \quad P_{srx} = f_{srx} A \geq P$$
$$Y \text{ axis: } \quad P_{sry} = f_{sry} A \geq P$$

P_{srx} = safe load on each chord in X axis at R_x, kips
P_{sry} = safe load on each chord in Y axis at R_y, kips
f_{srx}, A, P, and f_{sry} are as previously defined.

Step 6. If necessary, size the chord's stitch bracing. Try one stitch at mid-length, then two stitches at third points, etc. until the member is safe. $L_b \geq 2\text{'-}0\text{"}$.

$$P = P_s d_{sy}$$

P = total comp. load on end of chord(s), lb or kips
P_s = comp. load on end of stitch bracing, lb or kips
d_{sy} = depth of chord(s) in Y axis, in.

Metal Decking Design:

$$(\omega + 10\, d)\, \kappa_s\, L^2 \approx 2.5\, f_b\, S_d$$

ω = unit load (not including weight of concrete) on a 1 ft wide strip of decking measured $\perp$ to ribs, psf
d = total depth of concrete, in. Generally $d \geq 4$ in. for light loads on spans to 10 ft and up to 8 in. for heavy loads on spans to 15 ft.
κ_s = span factor. $\kappa_s = 1.09$ if deck is single span,

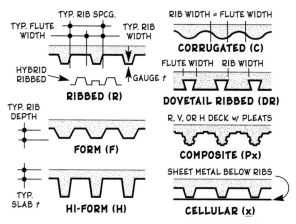

TYP. RIB SPCG.

RIB WIDTH = FLUTE WIDTH

TYP. FLUTE
WIDTH

TYP. RIB
WIDTH

CORRUGATED (C)

HYBRID
RIBBED

GAUGE *t*

FLUTE WIDTH   RIB WIDTH

RIBBED (R)

DOVETAIL RIBBED (DR)

TYP. RIB
DEPTH

R, V, OR H DECK w/ PLEATS

FORM (F)

COMPOSITE (Px)

TYP.
SLAB *t*

SHEET METAL BELOW RIBS

HI-FORM (H)

CELLULAR (x)

Fig. 3-8. Metal decking profiles.

     1.04 if 2 spans, 1.00 if 3 or more spans.

L = length of span, ft

f_b = safe unit bending stress for decking; unless otherwise noted, f_b = 20,000 psi.

S_d = unit section modulus of decking, in³/LF width. From Table 3-4 select a decking whose $S ≥ S_d$.

Composite Design:

Step 1. Compute the transformed section modulus of the beam and decking. The slab's effective width ≤ 0.25 beam span, 0.50 beam spacing, and 8.0 slab thickness.

   M? = M_{max} = $f_b S_x$ (two equations, two unknowns)

   M? = applicable moment formula

M_{max} = max. moment of applied load, in/kips

TABLE 3-4: ECONOMIC SECTIONS, METAL DECKING

DECKING	S_x[1], in^3	DECKING	S_x[1], in^3
H-14/7.5 × 12	3.858	R-20/3 × 2.5 × 8	0.568
H-16/7.5 × 12	3.099	DR-16/2 × 1 × 6.13	0.549
H-16/4.5 × 12	2.835	PF-18/2 × 12	0.547
H-14/6 × 12	2.793	PR-20/3 × 2.5 × 8	0.512
H-18/7.5 × 12	2.429	R-20/3 × 2.5 × 8	0.482
H-16/6 × 12	2.244	PF-16/1.5 × 6	0.480
H-18/4.5 × 12	2.175	PR-16/1.5 × 2.5 × 6	0.456
H-14/4.5 × 12	1.856	PF-22/3 × 12	0.455
H-16/3 × 12	1.769	DR-18/2 × 1 × 6.13	0.430
H-18/6 × 12	1.762	PF-20/2 × 12	0.428
H-20/4.5 × 12	1.548	R-18/1.5 × 2.5 × 6	0.425
H-16/4.5 × 12	1.491	HPR-22/3 × 2.5 × 8	0.415
H-18/3 × 12	1.352	R-16/1.5 × 2.5 × 6	0.412
H-18/4.5 × 12	1.174	R-18/2 × 2.5 × 6	0.388
PF-16/3 × 12	1.125	PF-18/1.5 × 6	0.385
R-16/3 × 2.5 × 8	1.098	PF-20/2 × 12	0.376
PF-16/3 × 12	0.975	R-22/3 × 2.5 × 8	0.366
H-20/3 × 12	0.957	PR-18/1.5 × 2.5 × 6	0.356
PF-18/3 × 12	0.899	R-18/1.5 × 2.5 × 6	0.324
R-16/3 × 2.5 × 8	0.883	DR-20/2 × 1 × 6.13	0.319
H-20/4.5 × 12	0.866	R-16/1.5 × 1 × 6	0.296
R-18/3 × 2.5 × 8	0.859	PF-22/2 × 12	0.295
PR-16/3 × 2.5 × 8	0.844	R-20/2 × 2.5 × 6	0.287
PF-18/3 × 12	0.784	R-20/1.5 × 2.5 × 6	0.275
PF-16/2 × 12	0.761	PF-20/1.5 × 6	0.266
R-18/3 × 2.5 × 8	0.679	PR-20/1.5 × 2.5 × 6	0.259
PR-18/3 × 2.5 × 8	0.676	R-16/1.5 × 1 × 6	0.249
PF-16/2 × 12	0.659	DR-22/2 × 1 × 6.13	0.247
PF-20/3 × 12	0.654	R-22/2 × 2.5 × 6	0.236
R-16/1.5 × 2.5 × 6	0.631	R-20/1.5 × 2.5 × 6	0.234
PF-18/2 × 12	0.625	PF-22/1.5 × 6	0.208
PF-20/3 × 12	0.572	R-18/1.5 × 1.75 × 6	0.204

1. Section modulus is for typical 1 ft width of decking measured ⊥ to ribs.

f_b = safe unit bending stress for steel used, ksi
S_x = transformed section modulus of beam section, in^3

Step 2. Knowing S_x, find the beam's economic section for composite design from Table 3-5.

Step 3. Find the horizontal shear acting through the studs in the slab from the formula on the next page.

TABLE 3-5: ECON. SECTIONS, COMPOSITE DESIGN						
ECON. SECTION	Total slab t 4 in.	5 in.	6 in.	ECON. SECTION	Total slab t 4 in.	5 in.	6 in.
W 36 × 170	713	748	781	W 21 × 50	136	146	157
W 36 × 160	670	702	733	W 18 × 50	125	134	145
W 36 × 150	628	659	688	W 21 × 44	120	129	138
W 33 × 152	603	633	661	W 18 × 46	114	123	133
W 33 × 141	559	587	613	W 16 × 45	104	113	123
W 36 × 135	558	586	612	W 14 × 48	99.6	109	120
W 33 × 130	512	538	562	W 18 × 40	99.4	108	116
W 30 × 132	481	506	531	W 16 × 40	92.9	101	110
W 33 × 118	461	484	506	W 14 × 43	89.3	98.1	108
W 30 × 116	421	443	465	W 18 × 35	86.0	93.4	101
W 30 × 108	388	409	429	W 16 × 36	82.8	90.4	98.4
W 30 × 99	354	373	392	W 14 × 38	80.4	88.5	97.0
W 27 × 94	316	334	351	W 14 × 34	72.1	79.3	87.0
W 24 × 94	290	307	325	W 16 × 31	71.9	77.9	84.9
W 27 × 84	282	297	313	W 12 × 35	68.6	76.1	84.1
W 24 × 84	259	274	290	W 14 × 30	63.6	70.1	76.9
W 24 × 76	234	248	262	W 16 × 26	59.7	65.4	71.3
W 24 × 68	209	221	234	W 12 × 30	58.8	65.3	72.1
W 21 × 68	189	202	215	W 14 × 26	55.2	60.9	66.9
W 24 × 62	184	196	209	W 12 × 26	51.4	57.1	63.1
W 21 × 62	173	185	197	W 14 × 22	46.5	51.4	56.5
W 24 × 55	164	175	186	W 12 × 22	42.7	47.7	52.8
W 21 × 57	156	167	179	W 10 × 22	38.8	43.8	49.0
W 18 × 50	149	160	173	W 8 × 24	36.7	42.3	48.2
W 18 × 55	137	147	159	W 12 × 19	36.7	41.0	45.5

$$V_{hc} = 0.425 \, f_c \, d \, (16 \, t + b_f)$$

V_{hc} = total horizontal shear in concrete slab, kips
f_c = safe stress in comp. for concrete slab, ksi
d = minimum depth of concrete slab, in.
t = total thickness of concrete slab, in.
b_f = width of steel flange supporting metal studs, in.

Step 4. Find the beam's number of required studs, find the studs' actual unit stress f_v, and size the studs, all from the formula below. If the ribs run perpendicular to the beam, select a stud spacing equal to the rib spacing, then solve for f_v and size the studs as follows:

$$h \, V_{hc} = 0.425 \, \kappa \, f_v \, w \, \eta \, (t/h - 1)$$

h = height of metal decking, in.
V_{hc} = total horizontal shear in concrete, kips
κ = ∥/⊥ factor. If ribs run ∥ to beam, κ = 0.7; if ribs run ⊥ to beam, κ = 1.0.
f_v = safe unit horizontal shear stress for stud steel, ksi. Actual f_v ≤ safe f_v.
w = width of decking ribs that rest on beam, in.
η = minimum number of studs along total length of beam: i.e. length of beam ÷ stud spacing
t = total thickness of concrete slab, in.

Select the stud size from the list below:

Stud size	Conc. f_c (ksi) ➔	3.0	3.5	4.0
½ in. dia. × 2 in. shank incl. head		5.1	5.5	5.9
⅝ in. dia. × 2 in. shank incl. head		7.0	7.5	8.1
⅝ in. dia. × 2½ in. shank incl. head		8.0	8.6	9.2
¾ in. dia. × 2½ in. shank incl. head		10.3	11.2	11.9
¾ in. dia. × 3 in. shank incl. head		11.5	12.5	13.3
⅞ in. dia. × 3 in. shank incl. head		14.2	15.3	16.4
⅞ in. dia. × 3½ in. shank incl. head		15.6	16.8	18.0

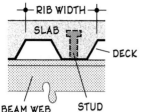

Fig. 3-9. Stud decking.

Step 5. If the decking ribs run parallel to the beam, find the maximum spacing of studs on the beam.

$$L = S\eta$$

L = length of span, in.
S = max. spacing of studs on beam flange, in.
η = min. number of studs

Open-Web Steel Joist Design:

Step 1. Map the joist and bay modules in plan. Try to make the joist spacing uniform and each bay module an exact multiple of a feasible joist spacing.

Step 2. Knowing the joist module, joist length, and loads, size the joists. Solve for S_x below, then find the economic section under the S_x column in Table 3-6. Then check the section for its live load limit and span limit.

$$(\omega_D + \omega_L)\, \kappa_j\, J\, (L + 8)^2 = 96\, f_b\, S_x$$

ω_D = unit dead load on joists, psf
ω_L = unit live load on joists, psf
κ_j = joist weight factor. $\kappa_j \approx 1.02$ for heavy loads on short spans to 1.07 for light loads on long spans for K Series joists, 1.03–1.09 for J joists, and 1.08–1.14 for DLH joists.
J = uniform spacing of joists, ft
L = length of span, in.
f_b = safe bending stress for joist steel, usually 30,000 psi
S_x = section modulus of joist section, in³

TABLE 3-6: ECON. SECTIONS, OPEN WEB JOISTS

ECON. SEC	S_x, in^3	Wt, plF	LL lim., κ_L	Span lim., ft
72 DLH 19	515	70	705	84-144
68 DLH 19	486	67	624	80-130
72 DLH 18	442	59	442	84-144
64 DLH 18	402	59	487	75-128
72 DLH 17	379	56	549	84-144
68 DLH 17	367	55	488	80-136
64 DLH 17	349	52	430	75-128
72 DLH 16	337	50	481	84-144
68 DLH 16	323	49	430	80-136
64 DLH 16	303	46	377	75-128
72 DLH 15	289	44	409	84-144
68 DLH 15	272	40	364	80-136
68 DLH 14	246	40	327	80-136
64 DLH 14	235	40	285	75-128
52 DLH 15	226	42	219	61-104
60 DLH 14	220	40	251	70-120
56 DLH 14	215	39	228	66-112
68 DLH 13	214	37	304	80-136
64 DLH 13	207	34	268	75-128
56 DLH 13	190	34	204	66-112
48 LH 15	183	36	167	56-96
52 DLH 13	176	34	174	61-104
64 DLH 12	170	31	222	75-128
60 DLH 12	164	29	195	70-120
56 DLH 12	156	30	167	66-112
44 LH 14	147	31	123	52-88
52 DLH 12	145	29	144	61-104
56 DLH 11	137	26	155	66-112
52 DLH 11	130	26	132	61-104
52 DLH 10	118	25	120	61-104
48 LH 12	113	25	104	56-96
44 LH 12	108	25	91.3	52-88
40 LH 12	106	25	80.4	47-80
36 LH 12	98.0	25	66.8	42-72
48 LH 11	90.3	22	83.2	56-96
44 LH 11	89.8	22	75.6	52-88
40 LH 11	87.4	22	66.6	47-80
36 LH 11	83.5	23	57.1	42-72
48 LH 10	83.4	21	77.0	56-96
44 LH 10	82.9	21	70.2	52-88

TABLE 3-6: ECON. SECTIONS, OPEN WEB JOISTS

ECON. SEC	S_x, in³	Wt, pLF	LL lim., κ_L	Span lim., ft
40 LH 10	79.7	21	60.9	47-80
36 LH 10	76.5	21	52.3	42-72
44 LH 09	75.1	19	63.4	47-80
32 LH 10	70.0	21	42.5	38-64
28 LH 09	58.6	21	30.4	33-56
40 LH 08	55.7	16	42.5	42-72
36 LH 07	49.5	16	34.0	42-72
32 LH 07	47.7	16	29.1	38-64
32 LH 06	42.6	14	26.0	38-64
28 LH 06	39.7	16	21.1	33-56
24 LH 06	35.3	16	15.7	28-48
28 LH 05	30.3	13	16.2	33-56
20 LH 06	28.9	15	10.6	22-40
24 LH 05	28.6	13	12.9	28-48
28 K 8	26.0	12.7	14.0	33-56
30 K 7	25.4	12.3	14.9	30-60
26 K 9	26.4	12.2	13.1	26-52
24 LH 04	24.7	12	11.2	24-48
28 K 7	23.7	11.8	12.8	28-56
24 LH 03	22.0	11	9.95	24-48
24 K 7	20.2	10.1	9.40	24-48
18 LH 04	20.0	12	6.58	18-36
26 K 6	19.6	10.6	9.98	26-52
20 LH 03	19.4	11	7.30	20-40
24 K 6	18.1	9.7	8.51	24-48
26 K 5	18.0	9.8	9.14	26-52
18 LH 03	17.3	11	5.79	18-36
24 K 5	16.6	9.3	7.74	24-48
18 LH 02	15.9	10	5.32	18-36
22 K 5	15.2	8.8	6.47	22-44
22 K 4	13.5	8.0	5.79	22-44
20 K 4	12.2	7.6	4.80	20-40
18 K 4	11.0	7.2	3.82	18-36
20 K 3	10.2	6.7	4.10	20-40
18 K 3	9.14	6.6	3.27	18-36
16 K 2	7.27	5.5	2.33	16-32
14 K 1	5.61	5.2	1.54	14-28
12 K 1	4.78	5.0	1.12	12-24
10 K 1	3.98	5.0	0.78	10-20
8 K 1	3.14	5.1	0.49	8-16

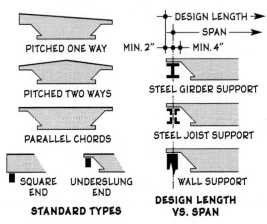

Fig. 3-10. Open-web steel joist details.

a. **Live load limit check:** $1,728,000,000\ \kappa_L/JL^3 \geq \omega_L$. Find κ_L (live load limit factor) for member. If **NG**, select a joist with a higher κ_L.

b. **Span limit check:** Compare actual span of member with span limits. If **NG**, select joist with next largest S_x within span limit.

Step 3. Size the open web joists' lateral bracing. Since different manufacturers may have slightly different specifications for their joists' lateral bracing, select the minimum size and maximum spacing of each pair of braces from manufacturers' catalogs.

Step 4. Knowing each joist's section number, size its horizontal X bracing —i.e. its minimum size and maximum spacing— from manufacturers' catalogs.

Step 5. Design the girder as follows:

a.   Load at each panel point:

$$24{,}000\,P = (\omega_D + \omega_L)\,\kappa_g\,J\,(L + 8)$$

P = total load on each panel point, kips

κ_g = girder weight factor. $\kappa_g \approx 1.02$ for heavy loads on short spans to 1.07 for light loads on long spans. w_D, w_L, J, and L are as previously defined.

b.   No. of joist spaces along girder: From Step 1.

c.   Depth of girder, in: Knowing the girder's span and uniform load, find its depth from Fig. 3-11.

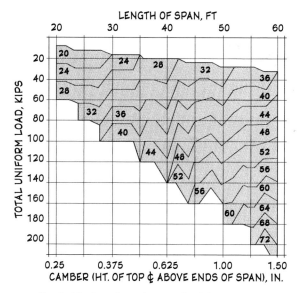

Fig. 3-11. Depth estimator for joist girders.

Steel Staircase Design:

$$2{,}300\, f_b\, S_x = (\omega_D + \omega_L)\, b\, L^2 \cos^2 [\tan^{-1} (r/t)]$$

f_b = safe unit bending stress for type of steel, psi

S_x = section modulus of each stringer, in^3. Solve for this value, then select the economic section from the feasible channels listed below:

Econ. sec.	S_x, in^3	Econ. sec.	S_x, in^3
MC 12 × 50	44.9	C 12 × 30	27.0
MC 12 × 45	42.0	MC 10 × 28.5 ...	25.3
MC 12 × 40	39.0	C 12 × 25	24.1
MC 12 × 35	36.1	C 12 × 20.7	21.5
MC 12 × 32.9	31.8	C 10 × 20	15.8
MC 12 × 30.9	30.6	C 10 × 15.3	13.5

ω_D = unit dead load on stairs, psf. $\omega_D \approx 40$ psf for concrete treads and steel steps with open risers, and 25 psf for treads of checker-plate steel or abrasive aluminum.

ω_L = allowable unit live load on stairs, psf

b = width of staircase, in. b = length of tread + thickness of spandrel on each side.

L = inclined length of staircase stringer, in. L = horizontal length of staircase ÷ cos [tan^{-1} (r/t)] or height of staircase ÷ sin [tan^{-1} (r/t)].

r = rise of steps, in.

t = run of steps, in.

Space Frame Design:

Step 1. Select the space frame module, usually by examining load capacities, span lengths, and support types in loading tables in manufacturers' catalogs.

Step 2. Knowing the frame's allowable load, span, module, and overhang, select the frame's column or wall supports from manufacturers' catalogs.

Step 3. Assuming an equilateral space frame (all struts or chords are equal), compute the frame's depth.

> **Triangular cells:** $d = 0.816\,L$
> **Rectangular cells:** $d = 0.707\,L$

d = depth of frame, from ₵ of base and top chords, in.
L = length of each space frame chord, in.

Light Metal Framing Design:
Sheel metal joists and rafters are lightweight, fireproof, and they contain voids for easy installation of enclosed pipes and wires. They may be designed as described below:

$$\omega\,J\,L^2 \approx 1{,}150\,f_b\,S$$

ω = total unit live and dead load on floor, psf
J = uniform joist spacing, usually 16 in. o.c.
L = length of span, in.
f_b = safe bending stress, usually 24,000 psi
S = section modulus of joist, from Table 3-7, in^3

TABLE 3-7: ECON. SECTIONS, LIGHT METAL JOISTS					
Joist Size, $b \times d$ in/t ga.	S_x in^3	Wt. lb/sf	Joist Size, $b \times d$ in/t ga.	S_x in^3	Wt. lb/sf
JWE-$2\frac{1}{2} \times 12/12$	6.01	6.53	JWE-$2\frac{1}{2} \times 8/16$	1.86	2.85
JWE-$2\frac{1}{2} \times 10/12$	4.62	5.80	JW-$2 \times 8/16$	1.69	2.63
JWE-$2\frac{1}{2} \times 12/14$	4.41	4.68	J-15/$2 \times 8/16$	1.51	2.48
JWE-$2\frac{1}{2} \times 10/14$	3.35	4.16	J-15/$8 \times 7\frac{1}{4}/16$	1.31	2.32
JWE-$2\frac{1}{2} \times 9\frac{1}{4}/14$	3.00	3.97	J-15/$8 \times 8/18$	1.24	1.99
JW-$2 \times 10/14$	2.92	3.82	J-15/$8 \times 7\frac{1}{4}/18$	1.06	1.87
JW-$2 \times 9\frac{1}{4}/14$	2.60	3.63	JW-$2 \times 6/16$	0.91	1.78
JW-$2 \times 8/14$	2.11	3.31	J-$1\frac{5}{8} \times 6/18$	0.80	1.66

Light Metal Framing Fastener Design:

$$V S = f_v L$$

V = total shear, bearing, or withdrawal load transmitted through framing connection, lb
S = maximum unit spacing of fasteners, in. o.c.
f_v = safe lateral strength of each fastener, lb. If the fasteners are power-driven nails, see Table 3-8;

TABLE 3-8: METAL FRAMING FASTENER LOADS

POWER-DRIVEN NAILS IN STEEL

Dia. in.	Min. steel t	Type of Load	Allow. load, lb/fastener Ga. t → 12	14	16	18	20
$1/8$	$1/4$	Withdrl/shr	375	375	375	375	310
	$3/8$	Withdrl/shr	500	500	500	410	310
	$1/2$	Withdrl/shr	620	620	510	440	310
$5/32$	$1/4$	Withdrl/shr	470	470	470	470	380
	$3/8$	Withdrl/shr	650	650	640	510	380
	$1/2$	Withdrl/shr	820	800	640	510	380
$3/16$	$1/4$	Withdrl/shr	570	570	570	570	460
	$3/8$	Withdrl/shr	800	800	770	620	460
	$1/2$	Withdrl/shr	990	970	770	620	460

POWER-DRIVEN NAILS IN CONCRETE

Dia. in.	Min. penetration, in.	Type of Load	Allow. load, lb/fastener f_c psi → 2,000	3,000	4,000
$1/8$	$3/4$	Withdrawal	93	120	145
		Shear	150	165	185
$9/64$	1	Withdrawal	160	200	250
		Shear	250	275	300
$1/8$	$1\frac{1}{4}$	Withdrawal	240	310	380
		Shear	360	400	440
$3/16$	$1\frac{1}{4}$	Withdrawal	320	425	405
		Shear	370	550	530
$1/4$	$1\frac{1}{2}$	Withdrawal	450	640	590
		Shear	515	780	730

if they are welds or screws, see Table 3-9.
L = length of framing anchored to base structure, in.

Steel Column Design:

Step 1. Tentativly estimate the column's size from

$$V P_\Delta \approx \kappa_t f_c A$$

V = total load on column, kips
P_Δ = the P-Delta Effect, a secondary load factor
κ_t = trial complication factor. Try between 0.25 (simple) and 0.65 (complex) depending on eccentric loads, side loads, column K factors, etc.
f_c = safe stress in compression for type of steel, ksi

TABLE 3-9: METAL FRAMING FASTENER LOADS

WELDS		Allow. load, lb/fastener [1]				
Type of Weld	Ga. t →	12	14	16	18	20
Fillet		1,030	740	590	470	350
Flare-bevel groove [2]		820	590	470	375	280

SCREWS	Dia.,	Type of	Allow. load, lb/fastener [1]				
Size	in.	Load Ga. t →	12	14	16	18	20
No. 6	0.106	Withdrawal	540	310	240	170	110
		Shr/bear'g	—	—	380	350	260
No. 8	0.125	Withdrawal	530	380	270	190	115
		Shr/bear'g	—	—	490	400	310
No. 10	0.153	Withdrawal	650	390	290	200	145
		Shr/bear'g	—	630	620	470	330
No. 12	0.177	Withdrawal	610	440	320	230	145
		Shr/bear'g	860	780	730	500	340

1. When joining steels of different gauges, use allowable load for lower gauge.
2. A flare-bevel groove is a weld between the edge of a small hole in one member and the flat of the attached member below.

A = minimum net area of trial steel section, in^2.

Step 2. Determine the column's K factors.

Step 3. Find the column's slenderness ratios.

$$X \text{ axis:} \quad R_x = K_x L/r_x$$
$$Y \text{ axis:} \quad R_y = K_y L/r_y$$

R_x, R_y = column slenderness ratio about each axis. The larger value governs.

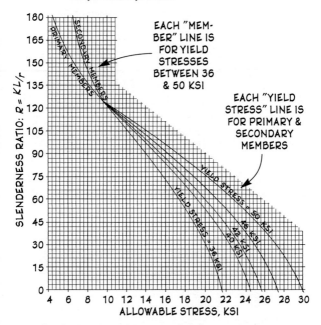

Fig. 3-12. Allowable stresses for steel columns.

K_x, K_y = column end condition K factor about each axis
L = unbraced length of column, in.
r_x, r_y = radius of gyration about each section axis, in.

Step 4. Find the yield stress for the column steel, then find the trial section's safe stress based on its governing slenderness ratio from the graph in Fig. 3-12.

Step 5. Find the trial section's maximum design load from the formula below:

$$V_d = P_\Delta [V_a + K_y V_x + K_x V_y + K_y V_{ex} e_x \,(^A/_{S_y}) + K_x V_{ey} e_y \,(^A/_{S_x})]$$

V_d = total design load on column, kips
V_a = axial load, if any, from above column, kips
V_x = total axial load on column in X axis, kips
V_y = total axial load on column in Y axis, kips
V_{ex} = eccentric load on column in X axis, kips
A = area of trial section, from steel tables, in^2
S_y = section modulus of trial section about Y axis, in^3
V_{ey} = eccentric load on column in Y axis, kips
S_x = section modulus of trial section about X axis, in^3
e_x, e_y = eccentricity of load in X or Y axis, in. For
      beam-to-column web, $e = 0.5\ t_w$. For beam-to-
      column flange, $e = 0.5\ d$.
      P_Δ, K_y, and K_x are as previously defined

Step 6. Compute the column's moment due to wind load.

     Load acts on column's top: $M = P L$
     Load acts on column's length: $M = 0.50\ W L$

M = moment of column due to lateral load, in-kips
P = concentrated load against top of column, kips
L = clear unbraced length of column, from Step 3, in.
W = total uniform side load against column (i.e.
      floor/floor height of facade area × width of fa-

cade btwn. two columns × unit wind load), kips

Step 7. Check the section for combined compression and bending as follows:

$$(V_d/_A f_c) + (M_x/_{S_y} f_c) + (M_y/_{S_x} f_c) \leq 1.00$$

M_x = moment of column side load in X axis, in-kips
S_y = section modulus of trial section in axis perpendicular to direction of moment, in^3
V_d, A, f_c, M_y, and S_x are as previously defined.

Central Axis of Built-Up Steel Sections:

$$A_t d = A_1 d_1 + A_2 d_2 + A_3 d_3 + ... A_Z d_Z$$

A_t = total area of built-up section, in^2
d = distance from reference axis of total section to central axis of total section, in.
A_1 = section area of steel section 1, in^2
d_1 = distance from central axis of section 1 to reference axis of total section, in.
A_2 = section area of steel section 2, in^2
d_2 = distance from central axis of section 2 to reference axis of total section, in.
A_3 = section area of steel section 3, in^2
d_3 = distance from central axis of section 3 to reference axis of total section, in.
A_Z = section area of steel section Z, in^2
d_Z = distance from central axis of section Z to reference axis of total section, in.

Column Pedestals, Small-Moment Design:

Step 1. Find the bearing plate's required area.

$$V = 0.25 A f_c$$

V = total vertical load on column, lb
A = minimum surface area of bearing plate, in^2
f_c = safe unit compression stress for concrete, psi

Step 2. Compute the length of the base cantilevering from the column's bearing area on all sides.

$$A = (2\,E + 0.95\,d)\,(2\,E + 0.80\,b)$$

A = minimum area of bearing plate, from Step 1, in^2
E = minimum extension of base from outer edge of column on all sides, in.
d = depth of column section, in.
b = breadth or width of column section, in.

Step 3. Compute the bearing plate's length and width.

$$L = 2\,E + 0.95\,d \qquad W = 2\,E + 0.80\,b$$

L = optimal length of bearing plate, in.
W = optimal width of bearing plate, in.
E, d, and b are as previously defined

Step 4. Compute the bearing plate's thickness.

$$f_y\,t^2 = 4\,f_c\,E^2$$

f_y = safe unit yield stress for steel, ksi
t = minimum thickness of bearing plate, in.
f_c = safe unit compression stress for concrete, ksi
E = minimum extension of base from outer edge of column on all sides, from Step 2, in.

Column Pedestals, Bi-Axial Moment Loads:

$$M_{max\text{-}total} = (M_{max\text{-}x}^2 + M_{max\text{-}y}^2)^{0.5}$$

M = max. moment against column in each axis, in-kips

Column Pedestals, Large-Moment Design:

Step 1. Knowing the column's depth d and width b_f, select a distance e (usually 2.50 in.) which locates the anchor bolt centers on each side of the column's flange.

Step 2. Knowing d, b_f, e, P_T (the column's total load), and f_{cc}, find m, the width of the mantle between the outer edges of the column and pedestal, from below. m should be about the same on all sides of the column.

$$P_t = f_{cc} (d + 2\ m) (b_f + 2\ m)$$

Step 3. Knowing d, b_f, e, P_t, and m, size the pedestal from

$$X \geq d + 2\ m \qquad Y \geq b_f + 2\ m$$

Step 4. Knowing X, e, m, the column's static dead load P_d, and its maximum moment M_{max} due to any eccentric load, bending, and lateral loads, find P_{anc}, the net force resisted by each symmetrical anchor bolt, from

$$P_{anc} (X - m)^2 = (X - 2\ m) [P_d (X - m) - M_{max}]$$

Step 5. Knowing d, e, P_{anc}, the pedestal's safe stress f_b, and the anchor bolts' safe stress f_t, find the anchor bolts' diameters from

$$P_{anc} = 0.785\ f_t\ \delta^2$$

Step 6. Find the pedestal's required thickness from

$$t_p = \left\{ \frac{3\ (b_f - t_w)^2}{4 + 12.8 \left(\dfrac{b_f - t_w}{2\ d - 4\ t_f} \right)^3} \right\}^{0.5}$$

t_p = min. thickness of column base or pedestal, in.
b_f = width of column section on top of pedestal, in.
t_w = thickness of column web, in.

d = depth of column section on top of pedestal, in.
t_f = thickness of column flange, in. If column is a
       pipe or other steel shape, t_f = thickness of the
       outermost part of its section.

Step 7. Design the braces that connect the anchor
bolts to the column. The braces are typically vertical angles or plates that are welded to the column's sides and
have a horizontal plate on top that contains a hole big
enough for the anchor bolt to slide through. The top
plate's thickness is found from

$$L \left(0.125 \, d_k \, f_{cc} \, b - P_{max}\right) = 1.34 \, f_b \, t_p^{\,2} \, (b_p - 1.5 \, \delta)$$

L = average length of span bridged by plate, in.
d_k = distance from ₵ of bolt to near edge of plate, in.
f_{cc} = specified strength of footing concrete, ksi

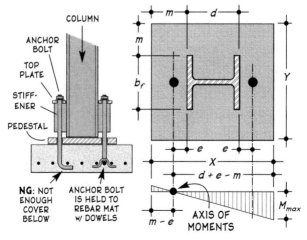

Fig. 3-13. Large-moment column pedestal details.

➔ß▣I▯▩♀✷⚒☞♀♥▥℃

b   = breadth or width of column base plate, in.
P_{max} = full axial load on column, kips
f_b = safe stress in bending for column, ksi
t_p = thickness of plate on top of angle, in.
b_p = breadth or width of plate on top of angle, in.
δ   = diameter of anchor bolt, in.

Step 8. Knowing P_{max}, b, d_k, f_{cc}, the weld thickness t_w, the electrode strength E, and the number of rows of welds η required to hold each anchor bolt's supporting plate to the face of the column, find the unit strength F_w of all the welds required in each row from

$$1.68 \ \eta \ F_w \ t_w \ E \ = \ d_k \ f_{cc} \ b - 8 \ P_{max}$$

Step 9. Specify the welds. Knowing the unit strength F_w of the required welds in each row against the column and the column's net tension load $T_{max} = (0.125 \ d_k \ f_{cc} \ b - P_{max})$, find the length L_w of each row of welds from

$$F_w \ L_w \ = \ T_{max} \ = \ 0.125 \ d_k \ f_{cc} \ b - P_{max}$$

Divide weld length L_w into three welds (one at each end of the angle and one in the center), round off each weld to the next highest ¼ in, and add ¼ in. to each end.

Bracing: If a steel structure is a braced frame, design it as described on page 43; if it is a rigid frame or infilled frame, design it as described on page 47.

Connections: Structural steel connections, in addition to being strong, should be simple: few parts, simple details, uniform arrangements, same size throughout the building. Fig 3-14 shows several common steel beam-to-column connections. The connectors may be bolts, rivets, or welds.

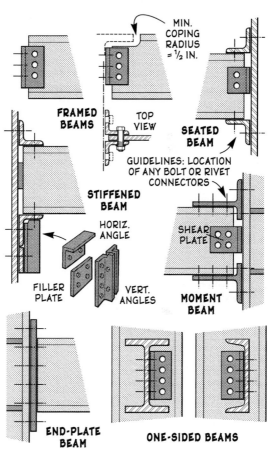

Fig. 3-14. Common steel beam-to-column connections.

Bolt or Rivet Connections, Unit Strength:

$$T = 0.785\, f_t \left(\delta - \frac{0.974}{\eta}\right)^2$$

T = tensile capacity of bolt, kips
f_t = safe unit tensile stress for type of bolt steel, ksi
δ = diameter of each bolt, in.
η = number of threads per in. in bolt shaft

Bolt or Rivet Connection Design:

Step 1. Determine the type of connection: *slip-critical* (the tightened bolt or rivet creates a clamping action on the connected parts which resists the applied load: F), *bearing, threads included* (the connector is a bolt whose threads lie within the connection's shear plane: N), or *bearing, threads excluded* (the connector has no threads in the connection's shear plane: X).

Step 2. Tentatively arrange the connection's fasteners in a pattern of rows and columns; then, knowing the fasteners' total load P_{tot} and number η, find each fastener load P from

$$P_{tot} \le \eta\, P$$

P_{tot} = total load of connector, kips
η = number of fasteners in connection
P = allowable load of fastener in connection, kips

Step 3. Knowing the type of connection and the allowable load of each fastener, find its minimum diameter from Fig. 3-15. If the bolt diameter $\ge 1\frac{1}{4}$ in, consider redesigning the connection with more fasteners.

Step 4. Knowing the connection's total load, the number and diameter of its fasteners, and the safe yield stresses of the steel used for each piece in the connec-

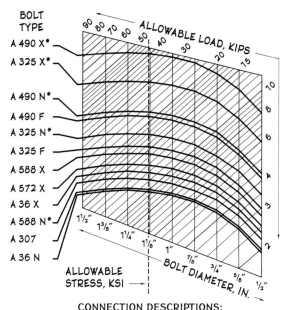

CONNECTION DESCRIPTIONS:

F = slip-critical (formerly friction) type
N = bearing type, threads included in shear plane
X = bearing type, threads excluded from shear plane

Allowable loads are for standard-size bolts.
Double shear values = 2 × single shear values.

For threaded parts of all other metals, $f_v = 0.17 f_u$ for type N connections and $0.22 f_u$ for type X connections.

The bolt types marked (*) are appropriate for long or short slotted holes perpendicular to direction of load; this is required in bearing connections.

Fig. 3-15. Allowable loads for steel bolts.

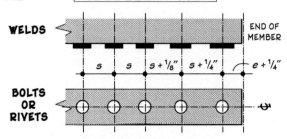

**Fig. 3-16. Optimal bolt, rivet, or weld
row spacing at end of connected member.**

tion, find the thicknesses of the plate(s) and web from

  a. Plate(s) of connection: $P_{tot} \leq \eta\, t_p\, f_{yp}\, \delta$
  b. Web of parent member: $P_{tot} \leq t_w\, f_{yw}\, \delta$

P_{tot} = total load of connector, kips
η = number of shear planes or plates in connection
t_p = total thickness of plate(s), in.
δ = diameter of each bolt or rivet, in.
f_{yp} = safe yield stress for plate steel, ksi
t_w = thickness of plate or web, in.
f_{yw} = safe yield stress for web or parent steel, ksi

Bolt Plate Design, Block Shear:

Step 1. Find the fasteners' minimum diameters based
on the connection's applied load.

$$P = 0.785\, \eta\, f_v\, \delta^2$$

P = total load supported by the connection, kips
η = number of bolts or rivets in connection
f_v = safe unit shear stress for steel used, ksi
δ = minimum diameter of each bolt, in.

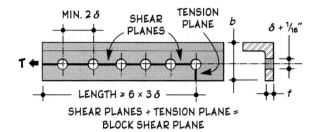

Fig. 3-17. Block shear in a steel angle connection.

Step 2. Solve the equation below and note which net section area is greater.

$$A_{nt} \geq ? \leq 0.6\, A_{nv}$$

A_{nt} = net section area of tension plane in member, in^2
A_{nv} = net section area of shear plane in member, in^2

Step 3. Solve the proper equation below to find the member's capacity for block shear. If $V_b \geq P$ from Step 1, the connection is safe in block shear.

$$A_{nt} \leq 0.6\, A_{nv}: \quad V_b = 0.45\, f_y\, A_{nt}$$
$$A_{nt} \geq 0.6\, A_{nv}: \quad V_b = 0.45\, f_y\, A_{nv}$$

V_b = maximum block shear stress of member, psi or ksi
f_y = safe unit yield stress for type of steel, ksi
A_{nt} = net section area of member in tension, in^2
A_{nv} = net section area of member in shear, in^2

Bolt Plate Design, Critical Net Section:
Fill out the schedule at the top of Fig. 3-18 (a sample scenario is inscribed), then find the shortest chain length which is the bolt plate's critical section.

Chain	Total width	− no. holes in chain	+ no. gage sp. in chain	× $s^2/4g$	= chain length
ABCD	12 in.	− 4	+ 0	× 1.59/4 × 3 =	8.00 in.
ABCGD	12 in.	5	2	1.59/4 × 3	7.42 in.
ABFCD	12 in.	5	2	1.59/4 × 3	7.42 in.
AEFGD	12 in.	5	2	1.59/4 × 3	7.42 in.
AEBFCGD	12 in.	7	4	1.59/4 × 3	5.84 in. ✚
AEHFIGD	12 in.	7	6	1.59/4 × 3	6.27 in.
AEIGD	12 in.	6	4	1.59/4 × 3	6.85 in.
AEHFGD	12 in.	6	4	1.59/4 × 3	6.85 in.

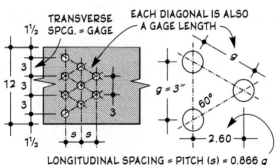

Fig. 3-18. Critical net section in a bolted plate.

Bolted Splice Plate Design:

Step 1. Find the fasteners' minimum diameters.

$$P = 0.785\, \eta\, f_v\, \delta^2$$

P = total load supported by all the bolts or rivets in the connection, lb or kips

η = no. of bolts or rivets in connection on each side of the parent members' seam-in-common

f_v = safe unit shear stress for A441 steel, ksi
δ = minimum diameter of each bolt or rivet, in.

Step 2. Check the parent tensile member for safe bearing stress. In the formula below, P should $\geq P$ of the initial load. Otherwise the parent member must be made thicker or wider. The member may also require investigation for block shear.

$$P = t_p f_b [b - \eta_{ns} (\delta + 0.125)]$$

t_p = thickness of each parent member, in.
f_b = safe bearing stress for parent member steel, ksi
b = width of parent member, in.
η_{ns} = no. of bolts in net critical section of connection
$\quad$ P and δ are as previously defined

Step 3. Find the thickness of the two plates on each side of the parent member.

$$P = \eta \, t_p f_b [b - \eta_{ns} (\delta + 0.125)]$$

η = number of plates in connection, usually 1 or 2
t_p = total thickness of plates, in.
b = full breadth or width of plates, in.
$\quad$ P, f_b, η_{ns}, and δ are as previously defined

Step 4. Investigate the pitch between the connectors for adequate length (see Fig. 3-18).

$$b \geq 3 \, \eta_{ns} (\delta + 0.125)$$

All terms are as previously defined.

Step 5. Find the longitudinal dimension, or length, of the plates on each side of the parent member.

$$L \geq 6 \, \eta_{lc} (\delta + 0.125)$$

L = total length of plates, in.

η_{lc} = number of connectors arranged longitudinally on each side of splice

δ = diameter of each bolt, in.

Bolted Framed Beam Connection Design:

Step 1. If the beam is framed to a girder, see if its top or bottom flange is coped. If so, subtract $k + \frac{1}{8}$ in. from the beam's full depth for further calculations below.

Step 2. Knowing the beam's end reaction R, its depth d, and its flange-to-fillet depth k, design the column or row pattern of fasteners on the angle flanges. Tentatively select the number of fasteners η_1 in equation **a** below, then solve for η_2 and η_3 in equations **b** and **c**.

a. $|\eta_1| = d - 2 \, (k + 0.125)$. $|\eta_1|$ means save only the integer of quantity η_1.

b. Try a bolt diameter. $\delta = \frac{3}{4}$ in the formula $R \leq 0.785 \, |\eta_2 \blacktriangleright| \, f_v \, \delta^2$. $|\eta_2 \blacktriangleright|$ means raise the quantity η to the next integer: e.g. $|5.6| = 6.0$.

c. Try a bolt diameter. $\delta = 1$ in the formula $R \leq 0.785 \, |\eta_3 \blacktriangleright| \, f_v \, \delta^2$.

If $|\eta_2 \blacktriangleright| \leq |\eta_1|$, then $|\eta_2 \blacktriangleright|$ is the optimal number of fasteners and they require only one column of fasteners. If $|\eta_2 \blacktriangleright| > |\eta_1|$, then the column/row pattern has two columns and its optimal number of rows is the next integer above $0.5 \, \eta_3$: e.g. if $\eta_3 = 8.67$, then $0.5 \times 8.67 = 4.33 \blacktriangleright 5$ rows.

Step 3. Knowing the number of columns and rows in each angle leg and thus the number of bolts or rivets in the leg, find the optimal diameter of the bolts or rivets from a choice of $\frac{3}{4}$, $\frac{7}{8}$, and 1 in. diameters from

$$R \leq 1.57 \, \eta \, f_v \, \delta^2$$

R = beam end reaction, kips
η = number of bolts or rivets in connector
f_v = safe unit shear stress for type of steel, ksi
δ = diameter of each bolt or rivet, in.

Step 4. Knowing k and δ, find the length L of each angle from

$$L = [\delta - 2 (k + 0.125)]$$

Step 5. Knowing R, L, η, δ, and the safe unit tensile stress f_t of the type of steel used for the angle, find the angle leg thickness t from

$$R \leq 0.6 f_t t [L - \eta (\delta + 0.063)]$$

Solve for t, then increase t to next highest number of $\frac{3}{8}$, $\frac{1}{2}$, $\frac{5}{8}$, $\frac{3}{4}$, $\frac{7}{8}$, 1, $1\frac{1}{8}$ in.

Step 6. Arrange the bolts or rivets on each angle leg according to the following pitch and edge distance requirements.

Pitch (connector spacing) requirements: min. pitch = $2\frac{2}{3}$ diameters, but 3 diameters is preferred and used widely. Also measure the beam-to-angle holes from the top of the beam angle leg down and the angle-to-column or girder holes from the bottom of the column angle leg up, as this puts more shear plane in front of the transferred loads.

Edge distance requirements: minimum 1.5 δ or $1\frac{1}{4}$ in, whichever is more; but an extra $\frac{1}{4}$ in. is safer.

Bolted Seated Beam Connection Design:

Step 1. Knowing the beam's end reaction R, yield stress f_y, and web thickness t_w, find the seat angle's length L and thickness t_L from Table 3-10.

Step 2. Knowing the beam's end reaction R and the fastener steel's safe unit shear f_v, determine the size and number of bolts in the seat angle's outstanding leg from

$$R \leq 0.785 \, \eta \, f_v \, \delta^2$$

R = beam end reaction, kips
η = number of bolts in leg of seat angle that rests against parent member. If $L = 6$ in, $\eta = 2, 4,$ or 6; if $L = 8$ in, $\eta = 3, 6,$ or 9.

TABLE 3-10: SEATED BEAM ANGLE LOADS

Seat angle, $f_y = 36$ ksi $L_1 \times L_2 \times t$, in.	$^3/_{16}$	$^1/_4$	$^5/_{16}$	$^3/_8$	$^7/_{16}$	$^1/_2$	$^9/_{16}$	$^5/_8$
L 8 × 8 × 1	19	34	47	60	26	44	60	78
L 6 × 6 × 1	18	32	43	57	26	40	56	74
L 8 × 8 × $^3/_4$	17	26	36	48	21	33	46	60
L 6 × 6 × $^3/_4$	16	24	33	44	19	30	43	78
L 8 × 8 × $^5/_8$	14	22	31	38	18	28	39	78
L 6 × 6 × $^5/_8$	13	20	29	34	16	25	36	78
L 8 × 8 × $^1/_2$	11	18	24	27	14	22	29	78
L 6 × 6 × $^1/_2$	10	16	21	24	12	20	25	78
L 8 × 8 × $^3/_8$	8.4	13	15	17	10	15	18	78
L 6 × 6 × $^3/_8$	7.5	11	13	15	9.1	13	16	18

Seat angle, $f_y = 50$ ksi $L_1 \times L_2 \times t$, in.	$^3/_{16}$	$^1/_4$	$^5/_{16}$	$^3/_8$	$^7/_{16}$	$^1/_2$	$^9/_{16}$	$^5/_8$
L 8 × 8 × 1	26	41	53	82	36	51	69	102
L 6 × 6 × 1	26	38	50	74	33	48	65	95
L 8 × 8 × $^3/_4$	22	31	42	60	27	39	53	77
L 6 × 6 × $^3/_4$	19	28	39	54	24	36	50	70
L 8 × 8 × $^5/_8$	18	26	35	50	22	33	43	65
L 6 × 6 × $^5/_8$	16	24	31	46	20	31	39	60
L 8 × 8 × $^1/_2$	14	21	25	40	17	26	31	48
L 6 × 6 × $^1/_2$	13	19	23	35	15	23	27	41
L 8 × 8 × $^3/_8$	10	14	16	22	13	17	19	25
L 6 × 6 × $^3/_8$	9.5	12	14	17	12	14	17	20

f_v = safe unit shear stress of bolt steel, ksi.
δ = min. bolt or rivet diameter, usually $\frac{3}{4}$, $\frac{7}{8}$, or 1 in.

Step 3. Knowing η, find the width b_v of the seat angle's vertical leg from the following: If η = 2 or 3, b_v = 4 in.; if η = 4 or 6, b_v = 6 in.; if η = 6 or 9, b_v = 8 in. The width b_h of the angle's horizontal leg is normally 4 in.

Bolted Stiffened Beam Connection Design:

Step 1. Knowing the beam's end reaction R, yield stress f_y, beam web thickness t_w, and flange-to-fillet depth k, find the beam end's minimum bearing length L_b from

$$L_b + k = 1.33 \, R/f_y \, t_w$$

After solving for L_b, increase L_b to the next highest integer to obtain stiffener width b_s, then add another in. to obtain the width of the horizontal angle's shelf leg L_h: e.g. L_b = 4.37 in. ➜ b_s = 5.00 in. + 1 ➜ L_h = 6.00 in.

Step 2. Knowing the beam's end reaction R, design the seat angle bolts or rivets according to

$$R \leq 0.785 \, \eta \, f_v \, \delta^2$$

R = beam end reaction, kips
η = number of bolts in vertical legs of shelf angles
f_v = safe unit shear stress of bolt steel, ksi. f_v for common bolt steels are A307 = 10 ksi, A325-F = 17.5 ksi, A325-N = 21 ksi, A490-F = 22 ksi, A490-N = 28 ksi, A325-X = 30 ksi, and A490-X = 40 ksi.
δ = min. bolt or rivet diameter, usually $\frac{3}{4}$, $\frac{7}{8}$, or 1 in.

Step 3. Knowing the shelf angle's number of bolts η, find the seat angles' vertical length L_v from

$$L_v = 1.5 \, \eta + 0.5$$

Step 4. Knowing the beam end reaction R, the shelf angle's safe yield stress f_y, and the stiffener width b_s (this is also the length of the shelf angle's central legs), find the shelf angle legs' minimum thickness t_a from

$$R \leq 0.9 \, f_y \, b_s \, t_a$$

After finding t_a, increase its value to the next highest multiple of $1/16$ in.

Step 5. Using the shelf angles as a guide, design the top angle. Let b_s equal the length of the top angle's legs and let t_a equal its thickness.

Bolted Moment Beam Connection Design:

Step 1. Knowing the beam's total live load, dead load, and wind or other lateral loads (or knowing the beam's full end moment M_e) as well as the beam's length L, depth d, and flange thickness t_f, find the beam end's horizontal load force F_h from

$$0.5 \, L \, (1.2 \, W_d + 0.5 \, W_l + 1.3 \, W_w) = F_h \, (d + 0.5 \, t_f)$$

Step 2. Knowing the horizontal force F_h, the beam's flange width b_f, and the top and seat plates' safe shear stress f_{vp}, design the top and seat plates. Usually find their size and number of bolts first, then draw the tee web's outline around the bolt's column/row pattern. First, find the bolt's diameter and minimum number from

$$R \leq 0.71 \, \eta \, f_v \, \delta^2$$

R = beam end reaction, kips

η = min. no. of bolts in tee web. This is an even number when the shelf is two back-to-back angles.

f_v = safe unit shear stress of bolt steel, ksi.

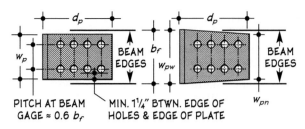

Fig. 3-19. Parallel vs. tapered connection plates.

δ = minimum bolt dia., in. δ is usually $\frac{3}{4}$, $\frac{7}{8}$, or 1 in.
The bolts' optimal number and diameter is found by tri-
al. The web's sides may be parallel or tapered (see Fig.
3-19). A tapered area is more efficient and can extend
beyond the edges of the beam flange, but it should not
be wider than the parent column's flange. Here assume a
tapered outline and design as described below.

Step 3. Select a plate width at row l_{p2} that satisfies spatial design criteria (the beam flange width b_f is usually
appropriate) and use this value in equation **b** below to
find the tee webs' thickness t_p. After rounding t_p to the
next highest multiple of $\frac{1}{16}$ in, use this value in equation
a to find the trapezoidal plates' narrower end width w_{pn}:

a. Tension plane l_{p1}: $F_h \leq 0.6\, f_y\, t_p\, [w_{pn} - 4\,(\delta - 0.125)]$
b. Tension plane l_{p2}: $F_h \leq 0.6\, \eta_r f_y\, t_p\, [w_{pw} - 4\,(\delta - 0.125)]$

After finding w_{pn}, increase its width to the next highest
one or two integers and use this value for w_{pw}, the wider
end width of the trapezoidal plates. If the plate is rectangular, select a length L_p that is $\frac{1}{2}$ in. less than b_f,
then solve for t_p and round it off as described above.

Step 4. Knowing the beam's horizontal load force F_h,

the tee web's safe unit shear stress f_{vp}, the tee webs' thickness t_p, the bolt diameters δ, and the number of bolts η, find the tee webs' horizontal length d_p from

$$F_h = 0.9 f_{vp} t_p [d_p - 0.5 \eta (\delta + 0.063)] \geq 1.5 \eta_r + 3$$

η_r = number of rows of bolts in plate

All other values are as previously defined.

Step 5. Design the top and seat members' bases; these are the vertical flanges that connect to the column. This involves finding each flange's thickness t_{pb}, width b_p, and length l_{pw} as well as determining the minimum number and diameter of its bolts as described below. Each base should be a vertical mirror of the other.

Base thickness t_{pb}: $\quad F_h \leq 0.9 f_v t_{pb} [l_p - 2 (\delta + 0.063)]$

After finding t_{pb}, round it up to the next $1/16$ in. if $t_{pb} \leq 1$ in. or the next $1/8$ in. if $t_{pb} > 1$ in.

Base width b_p:
$$F_h \leq 1.8 f_v t_{pb} [b_p - 0.5 \eta (\delta + 0.063)] \geq 1.5 \eta_r + 3.5$$

Base length l_{pw}: $\quad l_{pw} \geq$ length of tee web

Number of bolts: $\quad F_h \leq 0.785 \eta f_t \delta$

The optimal number and diameter of bolts is found by trial. η should be a multiple of 4 for each plate and δ is usually selected from $3/4$, $7/8$, and 1 in.

Step 6. Check if the column may require web stiffening.

Bolted One-Sided Beam Connection Design:

Step 1. If the beam connects to a column web, check to see if the column's web cavity is too narrow to accept a double-angle connection as follows:

One-angle check: $t_w + 10 \leq d_c - 2\,k_c$
         If **NG** ➜ one angle only

Beam width check: $2\,(b_f + t_w) + 5 \leq d_c - k_c - 0.25$
         If **NG** ➜ bolted connection is too wide ➜ use weld

t_w = web thickness of beam section, in.
d_c = total depth of column section, in.
k_c = distance from outer face of flange to web toe of
      fillet of column, in.
b_f = flange width of beam, in.

Step 2. Knowing the beam's end reaction R and its dimensions d, k, and t, design the connection's bolts or rivets. In equation **a** below, L_{max} = maximum distance between the beam's web toe fillets and thus is the angle's maximum length; so in equation **a** find L_{max}, then round this value to the next lowest $1/4$ in. Then in equation **b** use L_{max} to find the maximum number of bolts η that the angle can hold and round this value to the next lowest integer. Then in equation **c** use η to find the minimum bolt diameter δ and round this value up to the next highest multiple of $1/8$ in. $\eta \geq 3/4$ in.

    a. $d - 2\,k = L_{max}$
    b. $L_{max} = 3\,\eta + 3.5$
    c. $R \leq 0.28\,f_y\,\eta\,\delta^2$

Step 3. Knowing the beam's end reaction R, bolt diameter δ, number of bolts η in each angle leg, and angle leg length L_L, find the angle's thickness t_L from

$$R \leq 0.4\,f_y\,t_L\,[L_L - \eta\,(\delta - 0.063)]$$

After finding t_L, round it up to the next multiple of $1/16$ in. t_L must $\geq 3/8$ in. for $3/4$ and $7/8$ in. bolts and $1/2$ for 1 in. bolts. As one angle leg is a mirror of the other, both legs are now designed. Next, locate the bolt holes on the two angle legs as follows: on the beam leg locate the top hole ₵ $1\frac{3}{4}$ in. down from the top edge and space the other holes 3 in. apart downward; then on the column leg locate the bottom hole ₵ $1\frac{3}{4}$ in. up from the bottom edge and space the other holes 3 in. apart upward. This arrangement puts more of the legs' shear planes in front of the bolts' bearing surfaces.

Step 4. Check each angle leg for safe bearing and shear as follows:

a. Bearing check: $R \leq 0.6\, f_y\, t_w\, \eta\, \delta$
b. Shear check: $R \leq 0.4\, f_y\, c\, [L_L - 0.5\, \eta\, (\delta - 0.063)]$

c = typically 1 or 2 bolt columns in each angle leg

Step 5. Check if the column may require web stiffening.

Brackets, Pedestal Bracket Design:

Step 1. Knowing the bracket load and its bearing area, design the top plate. Centrally locate the load's bearing

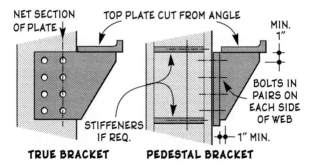

Fig. 3-20. Two types of steel brackets.

area on the plate, add $\frac{1}{2}$ in. all around, fit the plate concentrically against the column, then measure the load center's eccentricity L_e.

Step 2. Knowing the bracket load P and its eccentricity L_e, find the load's maximum moment on the connection.

$$M_{max} \leq P L_e$$

Step 3. Knowing the bracket load P, the bolts' safe shear stress f_v, and the bolt's safe tension stress f_t, tentatively select the plate-to-column bolt number η and diameter δ from equation **a** below. Round η up to the next even number and δ up to the next $\frac{1}{8}$ in; then in equation **b** find the bracket's actual tensile stress f_{ta} and compare this with allow. f_t. Finally, knowing M_{max} and f_t, from equation **c** find η_m, the connection's maximum number of bolts. If $\eta \geq \eta$ in equation **a**, revise.

    a. $P \approx f_v \eta \delta^2$
    b. $P = 0.785 f_{ta} \eta \delta^2$ ... $f_{ta} \leq f_t$
    c. $M_{max} \leq 0.25 f_t \eta_m{}^2$

Step 4. Knowing the bracket load P, the plate-to-column's number of bolts η, and the plate's safe unit shear stress f_v, find the side plate's minimum thickness t_p from

$$P \leq f_v t_p [3\eta + 1 - \eta (\delta - 0.125)] \quad ... t_p \leq 0.67 \delta$$

Step 5. Knowing the connection's number of bolts η, find the side plate's depth d from

$$d \geq 1.5 \eta + 1$$

Step 6. Knowing all the above, draw the bracket in elevation as shown in Fig. 3-21, then note angle $\angle$. If $\angle \leq$ 45°, consider increasing it to a more efficiently load-

➔ß▯I▯▦♀✳☞☞♀🏠🖐

bearing 45°, then redraw the bracket's stem plate and increase d above the value found in Step 5; as this creates a more stable bracket. $\angle$ and d can be made larger if desired for the same reasons. After measuring F and x in Fig. 3-21, find the stem plate's thickness t_s from the equations below:

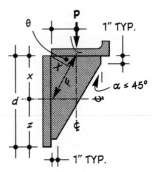

$\tan \angle = 0.5\, d/L_e$ ... find $\angle$

$\sin \angle = P/F$ ... find F

$\tan \angle = x/L_e$ ... find x

$t_s = 0.5\, F/f_c\, x$ ... raise t_s to next $\frac{1}{8}$ in.

Fig. 3-21.
Side view.

Step 7. Knowing all the above, dimension the pedestal in its front elevation.

Step 8. Investigate the possibility that the column may require web stiffening.

Brackets, True Bracket Design:

Steps 1–4 and **8** are the same as in pedestal bracket design.

Step 5. Knowing M_{max}, f_b, t_p, η, and δ, find each bracket's thickness from

$$M_{max} \leq 0.167\, f_b\, t_p\, [(1.5\,\eta + 1)^3 - (1.125\,\eta^3 - 4.5\,\eta)(\delta + 0.125)]$$

Step 6. Knowing the number of bolts η in each bracket, find its depth d from

$$d \geq 1.5\,\eta + 1$$

Step 7. Knowing the total load P on both brackets and the column's depth d_c, find the minimum thickness of the brackets' top plate as sketched and computed below:

$$P\,(d_c + t_p) = 2.4\,f_b\,L_b\,t_p{}^2$$

Hanger Design:

Step 1. Knowing the hanger load P and the bolts' safe unit tension stress f_t, tentatively select a bolt number that forms a bilaterally symmetrical pattern, then find the bolts' diameter from the formula below. After solving for δ, round this value to the next highest $\frac{1}{8}$ in.

$$P \leq 0.39\,f_t\,\eta\,\delta^2$$

Step 2. Graphically locate the hanger base, then determine its feasible length L and width b_e.

Step 3. Knowing the hanger load P (lb) and its spans X and Y (in) and assuming the modulus of elasticity E of

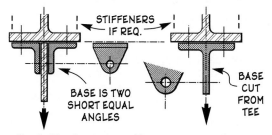

Fig. 3-22. Two types of hanger connections.

its steel = 29,000,000 psi, find its minimum thickness t_b from below. If the base is two angles, round t_b up to the next multiple of $1/8$ in, then select an angle whose dimensions satisfy t_b, X, and Y. If the base is a T section, select a W shape whose web $t \geq t_b$.

$$P Y^3 = 403,000 \, X \, t_b^3$$

Step 4. Design the hanger's lower portion. Depending on how the load is connected to the hanger, this part may be designed as a truss chord, hook, or cable assembly, as well as any sleeve nut, turnbuckle, clevis, or other bolt variation.

Step 5. Investigate the parent beam flange for safe net section through the hanger bolt holes by finding the beam's total moment at the point of its span where the hanger is installed, then solving the equation below:

$$M_{hanger} \leq 0.25 \, f_b \, t_f \, (d - t_f) \, [b_f - \eta \, (\delta - 0.063)]$$

f_b = safe unit bending stress of beam steel, ksi
t_f = thickness of beam flange, in.
d = depth of beam, in.
b_f = width of beam flange, in.
η = number of bolts in one row transverse to beam longitudinal axis
δ = diameter of bolt in row above, in.

Note: If the parent member is not a standard W shape, then $M_{hanger} \leq 0.5 \, f_b \times 0.5$ length between the parent member ℄ and the ℄ of part of parent member to which hanger is connected × the net section area of the part of the parent member to which the hanger is connected.

Step 6. Investigate that the beam above the hanger may require web stiffening (see page 170).

Bolted Column Splice Design:

Step 1. Compute the splice's design load. Solve for both equations, then use the larger value.

$$V_s = V_{lat} + 0.25\, V_d \qquad V_s = 0.50\, V_t$$

V_s = design load on column splice, kips. The larger value governs.
V_{lat} = total lateral load of upper column, if any, kips
V_d = total dead load of upper column, kips
V_t = design load of upper column, kips

Step 2. Determine the type of connection the splice should have (splices on outer flange, splices on inner flange, butt plate between shafts, etc.); then size the splice plates from

$$V_s \approx 1.5\, f_c\, b\, t$$

V_s = design load on column splice, from Step 1, kips
f_c = safe unit stress for bolts, ksi. Any lateral loads against the splice act as a shear load through the bolt sections.
b = trial width of plates on each side of column, in. Both plates should be same width, length, and thickness. Usually select a trial width of ±10 percent less than width of upper column flange.
t = width of plate on each side of column, in. Solve for this, then use next highest steel plate t.

Step 3. Determine the optimal number and diameter of the bolts that connect the plates to the column flanges.

$$V_s = \eta\, f_v$$

V_s = total load on column splice, from Step 1, kips
η = no. of bolts required in each half of splice
f_v = safe unit shear stress for type of steel used for

bolts, ksi. Find the safe stress for optimal bolt
diameter and minimum number of bolts required,
then select an even number of bolts based on an
efficiency factor of η bolts × f_v/V_s .

Step 4. Investigate the plates for lateral shear.

$$V_{lat} \leq 2.0\, f_v\, b\, t$$

V_{lat} = total lateral shear on splice (= lateral load), kips
f_v = safe shear stress for type of plate steel, ksi
b = effective width of bearing plate, in. This equals
       total width of plate – 2 holes in each horiz. plane
       × (hole dia. + $\frac{1}{8}$ in. tolerance for each hole).
t = thickness of bearing plate, from Step 2, in.

Step 5. If shims are between the upper column flanges
and the plates on each side, size them according to

$$t_s \leq 0.5\, (d_L - d_U)$$

t_s = optimal thickness of shim, in.
d_L = depth of lower column, in.
d_U = depth of upper column, in.

Butt or Fillet Weld Design:

Step 1. Having drawings of the connection assembly,
compute the unit strength of each weld from

    a. Butt welds: $V_w \geq 0.3\, E\, t$
    b. Fillet welds: $V_w \geq 0.3\, E\, w \sin\,(\tan^{-1} {}^h/_w)$

V_w = required unit shear strength of weld, kips/lin. in.
E = modulus of elasticity, usually 29,000,000 psi
t = minimum thickness of materials joined in weld or
       penetration of weld, whichever is less, in.
w = width of weld, in. h = height of weld, in.

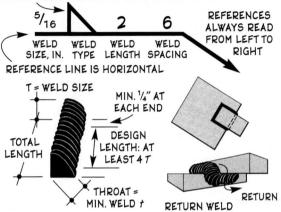

Fig. 3-23. Anatomy of a weld.

Step 2. Knowing the total effective load to be supported by the weld, compute its required net length from

$$P = L V_w$$

P = allowable load of truss chord, kips
L = required net length of both welds, in.
V_w = unit shear strength of welds, kip/linear in.

Step 3. If the connection has two welds A and B, one on each side, find the net length of each weld by taking moments about the welded member's axis.

$$y (L - L_b) = L_b (w - y)$$

y = length from axis of welded member to weld A, in.
L = required net length of both welds A and B, in.

L_b = net length of weld B, in.
w = width of welded member, in.

Step 4. If the connection has two welds, find the net length of weld A.
$$L_s = L_a + L_b$$

L_s = required net length of both welds A and B, in.
L_a = net length of weld A, in
L_b = net length of weld B, in.

Step 5. Design the length of each weld.

$$L_w \geq |4\,t + 0.5|_{0.25}$$

L_w = minimum length of each weld, in.
t = thickness of weld, in.

Welded Framed Beam Connection Design:

Step 1. Knowing the beam's depth d and its flange-to-fillet depth k, select the largest angle length that satisfies the equation below from the following dimensions: $5\frac{1}{2}$, $8\frac{1}{2}$, $11\frac{1}{2}$, $14\frac{1}{2}$, $17\frac{1}{2}$, $20\frac{1}{2}$, $23\frac{1}{2}$, $26\frac{1}{2}$, or $29\frac{1}{2}$ in.

$$L \leq d - 2k$$

Step 2. Knowing the beam's end reaction R and angle length L, from Table 3-11 select a thickness t_A for weld A at the smallest R_a that $\geq R$.

Step 3. Knowing the beam's end reaction R and angle length L, from Table 3-11 select a thickness t_B for weld B at the smallest R_a that $\geq R$.

Max. beam web t_w at weld t_A		
t_A	f_y = 36 ksi	f_y = 50 ksi
$\frac{3}{16}$	0.38	0.28
$\frac{1}{4}$	0.51	0.37
$\frac{5}{16}$	0.38	0.28

Fig. 3-24.

Step 4. Knowing f_y, the beam web t_w, and the beam-to-angle weld A thickness t_a, compare t_w to t_A in Fig. 3-24, which lists the minimum beam web thickness for each weld thickness at f_y = 36 and 50 ksi. If $t_w \geq t_A$, reduce R_a according to the formula below. Then if $R_{a-} \leq$ beam reaction R, select the next larger thickness for weld A than was chosen in Step 2. This situation occurs rarely.

$$R_{a-} = R_a \times \text{min. } t_w/\text{actual } t_w$$

Step 5. Compare the shear capacity of weld B with the shear capacity of the parent web according to the formula below. If the web is not thick enough or if another connection is on the web's other side, the web may not be strong enough to support the connection(s).

$$\frac{t_{pw} f_{vpw}}{0.21 \eta t_b E} \leq 1.0$$

TABLE 3-11: BEAM-TO-ANGLE WELD THICKNESSES

A: BEAM-TO-ANGLE WELD LOAD, kips

Thickness of weld A	5½	8½	11½	14½	17½	20½	23½	26½	29½
$^3/_{16}$	37	59	76	93	110	123	138	152	165
$^1/_4$	49	79	102	125	146	164	184	202	220
$^5/_{16}$	62	99	128	156	183	205	230	253	275

Angle length L, in. — Angle leg A = 3 in. → ← Angle leg A = 3½ in.

B: ANGLE-TO-PARENT MEMBER WELD LOAD, kips

Thickness of weld A	5½	8½	11½	14½	17½	20½	23½	26½	29½
$^1/_4$	14	32	53	76	101	125	149	173	197
$^5/_{16}$	18	40	67	95	126	156	186	217	247
$^3/_8$	22	48	80	115	152	187	223	261	296

Angle length L, in. — Angle leg B = 3 in. | B = 3½ in. | ← Angle leg B = 4 in.

t_{pw} = web thickness of parent member, in.
f_{vpw} = safe unit shear stress of parent member, ksi
η = no. of connections on each side of web, 1 or 2
t_b = thickness of weld B, in.
E = welding electrode strength. E usually = 70 ksi.

If this equation is **OK**, proceed to Step 6. If **NG**, make the weld larger. If possible lengthen the angle connector until the following relation is satisfied:

$$\frac{t_{pw}\, f_{vpw} \times \text{original angle length}}{0.21\,\eta\, t_B\, E \times \text{new angle length}} \leq 1.0$$

If lengthening the angle is not possible, make the angle wider, make weld B thicker, or extend weld B along the angle's top and bottom edges until the following relation is satisfied:

$$\frac{t_{pw}\, f_{vpw} \times \text{orig. angle width} \times \text{orig. } t_B \times \text{orig. weld } L}{0.21\,\eta\, t_B\, E \times \text{new angle width} \times \text{new } t_B \times \text{new weld } L} \leq 1.0$$

Step 6. Knowing the thickness of angle welds A and B, find the angle legs' thickness t_L by choosing the greater value from **a** and **b** below.

    a. $t_L = t_A + 0.125$ **b.** $t_L = t_B + 0.125$

Welded Seated Beam Connection Design:

Step 1. Knowing f_v and f_y as well as the beam's end reaction R, flange width b_f, and flange thickness t_f, find the seat angle's horizontal length L according to

    $L \leq b_f + 4\, t_f + 0.5$ ... Suggested L = 6 or 8 in.

Step 2. Knowing the beam's end reaction R and its seat angle's horizontal length L, determine the angle's weld thickness t_w and length of its vertical leg b_L from the formula below. Common angle sizes for this connector are 4 × 3½, 5 × 3½, 6 × 4, 7 × 4, and 8 × 4.

$$R = 0.12 \, E \, t_w \, (b_L + 2)$$

R = beam end reaction, kips
E = electrode designation
t_w = thickness of weld that holds seat angle to parent structure, in. $t_w \le 0.707$ parent structure t.
b_L = length of vertical leg of seat angle, in.

Step 3. Knowing the beam's web thickness t_w, flange width b_f and thickness t_f, and flange-to-fillet depth k, size the beam-to-seat angle connectors. These hold the beam to the seat angle by a weld or bolt on each side of the beam's web. If the connectors are bolts they are sized by the formula below, which ensures that the bolt washer does not ride up on the flange toe fillet. If the connectors are welds, they are normally ¼ in. welds laid along the edge of the beam flange from the end of the beam to the outer edge of the angle's horizontal leg.

Bolt: $0.5 \, (b_f - t_w) \ge 2.5 \, \delta + k - t_f$

Welded Stiffened Beam Connection Design:

Step 1. Knowing the beam's end reaction R, yield stress f_y, web thickness t_w, and flange-to-fillet depth k, find the seat plate's minimum horizontal width b_s from the formula below, then round its value up to the next ¼ in.

$$R = 0.75 \, f_y \, t_w \, (b_s + k - 0.5)$$

Step 2. Knowing the above values and the seat plate width b_s, find the beam load's eccentricity e from

$$e \ge b_s + 1.25 \, k - 0.5 \, {}^R\!/_{f_y \, t_w}$$

Step 3. Knowing the above values, find the seat plate's thickness t_s from the formula below, then round its value up to the next $\frac{1}{16}$ in.

$$t_s \geq 2.22 \,(3\,e - b_s)/f_y\, b_s^{\,2}$$
$$t_s \geq \text{beam web } t_w + 0.063 \text{ in.}$$

Step 4. Knowing R, t_w, and the seat plate's width b_s, find the weld length L_w and weld thickness t_w from

$$R \leq 37.8 \, t_w \,(L_w - b_s)$$

A good way to tentatively select t_w is to start with $\frac{1}{4}$ in. and add $\frac{1}{16}$ in. for each 90 kips of R. Feasible weld thicknesses are $\frac{1}{4}$, $\frac{5}{16}$, $\frac{3}{8}$, $\frac{7}{16}$, $\frac{1}{2}$, and $\frac{5}{8}$ in. The above formula also assumes the use of E70 electrodes. After finding L_w, locate 0.2 L_w beneath the seat plate on each side of the stiffener, 0.2 L_w on each side of the stiffener plate near its top, and 0.2 L_w on each side of the stiffener near its bottom. The six welds total 1.2 times the total load; the added 0.2 is a safety factor.

Step 5. If necessary resize the seat plate as follows:

a. If f_y = 36 ksi and electrodes are E70, $t_s \geq 2.0 \; t_{weld}$.
b. If f_y = 50 ksi and electrodes are E70, $t_s \geq 1.5 \; t_{weld}$.
c. If beam $f_y \neq$ stiffener f_y, the stiffener thickness must $\geq$ beam web $t_w \times$ beam $f_y \div$ stiffener f_y.
d. If two stiffener plates align on opposite sides of the web of the parent member, the stiffener's weld size $\leq$ 0.50 the parent member web thickness if the web f_y = 36 ksi and $\leq$ 0.67 the parent member web thickness if the web f_y = 50 ksi.

Welded Moment Beam Connection Design:

Step 1. Knowing the beam's total live load, dead load,

and wind or other lateral loads as well as the beam's length L, depth d, and flange thickness t_f, find the beam end's horizontal load force F_h from

$$0.5\ L\ (1.2\ W_d + 0.5\ W_l + 1.3\ W_w)\ =\ F_h\ (d + 0.5\ t_f)$$

Step 2. Make the top plate about 1 in. narrower than the beam's upper flange and the bottom plate about 1 in. wider than the beam's lower flange; this creates narrow welding ledges on the lower piece on each side. Then, knowing F_h, beam flange width b_f, and its safe unit shear stress f_v, determine the top and bottom plate's widths b_{tp} and t_{sp} and their thicknesses t_{tp} and t_{sp} as below:

Top plate b_{tp}:	$b_f - 1 \approx b_{tp}$
Top plate t_{tp}:	$F_h \le f_v\ b_{tp}\ t_{tp}$
Seat plate b_{sp}:	$b_f + 1 \approx b_{sp}$
Seat plate t_{sp}:	$F_h \le f_v\ b_{tp}\ t_{tp}$

Step 3. Knowing F_h and the beam's flange thickness t_f and assuming E70 electrodes, design welds A and B around the top and seat plates. Tentatively select a weld thickness for both plates that is at least $1/16$ in. thinner than the two plates' least thickness. Then:

$$F_h \le 14.8\ t_{wa}\ L_{wa}$$

t_{wa} = thickness of weld A, in.
L_{wa} = length of weld A, in.

After finding L_{wa}, lay part of its length across the plate's end and half of the rest along each side, then find the top plate length L_{tp} from

$$L_{tp} \le 0.5\ (L_{wa} - b_{tp}) + 2$$
The top plate can now be specified

Step 4. Design weld B. As $L_{wa} = L_{wb}$, lay half of L_{wb} on one side of the seat plate and the other half on the other side, add a return ≈ 2 × weld thickness at the plate's end, then find the seat plate's length L_{sp} from

$$L_{sp} \le 0.5\ L_{wA} + 2$$

Step 5. Design the connection's bracket bars (see Fig. 3-25): its width b_{bb}, length L_{bb}, and thickness t_{bb}.

> **Width b_{bb}:** 1¼ in. for small beams, 1½ in. for large
> **Length L_{bb}:** $L_{bb} \ge b_{sp}$
> **Thickness t_{bb}:** $t_{bb} = t_{tp} + ⅛$ in. or $t_f + ⅛$ in, whichever is larger

Step 6. Design the beam shear plate, a vertical plate that is normally bolted to the beam web. Knowing the beam's end reaction R, its safe unit yield strength f_y, and its web thickness t_w, tentatively select a web connector bolt diameter of ¾, ⅞, or 1 in, then find the number of bolts η from

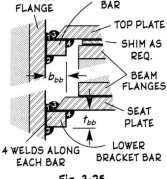

COLUMN FLANGE — UPPER BRACKET BAR — TOP PLATE — SHIM AS REQ. — b_{bb} — BEAM FLANGES — SEAT PLATE — t_{bb} — 4 WELDS ALONG EACH BAR — LOWER BRACKET BAR

Fig. 3-25.

$$R \le 0.71\ f_v\ \eta\ \delta^2$$

Then find the beam shear plate's length from

$$L_{bwsp} \le \text{beam depth} - 2\ k \quad \dots\ L_{bwsp} \ge 3\ \eta + 0.5\ \text{in}.$$

Step 7. Check the bolt bearing on the beam web from

$$R \ge 0.75\ f_v\ t_w\ \eta\ \delta$$

Then find the shear plate's thickness t_{bwsp} from

$$t_{bwsp} \geq \text{beam web } t_w \quad \dots \quad t_{bwsp} \geq t_w + {}^1/_{16} \text{ in.}$$

Step 8. Check for safe shear plate shear $f_{v\text{-}bwsp}$ from

$$R \leq 0.30\, f_{v\text{-}bwsp}\, t_{v\text{-}bwsp}\, [L_{bwsp} - \eta\,(\delta + 0.063)]$$

If $t_{bwsp} \geq t_w$ and plate $f_v \geq$ web f_v, bolt bearing is **OK**. Finally, check the shear plate width shear.

Step 9. Design weld C that connects the beam web shear plate to the parent member. Tentatively select a weld t_{wc} that is at least ${}^1/_{16}$ in. less than the two plates' least thickness. Then

$$F_h \leq 14.8\, t_{wc}\, L_{wc}$$
$$t_{wc} + 0.063 \text{ in.} \leq \text{column web } t$$
$$t_{wc} \times 2 \leq \text{shear plate } t$$

t_{wc} = thickness of weld C, in.
L_{wc} = length of weld C, in.

After finding L_{wa}, divide L_{wa} by 4, increase each quarter by ${}^1/_4$ in. and add ${}^1/_4$ in. to each end; then place two lengths along the sides, top, and bottom of the shear-plate-to-column-flange seam.

Step 10. Check that the column may require web stiffeners according to the formula below. When $A_{col\text{-}ws}$ is positive, web stiffeners are required.

$$A_{col\text{-}w} = [1.67\, F_h - f_{y\text{-}col}\, t_{cw}\,(t_b + 5\,k)]/f_{y\text{-}ws}$$

$A_{col\text{-}w}$ = potential section area of both stiffeners, in². If $A_{col\text{-}w}$ is +, $A_{col\text{-}w} \leq$ stiffener width × thickness.
F_h = horiz. load force of beam, from Step 3, kips
$f_{y\text{-}col}$ = safe unit yield stress of column steel, ksi
t_{cw} = thickness of column web, in.

t_b = thickness of beam flange, in.
k = beam flange-to-fillet depth, in.
$f_{y\text{-}ws}$ = safe unit yield stress of web stiffener steel, ksi

Step 11. If the column needs web stiffeners, size them as described below. All are the same size.

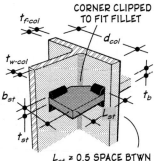

Stiffener thickness:
$t_{st} = 0.5\ t_{tp} \leq 0.5$ in.

Stiffener width:
$b_{st} \leq 0.33\ b_f$

Stiffener length if one-sided connection:
$L_{st} \geq 0.5\ d_{col}$

Stiffener length if back-to-back connection:
$L_{st} = d_{col} - 2\ t_{f\text{-}col}$

$L_{st} \geq 0.5$ SPACE BTWN FLANGES

Fig. 3-26. Column web stiffener details.

Stiffener-to-web weld thicknesses: min. $\frac{1}{4}$ in.

Stiffener-to-flange weld thicknesses: min. $\frac{5}{16}$ in. and make them equal

Stiffener weld length: The "required" calculations to find this length are needlessly complex for a short weld. Simply run four welds, two on top of and two beneath each stiffener.

Welded One-Sided Beam Connection Design:

Welded one-sided beam connections are usually superior to bolted or riveted ones because the angles can be narrower, which allows wider beams to fit into narrower column web cavities.

Step 1. Knowing the beam's depth d and flange-to-fillet depth k, find the connector angle's length from

$$L_a = d - 2k$$

Step 2. Knowing L_a, the beam's end reaction R, and that welds A and B are equal, select a weld thickness t_{wa} at the angle length and weld thickness whose smallest capacity $R_a \geq R$.

Step 3. Knowing R, the angle's safe yield stress f_y, and the angle length L_a, find the angle's thickness t_a from the formula below, then round t_a up to the next $\frac{1}{16}$ in.

$$R \leq 0.4 f_y t_a L_a$$

Step 4. Check if the column may require web stiffening (see pp. 169–170, Steps 10-11).

TABLE 3-12: ONE-SIDED BEAM CONN. WELD SIZES

A: BEAM-TO-ANGLE WELD LOAD, kips

Thickness of weld A	5½	8½	11½	14½	17½	20½	23½	26½
$\frac{3}{16}$	18	29	38	46	55	61	69	76
$\frac{1}{4}$	24	38	51	62	73	82	92	101
$\frac{5}{16}$	31	49	64	78	91	102	115	126

Angle leg A = 3 in. ──► ◄── Angle leg A = 3½ in.

B: ANGLE-TO-PARENT MEMBER WELD LOAD, kips

Thickness of weld B	5½	8½	11½	14½	17½	20½	23½	26½
$\frac{3}{16}$	5.4	12	20	28	38	47	56	65
$\frac{1}{4}$	7.3	16	26	38	50	62	74	86
$\frac{5}{16}$	9.1	20	33	48	63	78	93	108
$\frac{3}{8}$	11	24	40	57	76	93	111	130

∠ leg B = 3 in. │ B = 3½ in. │ ◄── Angle leg B = 4 in.

Square & Rectangular Knee Design:

Step 1. Knowing the sizes of the beam and column sections as well as the beam's maximum moment M_{max}, find its flange force F_1 according to

$$M_{max} = F_1 (d_b - t_f)$$

Step 2. Check the need of beam web stiffeners at seam $c\,d$ in Fig. 3-27A. F_{cd} = beam web capacity at seam $c\,d$.

$$F_{cd} = 0.58\ f_{yb}\ d_b\ t_{wb} \le F_1$$
If $F_{cd} > F_1$, stiffeners are required

Step 3. If seam $c\,d$ needs web stiffeners, tentatively size them as follows:

$$F_{cd} - F_1 = 0.60\ f_y\ b_{ws}\ t_{ws}$$
$$b_{ws} = 0.5\ (b_{fb} - t_{wb}) - 0.5\ \text{in.}$$
$$t_{ws} \ge \,^3\!/_8 \text{ in. } \le\ t_{fb}$$

Step 4. Check the need of column web stiffeners at seam $b\,d$ in Fig. 3-27B. F_{bd} = beam web capacity at seam $b\,d$.

$$M_{max\text{-}col} = F_4 (d_c - t_{fc})$$
$$F_{bd} = 0.58\ f_{yc}\ d_c\ t_{wc} \le F_4$$
If $F_{bd} > F_4$, web stiffeners are required

Step 5. If seam $c\,d$ needs web stiffeners, size them from

$$F_{bd} - F_4 = 0.60\ f_y\ b_{ws}\ t_{ws}$$
$$b_{ws} = 0.5\ (b_{fc} - t_{wc}) - 0.5\ \text{in.}$$
$$t_{ws} \ge \,^3\!/_8 \text{ in. } \le\ t_{fc}$$

Assuming $b_{fb} = b_{fc}$, the face of the column web stiffeners should be the same distance in from the column flange edges as are the beam web stiffeners.

Step 6. If web stiffeners are required at seams $b\,d$ or

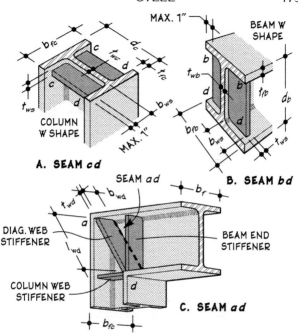

Fig. 3-27. Rigid knee connection details.

c d in Figs. 3-27A and 3-27B, they are also required at diagonal seam a d in Fig. 3-27C. Then size them from:

$$[(F_{cd} - F_1)^2 + (F_{bd} - F_4)^2]^{0.5} = 0.60 \, f_y \, b_{wd} \, t_{wd}$$
$$\text{wherein } t_{wd} \geq \tfrac{3}{8} \text{ in.}$$

The outer faces of the diagonal stiffeners should lie in the same vertical plane as the faces of the beam and column stiffeners; the column flange should be as thick as the beam flange; the beam stiffeners should be as thick as the inner column flanges and vertically align with them; and the column stiffeners should be as thick as the inner beam flanges and horizontally align with them.

Step 7. Design the connection's welds by (a) finding the maximum ultimate load transmitted from one piece-in-common to the next, (b) finding the weld force required at each weld seam, and (c) sizing each weld as follows:

a. **Maximum ultimate load resisted by each weld:**
$F_w \approx f_y \times$ section area of beam flange $= f_y\, b_f\, t_f$

b. **Unit weld force (kips/LF):**
$$f_w = \frac{F_w}{t \text{ of 2 sides to be welded} \times (\text{col. web } d - 2 \text{ col. flange } t)} = \frac{F_w}{2\, d_c - 4\, t_{fc}}$$

c. **Size and length of weld:** $f_w \geq 0.21\, E\, t_w$

f_w = unit weld force, from Step 7b, kips/LF
E = welding electrode capacity, usually 70 ksi
t_w = minimum thickness of weld, in.

Curved & Tapered Knee Design:

Step 1. Knowing the sizes of the beam and column sections as well as the beam's maximum moment M_{max}, find its flange force F_1 according to

$$M_{max} = F_1\, (d_b - t_f)$$

Step 2. If seam $b\,c$ needs web stiffeners, tentatively size them as follows:

a. Beam web capacity $F_{bc} = 0.58\, f_{yb}\, d_b\, t_{wb} > F_1$
b. $F_{bc} - F_1 = 0.60\, f_y\, b_{ws}\, t_{ws}$
c. $b_{ws} = 0.5\,(b_{fb} - t_{wb}) - 0.5$ in. ... $t_{ws} \geq \frac{3}{8}$ in. $\leq t_{fb}$

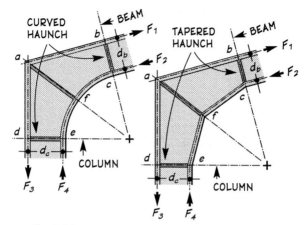

Fig. 3-28. Curved & tapered rigid knee details.

Step 3. Assuming web stiffeners are required at seam $d\,e$, tentatively size them as follows:

a. Column web capacity $F_{de} = 0.58\,f_{yc}\,d_c\,t_{wc} > F_4$
b. $F_{de} - F_4 = 0.60\,f_y\,b_{ws}\,t_{ws}$
c. $b_{ws} = 0.5\,(b_{fc} - t_{wc}) - 0.5$ in. ... $t_{ws} \geq \tfrac{3}{8}$ in. $\leq t_{fc}$

Step 4. If seam $a\,f$ needs web stiffeners, tentatively size them as follows:

a. $[(F_{bc} - F_1)^2 + (F_{de} - F_4)^2]^{0.5} = 0.60\,f_y\,b_{ws}\,t_{ws}$
b. $b_{ws} = 0.5\,(b_{fc} - t_{wc}) - 0.5$ in. ... $t_{ws} \geq \tfrac{3}{8}$ in. $\leq t_{fc}$

Step 5. Design the connection's welds. This is done as in the design of square or rectangular knees, Step 7.

Welded Column Splice Design:

Step 1. Compute the design load of the splice. Solve for both equations, then use the larger value.

$$V_s = 1.00\ V_{lat} + 0.25\ V_d \qquad V_s = 0.50\ V_t$$

V_s　= total design load on column splice, kips. The larger value governs.
V_{lat} = total lateral load of upper column, if any, kips
V_d　= total dead load of upper column, kips
V_t　= total design load of upper column, kips

Step 2. Size the weld at the seam of the two mating columns. If this is a full pen weld, its length ≈ the column's depth plus twice its width. The weld must also be thicker than the column's flange and web thicknesses. Knowing this, the upper column's b_{fc}, t_{fc}, and t_{wc}, and the electrode strength E, find the weld's thickness from

$$V_s = 0.21\ E\ [2\ b_{fc}\ (t_{fc} + \Delta t) + (t_{wc} + \Delta t)\ (d - 2\ t_{fc})]$$

Solve for Δt; then flange welds = $t_{fc} + \Delta t$ and web weld = $t_{wc} + \Delta t$. For each weld round the final values up to the next highest multiple of $\frac{1}{16}$ in.

Step 3. Although it is nearly impossible for the column to fail in shear if its weld is sized as described above, it is wise design to verify the column's safety in lateral shear according to the formula below:

$$V_{lat} \le 2.0\ f_v\ b\ t$$

V_{lat} = total lateral shear on column splice, equals lateral load, kips
f_v　= safe unit shear stress for type of steel, ksi
b　= effective breadth or width of bearing plate, in.
t　= thickness of plate on each side of column, in.

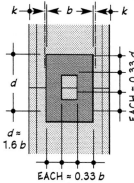

k → ← b → ← k

d

d ≈ 1.6 b

EACH ≈ 0.33 d

EACH ≈ 0.33 b

Fig. 3-29. Column shear plate details.

Step 4. Add a shear plate with a central pocket weld on each side of the column's web as sketched in Fig. 3-29. One's thickness should be slightly less than the column web thickness, and the plate-to-web weld thickness should be less than the plate thickness. If the abutting column webs have different thicknesses, the difference is usually so slight that the plate welds on each side can bridge the gap.

Highly Eccentric Plate Loads: Designing plates to support several eccentric load connections is easy if one does the following: (1) conceptualize each imposed load and its resisting force as a centroid where these forces are concentrated; (2) locate a central point anywhere amid any arrangement of load centroids; (3) measure the shortest distance between the central point and each load centroid; and (4) make a chart of each load force, its relative strength, the distance between the load and centroid, and the load's moment as follows:

Load force	Rel. strength of connection	d btwn load & centroid	Total load moment
Weld A	2.5 in. × W	× 21 in.	= 52.5 W
Weld B, etc.	9.0 in. × W	× 25.5 in.	= 230 W

Then simply sum the load moments about the centroid, solve for W, and find the strength of each connection.

Bolted/Welded Moment Beam Conn. Design:

Step 1. Knowing the beam's length L, depth d, flange thickness t_f, and its total gravity and lateral loads, find its horizontal load force F_h from

$$0.5 \, L \, (1.2 \, W_d + 0.5 \, W_l + 1.3 \, W_w) = F_h \, (d + 0.5 \, t_f)$$

Step 2. Determine the size and number of bolts in the beam's horizontal top and seat plates from

$$R = 0.71 \, \eta_r \, f_v \, \delta^2$$

R = beam end reaction, kips
η = req. no. of bolts in each plate (an even number)
f_v = safe unit shear stress of bolt steel, ksi
δ = min. bolt or rivet diameter, usually $\frac{3}{4}$, $\frac{7}{8}$, or 1 in.

Step 3. Design the beam's top and bottom seat plates as follows. Knowing the number of bolts in each plate, arrange them in two rows, then frame the rows with the plate's edges (min. $1\frac{1}{4}$ in. between hole edges and plate edges). The plate's sides may be parallel or tapered toward the outer end. If tapered, try a plate narrow-end width w_{pn} slightly less than beam flange width b_f, then use this value in equation **a** below to find each plate's thickness t_p. After rounding t_p up to the next $\frac{1}{16}$ in, use this in equation **b** to find the plate's wide-end width w_{pw}:

    a. $F_h \leq 0.6 \, \eta_r \, f_y \, t_p \, [w_{pn} - 4 \, (\delta - 0.125)]$
    b. $F_h \leq 0.6 \, f_y \, t_p \, [w_{pw} - 4 \, (\delta - 0.125)]$

After finding w_{pn}, increase it to the next integer. If the plate is rectangular, select a width w_p that $\approx \frac{1}{2}$ in. less than b_f, then solve for t_p and round off as above.

Step 4. Design the connection's two bracket bars (page 168, Step 5), beam web shear plate (page 168, Step 6), and any required web stiffening (page170, Step 11).

Bolted/Welded End-Plate Beam Connection Design:

Step 1. Knowing the beam's length L, depth d, flange thickness t_f, and its total gravity and lateral loads, find its horizontal load force F_h from

$$0.5 \, L \, (1.2 \, W_D + 0.5 \, W_L + 1.3 \, W_W) = F_h \, (d + 0.5 \, t_f)$$

Step 2. Knowing F_h and the beam's depth d, flange thickness t_f, and safe unit shear f_v, design the end plate-to-parent member bolts as follows. The number of bolts η is usually 8, but large joints may have 16 or even 24 bolts. Then find the minimum bolt diameter δ in the formula below and round its value up to the next $1/8$ in.

$$F_h \leq 0.393 \, f_v \, \eta \, \delta^2$$

Step 3. Knowing the beam flange width b_f, find the end plate width b_p from

$$b_p \leq 1.15 \, b_f$$

Step 4. Knowing F_h, the beam's safe unit shear f_v, depth d, and flange thickness t_f, and the end plate's width b_p, find the end plate's thickness t_p from

$$d \, F_h \leq 0.4 \, f_v \, t_p \, [d + t_f + (\delta + 0.75)] \, [b_p - 2 \, (\delta - 0.063)]$$

Step 5. After finding t_p, round it to the next highest $1/8$ in. Then check the end plate for safe shear according to

$$F_h \leq 0.8 \, f_y \, t_p \, b_p$$

Step 6. Knowing the beam's flange width b_f, flange thickness t_f, and web thickness t_w, design the top flange-to-end plate weld (see Fig. 3-30).

Length of weld:
$$L_w \geq 2\,(b_f + t_f) - t_w$$
Weld thickness:
$$F_h \geq 5.94\,f_y\,t_w$$

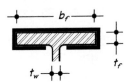

After finding t_w, round it to the next $1/8$ in. This fillet weld must $\leq 1/4$ in, or it must be a full pen weld all around.

Fig. 3-30.

Step 7. Knowing the end reaction R, length of the all-around weld L_w, yield stress f_y, and web thickness t_w, design the beam web-to-end plate fillet weld as follows:

Weld thickness: $R \leq 18\,L_w\,t_{weld}$
Length of weld: $F_h \geq 0.4\,f_y\,t_w\,L_{weld}$

After finding t_{weld}, round its value to the next highest $1/8$ in. After finding L_{weld}, divide this length in half, round each half to the next highest $1/4$ in, add $1/4$ in. to each end, then locate the welds on each side of the beam web.

Step 8. Check if the column may require web stiffening.

Pinned Connection Design:

Step 1. Draw an assembly of the pin componentry that is simple, concentric, and efficient. Indicate the supported member's potential range of rotation, clearance for fabrication and erection, and access for maintenance; then tentatively add feasible dimensions for the pin, eye plate, and gusset plate.

Step 2. Knowing the load forces of the members acting on the pin's gusset plate, find the loads' vertical and horizontal components, draw shear and moment dia-

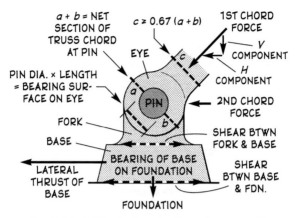

Fig. 3-31. Critical stresses in a pin connection.

grams in the vertical and horizontal planes through the
pin's axis, find the maximum vertical and horizontal
shears and moments, then find the maximum resultant
shear and moment on each of the two shoe plates from

Shear:	$V_{max\text{-}act}$	$= (V_{max\text{-}v}^2 - V_{max\text{-}h}^2)^{0.5}$
Moment:	$M_{max\text{-}act}$	$= (M_{max\text{-}v}^2 - M_{max\text{-}h}^2)^{0.5}$

Step 3. Knowing the pin steel's safe unit yield stress,
find the pin's safe unit stresses for shear, bearing (compression), tension, and bending moment as follows:

Shear:	f_v	$= 0.20\, f_y$
Bearing:	f_c	$= 0.30\, f_y$
Tension:	f_t	$= 0.38\, f_y$
Moment:	f_b	$= 0.33\, f_y$

Step 4. Knowing $V_{max\text{-}act}$, $M_{max\text{-}act}$, f_v, and f_b, find the

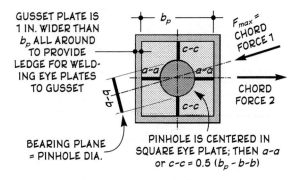

GUSSET PLATE IS
1 IN. WIDER THAN
b_p ALL AROUND
TO PROVIDE
LEDGE FOR WELD-
ING EYE PLATES
TO GUSSET

b_p

F_{max} =
CHORD
FORCE 1

c-c

a-a

a-a

b-b

CHORD
FORCE 2

c-c

BEARING PLANE
= PINHOLE DIA.

PINHOLE IS CENTERED IN
SQUARE EYE PLATE; THEN a-a
or c-c = 0.5 (b_p – b-b)

Fig. 3-32. Location of eye plate stresses.

pin's diameter δ from formula **a** below, then check the
pin's circular section area for safe shear from formula **b**:

    a. $M_{max\text{-}act} \leq 0.098 f_b \delta^3$
    b. $V_{max\text{-}act} \leq 0.785 f_v \delta^2$

Step 5. Assume that two truss chord forces F_1 and F_2
act on the gusset plate to which the eye plate is welded.
Then, knowing $V_{max\text{-}act}$ and the eye plates' f_v, f_c, and f_t,
design the two symmetrical eye plates on each side of
the gusset plate. First determine the shear, bearing,
and tension planes in the eye plates; then find the three
planes' dimensions from formulas **a**, **b**, and **c** below; then
use the plan dimensions to size the eye plate. In Fig.
3-32 the eye plate's shear plane is at the two lines a–a,
its bearing plane is at line b–b (which = pin diameter δ),
and its tension plane is at the two lines c–c.

    a. Bearing plane: $V_{max\text{-}act} \leq f_c t_e \delta$ find t_e
    b. Shear plane: $V_{max\text{-}act} \leq 2 f_v t_e (a\text{-}a)$ find a–a

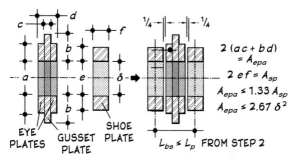

Fig. 3-33. Section through eye plate assembly.

c. **Tension plane:** $V_{max-act} \leq 2 f_t t_e (c-c)$ find $c-c$
d. **Eye plate w:** $b_p = \delta + 2 (a-a)$ find b_p
e. **Eye plate h:** $d_p = \delta + 2 (c-c)$ find d_p

t_e = thickness of eye plate, in.
$a-a$ = length of each shear plane in eye plate, in.
$c-c$ = length of each tension plane in eye plate, in.
b_p = breadth or width of eye plate, in.
d_p = height or depth of eye plate, in.

Then check the following dimension limits and revise b_p and d_p if necessary. $\delta \leq 8 t_e$.

$$0.67 \delta \leq \text{shear plane } c-c$$

Step 6. Knowing $V_{max-act}$, the pin diameter δ, the eye plate dimensions, and the shoe plate's yield stress f_y, design the shoe plate flanges. First draw an axial section of the eye plate assembly (see Fig. 3-33), then find its net section area A_{epa}, then find the net section area A_{sp} of each of the two shoe plate flanges from

$$A_{epa} \leq 0.75 A_{sp}$$

Then check that the length between the two shoe plate flange centerlines $\leq$ the pin axis length in Step 1 that was used to find $M_{max\text{-}act}$ in Step 2.

Step 7. Design the shoe plate flanges according to the following stresses in each flange (see Fig. 3-34):

Net shear plane:	$V_{max\text{-}act} \leq f_v\, b$	$(e\text{-}e)$
Bearing plane:	$V_{max\text{-}act} \leq f_c\, \delta\, b$	
Net tension plane:	$V_{max\text{-}act} \leq 2\, f_t\, b$	$(f\text{-}f)$
Base shear plane:	$V_{max\text{-}act} = f_v\, g\, b$	
ΣM at point P:	$V_{max\text{-}act} \times h = 0.167\, f_b\, b\, b_{bs}{}^2$	

Step 8. Knowing all the above, design the shoe plate's base. This involves satisfying the stress criteria described in **a, b, c, d, e, f,** and **g** below (see Fig. 3-35).

a. Beam shear plane: The pin connection's total gravity load may cause the base to fail in beam shear along plane a–a. Although this is a remote possibility, it must be investigated according to

$$P\left(L - {M^2}/{L}\right) \leq 1.33\, f_b\, b^2\, d^2$$

P = total load on pin connection, lb
L = length of shoe plate base, in.
M = out-to-out width of shoe plate flanges in direction parallel to L, in.
f_b = safe unit bending stress for shoe plate steel, psi
b = breadth or width of shoe plate base, in.
d = depth or thickness of shoe plate base, in.

b. Punching shear plane: If the shoe plate base is too thin, the pin's total gravity load may cause the base's central portion to separate or overturn from its outer portions along plane b–b. This possibility is investigated according to

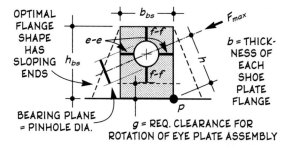

OPTIMAL FLANGE SHAPE HAS SLOPING ENDS

b_{bs}

e-e

h_{bs}

f-f

f-f

F_{max}

b = THICKNESS OF EACH SHOE PLATE FLANGE

h

P

BEARING PLANE = PINHOLE DIA.

g = REQ. CLEARANCE FOR ROTATION OF EYE PLATE ASSEMBLY

Fig. 3-34. Location of shoe plate flange stresses.

$$P \leq 1.8\, f_v\, d\, (M + N)$$

f_v = safe unit bending stress for shoe plate steel, psi
N = out-to-out width of shoe plate flanges in direction perpendicular to L, in.

P, d, and M are as previously defined.

c. **Strength of lateral rebars laid between opposing pin connections:** The total weight supported by the shoe plate base exerts a horizontal outward thrust that tries to push the two ground-level pin connections farther apart. If this thrust is counteracted by tensile rebars laid between the pin connections, find the rebars' size and number from the formula below:

$$P_{hor} \leq 0.47\, f_y\, \eta\, \delta^2$$

P_{hor} = horiz. component of pin connection load, psi
f_y = safe unit yield stress of rebar steel, psi
η = number of lateral rebars
δ = dia. of lateral rebars, in.

d. **Side bearing at edge of shoe plate base:** If part of the shoe plate base is below grade, the outward lateral thrust of the base will push against the below-grade substrate. If **c** above is satisfied, this thrust = 0. Otherwise, verify its safety according to

$$P_{hor} \leq 0.5 \, f_{bs} \, L \, (d_p - 6)$$

f_{bs} = safe unit bearing stress of substrate resting against side of the shoe plate base, psi or ksi

d_p = part of shoe plate base below substrate, in.

P_{hor} and L are as previously defined

e. **Anchor bolt shear:** The anchor bolts that hold the shoe plate base to its substrate must be large enough to resist the shoe plate's lateral outward thrust and deep enough to resist imbedment tearout due to the lateral thrust. Thus find the anchor bolt diameters from the formula below, and find their shaft length L_a below the shoe plate base from $L_a \geq 12 \, \delta$.

$$P_{hor} \leq 0.38 \, f_v \, \eta \, \delta^2$$

f_v = safe unit shear stress of anchor bolt steel, psi

η = number of anchor bolts in shoe plate base

δ = min. dia. of anchor bolts in shoe plate base, in.

f. **Bearing strength of shoe plate base substrate:** The material directly beneath the shoe plate base must bear the gravity load of everything above. This includes the total pin connection and all the weight it supports according to

$$P \leq 0.5 \, f_{bs} \, b \, L$$

All terms are as previously defined.

g. Σ moments at point G: At pt. G the vertical component of the angular thrust of F_{max} is counteracted by the upward counterthrust of the base's area × half its width × the substrate's safe bearing strength. Both the pin's footing and the substrate below must satisfy this relation.

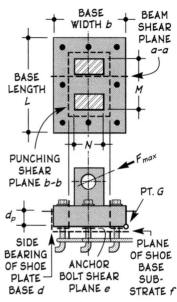

Fig. 3-35. Location of shoe plate base stresses.

Eyebar Design:

Step 1. Size the eyebar's shaft as described below.

Round section:	$P = 0.47\, f_{ye}\, \delta^2$
Rectangular section:	$P = 0.60\, f_{ye}\, b\, t$

P = total tensile load on eyebar, lb
f_{ye} = safe unit yield stress of eyebar steel, psi. If δ or

$t \leq 0.75$ in, $f_{ye} = f_y$; if ≤ 1.50 in, $f_{ye} = 0.92\, f_y$; if ≤ 4.5 in, $f_{ye} = 0.82\, f_y$.

δ = diameter of eyebar with round ring section, in.

b = width of eyebar with rectangular ring section, in.

t = thickness of eyebar with rectangular ring section, in.

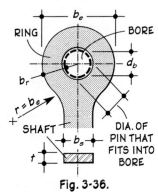

Fig. 3-36.

Step 2. Find the eyebar's bore diameter, ring width, and total width according to the formulas below:

> **Bore diameter:** $\delta_b \geq \delta_p + 0.031$
> **Ring width:** $P \geq 0.9\, b_r f_{ye}$
> **Total width:** $b_e \geq \delta_b + 2\, b_r$

δ_b = minimum diameter of bore, in.
δ_p = diameter of pin inserted into bore, in.
P = total tensile load on eyebar, lb or kips
b_r = width of ring around bore, in.
f_{ye} = safe unit yield stress of eyebar steel, psi or ksi.
  If eye $t \leq 0.75$ in, $f_{ye} = 1.0\, f_y$; if $t \leq 1.5$ in, $f_{ye} = 0.92\, f_y$; if $t \leq 4.5$ in, $f_{ye} = 0.84\, f_y$.
b_e = total width of eye, in.

Step 3. Verify that the eyebar's dimensions satisfy the relation below. If not, redesign it.

$$2.22\, P \leq t f_y (b_e - d_b) \leq 2.50\, P$$

Steel Cable Design: Also known as wire rope, steel cable has a number of helically arranged strands often wound around a central core of fiber, flexible plastic, or more steel strands. One's capacity or unit strength depends on its diameter, number and arrangement of strands, type of steel, type of core, and whether or not its steel is galvanized. Steel cable has two applications: (1) *standing* (fabric structures, hangers, etc.), and (2) *operating* (elevators, hoists, ski lifts, etc.). Important properties of standing cables are *exposure* (indoor, outdoor, or corrosive environments) and *crushing resistance* (ability to stand up to transverse loads that can damage the strands), while important properties of operating cables are *flexibility* (ability to endure repeated short-radius bending) and *wear resistance*. Below is a formula for designing operating steel cable.

$$P_b D = \kappa_C E \delta^2 \delta_s$$

P_b = total equivalent bending load of cable, psi.

D = dia. of drum or reel that cable spools onto, in.

κ_C = cable type coefficient based on type of steel cable used. A few values for κ_C are 0.380 for 6×7 fiber core cable, 0.437 for 6×7 IWRC or WSC cable, 0.405 for 6×19 fiber core cable, 0.400 for 6×37 fiber core cable, 0.470 for 6×37 IWRC cable, 0.370 for 8×19 fiber core cable, and 0.440 for flattened strand cable.

E = modulus of elasticity of steel cable, usually 12,000,000 psi

δ = diameter of steel cable, in.

δ_s = diameter of component strands of steel cable, in. δ_s for 6×7 cable = 0.106 δ; for 6×19 cable = 0.063 δ; for 6×37 cable = 0.045 δ; for 8×19 cable = 0.050 δ.

TABLE 4-1: REINFORCED CONCRETE DATA

SPECIFIED STRENGTH OF CONCRETE f_c, psi

STRESS	Formula	2,500	3,000	3,500	4,000
Shear (f_v): slabs, footings	$2 (f_c)^{0.5}$	100	110	126	141
Beams w no web reinf.	$1.1 (f_c)^{0.5}$	100	110	126	141
Joists w no web reinf.	$1.2 (f_c)^{0.5}$	61	66	77	86
Members w stirrups	$5 (f_c)^{0.5}$	250	274	316	354
Bearing (f_b): on full area ...	$0.25 f_c$	625	750	1,000	1,250
On $1/3$ area or less	$0.37 f_c$	938	1,125	1,500	1,875
Bending (f_c): tension ...	$1.60 (f_c)^{0.5}$	80	88	102	113
Compression	$0.45 f_c$	1,125	1,350	1,800	2,250
Mod. of elasticity (E)	$57,000 (f_c)^{0.5}$				
$\omega \approx 145$ lb/ft^3		2,880,000	3,640,000		
				3,150,000	4,070,000
Other densities ...	$33 \omega^{1.5} (f_c)^{0.5}$				
Formula coefficient (R) $f_y = 60$ ksi		161	204	271	295

Density, nonreinforced, standard gravel aggregate .. 145 lb/cf
Slag aggregate, 130; Cinder aggregate .... 110 lb/cf
Lightweight aggregates .... 35-100 lb/cf
Density, reinforced .... add 5 lb/cf to above values

REINFORCING BAR DIMENSIONS

BAR NO.	Dia., in.	Perim., in.	Sec. area, in^2	Wt, lb/LF
# 3	0.375	1.18	0.11	0.376
# 4	0.500	1.57	0.20	0.668
# 5	0.625	1.96	0.31	0.043
# 6	0.750	2.36	0.44	1.502
# 7	0.875	2.75	0.60	2.04
# 8	1.00	3.14	0.79	2.67
# 9	1.13	3.54	1.00	3.40
# 10	1.27	3.99	1.27	4.30
# 11	1.41	4.43	1.56	5.31
# 14	1.59	5.32	2.25	7.65
# 18	2.26	7.09	4.00	13.60

4. CONCRETE

Development Length of Tensile Reinforcing:

#3–#11 bars: $l_d \leq 12$ in, $0.004\ d_b\ f_y$, & $0.04\ A_b\ f_y/f_c^{0.5}$
#14 bars: $l_d \leq 12$ in, $0.004\ d_b\ f_y$, & $A_b\ f_y/f_c^{0.5}$
#18 bars: $l_d \leq 12$ in, $0.004\ d_b\ f_y$, & $0.11\ A_b\ f_y/f_c^{0.5}$
Comp. bars: $l_d \leq 12$ in, $0.004\ d_b\ f_y$, & $0.02\ d_b\ A_b\ f_y/f_c^{0.5}$
Top rebars w/ min. 12 in. concrete below: multiply $l_d \times 1.4$
Bars of spirals whose pitch ≤ 4 in: multiply $l_d \times 0.75$

l_d = minimum development length of tensile rebars, in.
A_b = section area of bars, in^2
f_y = yield strength of steel, usually 60 ksi
f_c = 28 day compressive strength of concrete, ksi
d_b = bar diameter, in.

Beam Bending Moment:

Step 1. Investigate the beam for safe width. If the depth is given, find the width according to Step 5 below.

$$L/b \leq 50$$

L = length of span, in.
b = breadth or width of beam, in.

Step 2. Compute the beam's total design load from

$$W_U = 1.4 \, W_D + 1.7 \, W_L$$

W_U = total design load on span, lb or kips
W_D = total dead load on beam, kips
W_L = total live load on beam, kips

Step 3. Compute the beam's maximum bending moment.

$$\boxed{M?} = M_{max} = f_c \, S_x$$

$\boxed{M?}$ = applicable moment formula, from beam tables
M_{max} = maximum moment of applied load, in/kips
f_c = specified strength of concrete, ksi
S_x = section modulus of beam section, in³

Step 4. Compute the beam's steel-to-concrete section ratio.

$$r = 47 f_c / f_y \, (87 + f_y)$$

r = maximum reinforcing ratio of steel to concrete
f_c = specified strength of concrete, ksi
f_y = safe yield stress of reinforcement, ksi

Step 5. Compute the beam's depth given its width. If the depth is known, find the beam's width.

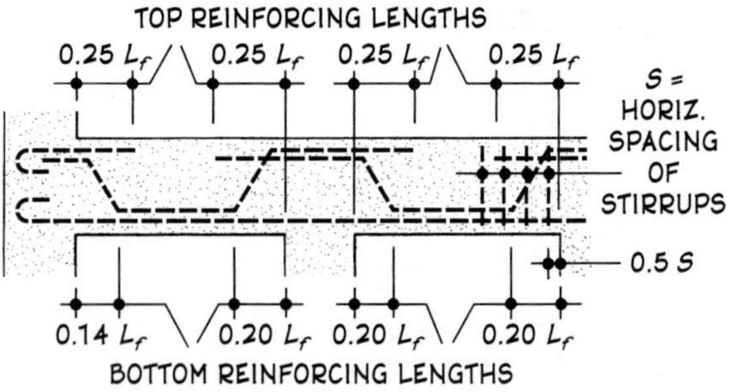

TOP REINFORCING LENGTHS

Fig. 4-1. Rebar length ratios in concrete beams.

$$M_{max} = 0.9 \, r \, f_y \, b \, d_e^2 \, (1 - 0.59 \, r \, f_y / f_c')$$

M_{max} = maximum moment of load, from Step 3, in-kips
r = maximum reinforcing ratio, from Step 4
f_y = safe yield stress of reinforcement, ksi
b = breadth or width of span, in.
d_e = effective depth of beam, in. Total depth = d_e + 2.5 min. cover.
f_c' = specified strength of concrete, ksi

Step 6. Compute the area of tensile reinforcing.

$$A_t = r \, b \, d_e$$

A_t = section area of tensile reinforcing, in^2
r = maximum reinforcing ratio, from Step 4
b = breadth or width of span, in.
d_e = effective depth of beam, in.

Step 7. Size the rebars. Select several sizes whose section area × an even number of bars ≥ A_t, then select the rebar size with the least total area.

Step 8. Check the minimum clear distance between rebars. Minimum spacing between bars is the bar diameter, 1.33 × aggregate size, or 1 in, whichever is most, with minimum $1\frac{1}{2}$ in. concrete cover on each side.

$$b = 3.00 + \delta \eta + s \, (\eta - 1)$$

b = breadth or width of span, in.
δ = diameter of selected rebars, in.
η = maximum number of rebars per row at designated δ. If η ≥ number of bars selected in Step 7, one row is **OK**. Otherwise reselect a larger bar diameter, or arrange bars in two rows and increase beam depth by $s + \delta$.
s = minimum clear distance between rebars, in.

194   ＋ℬ▯Ⅰ▯▦♀✳⚒ℂ💡❓🔢↻

Beam Shear:

Step 1. Compute the beam's design shear load. The expression $0.5\ W_u$ in the formula below is for the end reaction of a symmetrically loaded beam.

$$V = 0.5\ W_u - W_u\ d_e/L$$

V = maximum design shear load of beam, lb or kips
W_u = total design load on beam, lb or kips
d_e = effective depth of beam, in.
L = length of span, in.

Step 2. Compute the beam's design unit shear stress.

$$V = 0.85\ v\ b\ d_e$$

V = design shear load on beam, from Step 2, kips
v = design unit shear stress of beam, ksi
b = breadth or width of span, in.
d_e = effective depth of beam, from Step 1, in.

Step 3. Investigate the beam for safe shear.

$$v_u \leq f_v$$

v_u = design unit shear stress of beam, psi or ksi
f_v = safe stress in shear for concrete used, psi

Diagonal Tension: A reinforced concrete beam may develop diagonal cracks in its tensile zones subjected to maximum shear; then rows of U-shaped #3 or #4 bar *stirrups* are placed vertically near the ends of the span.

Step 1. Determine the spacing of stirrups if required.
   a. $v_u < f_v$ ➡ no stirrups required
   b. $v_u \geq f_v$ and $\leq 4 f_c^{0.5} + f_v$ ➡ s = 0.5 d_e
   c. $v_u \geq 4 f_c^{0.5} + f_v$ & $\leq 8 f_c^{0.5} + f_v$ ➡ s = 0.25 d_e

d. $v_u \geq 8 f_c^{0.5} + f_v$ ➡ increase d_e by
1.18 $v_u/(b f_c^{0.5} + f_v)$ & $s = 0.25 d_e$

v_u = design unit shear stress of beam, psi
f_v = safe shear stress of concrete, psi
f_c = specified strength of concrete, psi
d_e = effective depth of beam, in.
b = breadth or width of beam, in.
s = stirrup spacing, in. Round down to next ½ in.
Locate first stirrup 0.5 s from face of support.

Step 2. Compute the span's required stirrup length.

$$L_s = d + (0.5 L - d) (v_u - 0.5 f_v/v_u)$$

L_s = length of span from each end where stirrups are required, in.
d = total depth of beam, in.
L = length of span, in.
v_u = design unit shear stress of beam, psi
f_v = safe shear stress of concrete, psi

Step 3. Compute the required number of stirrups.

$$L_s = s |\eta|$$

η = required number of stirrups, units
L_s and s are as previously defined

Step 4. Compute the rebar size for each stirrup.

$$A_v f_y = 50 s b$$

A_v = min. section area of each stirrup, in². If $A_v \leq$ 0.11 ➡ #3 bars; if $0.11 \leq A_v \leq 0.20$ ➡ #4 bars.
f_y = safe unit yield stress for shear reinforcing, psi
s and b are as previously defined

Beam Deflection:

Step 1. Compute the beam section's moment of inertia.

$$I = \boxed{I?}$$

I = moment of inertia of concrete beam section, in^4
$\boxed{I?}$ = applic. moment of inertia formula from Table 1-4
b = breadth or width of beam, in.
d = total depth of beam, in.

Step 2. Compute the beam's initial deflection.

$$\Delta_I = \boxed{D?} \leq \kappa_\Delta L$$

Δ_I = maximum initial deflection of beam, in.
$\boxed{D?}$ = applicable deflection formula, from beam tables
κ_Δ = coeff. of allowable deflection, from Table 1-3

Step 3. Compute the beam's long-term deflection.

$$\Delta_L = \Delta_I [1 + W_D/(W_D + W_L)]$$

Δ_L = long-term deflection of beam, in.
W_D = total design dead load on beam, lb
    Δ_I and W_L are as previously defined.

Step 4. Compute the beam's allowable initial and long-term deflection. Both equations must be **OK**.

    a. Initial Δ: $\Delta_i \leq L \kappa_{\Delta i}$
    b. Long-term Δ: $\Delta_{lt} \leq L \kappa_{\Delta lt}$

$\kappa_{\Delta i}$ = coefficient of initial deflection, from Table 1-3
$\kappa_{\Delta lt}$ = coeff. of long-term deflection, from Table 1-3
    Δ_i, Δ_{lt}, and L are as previously defined

Bond Shear:

When a reinforced concrete beam flexes under a load, its rebars "pull" one way while the enveloping concrete "pulls" the other way, which creates a *bond shear* stress at the rebar/concrete interface.

$$V = 3.14\ f_{ub}\ \eta\ \delta\ (d_e - 0.33\ d_{ax})$$

V = maximum total shear on member, lb or kips

f_{ub} = safe unit bond shear stress for concrete and rebar size, from Table 4-2, psi. Solve for actual f_{ub}, then compare with allow. f_{ub}.

η = number of tensile rebars at critical section

TABLE 4-2: SAFE UNIT BOND STRESSES

TOP BARS: based on $u\ \delta = 3.4\ (f_c)^{0.5}$ & $u \leq 350$ psi

Rebar size	Strength of Concrete, f_c, psi						
	2,500	3,000	3,500	3,750	4,000	4,500	5,000
3	350	350	350	350	350	350	350
4	340	350	350	350	350	350	350
5	272	298	322	333	344	350	350
6	227	248	268	278	287	304	332
7	194	213	230	238	246	261	275
8	170	186	201	208	215	228	240
9	151	165	178	185	190	203	211
10	134	147	159	164	169	182	186
11	121	132	143	148	153	166	171

LOWER BARS: based on $u\ \delta = 4.8\ (f_c)^{0.5}$ & $u \leq 500$ psi

Rebar size	Strength of Concrete, f_c, psi						
	2,500	3,000	3,500	3,750	4,000	4,500	5,000
3	500	500	500	500	500	500	500
4	480	500	500	500	500	500	500
5	384	421	455	470	486	500	500
6	320	351	380	392	405	429	449
7	274	300	324	336	347	368	390
8	240	263	284	294	304	322	340
9	213	233	252	261	269	286	300
10	189	207	224	231	239	258	266
11	170	186	201	208	215	234	240

δ = minimum rebar diameter, in.
d_e = effective depth of structural member, in.
d_{ax} = vertical distance from outermost compression
face of structural member to neutral axis, in.

Location of Neutral Axis of Concrete Beam:

$$d_{ax} = \frac{d_e\, E_s\, f_c}{E_s\, f_c + E_c\, f_y}$$

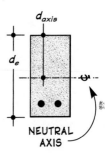

d_{ax} = vertical distance from outer compression face of reinforced concrete member
to neutral axis, in.

d_e = effective depth of beam, in.

E_s = modulus of elasticity of
rebar steel, psi

f_c = specified strength of
concrete, psi

E_c = modulus of elasticity of
concrete, psi

f_y = safe unit yield stress of
rebars, 50,000 psi

Fig. 4-2.

T-Beam Design: Optimal dimension ratios for T-
beams are:

▸ Flange width ≤ 0.25 span and ≤ 8.0 stem width.
▸ Flange thickness at tip ≥ 0.063 flange width, ≥
0.125 flange overhang on each side of stem, ≥ 0.5
stem width, and ≥ 0.016 span.
▸ Stem width ≈ 0.25–0.50 stem's effective depth.

Step 1. Compute the beam's design load.

$$W = 1.4\, W_D + 1.7\, W_L$$

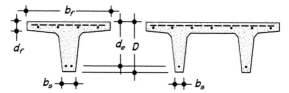

Fig. 4-3. Reinforced concrete T-beam details.

W = total design load on beam, lb
W_D = total dead load on beam, lb
W_L = total live load on beam, lb

Step 2. Compute the beam's maximum bending moment at midspan and, if the beam is continuous, its maximum negative moment at its supports.

$$\boxed{M?} = M_{max} = f_c\, S_x$$

$\boxed{M?}$ = applicable moment formula, from beam tables
f_c = specified strength of concrete, psi
S_x = section modulus of beam section, in³

Step 3. Estimate the span's effective depth at midspan from the formulas below. The lesser value governs.

$$\text{a.} \quad M_{max} = 0.067\, f_c\, d_e^3$$
$$\text{b.} \quad M_{max} = \kappa_r\, b\, d_e^2$$

M_{max} = maximum moment of applied load, in-lb
f_c = specified strength of concrete, psi
d_e = effective depth of stem (distance from top of stem to axis of tensile rebars), in.
κ_r = resiliency coefficient. κ_r = 178 at f_c = 2,500 psi, 223 at f_c = 3,000 psi, 324 at f_c = 4,000 psi, and 423 at f_c = 5,000 psi.
b = breadth or width of beam, in.

Step 4. Estimate the width of the stem at midspan.

$$b_s \approx 0.4 \, d_e$$

b_s = width of stem, use a whole number ≥ 8 in.
d_e = effective depth of stem, in.

Step 5. Design the stem's tensile reinforcement.

$$+M_{max} = 0.53 \, A_s \, f_y \, d_e$$

$+M_{max}$ = max. moment of applied load at midspan, in-lb
A_s = minimum area of reinforcement, in^2
f_y = safe unit yield stress of rebars, psi
d_e = effective depth of stem, in.

Step 6. Find the beam's actual unit shear stress f_v at its supports. If actual f_v > safe f_v, stirrups are required.

$$V = f_v \, b_s \, d_e$$

V = maximum shear at face of support, lb
f_v = actual unit shear stress at face of support, psi.
  Solve for this, then compare with beam's safe f_v.
  b_s and d_e are as previously defined

Step 7. Design the stem's tensile reinforcement over any fixed supports.

$$-M_{max} = 0.53 \, A_s \, f_y \, d_e$$

$-M_{max}$ = max. moment of load at face of support, in-lb
  A_s, f_y, and d_e are as previously defined

Step 8. Design the stem's stirrups if required.

$$s \, (V - f_v \, b_s \, d_e) = 0.60 \, A_s \, f_y \, d_e$$

s = maximum spacing of stirrups, in. $s_{max} \geq 0.5 \, d_e$.
  V, f_v, b_s, d_e, and A_s are as previously defined

Step 9. Estimate the width of the flange. If a trial value has been selected, investigate it for safe width.

$$b_f \leq 0.25\ L$$

b_f = maximum breadth or width of flange, equals beam spacing, in. Use next highest half integer.

L = length of span, in.

Step 10. Find the span's depth or thickness at its tip.

$$t_f = 0.63\ b_f$$

t_f = minimum thickness of flange at tip, in. Use next highest half integer.

b_f = breadth or width of flange, in.

Step 11. Find the flange's optimal depth at its base.

$$d_f \geq 0.125\ (0.5\ b_f - b_s) + t_f \geq 4\ \text{in.}$$

d_f = optimal depth of flange at base, in. Use next largest half integer.

b_f = maximum width of flange, in.

b_s = width of stem, 12 in.

t_f = thickness of flange at tip, in.

Step 12. Determine if the beam's initial and long-term deflection are safe.

Step 13. Design the flange's transverse reinforcement. Transverse rebar spacing $\leq 5 \times$ flange's minimum thickness or 18 in, whichever is less.

$$W\ L_o = 1.05\ A_s\ f_y\ d_e$$

W = total load on a transverse portion (usually a 12 in. strip) of the flange, lb

L_o = length of flange overhang, from ¢ of stem to tip of flange, in.

   A_s, f_y, and d_e are as previously defined

Step 14. Investigate the beam's unit bond stress. If computed V exceeds actual V, one solution is to select a larger number of smaller bars that would have a larger p_r while still satisfying A_s.

Top bars:	$\delta_r V \geq 2.60\, p_r\, d_e\, f_c^{0.5}$
Other-than-top bars:	$\delta_r V \geq 3.67\, p_r\, d_e\, f_c^{0.5}$

δ_r = diameter of rebars, in.
p_r = perimeter of rebars, in.
$\quad$ V, f_c, and d_e are as previously defined

Steel Beams Encased in Concrete Design:

In this structure a steel W or T shape is encased in a 2 to 3 in. cover of concrete whose top portion extends from its sides to form T-beam-like flanges that connect to similar flanges on each side.

Step 1. Tentatively select a steel shape that is enveloped in a concrete stem and integral floor slab; then note the steel shape's A, d, b_f, S_x, I_x, and f_b as well as the concrete's η (E_{steel}/E_{conc}) and f_c.

Step 2. At the beam's section of maximum moment (usually at midspan) compute its section modulus by finding the section's transformed width b_{cs}, from the following two equations, then selecting the lesser value.

$\quad$ **a.** $b_{csa} = 0.25\, L\, E_c/E_s$
$\quad$ **b.** $b_{csa} = (d_s\, d_c + b_c)\, E_c/E_s$

b_{csa} = composite section's transformed width at top of section, in.
L $\quad$ = length of span, in.
E_c $\quad$ = modulus of elasticity of concrete, psi
E_s $\quad$ = modulus of elasticity of beam steel, psi

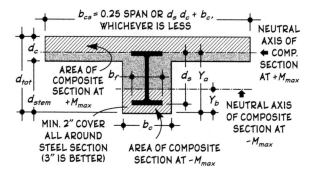

Fig. 4-4. Steel beam encased in concrete details.

d_s = full depth of steel beam, in.
d_c = depth of concrete slab at top of beam, in.
b_c = breadth or width of concrete stem, in.

Step 3. Locate the total section's neutral axis Y_a from

$$0.5\, b_{csa}\, y_a^2 = A_s (0.5\, d_{tot} - y_a)$$
$$\ldots \text{solve for } y_a \text{ quadradically}$$

b_{csa} = composite section's transformed width at top, in.
y_a = location of axis Y_a from top of section, in.
A_s = section area of rebar steel, in^2
d_{tot} = total depth of composite section, in.

Step 4. Find the section's moment of inertia I_{cs} from

$$\text{Total } I_{cs} = I \text{ of concrete} + I \text{ of steel}$$
$$I_{cs} = 0.33\, b_{csa}\, y_a^3 + [I_{W\text{-shape}} + A_{W\text{-shape}} (0.5\, d_{tot} - y_a)^2]$$

All the above terms are obvious or have been previously defined.

204 ➔ß▯I▯▦♀✳☞♡♙▯♋

Step 5. Find the section's section modulus S_{cs} from

$$\text{Total } S_x: \quad S_{cs} = S_{conc} + S_{steel}$$
$$S_{cs} = I_{cs}/y_a + I_{cs}/(d_{tot} - y_a)$$

All the above terms are obvious or have been previously defined.

Step 6. If the beam has a section of maximum negative moment, compute its section modulus. This may be done as in Step 2 by substituting the following terms:

For b_{csa} substitute b_{csb} = composite section's transformed width at base of section (shaded area at bottom of section), in.
For y_a substitute y_b = location of axis Y_b from bottom of composite section, in.

Step 7. Assuming the beam is uniformly loaded and has fixed supports, find its maximum positive moment from formula **a** below, then check that the actual f_b for concrete and steel ≤ allow. f_b by inserting in formula **b** allow. f_b for one material then solving for actual f_b of the the other. If the second material's actual f_b ≤ allow. f_b, the beam is **OK**.

$\quad$ **a.** $+M_{max} = 0.125 \ W_{tot-LL} \ L_{in} + 0.050 \ W_{tot-DL} \ L_{in}$
$\quad$ **b.** $+M_{max} = f_{b\text{-}steel} \ S_{steel} + f_{b\text{-}conc} \ (S_{conc} - S_{steel})$

All the above terms are previously defined.

Step 8. Find the beam's maximum negative moment $-M_{max}$ (usually at the face of an end support) from formula **a** below, then check that actual f_b for concrete and steel ≤ safe f_b similarly as was done for $+M_{max}$ in Step 7.

a. $-M_{max} = 0.083 \ W_{tot \ LL} \ L_{in}$
b. $-M_{max} \ E_{conc}/S_{conc} \ E_{steel} = $ act. $f_{b\text{-}conc}$ ≤ all. $f_{b\text{-}conc}$

Step 9. Check the total section for shear as follows:

   a. Vertical shear:

$$0.50\ W_{tot}\ (L - d_{tot}/L) \le f_{v\text{-}steel}\ A_s + 0.5\ f_c^{\,0.5}\ (b_{cs}\ d + b_c\ d_{stem})$$

   b. Horiz. shear at seam 1 (pt. of contraflexure):

$$0.30\ W_{tot} \le 0.12\ L_{in}\ f_c\ (x^2 + y^2)^{0.5} + 0.015\ f_c\ b_f\ L_{in}$$

   c. Horiz. shear at seam 2 (beam support):

$$0.30\ W_{tot} \le 0.12\ L_{in}\ f_c\ x + 0.015\ f_c\ b_f\ L_{in}$$

Step 10. Investigate the beam for safe deflection.

Ribbed Slab Design:

General dimensional ratios for ribbed slab floor and roof systems are:

- Rib breadth or width $b \ge 4$ in.
- Spacing between sides of adjacent ribs ≤ 30 in.
- Rib depth $\le 3.5 \times$ minimum width.
- Slab thickness ≥ 2 in.

Step 1. Determine the total design load on each rib.

$$W = 1.4\ W_D + 1.7\ W_L$$

W = total design load on each rib, lb
W_D = total dead load on each rib, lb
W_L = total live load on each rib, lb

Step 2. Compute the maximum positive and negative moments for each rib.

$$\boxed{\text{M?}} = M_{max}$$

$\boxed{\text{M?}}$ = applicable moment formula, from beam tables
M_{max} = maximum moment for each rib, in/lb, as below:

   W = design load on beam, lb
   P = weight of each point load on rib, lb
   L = length of span, in.

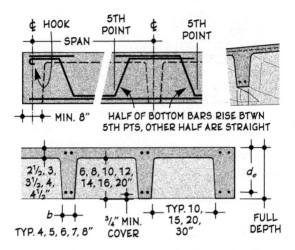

Fig. 4-5. Reinf. concrete ribbed slab details.

Step 3. Estimate the depth of each rib.

$$M_{max} \approx 0.075 \, f_c \, d_e{}^3$$

M_{max} = maximum moment for each rib, in-lb
f_c = specified strength of concrete, psi
d_e = effective depth of each rib, in. If $d_e \geq 13.5$ in, use 30 in. wide pans. d_e must also meet the following criteria:

Type of span	Min. d at f_y = 40 ksi	Min. d at f_y = 60 ksi
Simple	0.063 L	0.050 L
Semicontinuous	0.053 L	0.042 L
Continuous	0.048 L	0.038 L

Step 4. Find the width of each rib.

$$M_{max} = 0.15 \, f_c \, b \, d_e^{\,2}$$

M_{max} = max. moment of load at midspan of each rib, in-lb
b = minimum breadth or width of each rib, in.
f_c and d_e are as previously defined

Step 5. Knowing the width of each rib, determine or verify the ribs' ℄–℄ spacing and thus the width of the voids between them.

$$b_f = b + b_v$$

b_f = unit ℄–℄ spacing of ribs, in.
b = breadth or width of each rib, in.
b_v = width of voids or joist pans between ribs, in.

Step 6. Determine if the beam's initial and long-term deflection are safe. This is described on page 196.

Step 7. Design each rib's tensile rebars at midspan.

$$M_{max} = 0.53 \, A_s \, f_y \, d_e$$

M_{max} = max. moment of load at midspan of rib, in-lb
A_s = min. section area of rebars, in^2. Usually select two bars, then use A_s to find optimal size.
f_y = safe unit yield stress of rebars, psi
d_e = effective depth of each rib, in.

Step 8. Use the ribs' safe unit shear stress at its support to determine the ribs' minimum width b_s at its support. If this is greater than b at midspan, $b_s - b$ indicates how much horizontal taper each rib's sides can have at the face of each end support. Then find b_s from

$$W = 1.75 \, f_v \, b \, d_e + 0.012 \, s_r \, \omega \, d_e$$

W = total design load on each rib and slab (area between the ℄s of two adjacent ribs), lb
f_v = safe unit shear stress at rib's support, psi

➔ß▤I▢▨♀✳✂⒠♥♀⑩℃

b = min. width of rib at face of support, in.
d_e = effective depth of rib, in.
s_r = ₵–₵ spacing of ribs, in.
ω = unit live & dead load on area supported by rib, psf

Step 9. Design each rib's tensile rebars at its supports.

$$-M_{max} = 0.53\, A_s\, f_y\, d_e$$

$-M_{max}$ = max. moment of load at face of support, in-lb
A_s = min. area of reinforcement, in². As one lower
rebar is typically bent up to form part of the
top reinforcing, subtract A_s of the bent rebar
to find net A_s of the bottom rebar.
f_y and d_e are as previously defined

Step 10. Investigate each rib's unit bond stress according to the formulas below. Solve for f_c, then compare actual f_c with allow. f_c. If **NG**, try a larger number of smaller bars with a larger p_r that still satisfies A_s.

    a. Top bars: $\delta_r V \geq 2.60\, p_r\, d_e\, f_c^{0.5}$
    b. Lower bars: $\delta_r V \geq 3.67\, p_r\, d_e\, f_c^{0.5}$

δ_r = diameter of rebars, in.
V = maximum beam shear at face of support
p_r = perimeter of rebars, in.
    d_e and f_c are as previously defined

Step 11. Design the transverse reinforcement.

$$\omega\, s_r^{\,2} = 173\, A_s\, f_y\, d_e$$

A_s = min. section area of reinf., in². Usually wire mesh
or #3 rebars 18 in. o.c. is adequate.
    All other terms are as previously defined

Step 12. Knowing all the above, select the pan dimensions, then determine the final rib width, rib depth, and slab thickness.

    a. Pan width: $P_w \approx s_r - b_r$
    b. Pan depth: $P_d \approx 0.8 \, d$

P_w = estimated width of pan, in.
s_r = ¢-¢ spacing of ribs, in.
b_r = estimated width of each rib, in.
P_d = estimated depth of pan, 8, 10, 12, 14, 16, or 18 in.
    Slab t must ≥ 2.5 in. and should ≤ 4.5 in.
d = estimated total depth of rib, in.

One-Way Slab Design:

Step 1. Compute the design load on a 1 ft wide section of the slab in the direction of the rib-to-rib span.

$$W = 1.4 \, W_D + 1.7 \, W_L$$

W = total design load on unit section of slab, lb
W_D = total dead load on unit section of slab, lb
W_L = total live load on unit section of slab, lb

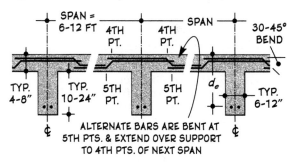

Fig. 4-6. Reinf. concrete one-way slab details.

Step 2. Find the slab's minimum effective depth.

$$W = 24\, d_e\, f_c^{0.5}$$

W = total design load on unit section of slab, lb
d_e = minimum effective depth of slab, in. Solve for
   this value, then use next highest half integer.
f_c = specified strength of concrete, psi

Step 3. Check the slab's total depth from $d \geq \kappa_t\, L$
wherein κ_t is listed below. Minimum total depth is 3.5 in.

Type of span	Min. d at $f_y = 40$ ksi	Min. d at $f_y = 60$ ksi
Simple	0.050 L	0.040 L
Semicontinuous	0.042 L	0.034 L
Continuous	0.036 L	0.029 L

Step 4. Design each rib's tensile rebars at midspan.

$$M_{max} = 0.53\, A_s\, f_y\, d_e$$

M_{max} = maximum moment of load at midspan of rib, in-lb
A_s = minimum area of reinforcement, in^2
f_y = safe unit yield stress of rebars, psi
d_e = effective depth of rib, in.

Step 5. Estimate the slab's total depth from

$$d = d_e + 0.5\, r_d + 0.75$$

d = total depth of slab, in. Solve for this value, then
   use next highest half integer.
d_e = minimum effective depth of slab, in.
r_d = rebar diameter, in.

Step 6. Determine if the beam's initial and long-term deflection are safe.

Step 7. Investigate the slab's shearing unit stress.

$$V = d_e (2 f_v b + 0.167 W_u)$$

V = maximum shear load on unit width of slab (usually equals half the total distributed load), lb
d_e = effective depth of slab, in.
f_v = safe unit shear stress of concrete, psi
b = unit width of slab, usually taken to be 12 in.
W_u = total distributed load on unit width of slab, lb

Step 8. Check the slab's unit bond stress from the formulas below. Solve for f_c, then compare actual f_c with allow. f_c. If **NG**, try selecting a larger number of smaller
bars with a larger p_r that still satisfies A_s.

    a. Top bars: $\delta_r V \geq 3.00\ p_r\ d_e\ f_c^{0.5}$
    b. Lower bars: $\delta_r V \geq 4.10\ p_r\ d_e\ f_c^{0.5}$

δ_r = diameter of rebars, in.
p_r = perimeter of rebars, in.
    V, f_c, and d_e are as previously defined.

Step 9. Design the slab's temperature reinforcement.

    a. Plain bars: $A_t \geq 0.0025\ b\ d$
    b. Deformed bars: $A_t \geq 0.0020\ b\ d$

A_t = minimum section area of temperature rebars, in².
    Solve for this, then size and space the bars.
    b and d are as previously defined

Step 10. Design the slab's rebar bends. Over continuous supports, every other bar is bent at 5th points of
span, then extended over the support to the 4th point of
the adjacent span.

Step 11. If the floor slab supports large concentrated
loads, investigate it for slab punching shear.

➤ß▓I▯▒☙♀☀✄☝♆♀▥℃

Two-Way Slab Design:
Two-way slabs are much like one-way slabs except the tensile rebars running one way run two ways and the slab's depth is increased slightly to accommodate the second layer of rebars.

Step 1. Determine the ratio of the slab's major-to-minor spans, then find the portion of the slab's load that is carried by the major span from the bar graph below.

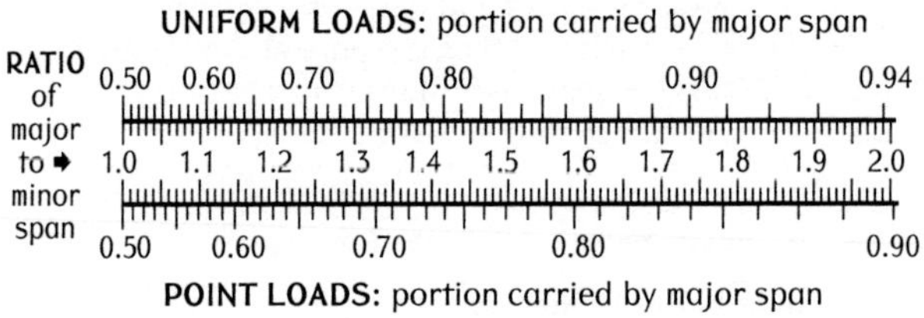

UNIFORM LOADS: portion carried by major span

POINT LOADS: portion carried by major span

Fig. 4-7. Rectangular slab load ratio bar graph.

Step 2. If the slab is rectangular, find the design loads W_x and W_y on its major and minor spans from formulas **a** and **b** below. If the bays are square, use only formula **a** to find W for both spans.

a. Load on major span: $W_x = A\, P_L\, (1.4\, \omega_D + 1.7\, \omega_L)$
b. Load on minor span: $W_y = A\, (1 - P_L)(1.4\, \omega_D + 1.7\, \omega_L)$

W_x = total design load on major span, lb
W_y = total design load on minor span, lb
A = area of each bay of slab, sf
P_L = portion of load carried by major span
ω_D = total unit dead load on slab, lb
ω_L = total unit live load on slab, lb

Step 3. Using W_x and W_y above in standard beam formulas, compute the maximum moments for the slab's major and minor spans.

Step 4. Tentatively estimate the slab's minimum depth from the formula below:

$$W = 24 \, d_e \, f_c^{0.5}$$

W = total design load on slab ($W_x + W_y$), lb or kips
d_e = minimum effective depth of slab, in. Solve for d_e, use next highest $\frac{1}{2}$ in, then add 1 in. minimum cover to obtain the floor's minimum total depth d_t.
f_c = specified strength of concrete, psi

Step 5. Investigate the total slab depth for safety.

$$4.0 \leq d_t \geq 0.0277 \, L_y$$

d_t = minimum total depth of slab, in. If this amount exceeds d_t from Step 4, use this value.
L_y = length of minor span, in.

Step 6. If any edge of the two-way slab system cantilevers beyond its perimeter support, find the cantilever's maximum feasible span according to

$$L_c \geq 0.21 \, L_x$$

L_c = maximum span of perimeter cantilever, if any, ft
L_x = length of major span, ft

Step 7. Compute the slab's area of reinforcement in each direction from

$$M_{max} = 0.53 \, A_s \, f_y \, d_e$$

M_{max} = max. moment of load each way at midspan, in-lb
A_s = min. area of rebars in each direction of slab, in^2
f_y = safe unit yield stress of rebars, psi
d_e = effective depth of slab, in.

214 ⮕ß▌I⬚▨♀✳✄Ⓔ♔♚🖭℄

Step 8. Check the safe unit shear stress at the slab's edge from the formula below. This is required only for the slab's major span. If actual f_v > allow. f_v, increase d_e.

$$M_{max\text{-}maj} = 0.0365\, L_x\, f_v\, d_e$$

$M_{max\text{-}maj}$ = maximum moment of major span, in-lb
f_v = max. actual unit shear stress for concrete, psi
L_x and d_e are as previously defined

Step 9. Check the unit bond stress between the slab's rebars and enveloping concrete by solving for f_c in the formula below then comparing actual f_c with allow. f_c. If actual f_c > allow. f_c, try a larger number of smaller bars with a larger p_r that still satisfies A_s.

$$V \geq 3.14\, f_c\, \eta\, \delta\, (d_e - 0.33\, d_{axis})$$

δ_r = diameter of rebars, in.
p_r = perimeter of rebars, in.
$V, f_c,$ and d_e are as previously defined

Step 10. Determine if the beam's initial and long-term deflection are safe.

Step 11. If the underside of the slab in the outer quarters of its span slopes slightly downward, its depth in the central half bay may be found from formula **a** below and its edge depth from formula **b** below.

    a. $3.5 \geq d_c \leq 0.65\, d_t$
    b. $d_p = d_t + 0.33\,(d_t - d_c)$

d_c = total depth of slab in central half bay, at least 3.5 in. Solve for this value, then use next highest half integer.
d_t = normal uniform total depth of slab, in.
d_p = total depth of slab at perimeter of bay, in.

Flat-Slab Floor Design: Divide each bay into a tic-tac-toe–like pattern of nine zones with the four columns supporting the bay being centered in the four corner zones (see Fig. 4-8). Then use the following moment equations for the nine zones as sketched below:

Zone 1 3 7 9 ..... M_{max} = −0.033 ωL^2 rebars both ways
Zone 2 8 .... M_{max} = +0.017 ωL^2 rebars both ways
Zone 4 6 .... M_{max} = −0.0083 ωL^2 rebars both ways
Zone 5 .... M_{max} = +0.0083 ωL^2 rebars both ways

Dimensional guidelines for flat-slab floors are:

▶   Slab thickness of floors ≥ 6 in. and ≥ 0.0032 L.
▶   Slab thickness of roofs ≥ 5 in. and ≥ 0.0025 L.
▶   Drop panel side ≥ 0.33 L (if bay is rectangular, use average of two sides). If drop panel is rectangular, long/short side ratio ≥ 2.0.
▶   Rebar spacing is usually 6–10 in. Avoid close spacing, maximum spacing ≤ 1.5 slab t, and try to have uniform spacing in all zones. #4 and #5 bars are best, and rebar bend angles are 30°.

Step 1. Determine the slab's major-to-minor span ratio, then find the portion of the slab load that is carried by the major span from the bar graph in Fig. 4-7.

Step 2. Determine the total unit design load carried by the major span on the slab area framed by each bay.

$$\omega = P_L (1.4 \, \omega_D + 1.7 \, \omega_L)$$

ω = total unit design load on slab's major span, psf
P_L = portion of slab load carried by major span
ω_D = total unit dead load on flat slab system, psf
ω_L = total unit live load on flat slab system, psf

Step 3. Select a trial thickness t for the slab from the

216

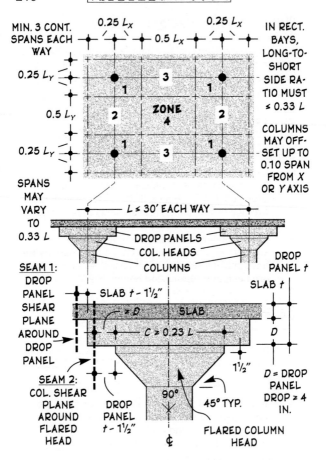

Fig. 4-8. Reinf. concrete flat slab floor details.

criteria below. Use the maximum value, then increase it
to the next highest increment of $\frac{1}{2}$ in.

    a. $t \geq (0.02\ L_x\ \omega^{0.5}/P_L) + 1.0$
    b. $t \geq 0.0032\ L_x$ for floors, $0.0025\ L_x$ for roofs
    c. $t \geq 0.15\ \omega^{0.5}/P_L$

t = minimum total thickness of slab, in.
L_x = length of major span, in.
    P_L and ω are as previously defined

Step 4. Investigate the total slab depth t for safety according to the formula below.

$$4.0 \leq t \geq 0.028\ L_y$$

t = minimum total depth of slab, in. If $t \geq t$ in Step 3,
    use this value.
L_y = length of minor span, in.

Step 5. Investigate the safe unit shear stress at the
slab's edge according to the formula below. Here V = total shear load on a 12 in. wide strip of the slab perpendicular to the major span. This calculation is required
only for the slab's major span. If actual f_v > allow. f_v, increase t accordingly.

$$\omega\ L_y = 252\ f_v\ (t - 1.0)$$

f_v = actual unit shear stress for concrete, psi
    ω, L_y, and t are as previously defined

Step 6. If any edge of the two-way slab system cantilevers
more than 24 in. beyond the plane of its perimeter supports, find the cantilever's maximum feasible span according to the formula below. If a longer cantilever is desired,
use L_c to find L_x in the formula above, then redesign the
cantilever thickness according to Steps 1-4.

$$L_c \geq 0.21\, L_x$$

L_c = maximum span of perimeter cantilever, if any, in.
L_x = length of major span, in.

Step 7. Determine if the beam's initial and long-term deflection are safe.

Step 8. Divide the bay into a tic-tac-toe–like pattern of nine zones as described in Fig. 4-8, then find the section area of reinforcement A_s in each zone from below.

Zone 1 3 7 9 .... $\omega\, L_x^2 \leq 16\, A_s f_y\,(t - 1.0)$
Zone 2 4 6 8 .... $\omega\, L_x^2 \leq 31\, A_s f_y\,(t - 1.0)$
Zone 5 .... $\omega\, L_x^2 \leq 63\, A_s f_y\,(t - 1.0)$

Zone 1 3 7 9 .. $\omega\, [L_y\,(1 - P_L)/P_L]^2 \leq 16\, A_s f_y\,(t - 1.0)$
Zone 2 4 6 8 .. $\omega\, [L_y\,(1 - P_L)/P_L]^2 \leq 31\, A_s f_y\,(t - 1.0)$
Zone 5 .... $\omega\, [L_y\,(1 - P_L)/P_L]^2 \leq 63\, A_s f_y\,(t - 1.0)$

A_s = minimum section area of reinforcement in each zone, in². Solve for A_s, then select a rebar diameter and even number of bars from $A_s \leq 3.14\, \eta\, \delta^2$. If the selected bars in adjacent zones are nearly the same size (e.g. #4s and #5s), make them all the larger size. $A_s \geq 0.0025$ section area of concrete.
f_y = safe yield stress of reinforcement, psi
$\omega, L_x, L_y,$ and t are as previously defined

Step 9. Check the unit bond stress in the rebars extending each way in each zone from the formula below. Solve for f_c, which should $\leq$ allow. f_c. If **NG**, try a larger rebar whose larger p_r leads to actual $f_c \leq$ allow. f_c.

$$\delta_r\, \omega\, L_y \geq 62\, p_r f_c^{0.5}\,(t - 1.0)$$

δ_r = dia. of rebars extending one way in each zone, in.
p_r = total perimeter of rebars extending in one direc-

tion of each zone, in.

f_c = specified strength of concrete, psi

ω, L_y, and t are as previously defined

Step 10. Estimate the drop panel's minimum width if square or rectangular, or its minimum diameter if round.

$$s \approx 0.35\,L_x$$

s = estimated length of drop panel side, in. Use a round-number value within ± 6% of computed s.

L_x = length of major span, in.

Step 11. Find D (in.), the drop or depth of the columns' drop panel. D must ≥ 4.0 in. Sizing the drop in this manner makes the panel safe in punching shear. The formula below assumes the bay and panel are square. If either is rectangular, $L^2 = X\,Y$, $s^2 = x\,y$, and $s = 0.5\,(x + y)$. After solving for D, increase it to the next highest ½ in.

$$\omega\,(L_x^2 - s^2) = 1{,}008\,s\,(t + D - 1.7)\,f_c^{0.5}$$

All unknowns are as previously defined.

Step 12. Estimate the diameter or minimum width at the top of the flared column heads. The flared head cone's apex typically has a 90° vertex angle.

$$c \approx 0.22\,L_x$$

c = estimated minimum width of column capital, in. Use a value within ±10% of the computed width.

L_x = length of major span, in.

Step 13. Find c (in.), the minimum diameter of the flared column head. Sizing this dimension as below makes the flared column head safe in punching shear along seam 2 as shown in Fig. 4-8. This formula assumes the bay is square. If it is rectangular, $L^2 = X Y$. After solving for c, increase its value to a practical number. Instead of solving for c quadratically, one may insert a trial value for c, then solve for f_c wherein actual $f_c \leq$ allow. f_c.

$$\omega [L_x^2 - 0.785 (c + 2 D)^2] = 810 (c + 2 D) (t + D) f_c^{0.5}$$

All unknowns are as previously defined.

Flat-Plate Floor Slab Design:
This simplest of two-way reinforced concrete slabs has uniformly flat ceilings supported by round or square columns with no capitals, brackets, or drop panels.

Step 1. Determine the ratio of the slab's major-to-minor spans, then find the portion of the slab's load carried by the major span from the bar graph in Fig. 4-7.

Step 2. Determine the total unit design load ω (psf) on the slab area framed by each bay.

$$\omega = P_L (1.4 \, \omega_D + 1.7 \, \omega_L)$$

ω = total unit design load carried by major span, psf
P_L = portion of slab load carried by major span
ω_D = dead load on system, psf
ω_L = live load on system, psf

Step 3. Knowing the length of the slab's major span and its service load, find the slab's minimum thickness from the graph in Fig. 4-9.

Step 4. Check the safe unit shear stress at the slab's edge as described below. Here V = total shear load on a 12 in. strip of the slab perpendicular to the major span. Perform this calculation only for the slab's major span. If actual $f_v >$ allow. f_v, increase t accordingly.

$$\omega \, L_y = 252 \, f_v \, (t - 1.0)$$

f_v = actual unit shear stress for concrete, psi
ω, L_y, and t are as previously defined

Step 5. If a slab edge cantilevers more than 24 in, find the cantilever's maximum feasible span from below. If a longer cantilever is desired, use L_c to find the equivalent L_x in the formula below, then redesign the cantilever's depth according to Steps 1-4.

$$L_c \geq 0.16 \, L_x$$

L_c = maximum span of perimeter cantilever if any, in.
L_x = length of major span, in.

Step 6. Determine if the beam's initial and long-term deflection are safe as described on page 196.

Step 7. Divide each bay of the structure into a tic-tac-toe—like pattern of zones, then design the slab's reinforcement as described on page 218.

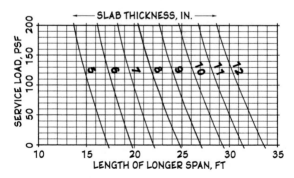

Fig. 4-9. Flat-plate slab thickness graph.

Step 8. Find the column's diameter from below. This formula assumes the bay is square. If rectangular, $L^2 = XY$. After solving for δ, increase it to a practical number. Instead of solving for δ quadratically, one may try values for δ, then solve for f_c wherein actual $f_c \leq$ allow. f_c.

$$\omega\,[L^2 - 0.785\,(\delta + 3)^2] = 792\,(t - 1.7)\,\delta\,f_c^{\,0.5}$$

Solve for δ quadratically.

All unknowns are as previously defined.

Waffle Slab Design:

Step 1. Determine the ratio of the slab's major-to-minor spans, then find the portion of the slab load carried by the major span from the bar graph in Fig. 4-7.

Step 2. If the slab is rectangular, find the total design loads W_x and W_y on its major and minor spans from formulas **a** and **b** below. If the bays are square, use only formula **a** to find W for both spans.

a. Load on major span: $W_x = A\,P_L\,(1.4\,\omega_D + 1.7\,\omega_L)$

b. Load on minor span: $W_y = A\,(1 - P_L)(1.4\,\omega_D + 1.7\,\omega_L)$

W_x = total design load on major span, lb
W_y = total design load on minor span, lb
A = rectangular area of each bay of slab, sf
P_L = portion of load carried by major span
ω_D = total unit dead load on slab, lb
ω_L = total unit dead load on slab, lb

Step 3. Determine each bay's rib width by selecting a feasible dome and rib width from Fig. 4-10 and using their dimensions in the formulas below. If the bay is not square, the ribs' widths and ¢–¢ spacing may differ in each direction.

a. DOME W + RIB W = ℄–℄ spacing of ribs
b. ℄–℄ rib spacing × no. ribs in each bay = width of bay

Step 4. Using W_x and W_y above, compute the maximum moments for the slab's major and minor spans.

$$\boxed{M?} = M_{max}$$

$\boxed{M?}$ = applicable moment formula from beam tables

Step 5. Determine the depth of each rib. If the bay is not square, find d_e in each direction, then use the larger value for the ribs in both directions.

$$M \leq 0.066\, f_c\, b\, d_e^2$$

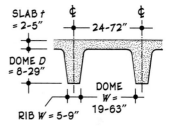

M = max. moment of load on each rib, in-lb

f_c = specified strength of concrete, psi

b = width of each rib, in.

d_e = effective depth of rib, from top of slab to ℄ of tensile rebars, in. Total depth $d = d_e + 0.5$ × tensile rebar $t + 1.5$ in. cover.

SLAB t = 2–5"

DOME D = 8–29"

RIB W = 5–9"

DOME W = 19–63"

24–72"

COMMON DOME SIZES, IN.

PLAN MODULE	TYP. DOME W	TYP. DOME D	RIB W
24 × 24	19 × 19	8, 10, 12, 14	5
36 × 36	30 × 30	8, 10, 12, 14, 16, 20	5
48 × 48	40 × 40	10, 12, 14, 16, 20, 24	5
60 × 60	50 × 50	10, 12, 14, 16, 20, 24	5

Fig. 4-10. Waffle slab dome details.

If a value for d is desired, use $d - 2$ in. for d_e in the formula $M \approx 0.17 f_c b_r d_e^2$ and solve for b_r, the width of each rib.

Step 6. Knowing the waffle slab's total depth, select a slab thickness and dome depth that satisfies the equation below. Then from Fig. 4-10 select a DOME D for the dome plan module size selected in Step 2 that creates a slab thickness of 2–5 in. depending on span dimensions of 25–60 ft. Also, DOME D ≈ 0.8 d.

$$\text{total depth } d = \text{slab thickness } t + \text{DOME D}$$

Step 7. Determine if the waffle slab's initial and long-term deflection are safe as described on page 196.

Step 8. Divide each bay into a tic-tac-toe–like pattern of nine zones as described on page 21 8; then find the minimum rebar area A_s for each zone from

$$\omega L_r^2 = 454 A_s f_y d_e$$

ω = total unit design load on each rib, lb
L_r = length of span of each rib, in.
A_s = area of tensile reinforcement in each rib, in^2
f_y = safe unit yield stress of rebar steel, psi
d_e = effective depth of rib, in.

Step 9. Investigate the reinforcement's unit bond shear as described on page 197.

Step 10. Check the safe unit seam shear at the perimeter of the filled coffers around the column heads.

    a. If bay is square:
$$\omega [L^2 + 4 m^2 - (x + 2m)^2] \leq 1{,}008 (x + 3)(t - 1.2) f_c^{0.5}$$

    b. If bay is rectangular:
$$\omega [XY + 4 mn - (x + 2m)(y + 2n)] \leq 504 (x + y + 6)(t - 1.2) f_c^{0.5}$$

ω = total unit design load on each rib, lb
L = length of ribs both ways if bay is square, in.
X = length of ribs in major span if bay is rect., in.
Y = length of ribs in minor span if bay is rect., in.
m = length of insets in shear seam around column, in.
n = width of insets in shear seam around each column as shown in Fig. 4-11 if bay is rectangular, in.
x = total length of shear seam around each column whether bay is square or rectangular, in.
y = total width of shear seam around each column if bay is rectangular, in.
t = total thickness of slab between ribs, in.
f_c = specified strength of concrete, psi

Step 11. Check the safe unit seam shear around each column that supports the waffle slab.

$$\omega(L^2 - C_a{}^2) \leq 252\, p\, d_e\, f_c{}^{0.5}$$

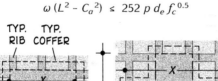

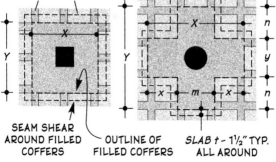

TYP. RIB   TYP. COFFER

X

Y Y n

x x n

m x

y

SEAM SHEAR AROUND FILLED COFFERS   OUTLINE OF FILLED COFFERS   SLAB t - 1½" TYP. ALL AROUND

Fig. 4-11. Reinf. concrete waffle slab details.

L = length of span if bay is square, in. If bay is rectangular, $L = XY$.

C_a = area enclosed by shear seam around column, in²
  If column is round, $C_a = 0.785 (c + 3)$.
  If column is square, $C_a = (s + 3)^2$.
  If column is rectangular, $C_a = (x + 3)(y + 3)$.

p = perimeter of shear seam around column, in.
  If column is round, $p = 3.14 (c + 3)$.
  If column is square, $p = 4 (s + 3)$.
  If column is rectangular, $p = 2 (x + y + 6)$.

  c = diameter of column if round, in.
  s = length of side of column if square, in.
  x = length of long side of column if rect., in.
  y = length of short side of column if rect., in.
    $\omega, X, Y, d_e,$ and f_c are as previously defined

Slab Punching Shear:

Step 1. Find the actual stress in the shear seam between the slab and column and compare it with its allowable stress.

$$A \omega = 2.9\, p\, d_e\, f_c^{0.5}$$

A = area of floor supported by column, sf
ω = total design unit load on floor, psf
p = perimeter of column, in. If column is square, $p = 4 s$; if rectangular, $p = 2 (l + w)$; if round, $p = \pi d$.
d_e = effective depth of floor, equals floor thickness at meeting of column − 1.0 in. minimum cover, in.
f_c = specified strength of concrete, psi

Step 2. If the column head is unsafe, design a square drop panel around the column beneath the floor. First find the panel's required depth in the equation below.

$$A \omega = 2.9\, p\, d_e\, f_c^{0.5}$$

A = area of floor supported by column, sf
ω = total unit design load on floor, psf
p = perimeter of column, in.
d_e = effective depth of panel, in. Total depth = d_e rounded to next highest 0.5 in. + 1 in. min. cover.
f_c = specified strength of concrete, psi

Step 3. If the column head is unsafe, find the required length of the panel's square side from

$$A \omega = 2.9 \, p \, d_e \, f_c^{0.5}$$

A = area of floor supported by column, sf
ω = total unit design load on floor, psf
p = perimeter of panel, in. If panel is square, $p = 4 \, s$.
d_e = effective depth of floor, equals floor t at meeting of column − 1.0 in. minimum cover, in.
f_c = specified strength of concrete, 3,000 psi

Step 4-6. Size the drop panel's rebar and check its safety in bond shear as described on page 197.

Reinforced Concrete Staircase Design: A

staircase's proper span is not its horizontal projection but its *inclined length*; and its load is usually not its gravity load but the load's *vector component perpendicular to the inclined span*. Although the horizontal length and gravity load may seem to cancel each other algebraically, in a moment equation the length is squared while the load is not and in a deflection equation the length is cubed. Thus, if a staircase riser/tread ratio is 7/10, a 12.2/10 length ratio becomes a 14.8/10 k moment ratio and a 18.5/10 k deflection ratio. In summary, a staircase is *an inclined span that supports an oblique load*; and one is designed as described below.

228 ➜ ß▥I▯▒♀☀⚓㉆💡🕯📖🔧

Step 1. Find the total load on the staircase span.

Step 2. Compute the staircase span's maximum moment.

$$1{,}150\, M_m = (\omega_D + \omega_L)\, b\, L^2 \cos^2 [\tan^{-1} (r/t)]$$

M_m = max. moment of applied staircase load, in-lb
ω_D = unit gravity (vert.) dead load on staircase, psf
ω_L = unit gravity (vert.) live load on staircase, psf
b = width of staircase, in.
L = inclined length of staircase, in. For spiral stair-
cases, L is a helix of radius r wherein $L = 6.28\, r$
× cos [$\tan^{-1} (r/t)$] × no. of revolutions of staircase. Take r 1.0 ft from steps' inside edge.
r = length of staircase riser, in.
t = length of staircase tread, in.

Step 3. Find the staircase slab's effective depth if its
steps are supported by spandrels on each side from the
formula below. If the staircase is a simple slab from side
to side, size its insteps as described in Step 5.

$$M_m = 0.066\, f_c\, b\, d_e^2$$

M_m = maximum moment of applied staircase load, in-lb
f_c = specified strength of concrete, psi
b = total width of any spandrels supporting staircase
steps, in. If steps are supported by two spandrels, width of each spandrel ≥ 0.5 b.
d_e = effective depth of spandrel(s), in. d_e is
measured perpendicular to incline of steps.
d_e + 1.5 in. = spandrel's total depth d.

Step 4. Determine if the staircase's initial and long-
term deflection are safe.

Step 5. Size the staircase slab's tensile rebars. If the
staircase has no spandrels but is a simple slab, its inset

thickness, tensile rebars, and temperature rebars based on the staircase length are found in Table 4-3. Otherwise, design the spandrel's rebars from

$$M_m = 0.53 \, A_s \, f_y \, (d - 1.5)$$

M_m = maximum moment of applied staircase load, in-lb

A_s = minimum area of tensile rebars in staircase spandrel(s), in². Solve for A_s, then select a rebar number (usually 1 or 2) and size whose total section area ≥ A_s.

f_y = safe unit yield stress of rebars, psi

d = minimum depth of spandrel(s) or step insets, in.

Step 6. Since one lateral rebar must be placed in each step for its length, size this rebar according to

$$A_s = 0.083 \, \omega \, f_y \, s^2 \, (d_i + 4)$$

A_s = minimum area of lateral rebar in each step, in².

d_i = effective depth of step inset, in.

ω, f_y, and s are as previously defined

TABLE 4-3: CONCRETE STAIRCASE DESIGN DATA

Inclined span, up to in.	Slab t at inset, in.	Tensile reinf. in. o.c.	Temp. reinf. in. o.c.
60	4	#3 at 8.5	#3 at 18
72	4	#3 at 6	#3 at 18
84	4.5	#4 at 9	#3 at 1
96	4.5	#4 at 7	#3 at 17
108	5	#4 at 6	#3 at 15
120	5.5	#4 at 5.5	#3 at 13.5
132	6	#5 at 8	#3 at 12
144	6.5	#5 at 7.5	#3 at 11
156	7	#5 at 7	#3 at 10
168	7.5	#5 at 6.5	#3 at 9
180	8	#5 at 6	#3 at 8

Step 7. Check the staircase for safe shear at the faces of its upper and lower supports.

$$W_g = 3.5\, A\, f_y^{\,0.5}$$

W_g = total gravity (dead + live) load of staircase, lb. Live load = stairs' Code-required floor load (usually 100 psf) × step width (ft) × horizontal projection of staircase length (ft).

A = section area of staircase concrete at face of top or bottom supports, in²

f_y = safe unit yield stress of steel reinforcement, psi

Step 8. Check the unit bond stress of the staircase's tensile rebars at their top and bottom supports in the formula below. Solve for f_c, then compare actual f_c with allow. f_c. If **NG**, select a larger number of smaller bars that have a larger p_r while still satisfying A_s.

$$\delta_r\, W_g = 3.67\, p_r\, d_e\, f_c^{\,2}$$

δ_r = diameter of tensile reinforcing, in²

p_r = total perimeter of rebars in tensile reinf., in²

d_e = effective depth of staircase section (vertical projection) that contains tensile reinforcing, in.

   W_g and f_c are as previously defined

Spandrels & Openings in Slabs:

Step 1. Assuming a rectangular opening a-b-c-d in a concrete slab, (1) divide the slab into a tic-tac-toe–like pattern of zones whose seams are at Z_1 to Z_8; (2) draw a dotted line halfway between each of the opening's sides a-b, b-c, c-d, and d-a and the nearest outside parallel Z seam to form the dotted-line rectangle a_r b_r c_r d_r; (3) draw diagonal lines from each corner a, b, c, and d of the opening to the corresponding corners a_r, b_r, c_r, and

d_r of the dotted-line rectangle; and (4) note the four trapezoidal areas ($a\ a_r\ b_r\ b$), ($b\ b_r\ c_r\ c$), ($c\ c_r\ d_r\ d$), and ($d\ d_r\ a_r\ a$) along the opening's four edges. Each trapezoid is the load area supported by the spandrel on its side of the opening.

Step 2. Find the maximum moments for each of the four spandrels that forms an edge of the opening from

$$M_m \leq 0.066\ \omega\ A\ L$$

M_m = max. moment of load on each spandrel a-b, b-c, c-d, and d-a, in-lb

ω = total unit design load on slab, psf

A = area of each trapezoidal area alongside the opening's four edges or spandrels, sf

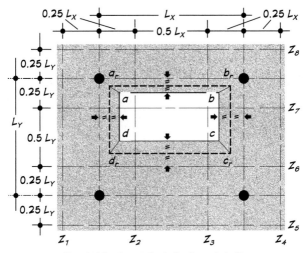

Fig. 4-12. Spandrel design details.

L = length of each spandrel, in. L = length m for
spandrels a-b and c-d, and L = length n for spandrels b-c and d-a.

Step 3. Find each spandrel's width b and depth d_e from

$$M_m \leq 0.066 f_c b d_e^2$$

M_m = max. moment of load on each spandrel, in-lb
f_c = specified strength of concrete, psi
b = width of each spandrel, in. $b \geq 8$ in.
d_e = effective depth of each spandrel from top of slab
to ¢ of tensile rebars, in. Total depth $d = d_e +$
0.5 tensile rebar $t + 1.0$ in. min. cover. d_e also $\geq$
2 × slab thickness t.

Step 4. Determine if each spandrel's initial and long-
term deflection are safe.

Step 5. Compute the minimum area of reinforcement A_s
for each spandrel according to the equation below.

$$M_m = 0.53 A_s f_y d_e$$

M_m = max. moment of load on each spandrel, in-lb
A_s = area of tensile rebars in each spandrel, in^2.
Select number and size of rebars that $\geq A_s$.
f_y = safe unit yield stress of rebars, psi
d_e = effective depth of spandrel, in.

Step 6. Investigate each spandrel's unit bond stress in
the formula below. Solve for f_c, then compare actual f_c
with allow. f_c. If **NG**, select larger rebars with a larger p_r
whose actual $f_c \leq$ allow f_c.

$$\delta_r V \geq 3.67 p_r d_e f_c^{0.5}$$

δ_r = diameter of tensile rebars in spandrel, in.
V = total shear load of each spandrel, lb

p_r = total perimeter of rebars each way in each zone, in.
d_e = effective depth of spandrel, in.
f_c = specified strength of concrete, psi

Concrete Hypar Design:

Step 1. Knowing the hypar's sides and height, note its perimeter $A\ B\ C\ D$, its peak corners A and C, and its base corners B and D.

Step 2. Find the total load supported by the hypar at each base from the formula below. Tentatively assume the membrane is $2\frac{3}{4}$ in. thick and the reinforced concrete weighs 160 pcf.

$$P_b\ =\ A\ (0.7\ \omega_D + 0.85\ \omega_L)$$

P_b = total load supported by each base, lb
A = horiz. projected area of hypar membrane, sf
ω_D = total unit dead load on membrane, psf. If concrete is $2\frac{3}{4}$ in. thick, $\omega_D = 2.75 \times 160/12$ + perhaps 5 psf roof waterproofing $\approx$ 40 psf.
ω_L = total unit live load on membrane, psf. Here the live load is usually a maximum snow load based on local climatic data.

Step 3. Determine the concrete's actual unit boundary shear stress at the edge of the membrane.

$$P_b\ L_L\ =\ 2\ v_{sb}\ H\ L_S$$

P_b = total load supported by each base, lb
L_L = length of hypar's longest side, ft
v_{sb} = actual unit shear at edge of membrane, lb/LF. This is the shear stress between the membrane and its usually thicker edge. The seam's unit length is 12 in. and its thickness is the membrane's thickness.

➔ ß▓I▯▦♀✳⚹⟟⊕♥♀▥↩

H = height of hypar, ft
L_S = length of the hypar's shortest side, ft

Step 4. Design the membrane from the formulas below. If the hypar is square or rectangular (i.e. not a quadrilateral), $f_{cv} = f_{tv}$ and $A_L = A_T$; then only one equation needs to be solved.

   a. $v_{sb} L_{a\text{-}l} = f_{cv} (L_S + L_L)$
   b. $v_{sb} L_{a\text{-}t} = f_{tv} (L_S + L_L)$

$L_{a\text{-}l}$ = length of hypar's longitudinal axis (longer diagonal between its opposite edges), ft
$L_{a\text{-}t}$ = length of hypar's transverse axis (shorter diagonal between its opposite edges), ft
f_{cv} = unit compression shear stress along each LF of membrane's edge in its concrete, lb/LF.
f_{tv} = unit tension shear stress along each LF of membrane's edge in its reinforcement, lb/LF.
   v_{sb}, L_L, and L_S are as previously defined

Solve for f_{cv} and f_{tv} *above*, then use these values below:

   c. Concrete design: $f_{cv}/A_c \leq 1.1 f_c^{0.5}$
   d. Rebar design: $f_{tv}/A_s \leq 0.6 f_y$

A_c = concrete area/LF of membrane edge, in². This typically = 2.75 × 12 in. Min. conc. t = two layers of rebar + min. 1 in. cover above and below.
A_s = rebar area/LF of membrane edge. Minimum rebar size = #3 and minimum spacing = 8 in.
f_c = specified strength of concrete, psi
f_y = safe unit yield strength of rebars, psi

Step 5. Size the membrane's edge members by sizing the concrete and rebars in each edge. Although each edge AB, BC, CD, and DE is designed separately, design is simpler if any edge lengths equal each other.

Edge $A\,B$: **Conc. area:** $A_{c\text{-}ab}\,f_c \geq f_v\,L_{ab}$

                Rebar area: $A_{s\text{-}ab}\,f_y \geq \dfrac{1.67\,f_v\,L_{ab}}{\cos\,(\tan^{-1} H_{ab}/L_{ab})}$

Edge $B\,C$: **Conc. area:** $A_{c\text{-}bc}\,f_c \geq f_v\,L_{bc}$

                Rebar area: $A_{s\text{-}bc}\,f_y \geq \dfrac{1.67\,f_v\,L_{bc}}{\cos\,(\tan^{-1} H_{bc}/L_{bc})}$

Edge $C\,D$: **Conc. area:** $A_{c\text{-}cd}\,f_c \geq f_v\,L_{cd}$

                Rebar area: $A_{s\text{-}cd}\,f_y \geq \dfrac{1.67\,f_v\,L_{cd}}{\cos\,(\tan^{-1} H_{cd}/L_{cd})}$

Edge $D\,A$: **Conc. area:** $A_{c\text{-}da}\,f_c \geq f_v\,L_{da}$

                Rebar area: $A_{s\text{-}da}\,f_y \geq \dfrac{1.67\,f_v\,L_{da}}{\cos\,(\tan^{-1} H_{da}/L_{da})}$

f_v = safe unit shear stress for concrete, psi

L_{ab}, etc. = length of edge $A\,B$, $B\,C$, $C\,D$, or $D\,A$, ft

$A_{c\text{-}ab}$, etc. = min. sec. area of concrete in edge, in^2

$A_{s\text{-}ab}$, etc. = min. sec. area of rebars in edge, in^2. Solve for this value, then select a size and number of rebars whose $A\,\eta \geq A_s$.

H_{ab}, etc. = height of each edge: difference in vertical dimension between each end, ft

       f_y and f_c are as previously defined

Step 6. Design the hypar's bases. Here the possibilities are too varied to be described by one format.

Reinforced Concrete Columns: Design considerations for reinforced concrete columns are:

▸ Each column must resist all lateral or eccentric moments associated with its loading condition.

▸ Each must be designed for min. 1 in. eccentricity and the actual eccentric load should be small.

▸ Each column end condition must ≤ 1.0 and its base must be rigidly anchored (rotation fixed).
▸ All rebars, ties, and spirals require 1.5 in. cover at interior exposures and 2.0 in. cover elsewhere.
▸ The ratio of vertical bar area to total column section area must be between 0.01 and 0.08.
▸ Lateral bracing (i.e. infills or shear walls) must lie within the building frame.

Total Column Design Load:

    a. $W_T = 1.05\ W_D + 1.3\ W_L + 1.3\ W_W$
    b. $W_T = 1.4\ W_D + 1.7\ W_W$

W_T = total design load on column, kips. The larger value governs.
W_D = actual or service dead load on column, kips
W_L = actual or service live load on column, kips
W_W = actual wind load on column (vert. proj.), kips

Biaxial Bending Moment on Columns: Biaxial
moments are usually a consideration only in round columns that support two-way slab systems.

$$M_T = (M_x^2 + M_y^2)^{0.5}$$

M_T = total biaxial bending moment for both axes, ft-lb
M_x = max. lateral moment of column in X axis, ft-lb
M_y = max. lateral moment of column in Y axis, ft-lb

Round Column Design:

Step 1. Compute the column's effective axial load. This value assumes no abnormal eccentric or side loads.

$$P_a = 1.33\ P_\Delta\ (1.4\ P_D + 1.7\ P_L)\ (1.1)^\kappa$$

P_a = effective axial load on column, kips
P_Δ = the P-Delta Effect, a secondary eccentric load factor as described on page 42. Unless otherwise noted, $P_\Delta = 1.08$.
P_D = service dead load on column, kips
P_L = service live load on column, kips
κ = location factor. $\kappa = 1$ for interior columns, 2 for perimeter columns, 3 for corner columns.

Step 2. Select a trial column diameter from

$$\delta \leq 1.10\,(P_a/f_c)^{0.5}$$

δ = estimated column diameter, in. $\delta \leq 10$ in. Above 16 in, δ is an even number.
P_a = effective axial load on column, kips
f_c = specified strength of concrete, ksi

Step 3. Compute the column's slenderness ratio.

$$S = 1.07 - 0.027\,L_u/\delta$$

S = slenderness ratio of column
L_u = unbraced length of column (clear distance from top of lower structure to underside of column capital or upper structure), in.
δ = trial diameter of column, in.

Step 4. Compute the section area of the column rebars.

$$P_a = 0.75\,S f_c A + A_s\,(f_y - 0.75\,S f_c)$$

A = total section area of column, in^2
A_s = section area of rebars, in^2
f_y = yield strength of steel reinforcement, ksi
P_a, S, and f_c are as previously defined

Step 5. Check the section area of reinforcing for safety. A_t must be between $0.01\,A$–$0.08\,A$. If $A_t \leq 0.01\,A$, either increase the area of tensile reinforcing or return to Step 2 and try a smaller column size. If $A_t ≥ 0.08\ A$, try a larger column size.

$$0.01 ≥ A_s/A ≤ 0.08$$

A_s = section area of steel reinforcing, in^2
A = total section area of column, in^2

Step 6. Size the vertical rebars. Minimum size and number is #5 and 6; maximum spacing = 6 in. o.c. Minimum concrete cover for round interior columns = 1.5 in.

    a. No. of rebars: $η ≥ 0.5\ (δ - 4)$

$η$ = minimum number of rebars.
$δ$ = diameter of column, in.

    b. Section area of each rebar: $A_s = η\ a$

A_s = section of rebars, in^2
$η$ = number of rebars
a = minimum section area of each rebar, in^2

Step 7. Design the spiral reinforcing. Minimum spiral wire size is #3 (the usual size), and the vertical spacing or pitch between each revolution of wire must be between 1.0 and 3.0 in.

$$0.89\ f_c\ S\ (δ - 3) = f_y\ a_s\ (δ - 4 - δ_s)$$

f_c = specified strength of concrete, psi
S = vertical spacing or pitch between each revolution of spiral reinforcing, in. Any $S ≤ 1.0 = 1.0$ in; any $S ≥ 3.0 = 3.0$ in.
$δ$ = diameter of column, from Step 5, in.
f_y = yield strength of reinforcement, psi
a_s = section area of spiral reinforcing, in^2
$δ_s$ = diameter of spiral reinforcing, 0.375 in.

Rectangular Column Design:

Step 1. Compute the column's effective axial load. This formula assumes no large eccentric or side loads.

$$P_a = 1.43 \, P_\Delta \, (1.4 \, P_D + 1.7 \, P_L) \, (1.1)^\kappa$$

P_a = effective axial load on column, kips
P_Δ = the P-Delta Effect, a secondary eccentric load factor. Unless otherwise noted, $P_\Delta = 1.08$.
P_D = service dead load on column, kips
P_L = service live load on column, kips
κ = location factor. $\kappa = 1$ for interior columns, 2 for perimeter columns, 3 for corner columns.

Step 2. Select a trial column according to

$$b \leq (P_a/f_c)^{0.5}$$

b = estimated min. thickness of column, in. If square, $b \leq 10$ in; if rect., $b \leq 8$ in. and $bd \leq 96$ in^2.
P_a = effective axial load on column, kips
f_c = specified strength of concrete, ksi

Step 3. Compute the column's slenderness ratio.

$$S = 1.07 - 0.027 \, L_u/b$$

S = slenderness ratio of column
L_u = unbraced length of column (clear distance from underside of upper structure to top of lower structure), in.
b = trial minimum thickness of column, in.

Step 4. Compute the vertical rebars' section area.

$$P_a = 0.70 \, S f_c A + A_s \, (f_y - 0.70 \, S f_c)$$

P_a = effective axial load on column, kips

240   ➔ ß▓ I ▯ ▦ ♀ ✳ ⚒ ☞ ⏻ ♀ ▥ ℃

S = slenderness ratio of column
f_c = specified strength of concrete, ksi
A = total section area of column, in^2
A_s = section area of steel reinforcing, in^2
f_y = yield strength of reinforcing, ksi

Step 5. Check the column size for safety. A_s must ≥ 0.01 A and ≤ 0.08 A. If A_s ≤ 0.01 A, either increase the area of reinforcing or return to Step 2 and try a smaller column size. If A_s ≥ 0.08 A, try a larger column size.

$$0.01 \geq A_s/A \leq 0.08$$

A_s = section area of steel reinforcing, in^2
A = total section area of column, in^2

Step 6. Size the vertical rebars. Minimum size is #4, maximum spacing is 6 in. o.c., and every corner and alternate rebar if any must be tied in both horizontal directions.

$$A_s = \eta\, a$$

A_s = section area of steel rebars, in^2
η = number of rebars
a = minimum section area of each rebar, in^2. Solve for a, then from Table 4-1 select rebar with lowest A_s above this amount.

Step 7. Determine the lateral tie bar size and spacing.

   Size: If vertical rebars are #10 or smaller, use #3 tie bars; if they are larger, use #4 tie bars

   Spacing: Use least distance of a, b, or c below:

   a. Spacing ≥ 16 vertical rebar diameters
   b. Spacing ≥ 48 tie bar diameters
   c. Spacing ≥ minimum column t

Reinforced Concrete Walls: Reinforced concrete walls are categorized structurally as follows:

1. **Unloaded.** Free-standing walls whose ground level on each side is the same or nearly so.
2. **Bearing.** Walls that support only vertical loads.
3. **Shear.** Walls that resist lateral thrusts (wind pressure, earth, seismic loads, etc.) against their ends.
4. **Retaining.** Walls that resist lateral earth thrusts against one side.
5. **Multiloaded.** These walls resist any combination of bearing, shear, and retaining loads.

Reinforced concrete walls are best designed by visualizing a 12 in. long section as a 1 ft wide column and assuming no slenderness ratio in the lengthwise direction.

Bearing Wall Design:

Step 1. Compute the wall's design load. If design loads were used to size the structure bearing on the wall, use them and omit this step.

$$W_U = 1.4\ W_D + 1.7\ W_L$$

W_U = total design load on wall. If load is continuous, W_U = pLF. If load is concentrated or at unit spacing, W_U = lb/unit

W_D = service dead load on wall. If load is continuous, W_D = pLF; if concentrated, W_D = lb/unit

W_L = service live load on wall. If load is continuous, W_L = pLF; if concentrated, W_L = lb/unit

Step 2. Select a trial wall thickness based on its height.

$$h \leq 20\ t$$

h = height of wall, in.
t = trial thickness of wall, in. nom. $t \geq 6$ in. nom.

Step 3. Find the wall's effective bearing length. Of the three criteria below, the least value governs.

a. If load is continuous, L_a = 12 in. Otherwise $L_a = \infty$.
b. If load is a series of concentrated loads, L_b = unit spacing between the loads.
c. $L_c = b + 4\,t$

Step 4. Check the wall for safe load.

TABLE 4-4: BEARING WALL DESIGN DATA			
WALL t, in.	Max. ht, ft	Economic reinf., Grade 60 rebars Vertical	Horizontal
6	12.5	#4 at 18 in. o.c.	#5 at 18 in. o.c.
7	14.6	#4 at 18 in. o.c.	#5 at 18 in. o.c.
8	16.6	#4 at 16 in. o.c.	#5 at 15 in. o.c.
9	18.7	#4 at 14 in. o.c.	#6 at 18 in. o.c.
10	20.8	#5 at 18 in. o.c.	#6 at 18 in. o.c.
11	22.9	* I: #3 at 18 in. o.c.	* I: #5 at 18 in. o.c.
		* O: #4 at 18 in. o.c.	* O: #4 at 18 in. o.c.
12	25.0	I: #3 at 17 in. o.c.	I: #5 at 17 in. o.c.
		O: #4 at 17 in. o.c.	O: #5 at 17 in. o.c.
13	25.0	I: #3 at 16 in. o.c.	I: #5 at 16 in. o.c.
		O: #4 at 16 in. o.c.	O: #4 at 16 in. o.c.
14	25.0	I: #3 at 15 in. o.c.	I: #5 at 14 in. o.c.
		O: #4 at 15 in. o.c.	O: #4 at 14 in. o.c.
15	29.1	I: #3 at 14 in. o.c.	I: #5 at 15 in. o.c.
		O: #4 at 14 in. o.c.	O: #4 at 15 in. o.c.
16	33.3	I: #4 at 13 in. o.c.	I: #6 at 18 in. o.c.
		O: #3 at 13 in. o.c.	O: #5 at 18 in. o.c.

* For walls ≥ 11 in. thick, "I" denotes size & spacing of rebars 3 in. from inner face of wall and "O" denotes size & spacing of rebars 3 in. from outer face of wall.

$$W_W = 4.62 \, t f_c \, [1 - (0.025 \, h/t)^2]$$

W_W = unit design load on wall, pLF
t = trial thickness of wall, in.
f_c = actual strength of concrete, psi. Solve for this
then compare with allowable f_c. If actual $f_c \geq$ allowable f_c, make the wall thicker.
h = height of wall, from Step 2, 160 in.

Step 5. Design the reinforcement based on the wall's thickness from Table 4-4.

Basement or Multiloaded Wall Design:

Step 1. Find the wall thickness required to resist the earth load against the wall's outer face from Table 4-5.

Step 2. If the wall is loadbearing, compute its design load from

$$W_U = 1.4 \, W_D + 1.7 \, W_L$$

W_U = total design load on basement wall, pLF
W_D = service dead load on basement wall, pLF
W_L = service live load on basement wall, pLF

Step 3. Compute the wall's added thickness due to any vertical loads.

$$W_U = 4.62 \, f_c \, t_v \, [1 - (0.025 \, h/t)^2]$$

W_U = total design load on wall, pLF
f_c = specified strength of concrete in wall, psi
t_v = added wall thickness due to any vertical load, in.
Round t_v to the next highest integer.
h = total height of wall, in.
t = thickness of wall due to lateral load, in.

Step 4. Compute the wall's added thickness due to any shear loads. This includes any longitudinal loads against its ends and any wall loads from above the first floor.

$$V_h \le 8.5\, t_s\, L\, f_c^{0.5}$$

V_h = horizontal shear load against wall, lb.

TABLE 4-5: MULTILOADED WALL DESIGN DATA

ΔV [1] ft.	Wall t, in.	Economic reinforcement, Grade 60 rebars Vertical	Horizontal
3	8	#3 at 18 in. o.c.	#4 at 18 in. o.c.
4	8	#3 at 16 in. o.c.	#4 at 18 in. o.c.
5	8	#3 at 14 in. o.c.	#4 at 18 in. o.c.
6	8	#3 at 12 in. o.c.	#4 at 16 in. o.c.
7	8	#4 at 18 in. o.c.	#4 at 13 in. o.c.
8	8	#4 at 17 in. o.c.	#5 at 11 in. o.c.
9	8.5	#4 at 16 in. o.c.	#5 at 16 in. o.c.
10	9	#4 at 15 in. o.c.	#5 at 15 in. o.c.
11	9.5	[2] I: #4 at 14 in. o.c.	[2] I: #5 at 13 in. o.c.
		[2] O: #3 at 14 in. o.c.	[2] O: #4 at 13 in. o.c.
12	10	I: #4 at 13 in. o.c.	I: #5 at 12 in. o.c.
		O: #3 at 13 in. o.c.	O: #4 at 12 in. o.c.
13	11	I: #4 at 12 in. o.c.	I: #5 at 11 in. o.c.
		O: #3 at 12 in. o.c.	O: #4 at 11 in. o.c.
14	12	I: #5 at 16 in. o.c.	I: #6 at 14 in. o.c.
		O: #4 at 16 in. o.c.	O: #4 at 14 in. o.c.
15	13	I: #5 at 15 in. o.c.	I: #6 at 13 in. o.c.
		O: #4 at 15 in. o.c.	O: #5 at 13 in. o.c.
16	14	I: #5 at 14 in. o.c.	I: #6 at 12 in. o.c.
		O: #4 at 14 in. o.c.	O: #5 at 12 in. o.c.

1. ΔV is the vertical difference between the heights of the wall's bases on each side.
2. For walls ≥ 11 in. thick, "I" denotes size & spacing of rebars 3 in. from inner face of wall and "O" denotes size & spacing of rebars 3 in. from outer face of wall.

t_s = added wall thickness due to any shear loads, in.
L = total length of wall, in.
f_c = specified strength of concrete in wall, psi

Step 5. Design the wall's rebars from Table 4-5.

Retaining Wall Design:

Step 1. Find the total height of the wall.

$$h = h_a + h_b$$

h = minimum total height of retaining wall, ft
h_a = height of wall above ground, ft
h_b = height of wall to below frost level, 3.5 ft

Step 2. Find the width of the wall's footing.

    a. Nonkeyed: $b = 0.67 (h + 4 s)$
    b. Keyed: $b = 0.75 (h + 4 s)$

b = breadth or width of retaining wall footing, ft
h = total height of wall, from Step 1, ft
s = slope of surcharge behind stem (rise/run of finished grade behind wall), ft/ft. $s \le 0.5$.

Step 3. Compute the width of the stem at its base.

$$a = 0.083 (h + 4 s) + 0.67$$

a = breadth or width of stem at base, ft
     h and s are as previously defined

Step 4. Compute the width of the footing's heel.

    a. Nonkeyed: $b_h = b - a$
    b. Keyed: $b_h = 0.375 (h + 4 s)$

b_h = breadth or width of footing heel, ft
b = breadth or width of footing for Type 1 wall, ft

a, h, and *s* are as previously defined

Step 5. Determine the footing's depth.

$$d = a$$

d = depth of footing, ft
a = width of stem at base, from Step 3, ft

Step 6. Compute the depth and width of the bottom key.

$$k = 0.67 a$$

k = depth and width of key if one is required, ft
a = width of stem at base, from Step 3, ft

Step 7. Design the stem's vertical reinforcing.

    a. Nonkeyed: $A_v \geq [0.045 (h + 4 s)]^{0.5}$
    b. Keyed: $A_v \geq [0.04 (h + 4 s)]^{0.5}$

A_v = minimum section area of vertical rebars in stem, in²/LF. Select optimal # and spacing from schedule below. *A* may equal A_v, A_h, A_{lat}, or A_{lon}.

    A to 0.133 in²/LF ➔ #3 bars spaced $^{1.32}/_A$ in. o.c.
        (NG for A_v)
    A to 0.207 in²/LF ➔ #4 bars spaced $^{2.40}/_A$ in. o.c.
    A to 0.293 in²/LF ➔ #5 bars spaced $^{3.72}/_A$ in. o.c.
    A to 0.400 in²/LF ➔ #6 bars spaced $^{5.28}/_A$ in. o.c.
    A to 0.527 in²/LF ➔ #7 bars spaced $^{7.20}/_A$ in. o.c.
    A to 0.667 in²/LF ➔ #8 bars spaced $^{9.48}/_A$ in. o.c.
    A to 0.847 in²/LF ➔ #9 bars spaced $^{12.0}/_A$ in. o.c.
    A to 1.040 in²/LF ➔ #10 bars spaced $^{15.2}/_A$ in. o.c.

    h and *s* are as previously defined

Step 8. Design the stem's horizontal reinforcing.

$$A_h \geq 0.36 a$$

A_h = minimum section area of horiz. rebars in stem, in²/LF. Select bar size and spacing from Step 7.
a = width of stem at base, ft

Step 9. Design the footing's lateral reinforcing.

    a. Nonkeyed: $A_{lat} \geq [0.045\,(h + 4\,s)]^{0.5}$
    b. Keyed: $A_{lat} \geq [0.030\,(h + 4\,s)]^{0.5}$

A_{lat} = minimum section area of lateral reinforcing in footing, in²/LF. Select optimal bar size and spacing from schedule in Step 7.
    h and s are as previously defined

Step 10. Design the footing's longitudinal reinforcing.

$$A_{lon} \geq 0.29\,a$$

A_{lon} = minimum section area of longitudinal reinforcing in footing, in²/LF, from schedule in Step 7.
a = width of stem at base, ft

Bracing Design: A reinforced concrete frame is adequately braced if its lateral structure resists at least six times the column's lateral stresses.

$$6\,E_s\,t_s\,[(0.48\,h_b/L_b)^3 + 0.083\,h_b/L_b] \leq$$
$$E_b\,t_b\,[(0.48\,h_s/L_s)^3 + 0.083\,h_s/L_s]$$

E_s = modulus of elasticity of structure, psi
t_s = thickness of structure $\perp$ to axis of brace, ft
h_b = height of brace, ft
L_b = length of brace, ft
E_b = modulus of elasticity of brace, psi
t_b = thickness of brace $\perp$ to axis of structure, ft
h_s = height of structure, ft
L_s = horizontal length of structure $\parallel$ to axis of brace, ft

Reinf. Concrete Dowel Connection Design:

One end of these usually small rebar assemblies is usually tied to rebars protruding from already-poured concrete and the other end is tied to the rebars of concrete soon to be poured.

Step 1. Knowing the size of each rebar in the parent structure, size its mating dowel in the secondary structure to satisfy the following:

a. $A_{sp} \leq A_{sd} \geq 1.15 \, A_{sc}$
b. $A_{sd} \geq 0.005 \, A_c$

A_{sp} = section area of each parent rebar, in^2
A_{sd} = section area of dowel rebar that each parent rebar ties to, in^2. The dowel rebar is typically one size larger than the parent rebar.
A_c = section area of parent concrete, in^2

Step 2. Determine if each dowel stem acts in compression or tension, then find its development length from

a. Compression: $L_d = 0.02 \, \delta \left[f_y / f_c^{0.5} \right] \geq 8.00$
b. Tension: $L_d = 0.04 \, A \left[f_y / f_c^{0.5} \right] \geq 8.00$

L_d = development length of each dowel stem, in.
    Select the larger number, then round any fraction to the next highest integer.
A = section area of dowel stem, in^2
f_y = specified yield strength of rebar, psi
f_c = specified strength of concrete, psi
δ = diameter of rebar, in.

Step 3. Determine the dowel's total length. In columns this equals its length in the column + its length down to the footing rebars + its length in the footing, and the footing lengths extend radially from the column.

Step 4. Determine each dowel's size and spacing.

Size: Use the larger of the mating rebars at each end.
Spacing: Use the same spacing as that of the mating
        rebars at each end. One spacing may be double
        the other if every bar in the larger spacing ties to
        every other bar in the smaller spacing.

Step 5. If the dowel extends from the top of base of a
staircase, find the dowel's angle of bend from

$$\angle = 180 - \tan^{-1} {}^r/_t$$

$\angle$ = angle of bend of dowel, °
r = height of riser, in. t = length of tread, in.

Rebar Hook Design:
Any tensile rebar less than
#14 requires a hook at each end. Compression rebars
require no hooks.

Step 1. Compute the hook's inside diameter from

$$\delta_i = \kappa\, \delta_r$$

δ_i = inside diameter of hook, in.
κ = size factor. κ = 6 if
   bars are #3–#8, 8 if
   bars are #9–#11.
δ_r = diameter of rebar, in.

Step 2. Compute the hook's
extension length from

$$e = 4\,\delta_r \geq 2.5 \text{ in.}$$

e = extension length of
   hook, in.
δ_r = diameter of rebar, in.

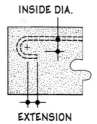

INSIDE DIA.

EXTENSION

**Fig. 4-13.
Rebar hook.**

Expansion Bolt Connection Design:

Step 1. Compute the bolt's allowable stress from

$$\eta\, f_e = \kappa\, R$$

η = no. of expansion bolts. Max. spacing ≤ 6 ft o.c., one bolt ≤ 2 ft from ends & both sides of corners.

f_e = actual unit bolt stress, withdrawal or shear, psi.

κ = load factor. κ = 1.0 if load is wind or seismic, 0.75 if any other load.

R = total reaction on bolts, withdrawal or shear, pLF

Step 2. Find the expansion bolt's minimum diameter and embedment from Table 4-6.

TABLE 4-6: ALLOWABLE EXPANSION BOLT LOADS

BOLT DIA.	←Min. dimensions, in.→				Type of Load	Allow. load, lb/bolt at conc. f_c, psi		
	Embed-ment	¢-¢ Spcg.	d	t		2,000	3,000	4,000
$\frac{1}{4}$	$1\frac{1}{2}$	$2\frac{1}{2}$	$1\frac{1}{4}$	2	W *	515	640	900
					S *	690	690	690
$\frac{3}{8}$	2	$3\frac{3}{4}$	$1\frac{7}{8}$	$2\frac{1}{2}$	W	970	1,210	1,700
					S	1,290	1,290	1,290
$\frac{1}{2}$	$2\frac{3}{4}$	5	$2\frac{1}{2}$	$3\frac{1}{4}$	W	1,400	1,750	2,440
					S	2,500	2,500	2,500
$\frac{5}{8}$	$3\frac{1}{4}$	$6\frac{1}{4}$	$3\frac{1}{8}$	4	W	2,300	2,900	4,100
					S	3,700	3,700	3,700
$\frac{3}{4}$	$3\frac{3}{4}$	$7\frac{1}{2}$	$3\frac{3}{4}$	5	W	3,100	3,900	5,500
					S	5,600	5,600	5,600
$\frac{7}{8}$	$4\frac{1}{2}$	$8\frac{3}{4}$	$4\frac{3}{8}$	6	W	3,500	4,400	6,100
					S	7,200	7,200	7,200
1	5	10	5	$6\frac{3}{4}$	W	4,800	6,100	8,500
					S	8,800	8,800	8,800

* W = withdrawal load parallel to axis of bolt;
S = shear load ⊥ to axis of bolt.

Anchor Bolt Connection Design:

Step 1. Compute the bolt's allowable stress from

$$f_v = S R_h$$

f_v = actual stress per anchor bolt, psi.
S = unit spacing of anchor bolts, ft o.c. Maximum
    spacing is 6 ft o.c., one bolt must be within 2 ft
    from ends & on both sides of corners.
R_h = horizontal reaction at top of wall, plf

Step 2. Find the anchor bolt's minimum diameter and
embedment from Table 4-7.

TABLE 4-7: ALLOWABLE ANCHOR BOLT LOADS [1]

BOLT DIA. in.	Min. Embed- mnt, in.	Min. Edge d, in.	Type of Load	ALLOW. LOAD, LB/BOLT			
				Solid Mas.	Grout'd Mas.	Conc., psi. 2,000	3,000
$\frac{1}{2}$	4	3	W [2]	680	950	950	950
			S [2]	350	2,000	2,000	2,000
$\frac{5}{8}$	4	$3\frac{3}{4}$	W	680	1,500	1,500	1,500
			S	500	2,750	2,750	3,000
$\frac{3}{4}$	5	$4\frac{1}{2}$	W	1,060	2,250	2,250	2,250
			S	750	2,900	2,940	3,560
$\frac{7}{8}$	6	$5\frac{1}{4}$	W	1,530	3,200	3,200	3,200
			S	1,000	3,350	3,580	4,150
1	7	6	W	2,080	3,200	3,200	3,200
			S	1,250	3,550	3,580	4,150
$1\frac{1}{4}$	8	$7\frac{1}{2}$	WW	2,700	3,200	3,200	3,200
			S	1,750	3,550	3,580	5,300

1. The loads in this table are for A307 bolts.
2. W = withdrawal load parallel to axis of bolt;
   S = shear load ⊥ to axis of bolt.

Reinforced Concrete Shelf Design:

Step 1. Determine the shelf's minimum length.

$$V_d = 0.25 \, f_c \, (b - 2)(s - 3)$$

V_d = design shear load on shelf or bracket, kips
f_c = specified strength of concrete, ksi
b = width of shelf, usually 2 in. wider than beam, in.
s = minimum projection of shelf or bracket, in.
   Minimum s = 10 in.

Step 2. Determine the corbel's minimum depth.

$$V_d = 0.25 \, f_c \, b \, d$$

d = depth of shelf or bracket, in. Min. d = 20 in.
   V_d, f_c, and b are as previously defined

Step 3. Size the corbel's shear reinforcing.

$$V_d = 0.70 \, \kappa \, A_s \, f_y$$

V_d = design shear load on shelf or bracket, kips
κ = coefficient of friction. κ = 1.4 for monolithic concrete, 1.0 for shelf concrete against higher-
   strength concrete, 0.7 for concrete against steel.
A_s = section area of shear reinforcing, in². Optimal
   number of bars is usually 2 or 4.
f_y = safe unit stress of reinforcement, ksi

Step 4. Size the shelf's tensile reinforcing.

$$2.33 \, V_d \, (s - 1) = A_t \, f_y \, \kappa \, (d - 4)$$

s = length of shelf or bracket, in.
A_t = section area of tensile reinforcing, in².
   A_t must $\geq A_s \geq 0.5 \, A_t$.
   V_d, f_y, κ, and d are as previously defined

Soil-Bearing Capacity under Footing:

$$P = A\,C_s$$

P = total load on footing incl. weight of footing, kips
A = minimum footing area, sf. If square, $A = b_{side}^2$.
C_s = bearing capacity of soil beneath footing, from Table 4-8, ksf

TABLE 4-8: PROPERTIES OF SOILS

TYPE of SOIL	Symbol	PERM., min/in. drop	BEAR'G ksf
Solid hard granite, gneiss, bedrock	RG	≈ ∞	80-160
Solid limestone, sandstone, slate....	RL	≈ ∞	50-80
Soft limestone, shale, crumbly slate	RS	≈ ∞	24-30
Hardpan, cohering inorganic soils	HS	60+	16-28
Boulders w/ rocks or sand	RB	2-4	12-16
Rotten or loose rock	RW	1.7-3	10
Compact gravel (rocks 2 mm-6 in.) ...	Gr	0.5-1	10
Compact sand (rocks 0.5-2 mm.)	Sa	0.8-2	7
Well-drained clean gravels	GW	1-2	10
Poorly drained clean gravels	GP	4-5	9
Silty gravels	GM	6-10	5
Clayey gravels	GC	8-20	4
Well-graded clean sands	SW	1-2	6
Poorly graded clean sands	SP	3-5	5
Silty sands	SM	5-12	4
Silt/sand/clay mix w/ plastic fines ...	SSC	15-35	3
Clayey sands, poor sandy clays	SC	20-30	3
Firm dry clay, fine inorganic soils	CD	30-50	8
Rocks w/ clay	CR	40-60	6
Inorganic silts, clayey silts	CS	20-30	4
Inorganic clays of low-medium plas ..	CL	≈ 40	3
Inorganic clays of high plasticity ...	CH	≈ 50	3
Rocks w/ organic soil	RO	5-15	4
Soft wet clay	CW	60+	3
Topsoil, peat, loam, organic soils ...	OH	5-20	2

Subsoil Stress Below Footing:

$$P d^3 = 2.09 f_{ss} (d^2 + x^2)^{2.5}$$

P = total gravity load on footing, lb
d = depth between underside of footing and locus of subsoil stress, ft
f_{ss} = unit subsoil stress at depth d below footing, psf
x = lateral distance if any from vertical proj. of ₵ of footing load to point of unit subsoil stress, ft

Lateral Bearing Load on Footing: Sometimes a foundation supports an oblique load that creates a lateral load against the footing's side, which must be resisted by the footing's sidesoil or added structure.

Step 1. Knowing the footing's tentative total depth d_t and the depth of its underside below grade, find c, the distance from finished grade to $2/3$ the footing's depth (i.e. the centroid of the footing's side where its lateral bearing load P is concentrated), then use c to find P.

$$d_t b_{diag} f_{sb} = 4 P^{0.5} [6,000 P^{0.5} (11,200 P + c b_{diag} f_{sb})^{0.5}]$$

d_t = total depth of footing, in.
b_{diag} = widest diagonal of footing, in.
f_{sb} = safe lateral bearing stress of ftg sidesoil, psf.
P = total lateral bearing pressure of footing against sidesoil, lb
c = vertical distance from finished grade to $2/3$ the footing's depth, in.

Step 2. Knowing the footing's total lateral bearing pressure P, the footing's side diagonal area A, and the footing sidesoil, find the sidesoil's safe unit stress f_{lsb} from $P = f_{isb} A$, then compare actual f_{isb} with allow. f_{isb} in the graph of Fig. 4-14.

Footing on Stronger-over-Weaker Soil:

$$A^{0.5} \geq (P/C_w)^{0.5} - 0.159 \, d \, C_s^{0.5}$$

A = minimum area of footing, sf. If footing is square, $A^{0.5} = b_{side}$, minimum length of one side.

P = total load on footing incl. weight of footing when placed on stronger-over-weaker soil, 100 kips

C_w = bearing capacity of weaker underlying soil, ksf

d = depth of stronger upper soil, 3 ft

C_s = bearing capacity of soil beneath footing, from Table 4-8, ksf

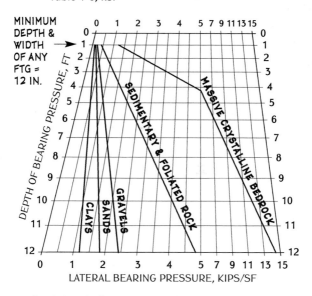

Fig. 4-14. Safe lateral bearing soil stress graph.

Reinforced Concrete Wall Footing Design:

Step 1. Compute the unit design load on the footing.

$$\omega = \kappa_f (1.4\,\omega_D + 1.7\,\omega_L)$$

ω = total unit design load on footing, pLF or kLF

κ_f = weight of footing factor. $\kappa_f \approx 1.0$ if dead load includes weight of footing, 1.08 if not.

ω_D = unit dead load on footing, excl. wt. of footing, pLF

ω_L = unit live load on footing, pLF

Step 2. Compute the footing's width.

$$b\,C = 12\,\kappa_f (\omega_D + \omega_l)$$

b = width of footing, in. Round off to next highest multiple of 4 in.

C = bearing capacity of soil, from Table 4-8, psf.

κ_f = weight of footing factor, from Step 1

ω_D = unit dead load on footing, from Step 1, pLF

ω_L = unit live load on footing, from Step 1, pLF

Step 3. Compute the footing's depth.

$$41\,b\,d_e\,f_c^{0.5} = \omega\,(b - w - 2\,d_e)$$

d_e = effective depth of footing, from top of footing to ₵ of rebar, in.

f_c = specified strength of concrete, psi

w = width of wall, in.

   b and ω are as previously defined

Step 4. Design the lateral reinforcing from the formulas below. Maximum spacing of rebars both ways is 18 in.

    a. $6.5\,A_{lat}\,b\,d_e\,f_y = \omega\,(b - w)^2$

    b. $A_{lat}\,f_y = 2{,}400\,d_e$

A_{lat} = minimum section area of lateral rebars, in²/LF. The larger value governs. After finding A_{lat}, select rebars and spacing from schedule below:

A_{lat} to 0.073 in²/LF ➔ #3 bars spaced 18 in. o.c.
A_{lat} to 0.133 in²/LF ➔ #3 bars spaced $1.32/_A$ in. o.c.
A_{lat} to 0.207 in²/LF ➔ #4 bars spaced $2.40/_A$ in. o.c.
A_{lat} to 0.293 in²/LF ➔ #5 bars spaced $3.72/_A$ in. o.c.
A_{lat} to 0.400 in²/LF ➔ #6 bars spaced $5.28/_A$ in. o.c.
A_{lat} to 0.527 in²/LF ➔ #7 bars spaced $7.20/_A$ in. o.c.
A_{lat} to 0.667 in²/LF ➔ #8 bars spaced $9.48/_A$ in. o.c.
A_{lat} to 0.847 in²/LF ➔ #9 bars spaced $12.0/_A$ in. o.c.
A_{lat} to 1.040 in²/LF ➔ #10 bars spaced $15.2/_A$ in. o.c.
A_{lat} to 1.500 in²/LF ➔ #11 bars spaced $18.7/_A$ in. o.c.
A_{lat} to 2.670 in²/LF ➔ #14 bars spaced $27.0/_A$ in. o.c.

f_y = specified yield strength of reinforcement, psi
b, d_e, ω, and w are as previously defined

Step 5. Design the longitudinal reinforcing.

$$A_{lon} = 0.0020\ b\ d$$

A_{lon} = minimum section area of longitudinal rebars for width of footing, in²/LF
b and d are as previously defined

Step 6. Determine the optimal rebar size and spacing.

$$b = S\,(\eta - 1) + 6$$

b = width of footing, from Step 1, in.
S = allowable rebar spacing, in.
η = number of rebars in width of footing. Minimum rebar size = #3 ($a = 0.11$ in²), and ideal spacing ≈ 6–16 in. Try η = several rebar sizes, then select lowest total A_{lon} that ≥ A_{lon} from above.

Reinf. Concrete Column Footing Design:

Step 1. Compute the footing's design load.

$$P = \kappa_f (1.4\, P_D + 1.7\, P_L)$$

P = total design load on footing, lb

κ_f = weight of footing factor. $\kappa_f \approx 1.0$ if dead load includes weight of footing, 1.08 if excluded.

P_D = total dead load on footing, excl. wt. of footing, lb

P_L = total live load on footing, plF

Step 2. Find the footing's minimum plan area.

$$A\,C = 144\, \kappa_f\, P$$

A = minimum plan area of footing, in^2.

C = bearing capacity of soil, ksf

    κ_f and P are as previously defined

Step 3. Assuming the column and footing are square, check the footing for punching shear (see Fig. 4-15).

$$8\, A\, d_e\, (b_c + d_e)\, f_c^{0.5} = P\,[A - (b_c + d_e)^2]$$

A = area of footing, sf

d_e = effective depth of footing, in. d_e = total depth – 3.5 in. minimum cover.

b_c = breadth or width of column, in.

f_c = specified strength of concrete, psi. Solve for actual f_v, then compare with given f_c.

P = total design load on footing, lb

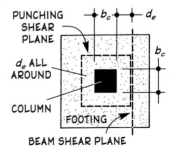

Fig. 4-15. Seam shears in column footing.

Step 4. Check the trial depth for beam shear (see Fig. 4-15).

$$3.4 \, A \, d_e f_c^{0.5} = P \, (s - b_c - 2 \, d_e)$$

d_e = effective depth of footing, in.
f_c = specified strength of concrete, psi.
s = shorter side of footing, in.
    A, P, and b_c are as previously defined

Step 5. Find the minimum area of reinforcing from the formulas below. The larger A_r governs. Maximum rebar spacing is 18 in. both ways, and outer bars must lie 3–6 in. from the edge of the footing.

    a. $7.25 \, A_r \, s \, d_e \, f_y = P \, (s - b_c)^2$
    b. $A_r f_y = 200 \, s \, d_e$

A_r = minimum section area of reinforcing, in^2/LF.
    The larger value governs.
f_y = specified yield strength of reinforcement, psi
    s, d_e, P, and b_c are as previously defined

Step 6. Determine the economical rebar size and spacing from

$$s = S \, (\eta - 1) + 6$$

s = shorter side of footing, from Step 4, in.
S = allow. rebar spacing, in.
η = number of rebars in width of footing. Minimum
    rebar size = #3 and optimal spacing ≈ 6-16 in.
    Select lowest total A_r that ≤ A_r from Step 5.

Combined Footing Design:
When two footings are near each other, or if one is near a property line or other obstacle that prevents one side of the footing from extending a normal distance from its column, the footings may be combined as described below.

Step 1. Compute the total design load on the combined footing from two columns A and B.

$$P = \kappa_f (1.4\, P_D + 1.7\, P_L)$$

P = total design load on footing, lb or kips

κ_f = weight of footing factor. $\kappa_f \approx 1.0$ if dead load includes weight of footing, 1.1 if excluded.

P_D = dead load on footing, excluding its weight, kips

P_L = total live load on footing, kips

Step 2. Locate the centroid of column moments by taking moments about the center of column B.

$$P_a\, d = e\, (P_a + P_b)$$

P_a = load from column A, kips

d = distance between ₵s of columns A and B, in.

e = distance from ₵ of load to ₵ of column B, in.

P_b = load from column B, kips

Step 3. Compute the length of the footing.

$$L = 2\, (e + s)$$

L = total length of footing, in.

e = distance from ₵ of load to ₵ of column B, in.

s = distance from column B to property line or other obstacle, in. If one column's footing area is not limited by a property line or obstacle, $s = 0$.

Step 4. Compute the footing's width from

$$144\, \kappa_f P = w\, C\, L$$

κ_f = weight of footing factor, from Step 1, 1.1

P = total design load on footing, kips

w = footing width, in. Increase to next multiple of 4 in.

C = bearing capacity of subsoil, from Table 4-8, ksf

L = total length of footing, in.

Step 5. Select a trial depth for the footing.

$$d \approx 0.06 \, (L + W)$$

d = trial depth of footing, in.
L = total length of footing, from Step 3, in.
W = width of footing, from Step 4, in.

Step 6. Arrange the rebars in the combined footing.

Subsequent Steps:
1. Draw shear and moment diagrams thro' the X axis.
2. Compute the maximum moment and shear for each stress.
3. Investigate the estimated depth for one-way shear, two-way shear, and maximum moment.
4. Design the longitudinal and lateral reinforcement.

Grilled Footing Design:
A large column footing may include two or more concentric tiers of several short steel beams bolted side-to-side with each tier perpendicular to the one below, then the tiers are enveloped in concrete to create a mass that can support a greater load per sf of area than a rebarred footing.

Step 1. Knowing the column load, size the footing as a typical footing including the rebars. When estimating the footing's total load, estimate the weight of the two tiers of grilles, then verify or refine afterwards.

Step 2. Lay out the plan of concentric column, billet, tier 1, tier 2, and footing as suggested in Fig. 4-16.

Step 3. Design the column's pedestal, billet, or base plate if it has one as described on pages 134–137.

Step 4. Design the top tier of grilles. If the column is a W shape, the top tier should have an odd number of evenly spaced beams running parallel to the column web with the center beam's web aligned with the column web. Then, knowing the uniform load on each beam (= total load on grille ÷ no. of beams), find M_{max}, select the economic section, then check for shear in **a**, **b**, and **c** below:

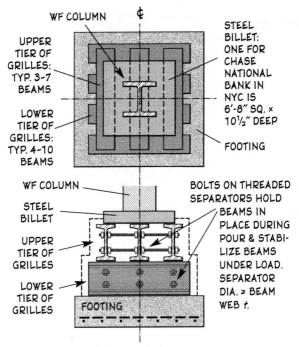

Fig. 4-16. Grilled column footing details.

a. $a_a = L - 8 \left[f_b \, S_x / p \right]$

a_a = length of column billet above top tier of grilles, in.

L = length of each beam in each tier of grillage, in.

f_b = safe unit bending stress of grillage steel, psi

S_x = section modulus of trial beam, in³. Solve for this, then select economic beam section, then use the selected beam's k and t_w in formula **b** below to find the minimum length of a_b.

P = total load on each tier of grillage, lb

b. $a_b + 2 \, k = {}^P\!/\!f_b \, t_w$

a_b = minimum length of billet, in. If $a_b < a_a$, increase length of billet to a_b or select a larger beam with a larger k and t_w, then use a_b in equation **c** below.

k = thickness of fillet in each grillage beam, in.

t_w = thickness of web in each grillage beam, in.

P and f_b are as previously defined.

c. $P(L - a_b) = 2 \, d \, f_v \, t_w \, L$

d = tentative depth of beam, in.

f_v = actual unit shear of each grillage beam, psi. Solve for this value, then compare with the beam's safe f_v. If actual f_v > safe f_v, select a beam with larger d and t_w.

P, L, a_b, and t_w are as previously defined.

Step 5. Design the lower tier of grillage. Again lay out a plan of a feasible number of short beams. If the column is a W shape, the lower tier should have an even number of evenly spaced beams running parallel to the column flanges with the two center beams' webs located directly beneath the column flanges. Then, knowing the uniform load of the first tier and its width b_b, size the lower beams similarly as in Step 4.

Step 6. Verify that the originally assumed weight of the grillage beams and enveloping concrete is adequate. If not, refine or redesign.

Foundations under Heavy Machinery: Some

factory machines are so large that they require massive individual foundations. Since such foundations are really large inertia blocks, the following may be used to design an inertia block for any operating machinery.

Step 1. Determine the foundation's design load from

$$W_T = 2.5\,(W_m + W_i) + W_f$$

W_T = total design load of foundation, lb
W_m = scaled weight of machinery, lb
W_i = effective weight of any impact load, lb. Compute impact load as described on page 29.
W_f = estimated weight of foundation, lb

Step 2. Find the foundation's depth according to

$$W_t\,L = 0.6\,f_c\,b\,d_e^2$$

W_t = total design load of foundation, lb
L = longer side of rectangular foundation base, ft
f_c = specified strength of concrete, psi
b = shorter side of rectangular foundation base, ft
d_e = effective depth of foundation, from top to mat of tensile rebars, in.

Step 3. Design the foundation's two-way grid of tensile rebars near its base. This grid can be duplicated for the foundation's top rebars.

$$W_t\,L = 4.2\,f_y\,A_s\,d_e$$

f_y = yield strength of steel reinforcing, psi

A_s = minimum section area of rebars, in². Solve for
    this, then select bars whose number × area ≥ A_s.
d_e = effective depth of foundation, in.
        W_t and L are as previously defined

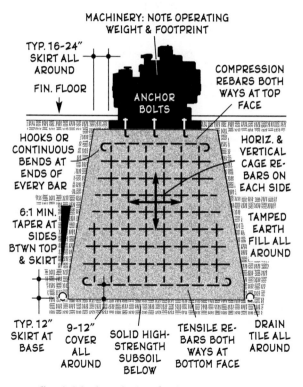

MACHINERY: NOTE OPERATING
WEIGHT & FOOTPRINT

TYP. 16-24"
SKIRT ALL
AROUND

FIN. FLOOR

COMPRESSION
REBARS BOTH
WAYS AT TOP
FACE

ANCHOR
BOLTS

HOOKS OR
CONTINUOUS
BENDS AT
ENDS OF
EVERY BAR

HORIZ. &
VERTICAL
CAGE RE-
BARS ON
EACH SIDE

6:1 MIN.
TAPER AT
SIDES
BTWN TOP
& SKIRT

TAMPED
EARTH
FILL ALL
AROUND

TYP. 12"
SKIRT AT
BASE

9-12"
COVER
ALL
AROUND

SOLID HIGH-
STRENGTH
SUBSOIL
BELOW

TENSILE RE-
BARS BOTH
WAYS AT
BOTTOM FACE

DRAIN
TILE ALL
AROUND

Fig. 4-17. Foundation for heavy machinery.

Step 4. Design the foundation's cage reinforcement.

$$A_s \geq 0.0025 \, A_c$$

A_s = min. section area each way in each grid of rebars, in². Max. rebar spacing = 12 in.

A_c = section area of concrete through each opposing pair of grids, in².

Step 5. Size the hooks at the ends of each rebar.

$$\delta_h \geq 14 \, \delta_r$$

δ_h = inside diameter of each hook, in.
δ_r = diameter of each rebar, in.

Reinforced Concrete Footing Piles:

A footing pile may be *bearing*, *friction*, and *caisson*. A bearing pile is driven until its bottom end reaches a stronger soil below. A friction pile develops its strength by the friction developed between the surface of its shaft and the surrounding soil. A caisson is made by driving a large tube into the ground, emptying the tube and excavating below its base a semi-spherical bell, then filling the tube and bell with concrete.

Bearing pile design: $\qquad P \approx 0.79 \, d^2 \, C$

P = bearing capacity of bearing pile, kips
d = diameter of bearing pile, ft
C = bearing capacity of refusal soil, ksf

Friction pile design: $\quad P \, (S + 1) \approx 2 \, W \, h$

P = bearing capacity of friction pile, kips
S = pile penetration for average of 5 final blows, in.
W = weight of pile-driver hammer, kips
h = height of drop for hammer, ft

When a cluster of friction piles are compactly spaced, the soil area required to support each pile may overlap the area required to support adjacent piles; then the piles' capacity must be reduced according to

$$P = P_s \{m\,n - (\angle/90)\,[m\,(n - 10) + n\,(m - 1)]\}$$

P = bearing capacity of all piles in a cluster, kips
P_s = bearing capacity of single pile, kips
$\angle$ = $\tan^{-1}$ of pile diameter ÷ ¢–¢ spacing of piles, °
m = number of rows in pile cluster
n = number of piles per row in pile cluster

Caisson Design: $\qquad 145\,P \approx C\,(H - 1)^2$

P = bearing capacity of caisson pile, kips
C = bearing capacity of refusal soil, ksf
H = height of caisson and bell, ft

Reinf. Concrete Footing Pile Cap Design:

Step 1. Determine the required number of piles.

$$\eta\,C = \kappa_f\,(P_D + P_L)$$

η = required number of piles. Round up to next highest integer.
C = bearing capacity of each pile, kips
κ_f = weight of pile cap factor. $\kappa_f \approx 1.0$ if dead load includes weight of cap, 1.1 if not.
P_D = unit dead load upon footing pile, kips
P_L = unit live load on footing pile, kips

Step 2. Select the best pile cap plan according to criteria **a** and **b** below:

    a. Centers of piles ≥ 2'-6" apart.
    b. Distance from pile ¢s to edges of cap ≥ 1'-3".

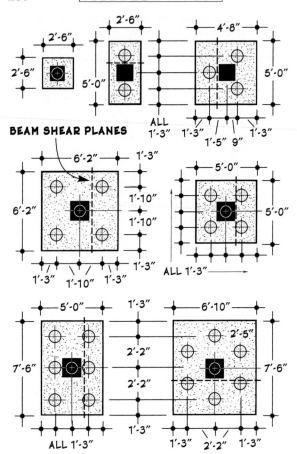

Fig. 4-18. Optimal pile cap plans.

Step 3. Compute the design load on each pile cap.

$$P\eta = \kappa_f (1.4\ P_d + 1.7\ P_l)$$

P = total design load on each pile, lb
P_d = total dead load on each pile, kips
P_l = total live load on each pile, kips
       η and κ_f are as previously defined

Step 4. Compute the pile cap's depth from

$$V = 1.70\ s\ d_e\ f_c^{0.5}$$

V = maximum shear force between column acting
      downward and piles resisting upward, lb.
s = length of longest side of pile cap, in.
d_e = effective depth of footing: distance from top of
      pile cap to ¢ of rebars, in. Min. d_e = 12 in.
f_c = specified strength of concrete, psi

Step 5. Design the reinforcing. Maximum spacing both
ways is 18 in. o.c., and outer bars must lie 3–6 in. from
the edge of the footing.

$$A_r f_y = 200\ s\ d_e$$

A_r = minimum section area of rebars each way, in^2
f_y = specified yield strength of reinforcement, psi
       s and d_e are as previously defined

Step 6. Determine the economic rebar size and spacing from

$$b = S (\eta - 1) + 6$$

b = width of footing, from Step 4, in.
S = allowable rebar spacing, in.
η = no. of rebars in width of footing. Ideal spacing ≈
      6–16 in. Try several rebar sizes, then select lowest
      total A_r that ≥ A_r from Step 5.

TABLE 5-1: ALLOW. MASONRY MORTAR STRESSES

MORTAR STRESSES in masonry	Allow. f_c, type of mortar, psi N	S	M
Compression, f_c, psi			
Brick, $f_c \geq 8,000$ psi (SW)	300	350	400
Brick, f_c = 4,500-8,000 psi (SW)	200	225	250
Brick, f_c = 3,000-4,500 psi (SW)	150	170	185
Brick, f_c = 2,500-3,000 psi (MW)	135	150	165
Brick, f_c = 1,500-2,500 psi (MW)	105	120	135
Brick f_c = 1,200-1,500 psi (NW)	95	110	120
Glazed facing brick	140	160	175
Firebrick (in refractory mortar)	—	—	500
Unburned clay, adobe brick	—	30	30
Gypsum masonry	20	20	20
Conc. block, hollow, grade A	85	90	100
Conc. block, hollow, grade B	70	75	85
Conc. block, grouted	230	240	270
Solid concrete units, grade S	100	115	125
Solid concrete units, grade N	140	160	175
Rubble or natural masonry	80	95	110
Coursed	100	120	140
Cut sandstone, cast stone	320	360	400
Cut limestone, marble	400	450	500
Cut granite, slate	640	720	800
Grout	200	200	200
Tension, f_t, all units: ⊥ to bed joints	28	36	36
Parallel to bed joints	56	72	72
Shear, f_v, all masonry solid units	56	80	80
Hollow units, average for width	19	27	27
Modulus of elasticity, E, psi, brick	800,000		
Concrete block	1,200,000		
All other units	800 f_c but not ≥ 3,000,000		
Glass block, NB only, min. $3\frac{1}{2}$ in. wide bed			
Exterior walls: max. unsupported area	144 ft²		
Max. unsupp. length 25 ft; Max. unsupp. ht	20 ft		
Interior walls: maximum unsupported area	250 ft²		
Maximum unsupported length & height	25 ft		

5. MASONRY

Nonreinf. Masonry Pillar and Pier Design:

$$P_e = t\,d\,f_c\,(1.25 - 0.05\,{}^h/_t)$$

P_e = effective axial load on masonry pillar or similar
structure, lb

t = minimum least dimension of above structure, in.
t must ≥ 0.1 h.

d = minimum largest dimension of pillar or projection
from wall, in. d + wall thickness must ≥ 0.1 h.

f_c = safe unit compr. stress for masonry units, psi

h = maximum unbraced height of above masonry, in.

TABLE 5-2: SAFE MASONRY UNIT STRESSES

TYPE OF MASONRY UNIT	Allow. f_c, psi
Solid clay units (brick)	1,500-14,000
Solid loadbearing conc. masonry unit, Grade N ..	1,800
Concrete block, Grade A, hollow or grouted	1,500
Concrete block, Grade N, hollow or grouted	1,350
Hollow clay units, Grade LB (1$\frac{1}{4}$ in. min. face shell)	1,350
Grouted or reinforced	1,500
Hollow clay units, Type I	2,500
Grouted or reinforced	2,000

Nonreinf. Masonry Bearing Wall Design:

Step 1. Determine the wall's thickness and height from

    a. Building Code Limit: $h \le 25\,t$
    b. Recommended Practice: $h \le 18\,t$

h = maximum height of masonry bearing wall, in.
t = minimum thickness of wall, in.

Step 2. Compute the wall's bearing capacity.

$$P_e = 2.4\,\kappa_i\,\kappa_n\,t\,f_{cm}\,[1 - (0.025\,{}^h/_t)^3]$$

P_e = effective axial load on masonry bearing wall, pLF
κ_i = inspection factor. κ_i = 1.0 for inspected work, 0.7 for uninspected work.
κ_n = net area factor. κ_n = 1.0 if masonry units are solid, 0.9 if grouted, 0.45 if hollow.
t = least thickness of masonry, in.
f_{cm} = safe unit stress in compression for masonry, psi.
h = maximum unbraced height of masonry, in.

Nonreinf. Masonry Nonbearing Wall Design:

Step 1. Compute the wall's minimum thickness or maximum height from

    a. Building Code Limit: $h \le 25\,t$
    b. Recommended Practice: $h \le 18\,t$

h = maximum height of masonry nonbearing wall, measured from lowest base on either side, in.
t = minimum thickness of wall, in. $t \ge 4$ in. nom.

Step 2. Find the width of the wall's lateral bracing.

$$h = \kappa_t\,(t + 6\,L_d)$$

h = height of masonry nonbearing wall, in.

κ_t = translation factor. κ_t = 1.20 if bracing is a corner, junction, or plan curve; 0.65 if bracing is pilasters, offsets, or niches.
t = minimum thickness of masonry, in.
L_d = minimum width of lateral bracing, in.

Step 3. Find the maximum spacing between the bracing.

$$L_u \leq 36\,t$$

L_u = maximum unbraced length of wall, ft
t = least thickness of wall, from Step 1, in.

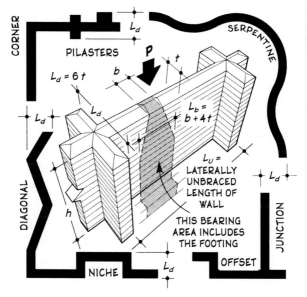

Fig. 5-1. Masonry NLB walls and lateral bracing.

Arch Design: A single arch's span-to-rise ratio should not exceed 9, and when four or more arches are aligned in series the span-to-rise ratio of each should not exceed 8; but 4 is much better.

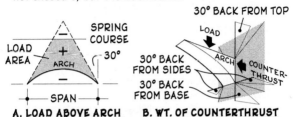

Fig. 5-2. Arch loads and counterthrusts.

$$L\,(W_D + W_L) \;=\; 8\,\kappa_L\,R\,C$$

L = length of span, in.

W_D = total dead load on arch [load area above arch × arch thickness × masonry unit weight (pcf)], lb.

W_L = live load on arch, lb. Consider only load resting on arch within projected area of dead load.

κ_L = live load factor. κ_L = 1.0 if W_L is uniform load, 0.5 if W_L is point or moving load.

R = rise or height of arch, in.

C = counterthrust of abutments (volume of counterthrust mass × unit weight: see Fig. 5-2B), lb.

Arches, Height of Masonry above Crown:

$$h \;=\; 0.2 + 0.25\,\kappa_s\,\kappa_m\,(0.5\,L + R)^{0.5} \;\geq\; 0.67 \text{ ft}$$

h = minimum height of masonry above or crown, ft. $h \geq 8$ in. or 0.67 ft.

κ_s = series factor. κ_s = 1.00 if arch is single, 1.41 if arch is one of a series.

κ_m = material factor. κ_m = 1.00 for cut stone, 1.13 for brick, 1.33 for field stone.

L = horizontal length of arch or length of span, ft.

R = height of semicircular or elliptical arch, ft. For semicircular arch, R = 0.5 × length of span.

Fireplace and Chimney Design:
The most efficient masonry fireplace that is easy to build is a Rumford fireplace. The formula below describes the relation between this fireplace's opening and its flue size.

$$s \geq 0.33 \, (A \, B)^{0.5}$$

s = side of flue if square (interior opening), in.

A = width of fireplace opening, in.

B = height of fireplace opening, in.

Reinforced Masonry Pillar and Pier Design:
A reinforced masonry pier may be *veneered core* (vertical rebars are placed inside an outer shell of masonry) or *formed core* (vertical rebars are inserted into unit block cavities). Veneered cores are designed as reinforced concrete columns, then the veneer is excluded from the column's thickness.

TABLE 5-3: RUMFORD FIREPLACE DIMENSIONS

FIREPLACE ELEMENT	Dimension
Firebox opng width, hearth width	1.0–1.62 firebox ht h
Hearth depth, backwall width, backwall ht	0.33 h
Hearth apron	width ≥ 1.0 h, depth ≥ 0.5 h
Throat depth .... 0.083 h rounded to nearest $\frac{1}{2}$ in.	
Smoke chamber ht, smoke chamber width at base	1.0 h

Step 1. Find the masonry's minimum thickness or maximum height from

$$h \leq 12\,t$$

h = maximum unbraced height of masonry, in.
t = least thickness of masonry, in. Least t = 16 in. nom. = $15\frac{5}{8}$ in.

Step 2. Compute the structure's vertical reinforcing. If the reinforcing is given, verify its safety.

$$0.01\,A \leq \eta\,A_s \leq 0.08\,A$$

A = section area of masonry pillar, post, or pier, in^2.
η = number of rebars in above construction
A_s = section area of vertical reinforcing, in^2. If $A_s \leq$ 0.01 A, use larger rebars or smaller pier; if $A_s \geq$ 0.08 A, use smaller rebars or make pier larger.

Step 3. Compute the structure's effective axial load.

$$P_e = t\,d\,f_{cm}\,(1.25 - 0.05\,{}^h/_t)$$

P_e = effective axial load on masonry column, lb
t = least thickness of column, in.
d = minimum depth of column section, in. d must $\geq$ 0.1 h and should preferably $\geq t$.
f_{cm} = safe unit compression stress for masonry, psi
h = maximum unbraced height of column, in.

Step 4. Compute the structure's actual axial load.

$$P_e = 1.43\,P_\Delta\,(1.4\,P_D + 1.7\,P_L)$$

P_e = effective axial load on column, lb.
P_Δ = the P-Delta Effect, a secondary eccentric load factor. Unless otherwise noted, P_Δ = 1.08.
P_D = service dead load on column, lb
P_L = service live load on column, lb

Reinforced Masonry Cavity Wall Design: A
cavity wall has at least one masonry withe on each side
of a planar void into which is placed a grid of horizon-
tal/vertical rebars, then the void is grouted.

Step 1. Determine the wall's height and thickness from

    a. Building Code Limit: $h \leq 25\ t$
    b. Recommended Practice: $h \leq 18\ t$

h = max. height of reinforced masonry cavity wall, in.
t = minimum thickness of wall, in.

Step 2. Find or verify the wall's minimum thickness or
the maximum load it will support.

$$P_e = 8.4\ (f_{c1}\ t_1 + f_{c2}\ t_2 + ... + f_{cz}\ t_z)\ [1 - (0.025\ ^h/_t)^3]$$

P_e = effective axial load on masonry cavity wall, PLF.
f_{c1}, f_{c2}, etc. = safe unit compression stress for
        masonry type 1, 2, etc., psi.
t_1, t_2, etc. = thickness of masonry type 1, 2, etc., in.
h = maximum height of masonry cavity wall, in.
t = minimum thickness of wall, 10 in.

Step 3. Design the wall's reinforcing according to the
simple schedule below:

Wall t, in.	Rebar size	Horiz. spcg.	Vert. spcg.
6	#4	32 in. o.c.	32 in. o.c.
7	#5	40 in. o.c.	48 in. o.c.
8	#5	32 in. o.c.	48 in. o.c.
9	#5	32 in. o.c.	32 in. o.c.
10	#6	40 in. o.c.	48 in. o.c.
12	#6	32 in. o.c.	40 in. o.c.
14	#7	40 in. o.c.	40 in. o.c.
16	#8	48 in. o.c.	48 in. o.c.
18	#8	40 in. o.c.	48 in. o.c.
20	#9	48 in. o.c.	48 in. o.c.

Step 4. Find the wall's laterally unbraced length from the formula below.

$$(W_w + W_m\, t)\, L_b{}^3 \;\le\; 12.8\; E\, t^3$$

W_w = wind load against wall (vertical projection), psf
W_m = weight of masonry, psf
t = thickness of wall, ft
L_b = maximum laterally unbraced length of wall, ft
E = modulus of elasticity of masonry, psi

Concrete Block Wall Design: Structurally a concrete block wall has three kinds of surface area:

1. **Support areas:** Vertical strips that lie directly below any structure bearing on the wall.
2. **Opening areas:** Wall areas that contain any openings more than 16 in. wide or high. Each such opening requires a header above that is designed as a reinforced concrete beam or concrete block bond beam that is grouted to at least 16 in. above the opening.
3. **Solid areas:** Vertical areas in the wall that contain no openings more than 16 in. wide or high. Blocks in these areas require no header, vertical reinforcing, or grouting.

Step 1. Determine the wall's minimum thickness for any areas with no openings more than 16 in. wide or deep.

$$h \;\le\; 20\, t$$

h = maximum height of wall, in.
t = minimum thickness of wall, in. Find this, then select next highest multiple of 2 in. nom.

Step 2. Compute the area of vertical reinforcing in the wall that have no openings.

$$\frac{0.313 \, W_t}{\kappa_n \, \kappa_i \, t \, f_m \, [1 - (0.025 \, {}^h/_t)^3]} + \frac{2.65 \, h \, W_w}{t \, f_b \, A_s} \le 1.00$$

W_t = total load on base of wall, PLF.

κ_n = net area factor. κ_n = 1.0 if masonry units are solid, 0.9 if grouted, 0.45 if hollow.

κ_i = inspection factor. κ_i = 1.0 for inspected work, 0.7 for uninspected work.

t = maximum thickness of wall, in.

f_m = safe unit compression stress for masonry, psi

h = maximum height of wall, in.

W_w = total lateral load against wall (vert. proj.), PLF

f_b = safe unit stress in bending for rebars, psi

A_s = section area of steel reinforcing, in²/LF

Step 3. Select a rebar size and spacing for the wall's vertical reinforcing that $\ge A_s$ above. The rebars and their grouted cells must be directly under any structure resting on the wall.

Step 4. Design the wall's horizontal reinforcing. A wall with vertical reinforcing requires horizontal reinforcing

TABLE 5-4: C-S AREAS OF REBARS IN MASONRY						
REBAR Unit	Area of horiz. or vert. rebar, in²/LF of wall					
SIZE spcg, in. ➔ 8		16	24	32	40	48
# 3	0.165	0.083	0.055	0.041	0.033	0.028
# 4	0.300	1.150	0.100	0.075	0.060	0.050
# 5	0.465	1.232	0.155	0.117	0.093	0.078
# 6	0.66	1.33	0.22	0.17	0.13	0.11
# 7	0.90	1.45	0.30	0.23	0.18	0.15
# 8	1.19	0.59	0.40	0.30	0.24	0.20
# 9	1.50	1.75	0.50	0.38	0.30	0.25
# 10	1.91	0.95	0.64	0.48	0.38	0.32
# 11	2.34	1.17	0.78	0.59	0.47	0.39

≥ 0.0007 vertical section area of wall. Either use rebars as listed in Table 5-4 or wire trusses according to the schedule below.

Wall t, in. nom.   Type of wire truss, all 8 in. vert. o.c.

6	9 ga. truss, ladder, or tab
8, 10	$3/16$ in. truss, ladder, or tab
12, 14	$3/16$ in. trirod truss or ladder
16, 18, 20	$3/16$ in. double rod truss or ladder

Step 5. Find the moment due to total gravity loads and lateral loads on each header.

$$M_t = 0.10 \, L^2 \, (W_v + W_h)$$

M_t = total moment due to vertical and horizontal loads on header, ft-lb

L = length of span, ft. L = width of opening + width of piers under each end of header. Width of pier usually = 0.67 ft for openings up to 6.0 ft wide, 1.33 ft for openings to 12.0 ft wide, and 2.0 ft for larger openings.

W_v = total dead and live load on header, lb. W_v = total roof load on header + weight of wall above header + weight of any garage door when suspended from header when open.

W_h = total wind load against header, lb. W_h = wind load on header + wind load against top half of any garage door below header.

Step 6. Compute the header's minimum depth, then compare with its actual depth. If minimum d ≥ actual d, the header masonry must be made thicker or higher.

$$M_t = 0.9 \, r f_y \, b \, d_e^2 \, (1 - 0.59 \, {}^{r f_y}/_{\kappa_n \, \kappa_i \, f_{cm}})$$

M_t = total moment of header load, from Step 1, ft-lb

r = maximum reinf. ratio. For Grade A concrete

block, $r = 0.0080$; for Grade N block, $r = 0.0072$.
f_y = safe unit yield stress of reinforcement, psi
b = width of header, in.
d_e = effective depth of beam, in.
κ_n = net area factor. $\kappa_n = 1.0$ if masonry units are
   solid, 0.9 if grouted, 0.45 if hollow.
κ_i = inspection factor. $\kappa_i = 1.0$ for inspected work,
   0.7 for uninspected work.
f_{cm} = safe unit compression stress for masonry, psi

Step 7. Compute the area of tensile reinforcing in the
header. Normally the economical reinforcing is horizontal rebars placed in a concrete block bond beam that
forms the header's lowest course.

$$A_t = r\, t\, d_e$$

A_t = section area of tensile rebars in header, in^2
r = maximum reinforcing ratio
t = width of header, in.
d_e = effective depth of header (full depth – length of
   tensile rebars from bottom edge), in.

Step 8. Size the rebars for the header bond beams based
on A_t above. A bond beam can hold one or two bars.

Step 9. Design the header's other reinforcing. Each
header requires (1) wire trusses or equal reinforcing in
every horizontal mortar joint for its full height, (2) one
or two compression rebars in a bond beam top course if
$0.33\, A_t \geq 0.11$, and (3) vertical rebars every 16 in.
horiz. o.c. if $0.15\, A_t \geq 0.11$.

Compr. reinforcing? $0.33\, A_t = \kappa \geq 0.11$ in.
Vertical reinforcing? $0.15\, A_t = \kappa \geq 0.11$ in.

Step 10. Find the minimum area of vertical reinforcing

for the piers on each side of each header.

$$\frac{12\,W_t}{\kappa_n\,\kappa_i\,t\,d\,f_m\,[1-(0.025\,^{h}/_t)^3]} + \frac{2.35\,M_t}{t\,f_b\,A_s} \leq 1.00$$

W_t = total live and dead load on base of pier, lb. W_t = 0.5 total load of header + weight of each pier.

κ_n = net area factor. κ_n = 1.0 if pier is grouted, 0.45 if pier is hollow.

κ_i = inspection factor. κ_i = 1.0 for Inspected work, 0.7 for uninspected work.

t = thickness of pilaster or pier, in.

d = depth of pilaster or pier, in.

f_m = safe unit stress in compression for masonry, psi

h = height of pier, equals height of opening, in.

M_t = total moment due to wind or other lateral loads on pier, ft-lb. M_t = wind moment on header & pier.

f_b = safe unit stress in bending for reinforcing, psi

A_s = section area of steel reinforcing, psi

Step 11. Design the pier's reinforcing. Select the smallest rebar area for a size and unit spacing that $\geq A_s$.

Concrete Block Shear Wall Design:
When reinforced concrete block walls with square or near-square plan shapes are located around elevator shafts, stairwells, and other stacked floor areas of equal size, they make excellent shear walls in multi-story buildings.

Step 1. Find the shear wall's minimum thickness.

$$h \leq 14\,t$$

h = max. ht. of reinf. concrete block shear wall, in.

t = minimum thickness of shear wall, in. Find this, then select next highest multiple of 2 in. nom.

Step 2. Design the wall's vertical reinforcing.

$$\frac{0.313 \, W_t}{\kappa_n \, \kappa_i \, t f_m \, [1 - (0.025 \, {}^h/_t)^3]} + \frac{2.65 \, h \, W_w}{t f_b \, A_s} \leq 1.00$$

W_t = total live and dead load on base of wall, pLF.
  W_t = unit live + dead loads on wall.
κ_n = net area factor. κ_n = 1.0 if wall is grouted, 0.45 if wall is hollow.
κ_i = inspection factor. κ_i = 1.0 for inspected work, 0.7 for uninspected work.
t = thickness of wall, in.
f_m = safe unit compression stress for masonry, psi
h = height of wall, in.
W_w = total lateral load against wall, pLF. W_w = unit wind or other lateral load resisted by wall × wind load width × wind load height ÷ wall length.
f_b = safe unit bending stress for rebars, psi.
A_s = section area of rebars, in²/LF. If A_s is too large (i.e. rebars are too big to fit into block cavities), try a thicker wall. If A_s is minus, try a thinner wall or install vertical rebars whose $A_s \geq 0.0020 \, t L$.

Step 3. Determine the size and spacing of vertical reinforcing. Select the smallest rebar area for a size and unit spacing that $\geq A_s$.

Step 4. Determine the size and spacing of horizontal reinforcing. If wire trusses are used, select the proper size and spacing from below:

Wall t, in. nom.	Type of wire truss, all 8 in. vert. o.c.
6	9 ga. truss, ladder, or tab
8, 10	$^3/_{16}$ in. truss, ladder, or tab
12, 14	$^3/_{16}$ in. trirod truss or ladder
16, 18, 20 ...	$^3/_{16}$ in. double rod truss or ladder

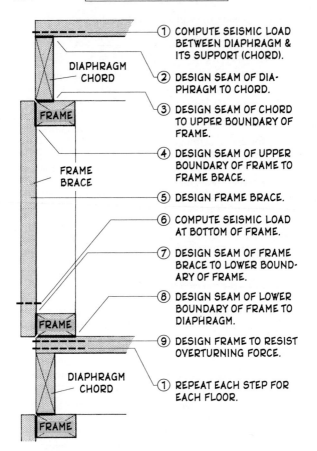

① COMPUTE SEISMIC LOAD BETWEEN DIAPHRAGM & ITS SUPPORT (CHORD).

DIAPHRAGM CHORD

② DESIGN SEAM OF DIA-PHRAGM TO CHORD.

③ DESIGN SEAM OF CHORD TO UPPER BOUNDARY OF FRAME.

FRAME

④ DESIGN SEAM OF UPPER BOUNDARY OF FRAME TO FRAME BRACE.

FRAME BRACE

⑤ DESIGN FRAME BRACE.

⑥ COMPUTE SEISMIC LOAD AT BOTTOM OF FRAME.

⑦ DESIGN SEAM OF FRAME BRACE TO LOWER BOUND-ARY OF FRAME.

⑧ DESIGN SEAM OF LOWER BOUNDARY OF FRAME TO DIAPHRAGM.

FRAME

⑨ DESIGN FRAME TO RESIST OVERTURNING FORCE.

① REPEAT EACH STEP FOR EACH FLOOR.

DIAPHRAGM CHORD

FRAME

Fig. 6-1. Seismic design sequence.

6. OTHER STRUCTURE

Aluminum: Common dimensions of aluminum structural members are:

▶ Angles (L) up to 8 × 8 × 1 in.
▶ I-beams (W and S shapes) up to 12 in. deep.
▶ I-beams and channels (C) up to 85 ft long.
▶ Sheets & plates up to 6 in. thick, 200 in. wide, and 45 ft long.

Structural aluminum design is analogous to structural steel design in many respects, excepting the conditions described below.

▶ An aluminum beam or column that experiences an excessive torsion load may quickly deform past its ability to return to its original shape; thus impact loads, oblique loads, web crippling, and large eccentric loads should be minimized and all lateral support should be maximized.
▶ When an aluminum beam subjected to combined compression and bending must support a large concentrated load, an excessive interaction occurs between web crippling and compressive buckling that requires the member to be designed according to

$$\left(\frac{\text{Applied moment}}{\text{Buckling moment}}\right)^{1.5} + \left(\frac{\text{Applied conc. load}}{\text{Web crippling load}}\right)^{1.5} \le 1.0$$

▸ When aluminum structure experiences numerous load cycles or heavy repeated loads, it fatigue-fails more readily than steel. Thus its design requires higher safety factors (1.8 for beam shear and bending, 2.0 for columns, and 1.5 for deflection); and members and connections should have a minimum number and size of notches, holes, and sharp re-entrant corners.

▸ Dimension tolerances of aluminum shapes, plates, and sheets vary more than those of steel.

▸ The coefficient of thermal expansion of aluminum is about twice that of steel.

Aluminum connections may be riveted, bolted, or welded. Aluminum rivets are usually driven cold by squeeze riveters; thus the rivet alloy should be slightly softer than the alloy of the connected pieces to minimize

TABLE 6-1: ALLOWABLE STRESSES FOR ALUMINUM

TYPE OF ALUMINUM SHAPE	Shear f_v	f_{vy}	Compression f_c	f_{cy}	Tension f_t	f_{ty}	Bending f_b	f_{by}
6001 shapes	11	20	17.5	35	35	38	31	56
6001 shts & pl.	11	20	17.5	35	35	42	32	58
6003 shapes	5	9	17	35	16	22	14.5	26
3003 shts & pl.	5.6	0	17	35	17	20	14	25
5456 shts & pl.	10.6	19	17	35	33	46	31	56
Rivets	10		17		17			

ALLOWABLE UNIT STRESSES, KSI [1,2]

1. Stresses without y are elastic stresses; stresses with y are yield stresses.
2. Aluminum's modulus of elasticity is 11,000,000 psi.

distortion around the connector. Rivet hole sizes should ≤ 1.04 rivet diameter, and minimum hole-to-edge distances ≥ 2 × rivet diameters. 7075 aluminum is the preferred alloy for aluminum bolts because it is stronger and more ductile than other alloys. Aluminum welds make superior joints and can be performed in the shop or field; but aluminum's high coefficient of thermal expansion requires fast weld cycles and other precautions to prevent distortion and buckling around the weld. Thus it is wise design to reduce allowable stresses for welded aluminum connections by 25 percent.

Fabric Structures: Fabric structures include awnings, canopies, tents, clearspans, bubbles, and sails. Here only sails are discussed further.

A sail fabric structure has three parts: its *membrane* (the fabric), *tensioning system* (the network of cables and related fittings that keep the membrane taut), and *tensile supports* (the anchors that hold the outer ends of the cables). Chief structural properties of fabrics are *grab tensile strength* (ability to resist a tensile force that is colinear with the total width of its surface), *strip tensile strength* (ability to resist a tension that is colinear with a small width of its surface), *trapezoidal tear strength* (ability to resist a racking stress that is colinear with its surface but not parallel to its warp or weft), and *tongue tear strength* (ability to resist a tensile force that acts in the direction of a colinear-surface force but oblique to its surface). An outline for designing fabric sail structures follows.

Step 1. Define the shape. Edges must be reinforced, and hooks and end fittings create stress concentrations where they meet the fabric. Also, an outdoor sail can collect a large area of rainfall and drain it in a very small area. Thus one's surface and downstream drainage should be mapped.

Step 2. Determine the loads, from interior fabric surface to cable vector. Remember that fabrics are easily damaged by winds and accumulations of snow.

Step 3. Select the fabric: this includes proper yarn, yarn size, yarn count, weave, waterproof coating, UV coating, dead load, roll width, seam construction, and light reflectivity. Interior sails should be fireproof, and light fixtures cannot be located near them.

Step 4. Select and size the fabric edge connections.

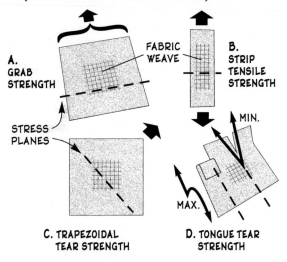

Fig. 6-2. Types of tear strengths in fabrics.

Each is considered in terms of function, strength, safety, weather resistance, constructability, cost, and aesthetics. Rotational freedom is often an important consideration. Large sails may require adjusting with cable turnbuckles and winches, which must be accessible.

Step 5.   Design the anchor. Examine every link in the chain of load transfer from cable connection to below the ground.

Step 6.   Draw and specify every connection in exact detail. A large percentage of sail fabric connection failures are caused by inexperienced contractors selecting what seems to be an "or equal" connector that is not at all what the designer intended.

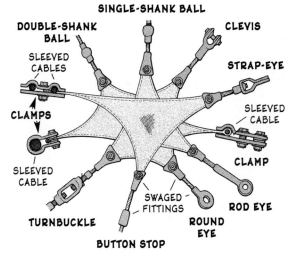

Fig. 6-3. Cable end fittings for fabric membranes.

Seismic Design: Regarding seismic design, a building's structure has three parts:

Frames: The building's vertical structure: columns, walls, and roofs exceeding 45°. Frames are categorized as *shear walls, braced frames, dual frames,* and *moment-resisting frames*; and dual and moment-resisting frames are rated as ordinary (OMRF), intermediate (IMRF), and special (SMRF), depending on the

---

TABLE 6-2: SEISMIC VALUES FOR BEARING WALL & BUILDING FRAME STRUCTURAL SYSTEMS

STRUCTURAL SYSTEM	R value	h limit	Z limit
BEARING WALL SYSTEMS			
w/ light steel tension-only bracing ...	4	65 ft	none
Light-framed walls w/ shear panels:			
Plywood walls to 3 floors high	8	65	none
All other light-framed walls	6	65	none
Shear walls: concrete or masonry ...	6	160	none
Braced frames for gravity loads:			
Steel	6	160	none
Concrete	4	—	< 0.30[1]
Heavy timber	4	65	none
BUILDING FRAME SYSTEMS			
Steel eccentrically braced frame	10	240	none
Light-framed shear walls:			
Plywood to 3 floors high	9	65	none
Other light-framed walls	7	65	none
Shear walls: concrete	8	240	none
Masonry	8	160	none
Steel concentrically braced frames ..	8	160	none
Concrete	8	—	< 0.30
Heavy timber	8	65	none

1. The term < 0.30 means this structural system is permitted only where seismic zone factors are less than 0.30.

added strength characteristics of their construction.

Diaphragms: The building frame's horizontal structure: floors and roofs up to 45°. Each diaphragm has a *skin* (its floor or roof surface) and *chords* (the structural members to which the skin is attached).

Seams: Meetings of diaphragms to frames. Most seismic structural failures occur at seams then radiate outward to cause progressive collapse of the building.

TABLE 6-3: SEISMIC VALUES FOR MOMENT RE-SISTING FRAMES & DUAL STRUCTURAL SYSTEMS

STRUCTURAL SYSTEM	R value	h limit	Z limit
MOMENT RESISTING (MR) FRAMES			
Special MR frames (SMRF):			
Steel or concrete	12	none	none
Intermed. MR frames (IMRF): conc. ...	8	—	< 0.30
Ordinary MR frames (OMRF): steel ...	6	160	none
Concrete	5	—	< 0.20[1]
DUAL SYSTEMS			
Shear walls: concrete w/ SMRF	12	none	none
Concrete w/ steel OMRF	6	160	none
Concrete w/ concrete IMRF	9	160	< 0.20
Masonry w/ SMRF	8	160	none
Masonry w/ steel OMRF	6	160	none
Masonry w/ concrete IMRF	7	—	< 0.20
Steel eccentrically braced frames:			
w/ steel SMRF	12	none	none
w/ steel OMRF	6	160	none
Concentrically braced frames:			
Steel w/ steel SMRF	10	none	none
Steel w/ steel OMRF	6	160	none
Concrete w/ concrete SMRF	9	—	< 0.30
Concrete w/ IMRF	6	—	< 0.30

1. The term < 0.30 means this structural system is permitted only where seismic zone factors are less than 0.20.

Step 1. Compute the seismic load of each structural unit (frame or diaphragm) in the architecture. In multi-story structures, these calculations must be made for every frame and diaphragm of every story, then the sum of all upper-story loads supported by each structural unit is added to each story load below.

Diaphragm 1 (roof): $P_{SG} = U + A\,(\omega_D + 0.25\,\omega_L + \omega_S)$

P_{SG} = total effective seismic gravity load of structural unit (frame or diaphragm), lb

U = sum of any upper-story seismic loads supported by structural unit, lb

A = surface area of structural unit, sf

ω_D = unit dead load of structural unit, psf

ω_L = unit live load on structural unit, psf

ω_S = unit snow load on structural unit, if $\geq$ 30 psf.

Frame 1a. (upper story, north-south walls):
$$P_{SG} = U + A\,(\omega_D + 0.25\,\omega_L + \omega_S)$$

P_{SG} = total effective seismic gravity load of structural unit (frame or diaphragm), lb

A = surface area of structural unit, sf

ω_D = unit dead load of structural unit, psf

ω_L = unit live load on structural unit, psf

U and ω_S are as previously defined

Frame 1b. (upper story, east-west walls):
$$P_{SG} = U + A\,(\omega_D + 0.25\,\omega_L + \omega_S)$$

P_{SG} = total effective seismic gravity load on structural unit, lb

A = surface area of structural unit, sf

ω_D = unit dead load of structural unit, psf

ω_L = unit live load on structural unit, psf

U and ω_S are as previously defined

Step 2. Find the value of the seismic subsoil factor.

$$\kappa_C = 1.14 \, \kappa_S^{0.6}/h^{0.3} \leq 2.75$$

κ_C = seismic numerical coefficient. If it is impractical
   to evaluate a building's period of vibration or
   site subsoil conditions, use κ_C = 2.75.

κ_S = site subsoil vibration coefficient. κ_S = 1.0 for
   dense, stiff, or rock-like soil; 1.2 for dense or
   stiff soil to 200 ft depth; 1.5 for unknown soil or
   soft to medium clay to 40 ft depth; and 2.0 for
   soft clay to below 40 ft depth.

h = height of building, ft.

Step 3. Compute the building's seismic load factor. If
the structure is uniform throughout, this value may be
used for every building frame and diaphragm. Otherwise, compute a separate κ_V for each structure.

$$\kappa_V R = Z \kappa_I \kappa_C$$

κ_V = seismic load factor of building frame

R = seismic resistance of building frame. Resilient
   ductile frames have high R values.

Z = seismic zone factor, from Fig. 6-4.

κ_I = building importance factor, from schedule below:

Building type	κ_i
Hospitals, fire & police stations, emergency vehicle garages, power facilities, communication centers, hazardous facilities	1.25
All other buildings	1.00

κ_C = seismic numerical coefficient, from Step 2

Step 4. Compute the seismic seam load between the bottom of the diaphragm and the frame below (seam ① in
Fig. 6-1). The formula below assumes uniform con-

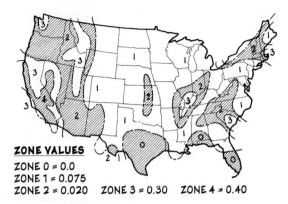

ZONE VALUES
ZONE 0 = 0.0
ZONE 1 = 0.075
ZONE 2 = 0.020   ZONE 3 = 0.30   ZONE 4 = 0.40

Fig. 6-4. Seismic zone map.

struction along the seam. Otherwise, find these loads by
Σ moments from the weights and moment arms of the different constructions along the seam.

$$\underline{S} = U + 0.5 \, \kappa_V \, P_{SG} + 0.5 \, h_f \kappa_V \, P_{SG}$$

$\underline{S}$ = seismic load at seam of diaphragm to frame, lb
U = sum of any upper-story seismic loads supported
by diaphragm or frame, lb
h_f = height of total building frame, ft
κ_V and P_{SG} are as previously defined

Step 5. Compare seismic seam load $\underline{S}$ with the loads
used in structural design. If conditions **a** and **b** below
exist, further seismic analysis is unnecessary, as $\underline{S}$ is
less than the loads for which the structure is designed.

a. Total live + dead load $\geq$ seismic load $\times$ 0.5 $\kappa_V \, P_{SG}$
b. Total wind load $\geq$ diaphragm shear load $\times$ 0.5 $h_f \kappa_V \, P_{SG}$

Step 6. Design the connection of the base of the diaphragm skin to the top of its chord (seam ② in Fig. 6-1). If the diaphragm is plywood sheathing on wood framing, find the required nail size, framing width, and boundary nail spacing from Table 6-4; or consider a glued-and-screwed connection using PL400 (bonding strength ≈ 230 psi of glued surface).

$$\underline{S} = \omega_s L$$

$\underline{S}$ = seismic seam load at meeting of diaphragm skin to top of diaphragm chord, lb

ω_s = unit seismic seam load at seam, plf

L = length of seismic seam, ft

Step 7. Design the connection at the seam of the diaphragm chord to the frame below (seam ③ in Fig. 6-1).

$$\omega_s S = 12 V$$

ω_s = unit seismic seam load at meeting of diaphragm chord to top of frame below, plf. Normally this equals ω_s from Step 6.

S = minimum spacing of connectors, in. o.c.

V = safe lateral strength of each connector at meeting of diaphragm to frame, lb

TABLE 6-4: DIAPHRAGM SHEAR LOADS, PLYWOOD						
STRUCTURAL SYSTEM	Common nail size	Min. nom. framing width, in.	MIN. STRESS, LB/LF, at boundary spcg. in. o.c.			
			8	6	4	3
(All data for this	6d	2	170	220	290	380
table is for min.		3	190	245	330	420
$^{15}/_{32}$ in. Douglas	8d	2	210	270	360	465
fir, Southern		3	240	305	405	525
pine or equal	10d	2	250	320	425	550
sheathing)		3	280	360	480	620

Step 8. Design the connection of the top of the frame to the frame brace (seam ④ in Fig. 6-1). If this is plywood sheathing nailed to a stud wall's top plate, its minimum nail spacing is described below. These values are for common nails hammered into $^{15}/_{32}$ in. or thicker sheathing on Douglas fir or Southern pine framing.

	Min. stress (pLF) per nail spacing			
COMMON NAIL SIZE	8 in. o.c.	6 in. o.c.	4 in. o.c.	3 in. o.c.
8d	220	280	430	550
10d	260	340	510	665

Step 9. Design the frame brace (seam ⑤ in Fig. 6-1). If this is plywood sheathing nailed to wall studs, the studs at 16 in. o.c. provide 32 LF of sheathing/framing connectivity; 8d nails 8 in. o.c. may be used to nail such sheathing to framing. Other frame braces may require detailed design, examples being reinforced concrete floors to columns and bearing walls of materials requiring steel tension bracing.

Step 10. Find the seismic load at the frame's base (seam ⑥ in Fig. 6-1) from

$$\underline{S} = U + \kappa_V P_{SG} + 0.5\, h_f\, \kappa_V\, P_{SG}$$

$\underline{S}$ = seismic seam load at base of frame, lb
U = sum of any upper-story seismic loads supported by diaphragm or frame, lb
h_f, κ_V, and P_{SG} are as previously defined

Step 11. Design the connection of the frame brace to the lower boundary of the frame (seam ⑦ in Fig. 6-1).

$$\underline{S} = \omega_s L$$

$\underline{S}$ = total seismic seam load at seam of frame brace to

lower boundary of frame, lb
ω_s = unit seismic seam load at seam, PLF
L = length of seismic seam, ft

Step 12. Design the connection of the bottom of the frame to the diaphragm below (seam ⑧ in Fig. 6-1)

$$\underline{S} = P_s \, \eta$$

$\underline{S}$ = total seismic seam load at meeting of bottom of frame to top of diaphragm below, lb
P_s = seismic shear load resisted by each connector, lb
η = number of connectors in seam

Step 13. Design the frame to resist overturning (seam ⑨ in Fig. 6-1). If any wall frame interbracing exists at any corners, each wall is adequately braced against overturning, assuming the corner boundary nailing is the same as at the top. If the frames are narrow due to wide openings, compute the pier rigidity of each frame as described on page 34. If the frame is unbraced against seismic shear loads for a length greater than 4 × its height, or if it includes unbraced walls or columns, or if the building is taller than wide, the frame must be designed to resist an overturning force as described on page 36.

Step 14. Compute the seismic seam load between the floor diaphragm and the frame below. If the floor is a concrete slab on a foundation wall, do as follows:

1. Compute the seismic seam load between the edge of the floor slab and the top of the wall according to Step 4 above.
2. Design the connection of the slab's anchor bolts to the top of the wall as in Step 7 above.

If the floor is wood framing over a crawl space:

1. Compute the seismic seam load between this diaphragm's boundary and its supports as in Step 4.
2. Design the connection of the diaphragm skin to the upper boundary of the diaphragm chord (floor sheathing to perimeter joists/blocking) as in Step 6 above.
3. Design the connection of the lower boundary of the diaphragm chord to the upper boundary of the structure below (joists to mudsills or pier caps) as in Step 7 above.
4. Design the connection of the lower boundary of the frame chord to the structure below (anchor bolts to foundation wall or piers) as in Step 7.

If the floor is an upper level, return to Step 4 and repeat each subsequent step for each floor to ground level. This sequence is shown schematically in Fig. 6-1. If seismic loads are not driven up by high Z, I, and C values in Step 3, structural or wind loads may be higher; then further seismic calculations are unnecessary. All this work is often simplified by using structural calculation data.

Seismic Anchorage of Mechanical Systems:

When earthquakes tremble, machinery inside buildings can be torn from their moorings and set into motion with the force of projectiles. Thus such componentry should be anchored by more than what is normally required for quiet-mode scenarios.

Step 1. Find the component's horizontal shear force due to an earthquake tremor from the following:

$$F_h = 0.4 \ W_m$$

F_h = estimated horizontal shear force of mechanical component due to seismic load, lb

W_m = operating weight of mechanical component, lb

Step 2. Size the component's base anchors to resist F_h. For floor-mounted units the connector is typically an anchor bolt that is sized as described on page 251.

Step 3. Find the component's vertical uplift force due to an earthquake tremor. If the component hangs from the ceiling, F_v is a downward force that is also added to the ceiling structure's normal design load.

$$F_v = 0.132\ W_m$$

F_v = vertical uplift force of mechanical component due to seismic load, lb
W_m = operating weight of mechanical component, lb

Step 4. If the component is floor-mounted, find its tension force due to overturning due to earthquake forces.

$$h\ F_h = b\ F_o$$

h = ht. of component from base to center of mass, ft
F_h = horiz. shear load of component due to seismic load, from Step 1, lb
b = average breadth or width (short side) of mechanical component, ft
F_o = tension force due to overturning seismic load, lb

Step 5. Size the mechanical component base anchors to resist the total uplift or downlift force caused by the tremor according to the following formulas:

    a. Floor-mounted: $F_{u-d} = F_v + F_o$
    b. Ceiling-mounted: $F_{u-d} = W_m + F_v$

All terms are as previously defined.

TABLE 7-1: R-VALUES OF BUILDING MATERIALS

MATERIAL	Thermal resistance, R per in. t
Fiberglass batts, 3.5; mineral wool loose fill	3.3
Styrofoam boards, 5.0; urethane or isocyanate bds	6.5
Vermiculite loose fill, 2.1; roof deck slabs	2.6
Reflective surface on batts or boards	+2.0
Mineral fiberboard, acoustic tile, perlite	2.7
Oak, maple, other hardwoods	0.9
Plywood, fir, pine, other softwoods	1.3
Granite, marble, other hard stones	0.06
Soft stones, sand, clay tile, conc. block, face brick	0.11
Gypsum, plaster, stucco, cement, common brick	0.20
Built-up roofing on plywood sheathing	1.5
Siding, shingles, 0.9; w/ insulated backing	+0.5
Uninsulated roofs and walls	≈ 3
Glazing: single pane	1.7/unit
Above w/ storm window	2.8/unit
Thermopane, $3/16$ in. airspace, 1.3; $1/2$ in. airspace	1.6
Insect screens over openable glazing	+1.5
Doors: wood solid-core, 1 in. thick, 1.6; $1\frac{1}{2}$ in. thick	2.0
$1\frac{3}{4}$ in. steel door w/ mineral fiber core	1.7
Above w/ urethane core	2.5
Any door w/ metal storm door, +1.1; wood stm dr	+1.7
Floors: $1/8$ in. asphalt or linoleum tile	0.05
1 in. ceramic tile or terrazzo floor	0.08
Cork tile floor, 0.3; $3/4$ in. hardwood floor	0.7
Concrete, 4 in. on 4 in. gravel, no insul. below	0.6
Concrete floor w/ 2 in. styrofoam below	11
Concrete floor w/ 4 in. styrofoam below	21
Carpet: synthetic, $1/4$ in. thick	1.0
Each added $1/4$ in. thickness	+0.4
Above carpets w/ $1/4$ in. underlayment	+0.7
Above carpets w/ $1/2$ in. underlyment	+1.5
Above carpets if wool ... multiply above values × 1.5	
Airspaces, $3/4$–4 in., vert. or horiz. heat flow up	0.8
Above w/ horizontal heat flow down	1.1

7. CLIMATE CONTROL

Air Density vs. Pressure (in. Hg):

$$D(459.7 + F) = 1.325\,\kappa_e\,B$$

Air Density vs. Pressure (psi):

$$D(459.7 + F) = 2.697\,P$$

D = density of air, pcf. Air at sea level at 68° and 760 mm pressure has a density of 0.073 pcf.

F = temperature of air, °F

κ_e = elevation coefficient, based on elevation above sea level, from bar graph below:

Elevation above sea level

1.00	0.962	0.925	0.890	0.856	0.824	0.793	0.763	0.734	0.705	0.677
0	1,000	2,000	3,000	4,000	5,000	6,000	7,000	8,000	9,000	10,000

κ_e = elevation coefficient

B = effective barometric pressure, in. Hg. If B is air's actual pressure (in. Hg.), disregard air's elevation above sea level, then $\kappa_E = 1.00$.

P = Actual air pressure, psi.

Solar Altitude: $\angle = \kappa_a - L$

∠ = solar altitude: vertical angle of sun above horizon at noon due south on 21st day of month, °

κ_a = solar altitude coefficient. κ_a = 66.5° for Dec 21, 69.5° for Nov & Jan 21, 78.5° for Oct & Feb 21, 90° for Sep & Mar 21, 101.5° for Aug & Apr 21, 110.5° for Jul & May 21, and 113.5° for Jun 21.

L = local latitude; round off to nearest half degree

Solar Azimuth: $H = S \tan \angle$

H = height of object casting the sun's shadow, ft
S = length of cast shadow, horizontal projection, ft
∠ = solar altitude: vertical angle of sun above horiz., °

Solar Trajectory or Sunpath Formulas:

Altitude of sunpath: $\sin \angle_v = \sin L \sin [23.5 \sin 0.98 (D - 81)] - \cos L \cos (15T) \cos [23.5 \sin 0.98 (D - 81)]$

Azimuth of sunpath:

$$\tan \angle_h = \frac{\sin (15\, T) \cos [23.5 \sin 0.98 (D - 81)]}{[23.5 \sin 0.98 (D - 81)] + \sin L \cos (15\, T) \cos [23.5 \sin 0.98 (D - 81)]}$$

$\angle_v$ = solar altitude: vertical angle of sun above horizon, °. At sunrise or sunset, $\angle_v = 0°$.

$\angle_h$ = solar azimuth: horiz. angle of sun from due south, °. Negative values indicate $\angle_h$ is east of south; positive values indicate $\angle_h$ is west of south.

L = latitude of site, °

D = day of year: number of day in year, as below:

Jan 1: 1	Feb 1: 32	Mar 1: 60	Apr 1: 91
May 1: 121	Jun 1: 152	Jul 1: 182	Aug 1: 213
Sep 1: 244	Oct 1: 274	Nov 1: 305	Dec 1: 335

T = time of day, decimal hr. At noon, T = 12.0.

Sun's Angle of Incidence on a Surface:

$$\sin \angle_A = \sin \angle_H \cos \angle_S + \cos \angle_H \sin \angle_S \cos (\angle_D + \angle_F)$$

$\angle_A$ = angle between incident sunrays and surface, °
$\angle_H$ = vertical angle of sun above horizon, °
$\angle_S$ = slope of planar surface to horizontal, °
$\angle_D$ = solar azimuth: angle of sun from due south, °
$\angle_F$ = orientation of planar surface from due south, °

Overhang Design: $H \cos \angle_a = L \tan \angle_v$

H = height of overhang's shadow on facade, measured down from lowest tip of overhang, in.
$\angle_a$ = angular difference between facade orientation and solar azimuth, °
L = horizontal length of overhang, in.
$\angle_v$ = vertical angle of sun above horizon, °

Hydrostatic Head: $P = A H$

P = total pressure against underside of const., lb
A = area of underside of construction, sf
H = hydrostatic head, psf

Channel Flow (Hydraulic Radius) Formulas:

Pipe flowing half full .... $R_h = 0.5\ r$
Pipe flowing full .... $R_h = 0.5\ r$
Box channel flowing full .... $R_h = b\ d/(b + 2\ d)$
Half-hex channel flowing full ... $R_h = 0.43\ r$
Any circular section .... $R_h = A/P_w$
Maximum waterflow in any
open channel section .... $508\ \kappa_R\ Q = \Delta^{0.5} \left(\dfrac{A^{1.67}}{P_w^{\ 0.67}} \right)$

r = radius of circular section, in.
b = width of box channel or rectangular section, in.
d = depth of box channel or rectangular section, in.
A = section area of channel waterflow, in²
P_w = wetted perimeter of channel waterflow, in.
κ_R = roughness coefficient of channel's inner surface, from Table 7-2.
Q = volume of waterflow, cfm
Δ = average slope of channel from inlet to outlet, vert. ft/horiz. ft. Δ should ≤ about 11° (2.33:12 pitch).

Gutter Design:

Ogee section .... $WR = 800\,\eta\,\kappa_\Delta\,w^{2.67}$
Half-round section .... $WR = 390\,\eta\,\kappa_\Delta\,\delta^{2.67}$
Rect. section .. $WR = 2,500\,\eta\,\kappa_\Delta\,(w\,d)^{1.67}\,(w+2\,d)^{-0.67}$
Any section .... $WR = 2,500\,\eta\,\kappa_\Delta\,(A)^{1.67}\,(P_w)^{-0.67}$

W = watershed area of roof drained by each gutter,

TABLE 7-2: CONDUIT ROUGHNESS COEFFICIENTS

PIPE OR CHANNEL SURFACE	Roughness coeff., κR
Sheet steel, alum., galv. metal piping or ducting	0.009
Copper, steel, neat cement, smooth plastic pipe	0.010
Finished concrete, planed wood, cast iron	0.012
Vitrified sewer, riveted steel, unplaned wood pipe	0.013
Unfinished concrete, poorly jointed conc. pipe	0.015
Smooth brick	0.016
Rough brick, tuberc'd iron pipe, smooth stone	0.017
Smooth earth, firm gravel	0.020
Rough earth, rubble	0.025
Laid untamped gravel	0.028
Muddy ditches, riverbeds w/ some stones & weeds	0.030
Earth with loose stones or weeds	0.035
Ditches & riverbeds w/ rough bottoms & thick veg.	0.040

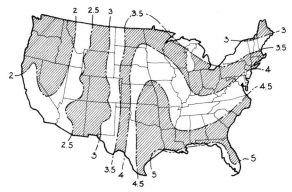

Fig. 7-1. Rainfall intensity map.

sf. *W* = horizontal area + 0.5 vertically projected area if roof slopes + 0.5 area of any facade above roof that drains into gutter.

R = maximum rainfall intensity, based on 50-year-frequency storm from Fig. 7-1, in/hr

η = number of leaders each gutter drains into

$κ_Δ$ = gutter drain slope coefficient based on pitch, from bar graph below:

Roof, footing drain, or storm drain slope or pitch, in/LF

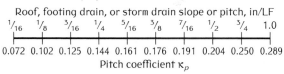

$^1/_{16}$	$^1/_8$	$^3/_{16}$	$^1/_4$	$^5/_{16}$	$^3/_8$	$^7/_{16}$	$^1/_2$	$^3/_4$	1.0
0.072	0.102	0.125	0.144	0.161	0.176	0.191	0.204	0.250	0.289

Pitch coefficient $κ_p$

w = min. top width of gutter if ogee or rect. section, in.

δ = min. diameter of gutter if half-round section, in.

d = minimum depth of gutter if rect. section, in.

A = section area of gutter if any section, in²

P_w = wetted perimeter of gutter if any section, in.

Vertical Gutter Leader Design:

Round sections: $\qquad$ $W R \approx 304 \, \delta^{2.67}$
Rectangular sections: $W R \approx 420 \, (w \, d)^{1.33}$

W = watershed area of roof drained by each leader, sf. W = horiz. area + 0.5 vert. area if roof slopes + 0.5 area of any facade that drains onto it.
R = maximum rainfall intensity, from Fig. 7-1, in/hr
δ = minimum diameter of round leader section, in.
w = width of rectangular section, in. $w \geq 2$ in.
d = depth of rectangular section, in. $d \geq 2$ in.

Sloping Leader Design: $\quad A_p \approx A_v \, (1 + \cos^2 \angle)$

A_p = required section area of nonvertical leader, in^2
A_v = section area of vertical leader, in^2
$\angle$ = angle from horizontal of leader, °

Foundation Drain Design: $\quad 5.6 \, n \, Q = \kappa_\Delta \, \delta^{2.67}$

n = surface roughness coeff. of drain, from Table 7-2
Q = water discharge rate into drain, gpm
κ_Δ = footing drain slope coefficient, depending on pitch, from bar graph on page 305
δ = minimum diameter of drain, in.

Storm Drain Design Formulas:

One watershed surface: $n \, (R \, W + 3.9 \, F) = 11.7 \, \kappa_\Delta \, \delta^{2.67}$
More than one watershed surface:

$$n \, (R \, W_1 \, \kappa_{P1} + R \, W_2 \, \kappa_{P2} + \cdots + R \, W_z \, \kappa_{Pz} + 3.9 \, F) = 11.7 \, \kappa_\Delta \, \delta^{2.67}$$

n = roughness coefficient of conduit, from Table 7-2
R = maximum rainfall intensity, from Fig. 7-1, in/hr.

W = watershed area drained by each surface, horiz. sf
κ_P = permeability factor (ground runoff coefficient)
for each surface drained, from data below:

Ground Surface	Runoff coefficient, κ_R
Forests	0.05–0.15
Saplings, orchards, chaparral	0.10–0.20
Gardens, lawns, meadows, ground cover	0.10–0.25
Gravel roads & walks	0.25–0.60
Loose block pavements, uncemented jts	0.40–0.50
Stone & brick pavements, uncemented jts	0.50–0.70
w/ tightly cemented joints	0.75–0.85
Asphalt & conc. pavements in good cond.	0.85–0.90
Watertight roof surfaces	0.95–1.00

F = no. of fixture units, if any, draining into conduit
κ_Δ = conduit slope coefficient depending on its slope
or pitch, from bar graph on p. 305
δ = minimum diameter of conduit, in.

Drywell Design: $W R \approx 188\, \delta\, h\, P$

W = horizontal area drained by drywell, sf
R = maximum rainfall intensity, from Fig. 7-1, in/hr.
δ = diameter of drywell, from inner faces of wall, ft
h = minimum height of drywell, from local frost depth
down to underside of base, in.
P = perc test result of adjacent soil, 4 min/in. drop.

Thermal Expansion Joint Design:

Step 1. Compute the maximum length of construction
allowed between each pair of expansion joints.

$$\Delta_e = 12\, \kappa_t\, E\, (\Delta t + 8)$$

Δ_e = maximum length of increase in expansion joint, in.
κ_t = coefficient of thermal expansion for construction

btwn two expansion joints, from Table 7-3, in/in.
E = maximum length of construction between joints, ft
Δt = max. temp. differential ($t_{max} - t_{min}$) of const., °F.

Step 2. Find the required number of expansion joints.

$$\eta = |(L/E) + \kappa_e + 1|$$

η = total number of req. expansion joints in const.
L = total length of construction, ft
E = maximum length of construction between joints, ft
κ_e = end factor. $\kappa_e = 0$ if construction containing
expansion joints abutts no construction at either
end, 1 if it abutts construction at one end, and 2
if it abutts construction at both ends.

TABLE 7-3: THERMAL EXPANSION COEFFICIENTS

MATERIAL		Rate of expansion, in×10⁻⁶/in°F.	
Ashlar masonry	3.5	Concrete masonry	6.7
Concrete	7.9	Limestone	3.8
Granite, common glass	4.7	Plate glass	5.1
Marble; slate	5.7	Sandstone	4.4
Tile, clay. brick	3.2	Plaster	9.2
Aluminum	12.8	Brass	10.4
Bronze	10.1	Copper	9.8
Iron, cast	5.9	Iron, wrought	6.7
Steel, structural	6.7	Steel, stainless	9.6
Lead	15.7	Zinc, rolled	17.3
Acrylics plastic	45.0	ABS plastic	60.0
Polybutylene (PB)	72.0	PVC plastic	30.0

WOODS	Exp. ⊥ grain	Exp. ‖ grain
Fir	0.000,002.1	0.000,032.0
Maple	0.000,003.6	0.000,027.0
Oak	0.000,002.7	0.000,030.0
Pine	0.000,003.0	0.000,019.0
Plywood	0.000,003.4	0.000,003.4

Heat Flow: There are four heat flows in a building:

1. **Conduction:** heat migrating through the building envelope's solid construction and insulation.
2. **Infiltration:** convection of heat via air through seams and openings in the building envelope.
3. **Auxiliary heat gain:** radiation within interior spaces via occupants' metabolism and Btus emitted from lights and machines.
4. **Solar heat gain:** sunshine arriving through glazing in the building envelope.

A comfortable indoor environment has a temperature between about 67° F in winter and 77° F in summer. The amount of heat flowing outdoors during the average coldest part of winter (winter design temperature) is a building interior's *design heating load*, while the amount of heat flowing indoors during the average warmest part of summer (summer design temperature) is its *design cooling load*. Design heating and cooling loads are used to size heating and cooling systems, while *energy audit* heating and cooling loads are used to estimate the energy cost of a proposed system or to compare systems.

Conduction-Infiltration Design Heating Load:

Step 1. Find the thermal resistance of each surface area of the building envelope construction as follows:

a. **Envelope has one construction type & no unheated voids:**
$$R = R_c + R_i t$$

b. **Envelope is more than one construction type:**
$$A R = A_1 (R_{c1} + R_{i1} t_1) + \ldots + A_Z (R_{cZ} + R_{iZ} t_Z)$$

TABLE 7-4: WINDCHILL EXPOSURE FACTORS

ENVELOPE IS:	Exposure factor: Exterior walls	Roofs
Well-shielded: solid windscreen around whole surface	1.0	1.03
Mostly shielded: few openings in surrounding windscreen	1.05	1.10
Partly shielded: ± 50% gaps in surrounding windscreen	1.10	1.15
Mostly exposed: little protection from direct or diagonal winds	1.15	1.30
Highly exposed: facade or roof on exposed hill; or upper part of tall building	1.30	1.60

TABLE 7-5: PERIMETER HEAT FLOW FRACTIONS

CONSTRUCTION	P per envelope surface
Masonry wall, rigid insul. one side or btwn withes ..	0.95
Concrete block wall, cavities filled w/ loose insul...	0.68
Curtain walls: glazing, 1.20; spandrels	0.77
Wood stud walls w/ batts in cavities	0.77
Above w/ rigid insul. outside	0.83
Metal stud wall w/ batts in cavities	0.80
Above w/ rigid insul. outside	0.87
Stud wall w/ much glass or doors	0.30
Wood or metal frame roof, batts in cavities	0.86
Above w/ rigid insul. on top	0.89
Concrete roof w/ rigid insulation on top	0.93
Roof insul. w/ large skylight, flue, or hatch area ...	0.42
Wood frame floor above crawlspace	0.83
Concrete floor slab, rigid insulation under & around edges	0.93
Large windows, 1.10; large doors (i.e. garage drs)	1.05
Wood frame construction w/ no insulation	1.00

c.   **An unheated void is between occupied indoor spaces & outdoors:**

$$R = R_c + R_i\, t + R_o$$

R = total thermal resistance of building envelope

$R_{c1, c2, c3... cZ}$ = unit R-value of each uninsulated envelope construction, per in. t, from Table 7-1

$R_{i1, i2, i3... iZ}$ = unit R-value of each envelope insulation, if any, per in. t, from Table 7-1

$t_{1, 2, 3... Z}$ = thickness of each envelope insulation, in.

A = surface area of total envelope construction, sf.

$A_{1, 2, 3... Z}$ = surface area of each envelope construction if more than one, sf

R_o = R-value of second part of envelope if unheated void is between indoors and outdoors.

Step 2. Find the temperature at the outer surface of the building envelope:

a.   **Envelope is above finished grade:**
$$T_o \approx 65 - \kappa_w (65 - T_d)$$

b.   **Envel. is a wall below fin. grade down to 20 ft:**
$$T_o \approx T_a - \kappa_d\, T_o\, (T_a - T_d) \approx 65 - \kappa_w (65 - T_d)$$

c.   **Envelope is a floor area within 20 ft of fin. grade measured down wall and in under floor:**
$$T_o \approx T_a - \kappa_{ad} (T_a - T_d)$$

d.   **Envel. is a wall or floor more than 20 ft below fin. grade measured down and in from ground:**
$$T_o \approx T_a$$

e.   **Envelope is floor area above an unfinished basement or crawlspace:**
$$T_o \approx T_i + 9 - \kappa_w (T_i - T_d)$$

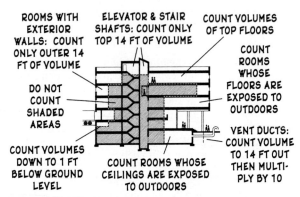

ROOMS WITH EXTERIOR WALLS: COUNT ONLY OUTER 14 FT OF VOLUME

ELEVATOR & STAIR SHAFTS: COUNT ONLY TOP 14 FT OF VOLUME

COUNT VOLUMES OF TOP FLOORS

COUNT ROOMS WHOSE FLOORS ARE EXPOSED TO OUTDOORS

DO NOT COUNT SHADED AREAS

COUNT VOLUMES DOWN TO 1 FT BELOW GROUND LEVEL

COUNT ROOMS WHOSE CEILINGS ARE EXPOSED TO OUTDOORS

VENT DUCTS: COUNT VOLUME TO 14 FT OUT THEN MULTIPLY BY 10

Fig. 7-2. Building interior air changes per hour.

TABLE 7-6: BUILDING INTERIOR AIR CHANGES/HR

TYPE OF SPACE*	Single glass or no weatherstrip	Storm sash or weatherstrip
No windows or exterior doors	0.7	—
One room surface exp'd to outdoors	1.2	0.8
2 room surfaces " " "	1.6	1.1
3 room surfaces " " "	1.9	1.3
Entrance halls	2.0	1.4
Rooms having ceilings & outer walls w/ plaster (not sheetrock) interior finish, stucco exterior finish, or vapor barrier .... mult. above amount × 0.4		
Rooms having exterior walls w/ all seams & utility penetrations sealed .... mult. above amount × 0.7		
Fireplace w/ loose damper .... add 2,500 ft³/V " " "		
w/ tight damper or glass drs ... add 1,000 ft³/V " " "		
Woodstove in non-airtight envel. add 1,500 ft³/V " " "		
in airtight envelope .... add 300 ft³/V " " "		

* Do not count shaded interior volumes in Fig. 7-2.

T_o = effective air temp. at outer surface of envelope, °F

κ_w = windchill exposure factor, from Table 7-4

T_d = winter design temperature, from Fig. 7-4, °F

T_a = average annual temp. of local area, from Fig. 7-3

κ_d = depth coeff., based on max. depth of soil (ft) at bottom of envelope surface, from bar graph below:

Maximum depth of soil at bottom of envelope, ft

0	2	4	6	8	10	12	14	16	18	20
1.00	0.75	0.57	0.45	0.35	0.27	0.20	0.16	0.11	0.06	0.00

κ_d = depth coefficient

κ_{ad} = depth coeff., based on average depth of soil d (ft) at bottom edge of envelope. Find maximum depth of soil d (ft) at bottom of envelope surface, then enter 0.5 d in bar graph above to find κ_{ad}.

T_i = ambient indoor temperature, °F.

Step 3. Compute the design heating load through the building envelope.

$$\mathbf{H}_{ci} = (A/R\,P + 0.018\,V\,\eta)\,(T_i - T_o)$$

$\mathbf{H}_{ci}$ = design heating load due to conduction-infiltration through area of envelope construction during cold weather, Btu/hr

A = surface area of envelope construction, sf

R = thermal resistance of building envelope, per in. t, from Table 7-1 or other data

P = perimeter heat flow fraction, from Table 7-5

V = volume of interior space(s) behind building envelope, as shown in Fig. 7-2, cf

η = no. airchanges/hr for room behind envelope. η = 0.022 $(T_i - T_o)$ × no. airchanges/hr from Table 7-6.

T_i = ambient indoor air temp. (thermostat setting, °F

T_o = effective air temperature at outer surface of envelope, °F

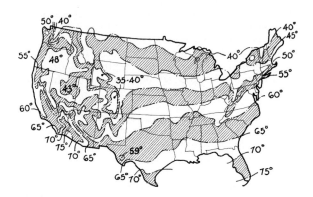

Fig. 7-3. Average annual temperature map.

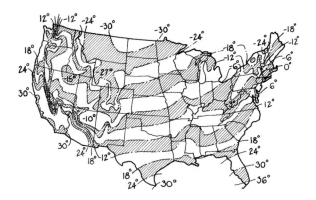

Fig. 7-4. Winter design temperature map.

Conduction-Infiltration Design Cooling Load:

Step 1. Find the average total thermal resistance of each part of the envelope construction, as follows:

a. **Envelope has one const. & no unheated voids:**

$$R = R_c + R_i t$$

b. **Envelope has more than one construction type:**

$$A R = A_1 (R_{c\,1} + R_1 t_1) + \ldots + A_z (R_{cz} + R_z t_z)$$

c. **An unheated void (attic, garage, etc.) is between indoors and outdoors:**

$$R = R_c + R_i t + R_o$$

R = total thermal resistance of envelope construction

$R_{c1,\,c2,\,c3\ldots\,cz}$ = unit R-value of each uninsulated envelope construction, per in. t, from Table 7-1

$R_{i1,\,i2,\,i3\ldots\,iz}$ = R-value of each envel. insulation, if any

$t_{1,\,2,\,3\ldots\,z}$ = thickness of each envel. insul. if any, in.

A = surface area of total envelope construction, sf. Ignore areas more than 1 ft below finished grade.

$A_{1,\,2,\,3\ldots\,z}$ = surface area of each envel. construction, sf

R_o = R-value of outer part of envelope construction if an unheated void is between indoors and outdoors, per in. t, from Table 7-1

Step 2. Find the temperature at the outer surface of the building envelope:

a. **Envelope surface is above grade and exposed to sunlight at least 2 hours daily:**

$$T_o \approx T_d - \kappa_{lo} + \kappa_u\,\kappa_i\,\kappa_c\,[^{1,200}/(6\,R + \omega)]$$

b. **Envelope surface is above grade and receives little sunlight daily (if grade is sloping, use average height of exposure):**

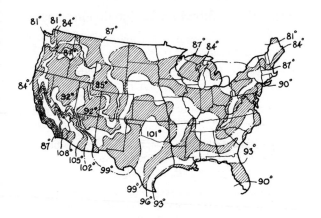

Fig. 7-5. Summer design temperature map.

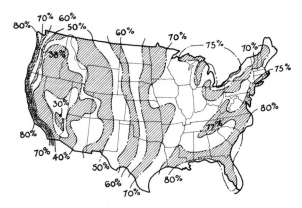

Fig. 7-6. Summer design humidity map.

$$T_o \approx T_d$$

c. Envelope surface is a wall below finished grade down to 20 ft below grade:

$$T_o \approx T_a + \kappa_d (T_d - T_a)$$

d. Envelope surface is a floor area within 20 ft of finished grade measured from ground level down the wall and in under the floor:

$$T_o \approx T_a + \kappa_{ad} (T_d - T_a)$$

e. Envelope surface is a wall or floor area more than 20 ft below finished grade measured down and in from ground level:

$$T_o \approx T_a$$

f. Envelope surface is a floor area above an unfinished basement or crawlspace:

$$T_o \approx T_i - 9 + \frac{(T_d - T_i)}{\kappa_w}$$

T_o = effective air temp. at outer surface of envelope, °F

T_d = summer design temperature, from Fig. 7-5, °F.

κ_{lo} = latitude-orientation factor (°F): adjustment of design temperature for latitude and orientation of site. Interpolate for intermediate values.

LAT,°N.	S	SE/SW	E/W	NE/NW	N	Horiz.
24	-6	3	0	2	1	1
32	3	1	0	1	1	1
40	1	0	0	2	1	1
48	4	3	1	0	0	0

κ_u = umbra fraction: portion of envelope that is unshaded during day. $\kappa_u = 1.0$ if unshaded all day; 0 if shaded all day. Interpolate for interm. values.

κ_i = bldg. envelope incidence factor, if envelope faces other than vertical or due south, from Fig. 7-8

κ_c = color coefficient. $\kappa_c = 1.0$ if envelope exterior is

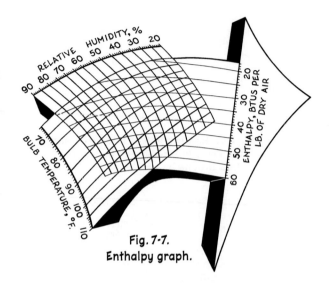

**Fig. 7-7.
Enthalpy graph.**

TABLE 7-7: METABOLISM OF HUMAN ACTIVITIES

OCCUPANT ACTIVITY	METABOLISM, btu/hr		
	Man	Woman	Child
Sleeping	250	210	190
Seated: quiet, as in theater	360	300	270
Writing or light work	480	410	360
Eating (incl. heat emitted by food)	520	450	400
Typing or clerical	640	540	480
Standing: slow walking	800	680	600
Light machine work	1,000	850	600
Heavy work, lifting	1,600	1,300	1,100
Walking, 3 miles per hr.	1,000	850	750
Jogging, gym athletics	2,000	1,700	1,500

Fig. 7-8. Building envelope incidence factors.

black or very dark, 0.8 if medium gray, 0.5 if light
or white, and 0.7 if glass.

R = R-value of envelope construction

ω = unit wt. of envelope const., psf of surface area

T_a = average annual temp. for region, from Fig. 7-3

κ_d = depth coeff. based on max. depth of soil at bottom of envelope surface, from bar graph on p. 313

κ_{ad} = depth coeff. based on average depth of soil at bottom of envelope. Find maximum depth of soil (ft) at bottom of envelope surface, then enter 0.5 depth in bar graph on p. 313 to find κ_{ad}.

T_i = ambient indoor temperature, °

κ_w = windchill exposure factor, from Table 7-4

Step 3. Compute the design cooling load through the building envelope.

$$\mathbf{C}_{ci} = 0.074\, V \eta\, (H_o + H_i) + A\, \kappa_f\, (T_o - T_i)/R\, P$$

$\mathbf{C}_{ci}$ = design cooling load due to conduction-infiltration through one area of envelope construction during warm weather, Btu/hr

V = volume of space(s) behind envel., from Fig. 7-2, cf

η = no. airchanges/hr for room(s) behind envelope, = 0.022 $(T_o - T_i)$ × no. airchanges/hr from Table 7-6

H_o = enthalpy of outdoor air during warm weather,

Btu/lb. From Fig. 7-5 find summer design temperature for local area, from Fig. 7-6 find summer
design humidity for local area, then from Fig. 7-7
find enthalpy (Btu/lb) for local area.

H_i = enthalpy of indoor air during warm weather, Btu/lb
A = surface area of envelope, sf
κ_f = fan factor. If ventilation fan is in envelope (i.e.
between a roof & suspended ceiling), $\kappa_f = 0.75$;
otherwise $\kappa_f = 1.0$.
T_o = air temperature at envelope outer surface, °F
T_i = ambient indoor temp., i.e. thermostat setting, °F
R = average thermal resistance of envelope
P = perimeter heat flow fraction, from Table 7-5

Conduction-Infiltration, Energy Audit:

Heating load: $24\ d_d\ \mathbf{H}_{ci} = \in (65 - T_d)$
Cooling load: $24\ d_d\ \mathbf{C}_{ci} = \in (T_d - 77)$

d_d = number of heating or cooling degree-days during
period of energy audit
$\mathbf{H}_{ci}$ = design heating load (conduction-infiltration) thro'
building envelope during energy audit, Btu/hr
$\mathbf{C}_{ci}$ = design cooling load (conduction-infiltration) thro'
building envelope during energy audit, Btu/hr
$\in$ = total heating or cooling energy used by building
during energy audit
T_d = winter design temperature at design heating or
cooling load, from Fig. 7-4, °F

Auxiliary Heat Gain: This is the heat added to in-
teriors by occupants, lighting, appliances, and other internal heat sources. In warm weather these gains are
usually maximum around the warmest time of day (mid-
afternoon), and thus are added to total cooling loads.

During cold weather they are usually minimal during the coldest time of day (before sunrise); thus only the gains occurring at this time are added to total heating loads. Conduction, infiltration, and auxiliary heat gain are often all that is needed to compute a building's total heating and cooling loads.

Auxiliary Heat Gain Formulas:

Design Heating Load:	$\mathbf{H}_a$ =	$M + H + 3.42\ W\ Q$
Design Cooling Load:	$\mathbf{C}_a$ =	$M + H + 3.42\ W\ Q$
Energy Audit Htg. load:	$\mathbf{H}_a$ =	$t\ (M + H + 3.42\ W\ Q)$
Energy Audit Clg. Load:	$\mathbf{C}_a$ =	$t\ (M + H + 3.42\ W\ Q)$

$\mathbf{H}_a$ = auxiliary heat gain in interior spaces at time of design heating load (usually 7 A.M.), Btu/hr

$\mathbf{C}_a$ = auxiliary heat gain in interior spaces at time of design cooling load (usually 3 P.M.), Btu/hr

t = period of energy audit heat flow, days

M = metabolism of occupants at time of design heating or cooling load, from Table 7-7, Btu/hr

H = average heat gain from appliances and motors in use at time of design heating or cooling load

W = average wattage of lighting in use at time of design heating or cooling load

Q = portion of lighting wattage emitted as heat at time of design heating or cooling load: $Q = 0.88$ for incand., 0.85 for quartz, 0.66 for fluorescent, 0.63 for mercury or metal-halide, 0.59 for sodium

Heat Loss or Gain thro' Ducting or Piping:

$$\mathbf{H}\ [R_c\ t_c + R_i\ t_i + (0.53 - 0.0014\ \Delta T)] = A\ \kappa_o\ \Delta T$$

$\mathbf{H}$ = heat loss or gain through wall of ducting or piping through which heat flows, Btu/hr

R_c = unit R-value of duct or pipe material, R/in. t.
R = 0.034 for steel, 0.029 for copper, 0.057 for aluminum, 0.91 for wood, 0.115 for conc.

t_c = thickness of duct or pipe material, in.

R_i = unit R-value of any insulation around duct or pipe, R/in. thickness

t_i = thickness of insulation around duct or pipe, in.

ΔT = temp. difference between inside and outside of duct or pipe, °F

A = surface area of duct or pipe, sf

κ_o = orientation coefficient for each duct or pipe surface whether it faces up, down, or to the side. κ_o = 1.00 for metal pipes and ducts w/ circular sections, 1.00 for sides of any rectangular material, 1.03 and 0.94 for wood tops & bottoms, and 1.08 & 0.93 for concrete tops and bottoms.

Energy Payback Span of Insulation:

$$\$_i \, E_f \; = \; \text{to } \$_o \, t \, (Q_u - Q_i)$$

$\$_i$ = initial cost of insulated installation, $

E_f = energy content of fuel used by installation or system, from Table 7-12, Btu/unit of energy

t_o = operating time of system that consumes the fuel, hours, days, months, years, etc.

$\$_o$ = operating cost of installation or system that consumes the fuel, $/day, month, etc.

t = timespan of payback span, days, years, etc.

Q_u = energy lost if installation is uninsulated, Btu/hr

Q_i = energy lost when installation is insulated, Btu/hr

Pickup Heating Load:
When interior spaces are unheated for an extended time during cold weather, heat drains out of the interior's solid masses as the en-

veloping indoor air temperature becomes lower; then when the heat turns back on, some of the Btus in the warming air flow back into the solids.

$$\mathbf{H}_p \approx P\,\mathbf{H}_{ci}$$

$\mathbf{H}_p$ = design pickup heating load for interior space(s) during cold weather, Btu/hr

P = pickup heating load fraction: portion of heat load absorbed by interior masses based on frequency of heat flow as listed below.

Type of heat flow	Pickup heating load fraction P
Heat off for 6 hr or nightly setback of 10° F	0.1
Heat off for 12 hr or nightly setback of 20° F	0.2
Heat off for 18 hr or nightly setback of 10° F	0.3
Heat off for 30 hr or more	0.4

$\mathbf{H}_{ci}$ = design conduction-infiltration heating load of interior space(s) during cold weather, Btu/hr

Solar Heat Gain: Solar heat gain is the sun's energy that enters indoors through glazing in the southerly surfaces of a building. This energy is about 300 Btu/sf·hr on a surface perpendicular to the arriving rays when the sky is clear and the sun is at least 15° above the horizon. As a site's elevation above sea level increases, the sun's energy increases (at mile-high Denver it is about 7 percent greater than at sea level). Although solar energy can significantly reduce the fossil-fuel energy required to keep a building's interior spaces comfortable during cold weather, the incoming rays will likely not reduce the overall size of a building's mechanical heating system; because the system's maximum heating load usually occurs just before dawn when no incoming radiance can reduce it. Thus solar heat gain is typically an *Energy Audit* calculation.

Step 1. Compute the incident clear-day insolation (solar heat gain) based on the site's latitude and timespan of the solar heat gain (usually its monthly totals as averaged on the 21st of each month).

$$\Phi_c \approx \Phi_g - 0.125 \, (\Phi_g - \Phi_s) \, (L - L_g)$$

Φ_c = net incident clear-day insolation for latitude of site and timespan of solar heat gain, Btu/day-sf

Φ_g = largest incident Insolation below site latitude; select from 24, 32, 40, or 48° in Table 7-8, Btu/day-sf

Φ_s = smallest incident insolation above site latitude; select again from Table 7-8, Btu/day-sf

L = latitude of site, decimal degrees

L_g = largest latitude value that is less than site latitude; select from 24, 32, 40, or 48°

Step 2. If added sunshine reflects from the ground in front of the solar glazing, compute the glazing's ground reflection factor.

$$\kappa_g \approx \kappa_s \, [\kappa_c + \kappa_r \, (0.7 - \kappa_c)]$$

TABLE 7-8: INSOLATION, BTUS/CLEAR DAY, SF

INSOLATION ON VERTICAL GLAZING

LATITUDE, °	Nov 21	Dec 21	Jan 21	Feb 21	Mar 21
24°	1,350	1,445	1,385	1,075	610
32°	1,450	1,515	1,490	1,310	900
40°	1,460	1,470	1,500	1,500	1,185
48°	1,280	1,095	1,310	1,540	1,395

INSOLATION ON GLAZING TILTING AT LOCAL LAT. + 20°

LATITUDE, °	Nov 21	Dec 21	Jan 21	Feb 21	Mar 21
24°	1,950	1,965	1,995	1,835	1,380
32°	1,855	1,915	1,890	1,885	1,570
40°	1,695	1,720	1,735	1,865	1,690
48°	1,385	1,395	1,415	1,775	1,725

κ_g = ground reflectance factor: portion of sun reflected onto solar glazing from ground in front, from Table 7-9. Use only if glazing is vertical or nearly so & is at or near ground, & if ground is fairly level in front of glazing; otherwise κ_g = 0.

κ_s = ground smoothness factor. κ_s = 1.0 if ground is fairly smooth, 0.5 if varied or slightly rocky. Interpolate for intermediate values.

κ_c = ground color factor, from Table 7-9

κ_r = snow cover reflectance factor, from Table 7-9

Step 3. Compute the solar heat gain thro' the glazing.

$$\Phi_a \approx 0.010\ \Phi_c\ t\ P A\ \tau\ \kappa_i \kappa_a \kappa_u\ (1 + \kappa_g)\ (1 + 0.000014\ E)$$

Φ_a = average solar heat gain through solar glazing during period of energy audit, Btu

Φ_c = incident clear-day insolation based on latitude of site and month of audit, from Step 1

t = period of energy audit, days

P = aver. % of local sunshine during period of audit

TABLE 7-9: GROUND REFLECTANCE FACTORS

NATURE OF GROUND outside glazing	κ
GROUND COLOR: black or near-black surfaces ...	0.05
Dark surface: brown, deep red, etc.	0.10
Medium dark surface: red brick, old wood, etc...	0.13
Vegetation, medium to dark green (most lawns) ..	0.17
Concrete, light foliage, light dirt, light sand, etc.	0.25
Sand, white or near-white	0.50
White smooth surface	0.70
SNOW COVER REFLECTANCE: less than 3 days/mo	0.00
Aver. 5 days/month, 0.10; aver. 10 days/month	0.20
Aver. 15 days/month, 0.30; aver. 20 days/month	0.40
Aver. 25 days/month, 0.50; Aver. all month long	0.60

A = surface area of glazing, sf

τ = coefficient of transmittance: portion of solar energy passing through glazing, from Table 10-7

κ_i = incidence factor: portion of sunlight absorbed by solar glazing if its surface varies from vertical or due south, from Fig. 7-9

κ_a = local clarity fraction: clearness of local atmosphere depending on location, smog, and other en-

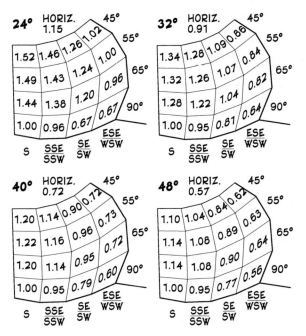

Fig. 7-9. Solar glazing incidence factors.

vironmental factors as described below:

Region or Condition	Clarity fraction in winter (κ_a)
Deep South	0.90
Florida, Gulf Coast, mid-south, West Coast	0.95
North'n plains, Rocky Mts, nr Canadian border	1.05
All other areas in conterminous 48 states	1.00
Cont. light smog or local haze	–0.1 from above
Continuous heavy smog	–0.2 from above

κ_u = umbra fraction: portion of collector area exposed to daily sun. κ_u = 1.0 if area is exposed to sun all day, 0 if area is in shade all day. Interpolate for intermediate values.

κ_g = ground reflectance factor, from Step 2

E = elevation above sea level, ft

Thermal Massing Design:
When the sun shines on a solid object surrounded by warm indoor air, the object absorbs the sun's energy; then after sunset the heat stored in the solid objects flows back into the interior air as it cools slightly. This can significantly reduce the fossil-fuel energy required to heat interior spaces,

TABLE 7-10: CAPACITANCE OF BUILDING MATERIALS

MATERIAL	Capacitance, Btu/cf · ° F.	Latent Heat of Fusion, ° F.
Red brick, 24.6; Fire brick	43.6	—
Sand, 18.1; Gypsum	20.3	—
Fresh Water, 62.4; Still air	0.01	—
Concrete, granite	31–32	—
Growing soil	13.9	—
Paraffin	38.4	3,570 at 115°
Glauber's salt	—	7,760 at 73°
Sodium Sulphate	—	6,600–9,000 at 65–89°

if they are enclosed in a thickly insulated building envelope with movable insulation over the windows.

Heating load: $H_{tm} = C V (T_a - T_e)$
Energy Auditing: $H_{tm} \approx 0.010\, t\, C V P (T_a - T_e)$

H_{tm} = latent heat stored by thermal massing for period of energy audit, Btus
C = capacitance of thermal massing: capacity to store thermal energy, from Table 7-10, Btu/cf·°F
V = volume of thermal massing, cf
T_a = temp. of massing at max. heat absorption, °F
T_e = temp. of massing at maximum heat depletion, °F
t = period of energy audit, days
P = average percentage of local sunshine during period of energy audit.

Total Solar Energy Savings: A solar heating system's cost-effectiveness is determined by computing its energy savings as below:

Step 1. Find the solar heating system's Solar Load Ratio for the period of the energy audit.

$$\kappa_{slr} = \Phi_a / (H_{ci} + H_p + H_{tm} - H_{ah})$$

κ_{slr} = Solar Load Ratio: ratio of solar heat gain to design heat loss through the building envelope
Φ_a = average solar heat gain through solar glazing during period of energy audit, Btu
H_{ci} = design heating load due to conduction-infiltration through building envelope during period of energy audit, Btu
H_p = design pickup heating load for interior spaces during cold weather during energy audit, Btu
H_{tm} = average latent heat stored due to thermal mass-

ing during period of energy audit, Btu

H_{ah} = design auxiliary heat gain added to interior spaces during period of energy audit, Btu

Step 2. Find the Heating Load Fraction from below.

Heating Load Fraction, κ_{hlf}

1.0 0.8 0.6   0.4   0.2   0.1   0.05   0.01

0   0.20 0.40 0.60 0.80 1.00 1.20 1.40 1.60 1.80 2.00 2.20 2.40

Solar Load Ratio, κ_{slr}

Step 3. Compute the cost of heating the solar architecture for the period of the energy audit.

$$\$_h \, \kappa_e \, \varepsilon \ = \ 100 \, \kappa_{hlf} \, \$_u \, (H_{ci} + H_p + H_{tm} - H_{ah})$$

$\$_h$ = cost of heating building during energy audit, $

κ_e = energy content of fossil-fuel energy used, from Table 7-12

ε = efficiency of backup heating, from Table 7-11, %

$\$_u$ = local unit cost of energy, dollars

      κ_{hlf}, H_{ci}, H_p, H_{tm}, & H_{ah} are as previously defined

TABLE 7-11: EFFICIENCY OF HEATING SYSTEMS

TYPE OF HEATING SYSTEM	Approx. efficiency, %
Electric baseboards, infrared electric units	90
Gas-fired furnaces w/ makeup air, gas-fired radiant ceiling units	80
Oil-fired furnaces w/ air ducts, hot water boilers w/ water baseboards	70
Wood or coal stoves (non-airtight), Rumford fireplaces	40
Above stoves, airtight	60
Fireplaces w/ conventional open hearths	20
Above w/ glass doors	40

Summary of Total Heating Loads:

$$\mathbf{H} = \Phi_h + \mathbf{H}_{ci} + \mathbf{H}_p + \mathbf{H}_{tm} - \mathbf{H}_{ah}$$

$\mathbf{H}$ = total heating load at design temp., Btu/hr

Φ_h = solar heat gain, Btu/hr

$\mathbf{H}_{ci}$ = design heating load due to conduction-infiltra-tion through building envelope during cold weather, Btu/hr

$\mathbf{H}_p$ = design pickup heating load for interior spaces during cold weather in Jan., Btu/hr

$\mathbf{H}_{tm}$ = latent heat stored by thermal massing, Btu/hr

$\mathbf{H}_{ah}$ = design auxiliary heat gain added to interior at heating load design temperature, Btu/hr

Summary of Total Cooling Loads:

$$\mathbf{C} = \mathbf{C}_{ci} + \mathbf{C}_{ah}$$

$\mathbf{C}$ = total cooling load at design temperature, Btu/hr

$\mathbf{C}_{ci}$ = design cooling load due to conduction-infiltra-tion through building envelope during warm weather, Btu/hr

$\mathbf{C}_{ah}$ = design auxiliary heat gain added to interior spaces at cooling load design temp., Btu/hr

  Much of the previous part of this chapter de-scribed how to quantify a building's thermal heating and cooling loads, and how to utilize solar energy to re-duce the fossil-fuel cost of keeping the building's inte-rior spaces warm during cold weather. The rest of this chapter describes how to use such previously deter-mined thermal loads to select and size a building's cli-mate control system so its interior spaces will remain constantly comfortable year-round.

Climate Control System Design Parameters:

Temperature: 67–78° year-round.
Humidity: 40–60 percent all year round.
Airflow: 10–50 fpm.
CO_2: should not exceed 800 parts per million.
Static air pressure: positive for spaces that generate
    clean air, negative for spaces that create foul air.
Pollution: low levels of dusts, molds, odors, noxious
    gases, microbes, chemicals, etc.
Adequate lighting: 50 fc in all service areas.

Heat Content Equations:

Elec. resistance heat	E_{MBtu} = ____	¢/kWh × 2.93
No. 2 fuel oil	E_{MBtu} = ____	$/gal × 7.14
Propane	E_{MBtu} = ____	$/gal × 10.9
Natural gas	E_{MBtu} = ____	¢/therm × 0.1

E_{MBtu} = million Btus of energy consumed

TABLE 7-12: ENERGY CONVERSION FACTORS

FUEL	COAL (lb)	OIL (gal)	PROPANE (therm)	ELEC. (kWh)	OAK (lb)	SOLAR (square)
COAL ...	14,600 Btus	0.160	0.195	4.28	3.73	0.487
OIL	6.23	91,000 Btus	1.213	26.7	23.3	3.033
PROPANE	5.137	0.824	75,000 Btus	21.97	19.2	2.500
ELECTRIC	0.234	0.038	0.046	3,413 Btus	0.87	0.114
OAK	0.268	0.043	0.052	1.15	3,910 Btus	0.130
SOLAR ...	2.055	0.330	0.400	8.79	7.67	30,000

Thermal Energy Storage System Design:

Step 1. Draw a daily load profile of the building's hourly heating loads based on design heating loads and local climate data as shown below.

Hr.	Temp. at hr, °F	Δt at hr, °F	Hourly htg load = design htg. load × $\Delta t_{hr} / \Delta t_{max}$ Btu/hr
7 a.m.	18	70 − 18 = 52	123,000 × 52/52 = 123,000
8 a.m.	21	70 − 21 = 49	123,000 × 49/53 = 116,000
9 a.m.	25	70 − 25 = 45	123,000 × 45/52 = 106,000, etc.

Step 2. Size the thermal heat reservoir from

$$H \approx 62.5 \, V \Delta t$$

H = total on-peak and off-peak heating load, Btu/hr
V = volume of thermal heat reservoir, cf of water
Δt = temperature differential of reservoir, °F

Step 3. Estimate the unit's required floor area. Knowing the unit's footprint, add 1 ft for perimeter construction/insulation plus a 3 ft access aisle all around.

Heat Recovery from Building Systems:

$$H_L \, \varepsilon \approx \epsilon \, \$ \, T$$

H_L = heat lost due to conventional operation, Btu/hr
ε = overall efficiency of heat recovery operation
ϵ = unit energy savings of recovery operation, Btu/hr
$\$$ = hourly value of recovered energy, dollars
T = timespan of recovery operation

Electric Heating Unit Design:

$$H \leq 3 \, L \, H_{cap}$$

H = design heating load of space, Btu/hr
L = req. length of electric baseboard heating, ft
H_{cap} = heating capacity of selected unit, watts/LF

Electric Baseboard Heating Unit Design:

$$\mathbf{H} \le 3\, H_{cap}$$

H = design heating load of space, Btu/hr
H_{cap} = heating capacity of selected unit, watts.
    Wattages of electric units are listed on the units
    and in manufacturers' catalogs.

Electric Heat Tracing Cable Design:

$$\Omega = 0.17\, d^2\, L\, (177 - T_o)$$

Ω = req. output of electric heat tracing cable, watts
d = diameter of pipe to be heated, in.
L = length of pipe to be heated, ft
T_o = lowest likely local subfreezing temperature, °F
    Use 5° below area's lowest recorded temp.

Electric Heating Cable for Radiant Slabs:

Electric heating cable for concrete slabs is typically made in capacities of 10, 20, 40, and 60 W/sf. Even in severely cold climates, 60 watt cable is usually satisfactory. Otherwise an elaborate system of piping containing heated antifreeze is usually devised.

Design snowfall, in/hr	Radiant slab output, Required W/sf at design temperature			
	30° F	20° F	10° F	0° F
0–1	25	35	43	51
1–2	46	55	64	74
2–3	68	79	90	98

➜ ß ▪ I ▯ ▦ ♀ ☀ ⬟ ⬆ 💡 ? 🗐 🖒

Radiant Floor Heating System Design:

Step 1. Size the system's piping as described below:

Mains: For small floorplans use $\frac{3}{4}$ in. piping. Otherwise size the mains according to pages 375–377.

Circuits: These are parallel runs of typically $\frac{1}{2}$ in. flexible copper or plastic tubing. Determine the optimal spacing between runs from

$$H\,S \;=\; 17\,\kappa_h\,A\,(T_s - T_r)$$

H = design heating load of interior spaces above radiant floor water heating system, Btu/hr

S = optimal spacing of parallel runs in piping, in. If $S \leq 6$ in, floor water radiant heating is not strong enough to satisfy load ➜ select another system or supplement floor heating with other systems. If $S \geq 18$ in, select a lower water temperature.

κ_h = comparative heating value of water if it contains glycol. If water contains no glycol, $\kappa_h = 1.0$; if 30% glycol, $\kappa_h = 0.976$; if 50% glycol, $\kappa_h = 0.904$. Interpolate for intermediate values.

A = floor area of system, sf. Subtract 1 ft from perimeter of heating area all around.

T_s = supply or initial water temperature of system, °F. Feasible T_i usually $\approx$ 95–120° F.

T_r = return water temperature of system, °F.

Step 2. Determine the system's pipe flow requirements.

$$H \;=\; 490\,\kappa_h\,Þ\,(T_s - T_r)$$

H = design heating load of occupancy, Btu/hr

$Þ$ = required pipe flow of system, gpm

T_s = supply or initial water temp. of system, °F.
κ_h and T_r are as previously defined

Hydronic Snow-Melting System Design:

$$A \approx 2.45 \, Q \, (T_i - T_o)$$

A = floor area of surface receiving snowfall, sf
Q = required waterflow to melt snow from area, gpm
T_i = highest temperature of liquid in piping, °F. This is usually 35–40°.
T_o = lowest temperature of liquid in piping, usually the region's winter design temperature, °F

Radiant Ceiling Heating System Design:

Gas-fired unit design: $H \approx L \, H_{cap}$
Infrared unit design: $190 \, H \approx V \eta \, (T_i - T_o)$

H = design heating load of interior space(s), Btu/hr for gas-fired units, watts for infrared units
L = required linear footage of selected unit, ft
H_{cap}= heating capacity of selected unit, Btu/LF. Typical capacity for high-firing mode ≈ 3,000 Btu/LF. Use more specific figures from manufacturers' catalogs when available.
V = volume of space to be heated, cf
η = number of air changes per hour (ach). For areas near building entries, assume 6 ach unless otherwise noted.
T_i = design indoor temperature, °F
T_o = design outdoor temperature, °F

Electric Heating/Cooling System Design:

Design heating load: $H \leq 4 \, \eta \, H_{cap}$
Design cooling load: $C \leq 3 \, \eta \, C_{cap}$

H = design heating load of interior space(s), Btu/hr

C = design cooling load of interior space(s), Btu/hr
η = number of units required to condition space
H_{cap}= heating capacity of selected heating unit, watts
C_{cap}= cooling capacity of selected cooling unit, watts

Hot Water Heating System Design:

Boiler design: $H_{cap} \geq$ **H** $(1.25 + 0.000,034\ E)$

H_{cap}= heating capacity of selected boiler, Btu/hr
H = design heating load of space, Btu/hr
E = elevation above sea level, ft. If less than 1,000 ft, use $E = 0$.

Boiler floor area: $A \approx (L + 5)(W + 5)$

A = approximate floor area for boiler and perimeter access, sf
L = length of boiler base, from catalog, ft
W = width of boiler base, from catalog, ft

The above formula may be used to estimate the floor area for most floor-mounted furnaces or boilers.

Baseboard heating length: **H** $\leq L\ H_{cap}$

H = design heating load of space, Btu/hr
L = total length of heating units in space, ft
H_{cap} = heating capacity of selected unit or rating as listed in product catalog, Btu/hr-LF

Steam Heating System Design:

Step 1. Knowing the building's total design heating load, find the heating capacity of the system from

$$H_{cap} = 1.6\ \mathbf{H}\ \frac{(T_{max} + Q - T_{min})}{(T_{ent} + Q - T_{exit})}$$

H_{cap} = heating capacity of selected unit, Btu/LF.

H = design heating load of interior space(s) or building, Btu/hr

Q = heat of vaporization/condensation of H_2O; this = 970 Btu/lb of H_2O if system operates at normal atmospheric pressure. If otherwise, find Q from the bar graph below.

Air pressure, in. Hg or psig

◄ in. Hg vacuum ─►│◄─── psig pressure ──────►

20	10	4	2	0	1	2	3	4	5	10	15	50
161	192	205	209	212	216	218	222	225	227	240	250	281

Heat of vaporization/condensation, Btu/lb of H_2O

T_{max} = maximum temperature of steam in boiler, °F. This is usually at least 20–25° above the boiling point of water.

T_{min} = temperature of incoming water, °F. This is initially the temperature of the building's cold water supply, but after initial cycling it is more likely to be 150–170°F.

T_{ent} = temp. of steam as it enters the radiators, °F. This should be a few degrees above the water's boiling point.

T_{exit} = temperature of water as it exits the radiators, °F. This should be below the water's boiling point; but the cooler the water is while it is still in the radiator, the more heat it gives to adjacent interior space. Optimal T_{exit} = 150–170°.

Step 2. Determine the unit pressure drop per 100 LF of the system's piping (Δp below). This is usually 1–8 oz/in² depending on the system's total heating capacity and the length of its supply piping. Generally the larger the system, the greater the pipe pressure drop between the boiler and the remote radiator; and the steam's unit pressure drop (ΔP below) must always exceed this amount (otherwise the steam won't reach the remote radiator). In most small systems ($H_{cap} \leq 250,000$ Btu/hr), $\Delta p \approx 2$ oz/in^2. Once Δp is determined, find the system's total pressure drop from

$$\Delta P \geq 0.02\, \Delta p\, L$$

ΔP = pressure of steamflow in system, oz/in^2 or psig

Δp = unit pressure drop of steamflow per 100 LF of pipe, oz/in^2

L = length of piping from boiler to remote radiator, ft

Step 3. Determine the amount of the building's total heating load that flows through each pipe in the system, then size each pipe according to

$$C\, \sigma_{vs} \geq 19.6\, Q\, v\, \delta^2$$

C = portion of system's design heating capacity that flows through each pipe section, Btu/hr

σ_{vs} = specific volume of steam at system pressure, cf/lb. This is found by entering the system's total pressure of steamflow (psig) found in Step 2 in the bar graph below:

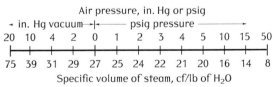

Air pressure, in. Hg or psig

◄ in. Hg vacuum ─►│◄─── psig pressure ───►

20	10	4	2	0	1	2	3	4	5	10	15	50
75	39	31	29	27	25	24	22	21	20	16	14	8

Specific volume of steam, cf/lb of H$_2$O

Q = heat of vaporization/condensation of H$_2$O; this = 970 Btu/lb of H$_2$O if the system operates at normal atmospheric pressure. If otherwise, find Q

from the bar graph in Step 1.

v = velocity of steamflow through piping, normally 100–140 fps. Velocities to 200 fps are OK in industrial and other settings where pipe noise is not a major concern. Normally this is set at about 125 fps, then the formula is solved for δ below; then after δ is sized the formula is rerun to solve for v to see if its value is OK.

δ = diameter of pipe through which steam flows (interior dimension), in. Solve for this value, then increase to nearest standard diameter.

Formulas for sizing low-pressure system steam piping:

One-pipe sys., supply risers, upfeeds [a] $C = 11\,Q\,\delta^{2.55}$
Radiator valves, vert. connections [b]... $C = 7\,Q\,\delta^{2.58}$
Radiator & rise runouts .... $C = 7\,Q\,\delta^{2.37}$
Branch vertical piping [c] .... $C = 14\,Q\,\delta^{2.70}$
Branch horizontal piping .... $C = 14\,Q\,\delta^{2.57}$
2-pipe sys. (1–6 psig boiler pr.) .. $C = 76\,\Delta p^{0.54}\,\delta^{2.60}$

    a. If $\Delta p \geq 0.063$ psi/100LF, use formula 6.
    b. Pipe diameter must ≤ 2 in.
    c. If $\Delta p \geq 0.042$ psi/100LF, use formula 6.

Step 4. Lay out the piping system. Make sure enough space exists around every part, especially at the ends of long runs, because steam piping experiences much more thermal expansion than normal piping due to the higher temperatures involved. Supply pipes should pitch up in the direction of flow at least $1/4$ in/10 LF (but $1/8$ in/LF is better), and return piping should pitch down in the direction of flow at least $1/2$ in/10 LF. Every LF of length must be drainable by drain or blowoff valves installed at the lowest elevations of each run.

Air Heating System Design:

Furnace capacity: $H_{cap} \geq$ **H** $(1.15 + 0.000,034\ E)$
Duct design: **H** $\leq\ 0.65\ A\ \kappa_d\ (T_h - T_i)$

H_{cap} = heating capacity of selected furnace, Btu/hr.
       Use net ratings as listed in product catalogs.
H   = design heating load of space or heating
       capacity of selected furnace, Btu/hr
E = elevation above sea level, ft
A = min. section area of duct (not incl. insul.), in^2
κ_d = duct velocity factor, from Table 7-13
T_h = temperature of heated air, °F
T_i = temperature of indoor air, assume 68°F unless
       otherwise noted

If the duct is more than 40 ft long or its aspect ratio (ratio of width to depth) exceeds 2.5, its size should be increased as described on page 348.

Location of registers: Locate wall registers close to floors and under windows. Locate floor registers near exterior walls and under windows. Grilles should direct airflow across nearby walls or floors.

Air Cooling System Design:

System capacity if cooling load is Btu/hr:
      $12{,}000\ C_{cap} \geq \mathbf{C}_{btu}\ (1.15 + 0.000,034\ E)$
System capacity if cooling load is tons:
      $C_{cap} \geq \mathbf{C}_{ton}\ (1.15 + 0.000,034\ E)$
Duct size if cooling load is Btu/hr:
      $\mathbf{C}_{btu} \geq\ 15\ \kappa_d\ A$
Duct size if cooling load is tons:
      $800\ \mathbf{C}_{ton} \geq\ \kappa_d\ A$

C_{cap} = cooling capacity of selected AC unit, tons
$\mathbf{C}_{btu}$ = design cooling load, Btu/hr
$\mathbf{C}_{ton}$ = design cooling load, tons
E = elevation above sea level, ft
κ_d = duct velocity factor, from Table 7-13
A = minimum section area of duct (not incl. insul.), in^2

If the duct exceeds 40 ft in length or its aspect ratio (ratio of width to depth) exceeds 2.5, its size should be increased as described on page 348.

Location of registers: Locate registers in ceilings or at least 6'-6" high on walls. Ceiling registers should be round or square and near the center of the zone; wall registers should be no farther than 10 ft apart to prevent dead air spots. Grilles should prevent drafts from forming in the lower 6 ft of the zone, which is best done by directing air across nearby wall or ceiling surfaces.

Static Air Pressure (s.a.p.) Loss Formulas for HVAC Ducting:

Total s.a.p. loss: $\Delta P_T = \Delta P_i + \Delta P_d - \Delta P_r$

Initial s.a.p. loss based on airflow velocity:
$$\Delta P_i = (\mathcal{V}_i/4005)^2$$

Initial s.a.p. loss based on airflow volume:
$$\Delta P_i = (Q_i/4005\ A_i)^2$$

Unit or total s.a.p. loss in duct:
$$10,700,000\ \Delta P_d\ s^{1.22} = \kappa_r\ L\ \mathcal{V}_i^{1.82}$$

S.a.p. regain at duct outlet when $\mathcal{V}_f > \mathcal{V}_o$:
$$\Delta P_r = 0.75\ [(\mathcal{V}_i/4005)^2 - (\mathcal{V}_o/4005)^2]$$

S.a.p. regain at duct outlet when $\mathcal{V}_f < \mathcal{V}_o$:
$$\Delta P_r = -1.1\ [(\mathcal{V}_o/4005)^2 - (\mathcal{V}_i/4005)^2]$$

ΔP_T = total static air pressure (s.a.p.) loss from start to end of contin. length of HVAC ducting, in. wg.

ΔP_i = initial s.a.p. loss at start of duct, in. wg. This loss is usually due to the operating pressure of the discharge fan.

ΔP_d = unit s.a.p. loss due to duct friction.

ΔP_r = s.a.p. regain at duct outlet, in. wg.

v_i = initial velocity of airflow in duct, fpm or cfm

Q_i = initial volume of airflow in duct, cfm

A_i = initial section area of ducting, sf

s = width of one side of duct if square, in. If duct is rect., $s = 0.5\ b\ d$; if duct is round, $s = 0.785\ \delta$.

κ_r = inner wall surface roughness coefficient. $\kappa_r = 0.009$ for galvanized sheet steel.

L = length of ducting, either total length (ft) or unit ft

v_o = velocity of airflow at duct outlet, cfm

Air Heating/Cooling System Design:

Typical HVAC system operating temperatures are:

Heating air .... 120–145° F
Heating indoor temperature ... 68° F at 50% r.h.
Cooling air .... 50–60° F
Cooling indoor temperature ... 77° F at 50% r.h.

TABLE 7-13: DUCT VELOCITY FACTORS

BUILDING TYPE	Main	Branch	Outlet
Residences	6.5	5	3.5
Theaters, assembly areas	8	6	4
Apartments, hotel & hospital bedrooms	10	7	4
Private offices, libraries, schools	12	8	6
General offices, restaurants, stores ...	15	9.5	7
Average retail, cafeterias	18	12	9
Industry, recreation, service, rest rooms	22	18	12

Low-Velocity Air Ducting Systems:

HVAC low-velocity air ducting is usually defined by the static air-flow pressure (s.a.p.) differential between the discharge fan and remote outlet. This differential is typically divided into the following three classes or systems:

Low pressure: s.a.p. 2.50–3.75 in. wg.
Medium pressure: s.a.p. of 3.75–6.75 in. wg.
High pressure: s.a.p. of 6.75–12.75 in. wg.

Static air pressure is the key to successful system design, because once all the ducts' theoretical airflows are known, the s.a.p. differentials—and thus airflows—at each outlet can be adjusted as desired.

Low-Velocity Systems, Preliminary Design:

Step 1. Estimate the building's required air supply.

$$Q \approx \eta \, [12 \, L_n + 12 \, L_e + 21 \, L_s + 24 \, L_w + (L_n - 24)(L_e - 24)]$$

Q = estimated required building supply air, cfm
η = no. of floors in building (perimeters aligned)
L_n = length of north facade, ft. $\quad L_n \geq 48$ ft.
L_e = length of east facade, ft. $\quad L_e \geq 48$ ft.
L_s = length of south facade, ft. $\quad L_s \geq 48$ ft.
L_w = length of west facade, ft. $\quad L_w \geq 48$ ft.

Step 2. Estimate the air handling unit's cooling load.

$$1,200 \, C \approx Q \, (3 + 4 \, S_a)$$

C = estimated air handling unit load, tons
Q = required building supply air, cfm
S_a = portion of outside air used as supply air

Step 3. Estimate the air handling unit's height and width (based on the unit's chilled-water coil surface area).

$$Q \approx 400 \, A$$

Q = required building supply air, cfm
A = req. surface area of unit's chilled water coil, sf

Unit height: $h \approx 4$ ft if $A \leq 30$ sf, 6 ft if $A \leq 72$ sf, 9 ft if A ≤ 108 sf, and 12 ft if $A \leq 144$ sf. If $A \geq 144$ sf, install more than one unit. Here $A = 60$ sf ➡ $h \approx 6$ ft. Add minimum 3 ft clearance above unit.

Unit width: $A = h \, w$. If $A = 60$ sf and $h = 6$ ft, then $60 \approx$ $6 \, w$ ➡ $w \approx 10$ ft. Add 3.5 ft access aisles each side.

Unit length: Rough out the HVAC system, determine the unit's required components and estimate their depths, then add them to obtain the unit's estimated length.

Low-Velocity HVAC System Design:
The following method of designing low-velocity HVAC ducting is the *equal friction method*. It is superior to the *static-regain method* for most low-volume HVAC systems.

Step 1. Locate the ducting grilles or outlets in their most feasible positions on each floor. In large floor areas this is usually done by arranging them in a grid pattern, then determining the most feasible branch ducting runs to each outlet. Rest rooms, elevator shafts, stairwells, and electrical closets all require outlets.

Step 2. Determine the portion of the building's heating load that must be delivered to each outlet on each floor by analyzing the data that determined the building's total heating and cooling loads. *A crucial consideration*: although each duct outlet in a uniform grid pattern may serve an equal zone area, *their heating and cooling loads may vary widely*, because zones bordered by exterior walls, bottom floors, and roofs typically require different loads. In fact, zones behind one facade may require heating while similarly occupied zones behind another facade in the same building may require cooling; thus the system may need to provide warm and cool air at the same time. The chief solution to this is to design the system to satisfy cooling loads, then install in each zone's branch duct a splitter damper with reheat coils.

Step 3. Knowing the building's total heating and cooling loads and v_{max}, and tentatively assuming that the primary feeder duct at the face of the discharge fan is square, size this duct from the two formulas below. The larger size governs.

    a. Heating load: $\quad s \geq 12.4 \left[H/v_{max} (T_h - T_i) \right]^{0.5}$
    b. Cooling load: $\quad s \geq 2.58 \left(C/v_{max} \right)^2$

s = clear inside width of one side of duct section if it is square, in.
H = design heating load of HVAC system, Btu/hr
C = design cooling load of HVAC system, Btu/hr
v_{max}= maximum recom. velocity of ducting airflow, fpm
T_h = temperature of heated air, assume 140° F unless otherwise noted
T_i = optimal temperature of indoor air, ° F. Assume 68° F for heating load.

Step 4. Knowing s and v_{max}, find the ducting's unit s.a.p. loss due to duct friction from

$$10{,}700{,}000 \, \Delta P \, s^{0.122} = \kappa_r \, L \, v_{max}^{1.82}$$

ΔP = unit s.a.p. loss due to duct friction, in. wg/LF of ducting. Find ΔP for unit duct length = 1.00 ft, then use ΔP as reference in later calculations.
κ_r = inner wall surface roughness coefficient of duct.

κ_r for galvanized sheet steel = 0.009.

L = length of duct, ft.

    s and v_{max} are as previously defined

Step 5. Make a schedule of the duct lengths that comprise the system's longest ducting run from discharge fan to remote outlet; then (1) give each duct segment in the run a name; (2) enter their lengths; (3) list the cooling load required at each outlet; then (4) find the airflow required to meet each cooling load from **a** or **b** below:

    a. Cooling load: $\mathbf{C}_o$ = 20.2 Q

    b. Heating load: $\mathbf{H}_o$ = 0.87 Q $(T_h - T_i)$

$\mathbf{C}_o$ = cooling load of each outlet, Btu/hr, if the system's cooling load governed the sizing of the primary duct's side s in Step 3

$\mathbf{H}_o$ = heating load of each outlet, Btu/hr, if the heating load governed the sizing of the primary duct's side s in Step 3

Q = volume of airflow required at each outlet, cfm

    T_h and T_i are as previously defined

Continue making the ducting schedule as follows: in column (5), knowing the required cooling or heating airflow for each outlet, sum the airflows that branch from each duct split by working upstream from the remotest ducts toward the central feeder ducts and eventually to the discharge fan; in column (6) enter the two airflow rates that stem from each duct split; then in column (7) list the percent airflows at each duct split in (6) that flow into the longer and shorter runs. Optimal duct register velocities for air ducting systems are broadcast studios ≈ 300–500 fpm, sleeping areas ≈ 500–700 fpm, movie theaters ≈ 1,000 fpm, offices and small retail ≈ 1,000–1,250 fpm, and recreation/industrial/service ≈ 2,000 fpm.

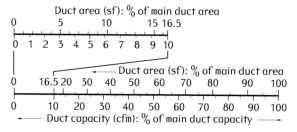

Duct sizing bar graph.

Step 6. From the duct sizing bar graph above find the equivalent section area of each branch duct if it is square that will maintain equal duct friction after each duct split. This time start at the discharge fan and work downstream toward the outlets. Then in column (8) enter each duct's equivalent section area in the schedule.

Step 7. Starting at the fan face and working downstream to the outlets, find each duct's section area by squaring the primary duct's sides from Step 3, then multiplying this by the percent airflow in each downstream split that was listed in column (7) of the schedule.

Step 8. Determine the most feasible sections for each length of ducting. Until now every duct section has been considered as square; but they are often more efficient and economical if round, and in narrow areas they may need to be rectangular. Do this as described below:

   a. If section is square: $A_\square = s^2$

   Wherein s = length of one side. Solve for s, then:
      If $s < 48$ in, select next largest multiple of 2 in.
      If $s \geq 48$ in, select next largest multiple of 4 in.

b. If section is round: $A_\circ = 0.933\,\delta^2$

Wherein δ = section's diameter. Solve for δ, then:
  If $\delta < 48$ in, select next largest multiple of 2 in.
  If $\delta \geq 48$ in, select next largest multiple of 4 in.

c. If section is rectangular: $A_\square = a\,b$

Wherein a and b are the rectangle's sides, $a > b$,
  and $b \geq 6$ in. Select a reasonable value for a,
  then find b from $b = A_\square \div a$, then
  If a or $b < 48$ in, select next largest mult. of 2 in.
  If a or $b \geq 48$ in, select next largest mult. of 4 in.

If a rectangular section's aspect ratio (longer-to-short-
er side ratio) ≥ 2.0, increase its section area as described below.

d. $a_{new}\,b_{old} = A_{old}\,\{1 + 0.072\,[(A_{old}/b^2) - 1]\} = A_{new}$
  Knowing b and A_{old}, solve for a or A_{new}.

If any duct is fitted with acoustic liners, its section is the
minimum clear width inside the liner. If a final duct segment ≤ 12 ft long and its airflow is 25–175 cfm, it may be
sized as a 3 or 4 in. diameter flexible conduit; then,
knowing its airflow, find its effective pressure drop ΔP
from the flexible conduit sizing bar graph below.

Flexible conduit sizing bar graph.

Step 9. Find the effective length L_e of each duct segment. If the segment has a normal number of fittings, L_e may be found from

$$L_e \approx 1.2\ L$$

L_e = equivalent length of ducting: length of duct plus safety factor for normal no. of fittings, ft
L = actual length of ducting, ft

Step 10. Determine the duct's unit s.a.p. drop due to duct friction depending on the shape of the duct's section as described below:

a. Circular duct:
$$\Delta P_d = 0.00137\ ^{(1 - 0.000034\ E)}\ \kappa_r\ L_e\ Q^{1.82}/_{\delta^{4.86}}$$

b. Square duct:
$$\Delta P_d = 0.00076\ ^{(1 - 0.000034\ E)}\ \kappa_r\ L_e\ Q^{1.82}/_{s^{4.86}}$$

c. Rectangular duct:
$$\Delta P_d = 0.00076\ ^{(1 - 0.000034\ E)}\ \kappa_r\ L_e\ Q^{1.82}/_{(a\ b)^{2.43}}$$

ΔP_d = unit s.a.p. drop in duct due to airflow friction loss, in. wg/LF
E = elevation of building site above sea level, ft. Any estimate of E within a few hundred ft is **OK**.
L_e = equivalent length of ducting, ft
Q_i = initial airflow in duct at discharge fan face, cfm.
κ_r, δ, s, a, and b are as previously defined

Step 11. Find the duct's initial static air pressure loss due to its initial velocity from the formula below:

$$\Delta P_i = 0.0013\ (1.0 - 0.000034\ E)\ (Q_i/_{A_i})$$

ΔP_i = initial s.a.p. loss due to operation of discharge fan, in. wg/LF
A_i = sec. area of duct at face of discharge fan, in^2. All other values are as previously defined.

Step 12. For each ducting outlet find the static pressure regain, or "gush effect", at its face. Thus, before the static pressure regain of each duct segment can be found, the airflow velocity at its beginning and end must be known as described below:

  a. **Inlet velocity:** $v_i = 144\, Q_i/A_i$
  b. **Outlet velocity:** $v_o = 144\, Q_o/A_o$

Q_i = initial volume of airflow rate in duct at inlet, cfm.
A_i = section area of duct at inlet, in^2
Q_o = final volume of airflow in duct at outlet, cfm.
A_o = section area of duct at outlet, in^2

Knowing the outlet airflow's initial and final velocities v_i and $v_\emptyset$, find the outlet's static pressure regain from

  c. **If $v_i \geq v_o$ (the usual situation):**
$$\Delta P_r = 0.75\,(1 - 0.000034\, E)\,[(v_i/4{,}005)^2 - (v_o/4{,}005)^2]$$

  d. **If $v_i < v_o$:**
$$\Delta P_r = 1.10\,(1 - 0.000034\, E)\,[(v_i/4{,}005)^2 - (v_o/4{,}005)^2]$$

ΔP_r = static pressure regain at outlet, in. wg
    All other values are as previously defined.

Step 13. Find the total s.a.p. loss at each outlet from
$$\Delta P_t = L_e\,\Delta P_d + \Delta P_i - \Delta P_r$$

ΔP_t = total static air pressure loss at outlet, in. wg/LF
L_e = equivalent length of duct, from Step 9, ft
ΔP_d = unit static air pressure drop in ducting due to airflow friction loss, from Step 10, in. wg/LF
ΔP_i = initial s.a.p. loss due to operating pressure of discharge fan, from Step 11, in. wg/LF
ΔP_r = s.a.p. regain at outlet, from Step 12, in. wg/LF
    All other values are as previously defined.

Step 14. Design each outlet grille by (1) determining the outlet's optimal throw by analyzing the space its airflow is entering, (2) estimating the outlet grille's throw from formulas **a b c d** below, (3) comparing the optimal throw with actual throw, and (4) refining if necessary.

    a. Straight throw (outlet vanes are =):
$$T = 0.0015 \; v^{1.5}$$

    b. Spread throw (outlet vanes are ?):
$$T = 0.0028 \; v^{1.5}$$

T = throw of vaned outlet, ? ft
v = outlet airflow velocity, fpm

    c. To find the outlet's airflow velocity:
$$Q = v A$$

    d. To find the grille's full area:
$$A_{tot} \, \kappa_{nfa} = A_{nfa}$$

A_{tot} = required total face area of grille, in²
κ_{nfa} = net free area factor of grille. If a grille's open spaces occupy 60% of its face area, $\kappa_{nfa} = 0.60$.
A_{nfa} = net free area of grille, in²

Step 15. Design the return grilles for each outlet. First, find the net free area of each return air grille from

$$A_{nfa\text{-}r} = 0.8 \, A_{nfa\text{-}s}$$

Then find the return grille's required total face area from below. Again say the selected grille's open spaces occupy 60 percent of its face area.

$$A_{tot} \, \kappa_{nfa} = A_{nfa\text{-}r}$$

If the grille is circular: $\quad A_o = 0.785 \, \delta^2$

The return air grille should be located where it will promote maximum air circulation throughout the space between it and the supply air grilles. Sometimes it is wise design to have two return air grilles instead of one.

Structural Weight of Ducting:

Step 1. Tabulate the area of every surface of the ducting assembly as shown on its mechanical drawings.

Step 2. From Table 7-14 find the ducting's thickness based on the minimum dimension of its largest surface.

Step 3. Find the unit weight of the ducting metal. Then, knowing the ducting's surface area, find its total weight.

Step 4. Add to the above amount the weight of the other materials the ducting is made of: shells, vanes, fire dampers, seam strips, girth reinforcing, corner reinforcing, diagonal bracing, stay bracing, support bracing,

TABLE 7-14: SHEET METAL WEIGHTS, THICKNESSES

UNIT WT, PSF, AT EACH GAUGE THICKNESS

METAL TYPE	26	24	22	20	18	16	14
Hot rolled steel	0.750	1.000	1.250	1.500	2.000	2.500	3.125
Galvan. steel	0.906	1.156	1.406	1.656	2.156	2.656	3.281
Stainless steel	0.790	1.050	1.310	1.580	2.100	2.630	3.280
Aluminum	0.015	0.288	0.355	0.456	0.575	0.724	0.914
Copper	0.737	0.932	1.178	1.484	1.869	2.355	2.972

THICKNESS, IN, AT EACH GAUGE THICKNESS

METAL TYPE	26	24	22	20	18	16	14
Hot rolled stl	0.018	0.024	0.030	0.036	0.048	0.060	0.075
Galvan. steel	0.022	0.028	0.034	0.040	0.052	0.064	0.080
Stainless stl	0.019	0.025	0.031	0.038	0.050	0.063	0.078
Aluminum	0.015	0.020	0.025	0.032	0.040	0.051	0.064
Copper	0.016	0.020	0.025	0.032	0.040	0.051	0.064

access door framing, acoustic mounts, probably a bucket of screws and bolts, probably insulation on the outside, and possibly acoustic lining on the inside. In lieu of more articulate data, a fair estimate of all these materials' weights is 2.2 × sheet metal's estimated weight.

High-Velocity HVAC System Ducting Design:

High-velocity HVAC system design involves several initial considerations before design, as follows:

▸ Network symmetry greatly improves balanced airflow throughout the ducting. It also reduces design and layout time, construction costs, and onsite balancing of system componentry.

▸ Is the system a 12-hr or 24-hr operation? 12-hr operations are primarily for daytime occupancies (e.g. offices), while 24-hr operations are typically for hospitals, apartments, and other occupancies with overnight sleeping areas. 12-hr operations usually have higher duct airflows because their occupants can tolerate more noise.

▸ The design friction loss from the discharge fan to the branch header just before the first riser takeoff should be as nearly equal as possible.

▸ The longest run should have the highest airflow velocities.

▸ The length-to-diameter ratio of each duct run should be about the same throughout the system.

▸ A good design velocity for all terminal runs is 2,000 fpm.

Step 1. Find the system's design heating and cooling loads from the two equations below:

Heating load: $H_{cap} \geq$ **H** $(1.15 + 0.000034\ E)$
Cooling load: $C_{cap} \geq$ **C** $(1.15 + 0.000034\ E)$

H_{cap} = design htg. capacity of selected system, Btu/hr
C_{cap} = design clg. capacity of selected system, Btu/hr
H   = design heating load of the architecture, Btu/hr
E = elevation of site above sea level, ft. If $E \leq 2,000$
      ft, use $E = 0$
C   = design cooling load of the architecture, Btu/hr

Step 2. Locate the duct outlets in every zone throughout the building, then draw a tentative ducting network from each primary fan to the outlets its serves. This network should be as simple and symmetrical as possible.

Step 3. Knowing the building's design heating and cooling loads, determine the primary duct's diameter at the discharge fan face from the two formulas below. Initial velocity for 12-hr operation is 3,000–5,000 fpm and for 24-hr operation is 2,000–3,000 fpm, but maximum velocities may be as high as 6,000 rpm.

Heating load: $\delta = \left[\dfrac{196\ \mathbf{H}}{v_{max}\ (T_h - T_i)} \right]^{0.5}$

Cooling load: $\delta = \left[\dfrac{8.50\ \mathbf{C}}{v_{max}} \right]^{0.5}$

δ = diameter of round duct at discharge fan face, in.
H   = design heating load of the architecture, Btu/hr
C   = design cooling load of the architecture, Btu/hr
v_{max} = maximum velocity of airflow in ducting, fpm
T_h = temp. of heating load airflow, usually 140° F.
T_i = ambient indoor temperature of occupancy during
      winter heating season, usually 68° F.

Step 4. Knowing δ and v_{max}, find the duct's equivalent friction loss per linear ft from

$$9,577,000 \, \Delta P \, \delta^{1.22} \; = \; \kappa_r \, L \, \mathcal{V}_{max}{}^{1.82}$$

ΔP = unit duct friction loss due to airflow, in. wg/LF

δ = dia. of round duct at discharge fan face, in.

κ_r = roughness coefficient of inner surface of ducting, from Table 7-2. κ_r = 0.009 for galv. sheet steel.

L = length of ducting, ft. Here solve equation for ΔP at L = 1.00 ft, then use ΔP as a reference value in subsequent calculations.

$\mathcal{V}_{max}$= maximum velocity of airflow in ducting, fpm

Step 5. Make a schedule of the duct lengths for the HVAC system's longest ducting from its discharge fan to its remote outlet. The remainder of this system design sequence is brief, as it is similar to that performed for low-velocity ducting, and because high-velocity ducting usually requires fewer calculations due to its usually greater symmetry.

a. Duct section area at remote outlet: $Q = \mathcal{V} A$

From the duct sizing bar graph on page 347, when a duct divides in half (symmetry), each branch duct's section area = 58 percent of the stem duct's section area. Thus, at each symmetrical duct split, the total outflow area equals 58% + 58% = 116%, or 1.16; or

b. Revised duct section area: $1.16 \, Q = \mathcal{V} A$

Here select a slightly *smaller* duct diameter, as this slightly increases the incoming velocity, which is considerably less at the outlets than at the primary discharge fan. Continue upstream and perform this calculation at every duct split to the discharge fan. Ideally the airflow velocity at each split will increase gradually until it approaches the velocity at the discharge fan.

Return Duct Design: In an enclosed central air system, the return airflow and thus the section area of each inlet and return duct ≈ 0.8 × supply section area.

$$A_r \geq 0.80 \, a \, b$$

A_r = minimum section area of return duct, in^2
a = wider dimension of duct, in.
b = narrower dimension of duct, in.

Air-Water Heating/Cooling System Design:

In these complex systems, a large air handling unit sends fresh air at high speeds through VAV ducting to all zones; then in each zone an air duct and two pipes containing heated and chilled water converge in one or more fan-coil units that portion the required conditioning to the occupancy. Thus the ducting is designed similarly as high-velocity air ducting systems.

Heat Pump Design: Heat pump operation is a four-step cycle in which a refrigerant at room temperature (1) is supercooled by expansion to temperatures that may be below 0° F, (2) absorbs heat via a network of coils (the absorber or cold end) immersed in a medium whose temperature is usually 35–45°, (3) is compressed which raises its temperature to well above 100°, then (4) radiates its heat through a network of coils (the radiator or hot end) that are immersed in a medium that rewarms the refrigerant to room temperature. The flow can be reversed, which allows air conditioners to act as heaters in cold weather; and the cycling either way is governed by a thermostat. A heat pump is classified according to the placement of its absorber and radiator. For example, in an *air-to-air heat pump* the absorber is placed

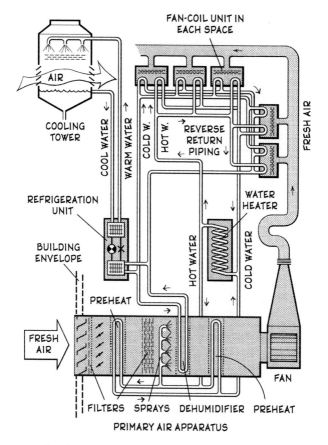

FAN-COIL UNIT IN
EACH SPACE

AIR

COOLING
TOWER

COOL WATER

WARM WATER

COLD W.

HOT W.

REVERSE
RETURN
PIPING

FRESH AIR

REFRIGERATION
UNIT

WATER
HEATER

BUILDING
ENVELOPE

HOT WATER

COLD WATER

FRESH
AIR

FAN

FILTERS   SPRAYS   DEHUMIDIFIER   PREHEAT

PREHEAT

PRIMARY AIR APPARATUS

Fig. 7-10. Air-water heating & cooling system.

where cold air passes through it and the radiator is located where air requiring warmth passes through it; in a *water-to-air heat pump* the absorber is immersed in a pond, well, or other body of water; and in a *ground-coupled heat pump* the absorber is buried several feet in the ground. The absorber may also be mounted in chimneys, graywater holding tanks, or solar collectors as a way of reusing the rejected heat from such sources.

Heat pump ducting and registers are the same as those in other air heating or cooling systems, and supply and return air volumes are usually equal.

Unit capacity, heating load: $H_{cap} \geq 1.15\,\mathbf{H}$
Unit capacity, cooling load: $C_{cap} \geq 1.15\,\mathbf{C}$
No. of units:
$$|P_{cap}/50{,}000| + 1 \geq \eta \geq |P_{cap}/15{,}000| + 1$$

Duct size, heating load in Btu/hr:
$$\mathbf{H}_{btu} \leq 0.65\,\kappa_d\,A\,(T_h - T_i)$$

Duct size, cooling load in Btu/hr:
$$\mathbf{C}_{btu} \leq 15\,\kappa_d\,A$$

Duct size, cooling load in tons:
$$800\,\mathbf{C}_{ton} \leq \kappa_d\,A$$

H_{cap} = heating capacity of selected unit, Btu/hr
C_{cap} = cooling capacity of selected unit, Btu/hr
$\mathbf{H}$ = design heating load of interior spaces, Btu/hr
$\mathbf{C}$ = design cooling load of interior spaces, Btu/hr
P_{cap} = design heating/cooling capacity of heat pump, Btu/hr. Use larger number of H_{cap} and C_{cap}.
η = number of units required, units
$\mathbf{H}_{btu}$ = heating capacity of selected unit, Btu/hr
$\mathbf{C}_{btu}$ = cooling capacity of selected unit, Btu/hr
$\mathbf{C}_{ton}$ = cooling capacity of selected unit, tons

κ_d = duct velocity factor, from Table 7-13
A = min. section area of duct (not incl. insul.), in^2
T_h = temperature of heated air, °F
T_i = temperature of indoor air, °F

Note: If the ducting exceeds 40 ft in length or its aspect ratio (ratio of its width to depth) ≥ 2.5, its size should be increased as described on page 348.

Water Cooling Systems:

In semi-arid regions that are more than about 4,000 feet above sea level (this includes one-third of the conterminous United States), a building's interior spaces can be cooled in warm weather with naturally chilled water. In summer these regions often experience clear night skies that are 30–50° cooler than mid-afternoon temperatures; thus if water is sprayed or trickled onto a building's roof from midnight till sunrise it becomes chilled, then the following afternoon the chilled water circulates through cooling coils exposed to fan-driven air. Such a *night roof spray cooling system* is simple and affordable, is easily designed and built, requires little architecture other than a nearly flat roof, keeps roofs clean, and protects the building from fire. An experienced manufacturer of these systems is Integrated Comfort, Inc. of Davis, CA.

Humidification System Design:

In a typical humidifier or evaporative cooler, a plume of water droplets ejected into a gently moving airstream evaporates and cools the surrounding air. Ideally the airstream moves at about 500 fpm at least 18 in. below ceilings and 8 ft from any seated occupants. Each unit should have a fan or other means of circulating the cooled air, and it should have a humidistat.

→ß▯Ⅰ▯▦♀❋⤨◉♀▥ℭ

$$12,000\ H\ =\ \eta\ Q\ (h_i\ c_i\ -\ h_o\ c_o)$$

H = design humidification load for occupancy, lb/hr
η = number of occupants in space
Q = req. airflow for occupancy, from Table 7-16, cfm
h_i = optimal indoor relative humidity, usually 50%
c_i = water content of saturated indoor air at optimal indoor temp. (usually 70°), from Table 7-15, gr/cf
h_o = design outdoor rel. humidity for site, usually 40%
c_o = water content of saturated outdoor air, usually at winter design temperature from Fig. 7-4

Dehumidification System Design:
Dehumidifiers remove water from warm humid air to make it feel cooler, eliminate hazards such as slippery floors, and minimize mildew growth indoors. There are three general kinds of dehumidifiers: *chillers*, *absorbers*, and *desiccant dryers*. Chillers utilize a refrigerant to cool moving air. Absorbers remove water from the air with hygroscopic chemicals which later have the collected moisture removed from them. Desiccant dryers have a water-ab-

TABLE 7-15: WATER CONTENT OF SATURATED AIR

t_o °F	c_o gr.	t_o °F	c_o gr.	t_o °F	c_o gr.	t_o °F	c_o gr.	t_o °F	c_o gr.
10	0.29	34	2.29	54	4.72	74	9.15	94	16.9
5	0.35	36	2.47	56	5.06	76	9.75	96	17.8
0	0.48	38	2.66	58	5.41	78	10.4	98	18.9
5	0.61	40	2.86	60	5.80	80	11.0	100	20.0
10	0.78	42	3.08	62	6.20	82	11.8	102	21.1
15	0.99	44	3.32	64	6.62	84	12.5	104	22.3
20	1.24	46	3.56	66	7.07	86	13.3	106	23.6
25	1.56	48	3.83	68	7.57	88	14.1	108	24.9
30	1.95	50	4.11	70	8.10	90	14.9	110	26.3
32	2.13	52	4.41	72	8.59	92	15.8	112	27.8

sorbing chemical spread on a slowly rotating porous wheel, half of which passes through a duct carrying humid air, while the other half passes through a hot or dry airstream that removes the collected water.

$$12,000 \ D \ = \ \eta \ Q \ (h_o \ c_o - h_i \ c_i)$$

D = design dehumidification load for occupancy, lb/hr
η = number of occupants in space
Q = req. airflow for occupancy, from Table 7-16, cfm
h_o = summer design outdoor rel. humidity for site, %
c_o = water content of saturated outdoor air at summer design temperature t_o, gr/cf. Find t_o from Fig. 7-5, then find c_o from Table 7-15.
h_i = optimal indoor relative humidity, usually 50%
c_i = water content of saturated indoor air at optimal indoor temperature (usually 75°), gr/cf. From Table 7-15, c_i for 75° F = 9.45 gr/cf.

Ventilation: Ventilation may be as simple as an open window or as complex as a filtered HVAC system that serves a hermetically sealed 'air aquarium.' Design guidelines for mechanical systems are:

▸ Intake louvers must be protected from entry or obstruction by insects, birds and nests, rodents, debris, updrafting rain, and swirling snow.
▸ Exhaust louvers cannot be near building entrances, operable windows, or intake vents.
▸ Supply air should be sent to where occupants are located more than the room they occupy.
▸ Installing CO_2 sensors saves energy.
▸ Recirculating and filtering part of the enclosed air to dilute indoor contamination usually costs less than using large volumes of outdoor air.

Ventilation Through Double-Hung Windows:

Step 1. Find the window's volume of incoming airflow.

$$Q \approx v A \varepsilon$$

Q = volume of incoming airflow thro' open window, cfm
v = velocity of airflow, fpm. 1 mph = 88 fpm. Prevailing windspeed usually ≈ 0.6 ambient breezespeed.
A = maximum free area of open window, sf.
ε = efficacy of opening. ε = 0.90 if opening faces prevailing winds, 0.55 if it is ⊥ to prevailing winds, and 0.15 if it faces away from prevailing winds. Interpolate for intermediate values.

Step 2. Determine the room's fresh air requirements from Table 7-16.

Step 3. Determine the height of the sash opening that is required to satisfy the room's fresh air requirements.

$$A_{req} Q \geq A Q_{req}$$

A_{req} = Required area of window opening, sf. (For most open windows this area is very small).
Q = Volume of incoming airflow thro' opening, cfm
A = Maximum free area of open window, sf
Q_{req} = fresh air requirement of room behind opng, cfm

Ventilation through Casement Windows:

$$Q \leq v w h \varepsilon$$

Q = volume of incoming airflow, cfm
v = velocity of airflow, fpm.
w = width of wind-scoop area when window is half open, ft. Half open ≈ 45°. Thus w = sash width × sin 45° – horiz. distance from sash's frame inset

to outer surface of building finish.

h = height of wind-scoop area, ft

ε = efficacy of opening. $\varepsilon = 0.90$ if opening faces prevailing winds, 0.55 if it is $\perp$ to prevailing winds, and 0.10 if it faces from prevailing winds. Interpolate for intermediate values.

Ventilation through Belvedere:

A belvedere induces natural airflow via the *aerosol effect* and the *stack effect*. The aerosol effect is a suction created by prevailing winds blowing through the belvedere's slatted vertical openings located above the horizontal opening at the belvedere's base; while the stack effect is the volume of air drawn up due to the temperature difference between the room's lowest and highest levels because the warmer air is less dense and rises.

Aerosol effect: $Q_a \approx 44\, A\, \varepsilon$

Stack effect: $Q_s \approx 70 + 3.7\,(h\,\Delta T)^{0.62}$

Q_a = volume of exiting airflow due to aerosol effect, cfm

A = area of opening, sf. Find (1) area of space between slats in one of the belvedere's walls and (2) area of horizontal opening at belvedere's base, then use the smaller value.

ε = efficacy of opening. $\varepsilon = 0.90$ if opening faces prevailing winds (usually the case with belvederes)

Q_s = volume of exiting airflow due to stack effect, cfm

h = height of temperature differential, ft

ΔT = temp. differential between lower & higher level, °F

Total ventilation airflow: $Q_T \approx Q_a + Q_s$

Q_T = total volume of exiting airflow due to aerosol and stack effect, cfm

Q_a and Q_s are as previously defined

364 ⟶ ß▯ I▯ ▤ ♀ ⤬ ⮑ ☀ ♀ ▥ ↻

Ventilation through Solar Chimney:

A solar chimney induces natural airflow via the *stack effect* as described above, which is quantified from

$$Q_s \approx 70 + 3.7 \, (h \, \Delta T)^{0.62}$$

Q_s = volume of exiting airflow due to stack effect, cfm
h = height of temperature differential, ft
ΔT = temp. diff. between lower and higher level, °F

TABLE 7-16: FRESH AIR REQUIREMENTS [1]

ACTIVITY	Min. airflow, F_o = cfm/occupant
Inactivity: reclining, sleeping, reading	10
Passive activity: classrooms, other listening	15
Light activity: eating, lobbies, retail areas	20
Moderate activity: light recreation, locker rooms, bars, private offices w/ smoking	25
Active work: shipping, dancing, machine work	30
Strenuous activity: gyms, conf. rooms w/ smoking	50
Smoking lounges, other indoor smoking areas	60

FLOOR AREA	Min. airflow, F_a = cfm/floor area
Corridor	0.33 ft³/min/ft² floor area
Garages	1.5 ft³/min/ft² floor area
Commercial kitchens	4.0 ft³/min/ft² floor area

SPATIAL UNIT	Min. airflow, F_u = cfm/ spatial unit
Ladies' rooms	35 ft³/min per toilet
Men's rooms	50 ft³/min per toilet or urinal
Canopy or fume hoods	60 ft³/min/sf of hood face area

AIR CHANGES/HR	Min. airflow, F_h = no. air changes/hr
Localized bad air	6-60 air changes/hr
Factory operations	obtain specific data for each analysis
Smoke exhaust systems	6 ac/hr outside air

1. Recom. airflow for any occupancy ≈ 1.5 ft³/min-occ.

Ventilation Design Formulas:

Required air per occupant: $\quad Q \geq F_o \, \eta$
Required air per floor area: $\quad Q \geq F_a \, A$
Required air per spatial unit: $\quad Q \geq 1.15 \, F_u \, \eta$
Required air per air changes: $\quad Q \geq 0.02 \, F_{ac} \, V$

Q = req. airflow delivery rate, (fresh or exhaust air), cfm
F_o = unit fresh air requirement per occupant, from Table 7-16, cfm
η = number of occupants in space
F_a = unit fresh air requirement of floor area, cfm
A = total floor area, sf
F_u = required fresh air for spatial unit (toilet, urinal, stove hood, etc.), cfm
η = number of spatial units served
F_{ac} = unit fresh air requirement, no. of air changes/hr. Multiply by safety factor of 2.5 unless specific data is given.
V = volume of ventilated space: $L \times W \times H$, cf

Ventilation Design, Supply Duct Size:

$$Q \leq A \, \kappa_d$$

Q = req. airflow delivery rate, (fresh or exhaust air), cfm
A = min. section area of duct (not incl. insulation), in^2
κ_d = duct velocity factor, from Table 7-13

If the duct exceeds 40 ft in length or its aspect ratio (ratio of its width to depth) ≥ 2.5, its size should be increased as described on page 348.

Ventilation Design, Exhaust Fan Size:

$$Q_{exi} + Q_{add} \geq Q_{tot}$$

Q_{exi} = ventilation rate of existing exhaust system, cfm
Q_{add} = additional ventilation required, cfm
Q_{tot} = total ventilation req. of exhaust system, cfm

Ventilation Design, Exhaust Duct Size:

$$Q \leq 0.8\, A\, \kappa_d$$

Q = req. airflow delivery rate, (fresh or exhaust air), cfm
A = min. section area of duct (not incl. Insulation), in^2
κ_d = duct velocity factor, from Table 7-13

Ventilation Requirement Based on CO_2 Concentration:

$$500\, Q = \Theta\, \eta\, (C_i - C_o)$$

Q = optimal ventilation load based on CO_2 conc., cfm
Θ = fresh air requirement per occupant based on activity from Table 7-16, cfm/occ
η = number of occupants in zone
C_i = indoor CO_2 setpoint, use 1,000 ppm unless otherwise noted
C_o = outdoor CO_2 level, typically 350–450 ppm

Ventilation Design, Indoor Parking Areas:

$$A\, h\, C_o\, Q \approx 486\, \eta\, \kappa_v\, \epsilon\, t$$

A = floor area of enclosed parking area, sf
h = clear floor-to-ceiling height of area, ft
C_o = max. level of carbon monoxide in enclosed parking area, ppm. This should never exceed 25 ppm.
Q = req. airflow of ventilation system, air changes/hr
ϵ = emission rate per vehicle, gr/min. ϵ varies considerably according to size of vehicle engine,

whether engine is hot or cold, ambient air temperature at time of engine startup (e.g. season of year), and age of vehicle (older vehicles generally have higher Є rates). Typical CO emissions of average-size auto engines are listed below:

Type of engine/starting/season	Emissions, gr/min
Cold-engine starting in summer (90° F)	3.7 gm/min
Hot-engine starting in summer	1.9 gm/min
Cold-engine starting in winter (32° F)	18.9 gm/min
Hot-engine starting in winter	3.4 gm/min

η = number of parking spaces in area
κ_v = fraction of vehicles operating at one time
t = operating time for each car from dropoff to parking or from parking to pickup, sec

Air Filtration: Filters are installed in climate control systems to remove particulates, microbes, gases, odors, and toxic chemicals. Each is typically rated in terms of *arrestance* (ability to remove lint, dust and other particles out of the airstream), *efficiency* (ability to remove sub-visible particles such as carbon black and fly ash), *airflow resistance* (the degree to which the filtering slows the airflow, thus requiring its fan and motor to be correspondingly stronger to maintain the required airflow), *airstream velocity* (typically 125–150 fpm for high-efficiency filters to 500 fpm for medium-efficiency ones and to 625 fpm for low-efficiency units), and *lifespan*. Since no one filter removes every pollutant, they are often combined to remove an acceptable percentage of whatever impurities that may exist in an indoor space.

　　The more efficient the filter, the more it slows the airflow; but increasing filter efficiency also reduces supply air requirements and thus the size of ducts, fans, boilers, and other system components. Since many filters become clogged over time, computerized s.a.p. sensors can be placed before and after one that notify service personnel when its initial ΔP has increased by a prescribed amount; then the filter is efficiently replaced. Air filters are typically selected as follows:

▸ Determine the size, concentration, and character of contaminants in the supply and return air.
▸ Determine the size of the particles to be removed and the optimal removal efficiency.
▸ Select a unit that combines the optimal efficiency and economy of operation.

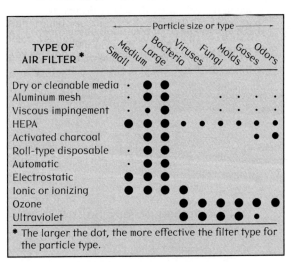

TYPE OF AIR FILTER *	Small	Medium	Large	Bacteria	Viruses	Fungi	Molds	Gases	Odors
Dry or cleanable media	·	●	●						
Aluminum mesh	·	●	●			·	·	·	·
Viscous impingement	·	●	●			·	·		·
HEPA	●	●	●	●	·	·	●		
Activated charcoal		·	●	●				●	●
Roll-type disposable	·	●	●						
Automatic	·	●	●						
Electrostatic	●	●	●						
Ionic or ionizing	●	●	●						
Ozone				●	●	●	●	·	●
Ultraviolet				●	●	●	●	·	

* The larger the dot, the more effective the filter type for the particle type.

Fig. 7-11. Ability of filters to remove pollutants from indoor air.

Air Filter Design: $100 \, Q_d = Q_e \, (100 - F)$

Q_d = initial design airflow in duct, fpm

Q_e = effective filtered airflow in duct, fpm

F = adsorption efficiency of filter in duct, %. After finding F, use this value in the Filter Airflow Resistance Graph of Fig. 7-12 to find the duct's effective airflow increase; then add this amount to the duct's normal airflow before sizing its section. For electronic, ionizing, or charged media filters, multiply the ducting's effective airflow increase value by 0.20.

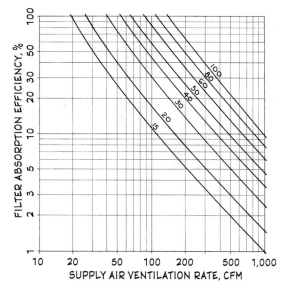

Fig. 7-12. Filter airflow resistance graph.

TABLE 8-1: PLUMBING FIXTURE REQUIREMENTS

OCCUPANCY & NO.	LAVS. M	F	TOILETS M	F	URINALS M	FTNS No./occ.
ASSEMBLY: auditoriums, courtrooms, gyms, etc.						
To 100	1	2	1	2	1	1/75
To 200	2	3	1	4	1	"
To 500	3	5	2	8	2	"
500+	1/175	1/100	1/250	1/65	1/250	"
BATHS OR SHOWERS, M or F: dorms, gyms, clubs, etc.: 1 per 8–30 occ.+ 1 per 20 above 30 occ.						
EATING PLACES: restaurants, dining halls, etc.:						
To 50	1	1	1	2	1	1/75
To 100	1	2	1	3	1	"
100+	1/125	1/80	1/200	1/50	1/200	"
Each kitchen must have a rest room w/ lav. & toilet						
HOSPITALS: ward or patient rooms, per floor:						
Per patient 1/10		1/10	1/8	1/8	0	1/75
INDUSTRIAL: warehouses, factories, etc., per fl.:						
To 50	1	2	1	2	1	1/75
To 100	2	3	1	4	1	"
To 250	3	5	2	8	2	"
250+	1/60	1/50	1/100	1/30	1/100	
NIGHT CLUBS: lounges, bars, casinos, etc.						
1/150	1/100		1/150	1/75	1/150	1/75
OFFICES: public & employees, per floor:						
To 50	1	2	1	2	1	1/75
To 125	2	3	1	4	1	"
To 300	3	5	2	8	2	"
300+	1/75	1/65	1/150	1/40	1/150	"
RELIGIOUS: churches, synagogues, mosques, etc.						
	1/150	1/100	1/150	1/75	1/150	1/75
SCHOOLS: nursery, elementary, per floor:						
	1/50	1/50	1/100	1/35	1/40	1/75
Middle school, high school, adult ed., per fl.:						
	1/60	1/50	1/100	1/45	1/60	1/75

8. PLUMBING

Waterflow Rate, Gal/min vs. Diameter:

$$Þ = 15\, d^2$$

Þ = waterflow rate in pipe at normal temperature and pressure, gpm

d = optimal inside diameter of copper, steel, or plastic pipe, in.

Waterflow Rate, Gal/min vs. Diameter:

$$Þ_{gpm} = 2.45\, Þ_{fps}\, d^2$$

$Þ_{gpm}$ = volume of waterflow in pipe, gpm

$Þ_{fps}$ = velocity or waterflow in pipe, fps

d = nominal inner pipe diameter, 2.5 in.

Required Number of Plumbing Fixtures:

Step 1. Find the occupancy load per floor.

$$\Theta = F\eta$$

Θ = total occupancy load of building

F = occupancy load per floor, occupants

η = number of floors in building

Step 2. Find the required number of plumbing fixtures for each floor from Table 8-1.

Plumbing Fixture Unit Requirements:

$$F_T = F_1 + F_2 + ... + F_z$$

F_T = total number of fixture units in plan, f.u.

$F_1, F_2, F_{etc.}$ = number of fixture units for each plumbing fixture, from Table 8-2

TABLE 8-2: PLUMBING FIXTURE UNIT VALUES

FIXTURE	FIXTURE UNITS, priv.	pub.	psf min. pressure
Toilet: flush tank	3	4	8
Flush valve	6	8	15
Urinal: flush tank	2	4	15
Flush valve	2	8	15
Lavatory or wash sink	1	2	8
Dental lavatory	1	1	8
Res. kitchen waste grinder	1	1	8
Self-closing faucet	1	1	12
Bathtub: no shower	2	4	8
With shower	2	4	12
Stall shower	2	2	12
Bidet	3	–	8
Bathroom: lav, tub, flush tank w.c.	6	12	8
Above w/ flush valve w.c.	8	15	10
Kitchen or service sink	2	3	8
Dish or clothes washer	2	3	8
Bar sink	1	3	8
Drinking fountain	–	1	15
Water cooler	–	1	8
Hose bibb	2	4	30
Fire hose	0	0	30
Lawn sprinkler	Coverage area × 0.3 gal/hr-ft²		

Initial Estimate of Building Water Demands:

Aver. demand: $B_{awd} \approx \eta\, \theta_{awd}\, [1 + 0.00077\, (T_d - 65)] + S$
Peak demand: $B_{pwd} \approx \eta\, \theta_{pwd}\, [1 + 0.00115\, (T_d - 65)] + S$

B_{awd} = average water demand of building, gal/day
B_{pwd} = peak water demand of building, gpm
η = number of occupants in building
θ_{awd} = aver. water demand/occ., from Table 8-3, g/day
θ_{pwd} = peak water demand/occ., from Table 8-3, gpm
T_d = summer design temperature for building site, from Fig. 7-5, °F.
S = aver. or peak water demand of any special loads

Pressure at Base of Water Supply Pipe:

$$\Delta P = 0.433\, \Delta h$$

ΔP = pipe pressure drop due to increased height, psi
Δh = change in height that induces pressure drop, ft

TABLE 8-3: ESTIMATED WATER SUPPLY DEMANDS

OCCUPANCY	Average demand, gal/day-occ.	Peak demand, gal/min-occ.
Assembly, theaters, lectures	5 per seat & empl.	0.17
Churches, mosques, synag.	5 + 5 for food serv.	0.12
Factories, no showers	15	0.12
w/ showers	25	0.50
Hospitals	175	0.50
Hotels, motels	75	0.43
Offices, stores, airports, etc.	10 + 5 for food serv.	0.09
Residences: homes, apts	100	0.33
Restaurants, dinner only	20	0.15
Two meals/day, 35; 3/day	50	0.13
Schools, w/ food service	25	0.12
w/ gym & showers	30	0.40

Contained Weight of Piping:

$$\omega_t = \omega_p + 0.34 \, d^2$$

ω_t = total unit weight of pipe & contained water, PLF
ω_p = unit weight of pipe, PLF
d = nom. pipe diameter, from Table 8-4, in.

Equivalent Length of Piping Elbows:

$$L_e \approx L + 1.33 \, \eta \, \delta$$

L_e = equivalent length of pipe with elbows, ft
L = actual length of pipe with elbows, ft
η = number of elbows in length of pipe
δ = diameter of piping, in.

TABLE 8-4: CONTAINED WEIGHTS OF PIPING

PIPE DIA. nom. in.	STEEL Schedule		COPPER Type			PLASTIC Type		
	40	80	K	L	M	ABS	PVC	CPVC
$3/8$	0.65	0.80	0.32	0.26	0.21	0.16	0.20	0.23
$1/2$	0.98	1.19	0.44	0.39	0.31	0.25	0.32	0.36
$3/4$	1.36	1.66	0.83	0.66	0.55	0.38	0.50	0.56
1	2.05	2.48	1.18	1.01	0.84	0.60	0.78	0.88
$1^1/4$	2.92	3.55	1.57	1.44	1.25	0.95	1.23	1.40
$1^1/2$	3.21	4.39	2.11	1.91	1.73	1.25	1.62	1.83
2	5.10	6.30	3.36	3.09	2.83	1.94	2.51	2.84
$2^1/2$	7.86	9.49	4.94	4.55	4.15	2.85	3.68	4.17
3	10.77	13.11	6.87	6.31	5.70	4.22	5.45	6.17
4	16.30	19.96	11.56	10.56	9.92	6.96	9.00	10.17
5	23.28	28.65	17.47	15.70	14.84	10.62	13.73	15.53
6	31.48	39.86	25.07	21.81	20.66	15.01	19.39	21.95

Equivalent Length of Piping Gate Valves:

$$L_e \approx 6\,\delta$$

L_e = equivalent length of gate valve, ft
δ = diameter of gate valve, in.

Supply Piping Design:

Step 1. Estimate the pipe pressure drop due to coldwater flow friction.

$$L\,\Delta P \approx 57\,P_i - 67\,P_h - 29\,H$$

L = effective length of pipe (includes safety factors for normal meter pressure drop and normal number of fittings), ft
ΔP = estimated pipe pressure drop for length of run, psi
P_i = initial or minimum water pressure, psi
P_h = req. pressure at highest or farthest outlet, psi
H = height of flow, or head, ft

Step 2. Convert any nonfixture unit flow to equivalent fixture unit flow.

$$Þ_e \approx \kappa_f\,(F_c + 0.071\,F_n)$$

$Þ_e$ = total equiv. fixture unit flow through pipe, f.u.
κ_f = pipe friction factor. κ_p = 2.0 if pipe is cast iron, wrought iron, galvanized iron, or steel; 1.0 if pipe is copper or brass.
F_c = coldwater fixture unit flow, f.u.
F_n = equivalent nonfixture unit flow, if any, gal/day

Step 3. From Fig. 8-1 find the minimum pipe diameter from the intersection of the vertical *fixture unit line* with the horizontal *pressure drop line*. At this point also note the water velocity in fps.

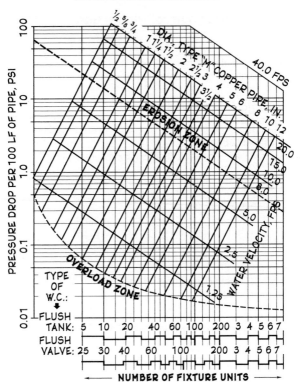

EROSION ZONE: AT VELOCITIES ABOVE UPPER DOTTED LINE, PIPE EROSION MAY OCCUR; CHOOSE LARGER DIAMETER PIPE.
OVERLOAD ZONE: AT VELOCITIES BELOW LOWER DOTTED LINE, SYSTEM LOAD IS TOO GREAT OR INCOMING PRESSURE IS TOO LOW; REDESIGN SYSTEM.

Fig. 8-1. Pipe diameter sizing graph.

Step 4. If the water velocity ≥ 8 fps, resize the pipe as below. In most systems optimal velocity is 4–6 fps; as above this pipe erosion can occur, and below this solid wastes tend to accumulate in the piping.

$$d_r \geq 0.0156 \, d \, v^{0.5}$$

d_r = resized pipe diameter, if necessary, in.
d = previous pipe diameter, from Step 3, in.
v = flow velocity through pipe, fps

Pipe Length Change due to Temperature Change:

$$\Delta L = \kappa_t \, L_L \, \Delta t$$

ΔL = change in pipe length due to change in temp., in.
κ_t = thermal expansion coefficient for pipe material, from Table 7-3, in/in.
L_L = length of pipe at lower temperature, in.
t = change in pipe temp., °F. Δt may occur in supply or waste runs.

Pipe Chase Size due to Thermal Expansion:

> **Chase Width:** $W \geq \kappa_w \, (\delta + \kappa_f)$
> **Chase Depth:** $D \geq \kappa_d \, (\delta + \kappa_f)$

W = optimal width of chase section, in. Round up to next 0.5 in.
D = optimal depth of chase section, in. Round up to next 0.5 in.
κ_w = chase width factor. $\kappa_w = 1.6$ for supply, 1.4 for waste, and 1.2 for vent piping.
κ_d = chase depth factor. $\kappa_d = 1.3$ for supply, 1.2 for waste, and 1.1 for vent piping.
δ = pipe diameter, in.

κ_f = pipe function factor. κ_f = 2.0 if pipe is supply, 1.4 if waste or vent.

If a hot and cold supply pipe are in one chase, add $2 \times (d_{hot} + d_{cold})$ in. to the pipes' required chase width (or depth if one pipe is above the other). If two waste or vent pipes are in one chase, subtract 2 in. from the required width for both pipes.

Water Hammer Arrester Design:

Threaded base connection: $C \approx F^{0.67}$
Soldered base connection: $C \approx F^{0.74}$

C = required air volume of water hammer arresters with threaded or
   soldered bases in plumbing system, in^2
F = number of fixture units in plumbing system, 36

The following formula is used to find the feasible pressure, and thus the diameter, of a water supply pipe with no arresters. This formula is particularly important for hot water plastic piping.

$$v L = 14.3 \, t \, (P_i + \Delta P)$$

v = maximum velocity of waterflow, fps
L = length of water supply piping, ft. Count only length from outlet upstream to next-to-last reduction of pipe diameter: e.g. if pipe reduces from 1 to $\frac{3}{4}$ in. diameter 30 ft upstream of outlet and reduces from $1\frac{1}{4}$ to 1 in. 26 ft farther upstream, $L = 30 + 26 = 56$ ft.
t = cycle time for opening or closing valve, sec. Most occupants take about 1.5 sec to close a standard hot or cold water plumbing fixture valve. Larger-diameter commercial valves operated by service

personnel take longer. A rational rule of thumb
for design: $t \approx$ pipe diameter × 1.4.

P_i = water pressure at valve when fully open, psi

ΔP = water pressure increase at valve due to pressure
surge caused by shutoff, psi. $P_i + \Delta P$ must $\leq$ piping's maximum safe pressure.

Pump Design, Net Actual Head of System:

$$H \approx H_a - H_f + H_s - H_v$$

H = net actual
height of pump
waterflow, ft

H_a = local atmos-
pheric head at
normal atmos-
pheric condi-
tions. At sea
level H_a usually
equals 33.95 ft.
At other eleva-
tions H_a may be
adjusted ac-
cording to
$(1 - 0.000034\ E)$.
If pump's net dis-
charge head is
required, $H_a = 0$.

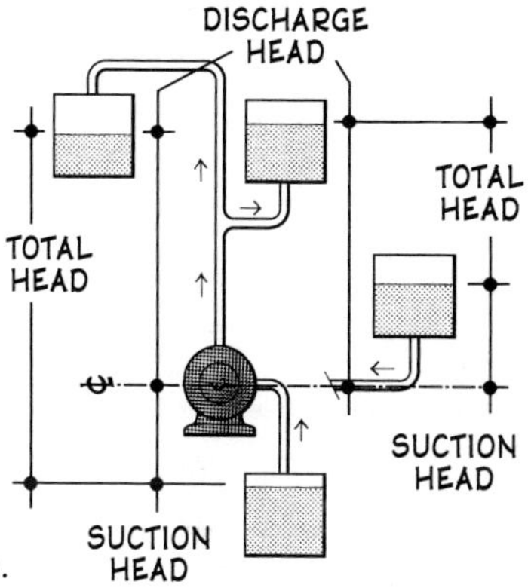

Fig. 8-2. Types of heads
in water pump systems.

H_f = pipe friction head:
energy loss of the liquid flowing through the suction pipe due to wall resistance of the pipe, fittings, valves, and entrance conditions. In small
systems this typically $\approx$ only 2-3 ft.

H_s = static suction lift head: vertical distance btwn

horizontal ¢ of pump impeller and reservoir's free
surface, ft. If reservoir's free surface is below
the impeller, H_s is +; if above the impeller, H_s is –
and is known as the *static suction head*.

H_v = vapor pressure head: vapor pressure of water in
air at normal atmospheric conditions (14.7 psi at
70° F), which causes the local atmospheric head
to be slightly less. H_v typically = 0.84 ft.

Pump Design, Required Horsepower:

$$40 \, ⱧP \, \varepsilon \approx \sigma \, Þ \, \kappa_\upsilon \, H$$

ⱧP = required pump horsepower, ? hp

ε = pump efficiency, %. Use 65% unless specific data
is available.

σ = specific gravity of liquid pumped. σ of water = 1.0.

Þ = pump capacity or flow, gpm

κ_υ = water viscosity factor, from bar graph below:

Normal water temperature

32°	50°	75°	100°	125°	150°	175°	200°	212°
2.00	1.41	1.00	0.75	0.59	0.49	0.40	0.35	0.33

κ_υ = water viscosity factor

H = total discharge height (head) or vertical distance
between pump and level of pumped liquid, ft. 1 ft
of head = 0.433 psi.

Pressure Relief Valve Design, Cavitation:

$$\kappa_c \, (P_i - P_o) \approx 2 \, (P_o + 14.7)$$

κ_c = cavitation constant. If $\kappa_c \leq 1.0$, cavitation will
likely occur and more than one pressure relief
valve should be installed in series.

P_i = valve inlet pressure, psi
P_o = valve outlet pressure, psi

Water Supply Delivery Rate of Drilled Well:

$$\text{Þ} \approx 0.2 (F + 0.071 F_n)$$

Þ = supply water delivery rate, gpm
F = number of fixture units served, units
F_n = nonfixture unit hot water req. for commercial or
     industrial processes, if any, gpm

Small Water Supply Tanks:
There are several common methods of sizing pressurized water supply tanks in small buildings: (1) capacity ≈ 10 × peak water delivery rate (gpm), (2) 25 gallons per occupant in residences, and (3) 15 minutes of storage per commercial occupant at peak water demand plus a fire protection reserve. Since water is densest at 39° F and expands by 1/23 its volume from 39–212° F, every water tank requires a 10 percent expansion airspace at its top.

Volume of Cylindrical Tank or Pipe:

$$2{,}200\ V = L\ \delta^2$$

V = volume of cylindrical void, as in a water tank or
     length of pipe, cf. 1 cf of liquid = 7.49 gal.
L = height of tank or length of pipe, in.
δ = clear inside diameter of tank or pipe, in.

Water Pressure Tank Design:

$$C \approx 5 (F + 0.071 F_n)$$

C = required capacity of water pressure tank, gal

F = number of fixture units served, units
F_n = nonfixture unit hot water required for commercial or industrial processes, if any, gpm

Large Water Supply Tanks: There are four kinds of large water tanks in building plumbing systems:

Gravity tank: a nonpressurized reservoir of water located above the plumbing system (usually on the roof or a nearby tower) that satisfies fixture pressure requirements by downfeeding or gravity.

Suction tank: a hermetically sealed reservoir accompanied by one or more pumps that continually supply water of adequate pressure to all fixtures in the building or zone.

Surge tank: a gravity or suction reserve that smoothes out jagged peak demands and erratic pressure variations in the water supply.

Booster pump: continuously running pumps with variable-speed drives that maintain near-constant water supply pressures.

Gravity Tank Design, Tank Capacity:

$$V_w \approx 4.25\, D_p$$

V_w = total volume of water gravity tank reservoir, cf
D_p = peak demand of water supply, gpm

Gravity Tank Design, Pump Capacity:

$$D_p = C\,\eta$$

D_p = peak demand of water supply, gpm
C = required pump capacity for gravity tank, gpm
η = optimal number of pumps in system

Suction Tank Design, Tank Volume:

Step 1. Find the tank's required volume.

$$400\, D_p \approx \eta\, C\, V_w\, H$$

D_p = peak demand of water supply, gpm
η = number of pumps in system
C = number of pump cycles per hour
V_w = water volume of suction tank, cf
H = total water discharge height or head, ft

Step 2. Find the tank's total air-water volume.

$$P_{min}\,(V_t - V_w) = 0.01\, V_w\, W_c\, P_{max}$$

P_{min} = minimum pressure of water supply, assume psi
V_t = total air-water volume of suction tank, cf
V_w = water volume of suction tank, 652 cf
W_c = water withdrawal capacity of suction tank, %
P_{max} = maximum pressure of water supply, psi

Suction Tank Design, Req. Pump Capacity:

$$D_p \approx C\,\eta$$

D_p = peak demand of water supply, gpm
C = required pump capacity for suction tank, gpm
η = optimal number of pumps in system

Suction Tank Design, Req. Pump Power:

$$92\ \text{HP}\ \varepsilon \approx C\, P_{max}$$

HP = required horsepower of suction tank pump, hp
ε = pump efficiency, %
C = capacity or maximum waterflow of pump, gpm
P_{max} = maximum pressure of water supply, psi

Suction or Surge Tank Design:

$$W = V_L - V_L P_{L/P_H}$$

W = withdrawal rate of tank per operating cycle, gal.
   6 W should ≤ peak hourly demand on plumbing sys.
V_L = air volume in tank at its lowest pressure, cf
P_L = lowest air pressure in tank, psi
P_H = highest air pressure in tank, psi

Surge Tank or Emergency Reserve Size:

$$V_r = 2.9 (D_p - Þ)$$

V_r = optimal volume of tank or reserve, cf
D_p = peak demand of water supply, gpm
Þ   = water supply delivery rate, gpm.

Booster Pump Design, Required Power:

Step 1. Find the booster pump's required horsepower.

$$325,000 \; ℙ \approx C \, ℰ \, W_p$$

$ℙ$ = required horsepower of booster pump, hp
C = capacity or maximum waterflow of pump, gpm
$ℰ$ = pump efficiency, %. $ℰ$ normally ≈ 65%.
W_p = maximum pressure of water supply, psi

Step 2. For multipump systems, select the optimal number of pumps according to the MMRD schedule below. The smallest pump should ≈ 10–30 percent of total load, $η - 1$ pumps should ≈ 80 percent of total load, and total pump capacity should ≥ 110 percent of total load.

   If 2 pumps: % load for each pump = 30 + 80
   If 3 pumps: % load for each pump = 25 + 55 + 55

If 4 pumps: % load for each pump = 15 + 35 + 35 + 35
If 5 pumps: % load " " " = 15 + 25 + 25 + 25 + 25
If 6 pumps: % load " " " = 12 + 20 + 20 + 20 + 20 + 20

Water Softener Design:

$$C = D_a\, t\, (H - 4.0)$$

C = regeneration capacity of water softener system,
grains. Solve for this value, then from specs below select unit with next largest capacity above
computed value. If C exceeds the largest capacity, use more than one unit.

Max. Cap., gr	Max. iron, gr/gal	Max. mangan- ese, ppm	Unit size, in. $D \times W \times H$	Wt. when full, lb
16,000	40	2	18 × 25 × 42	430
24,000	50	3	18 × 26 × 51	480
32,000	75	5	18 × 27 × 55	510
64,000	100	5	18 × 36 × 55	590
96,000	100	5	18 × 38 × 61	690
128,000	100	5	18 × 42 × 55	800

D_a = occupancy's aver. water supply demand, gal/day
t = water softener cycle time, days. For standard
residential units, solve for lower and upper limits
at t_L = 2 days and t_U = 6 days.
H = hardness of water, grains/gal

Water Heater Design:

Step 1. Find the water heater's theoretical capacity.
Once C below is solved, it may need adjusting due to
the unit's entering, ambient, and exiting temperatures.

Gas heaters: $220\,(F + 2\,F_n) \approx C_g\,(T_h - T_c)$
Electric heaters: $245\,(F + 2\,F_n) \approx C_e\,(T_h - T_c)$

F = number of hot water fixture units served, units
F_n = required nonfixture unit hot waterflow, gpm
C_g = capacity of gas hot water heater, gal
C_e = capacity of electric hot water heater, gal
T_h = temperature of heated water, °F
T_c = temperature of cold water, °F

Step 2. Find the water heater's effective capacity from the fixture unit diversity bar graph below.

Theoretical unit capacity

Diverse or effective unit capacity

Solar Water Heating Design:

Step 1. Determine the system's optimal collector area from the Solar Collector Area Graph of Fig. 8-3. This is for energy-conservative household use of hot water.

Step 2. Size the solar hot water reservoir from

> **Unit capacity, gallons:** $C \approx 2A$
> **Unit capacity, cubic ft:** $C = 0.27A$

C = storage capacity of reservoir, gal or cf
A = optimal area of solar collector glazing, sf

Irrigation System Design:

$$9,500\, \varepsilon\, Q = A\, D\, C\, W$$

ε = biotic efficiency of rainfall application or irrigation event, depending on local climatic condition as follows: low desert = 0.60; high desert = 0.65; hot dry = 0.70; temperate = 0.75; cool = 0.80. If

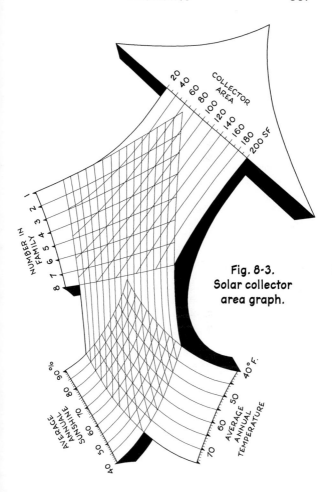

Fig. 8-3.
Solar collector
area graph.

irrigation events are necessary, ε will likely be
hot dry or ≤ 0.70.

Q = required irrigation waterflow, gpm. This equation
is typically solved for this value, which is then
used to size the irrigation's required piping.

A = area of plant strata to be irrigated, sf

D = depth of roots in plant strata, ft. 1.3 ft is a general value. $D ≈ 1.0$ ft for short plant strata (e.g.
close-cropped lawns) in dry soil.

C = capacity of subsoil to retain water, in/ft depth.
Typical values are coarse gravelly soil = 0.5, fine
sand = 1.0, sandy loam = 1.5, loam = 2.0, clayey
loam = 2.2, and fine topsoil = 3.0 in/ft depth.

W = portion of water depletion that maintains non-
wilting plant strata, %. Typical values are 50%
for medium-value turf and 75% for low-value turf.
Use more articulate data when available.

Swimming Pool Design:

Step 1. Knowing the pool's shape, compute its surface
area. If the area requirements depend on the pool's occupancy load, it may be sized from

$$A = 25 B$$

A = min. area of pool based on occupancy load, sf

B = max. number of bathers planned to use the pool

Step 2. Knowing the pool's surface area, determine the
minimum depth in every part of its area as follows:

Wading areas for children .... 12–24 in. deep
General shallow areas .... min. 3'-6" deep
Where diving is permitted from pool edge .. 9'-0" deep
Plummet depths & widths beneath diving boards:
    Beneath 1 meter boards ..... 11'-0" deep, 20' wide

Beneath 3 & 5 meter boards .. 12'-0" deep, 24' wide
Beneath 10 meter towers .... 15'-0" deep, 28' wide
Tank has roundfloor-to-wall seams vert. radii ≤ 2'-0"
Floor inclines .... max. 1:12 down to 4'-6" deep
From 4'-6" deep max. 1:3 down to pool's max. depth

Step 3. Knowing the pool's surface area and its depth in every area, find its volume.

Step 4. Knowing the pool's volume, determine the capacity of its circulation pump. The pool water requires at least three turnovers per day to keep it fresh.

$$V_p = 480 \ C_p$$

V_p = volume of swimming pool, gal
C_p = capacity of circulating pump, gpm. This is usually a double-suction centrifugal pump, as reciprocating pumps produce pulsations in the filters and single-suction pumps generally wear out faster. In public pools two pumps of required capacity are usually installed; then continuous operation is ensured if one pump needs servicing.

Step 5. Determine the circulating pump's full discharge head. The pump must deliver at least 15 psi pressure to each pool inlet after overcoming friction losses due to piping, fittings, filters, and possible heating.

a. Head in ft: $H_{ft} \geq 1.1 \ (35 + L_{pf} + L_f + L_h)$
b. Head in psi: $H_{psi} \geq 0.48 \ (35 + L_{pf} + L_f + L_h)$

H_{ft} = total discharge head of pump, ft.
H_{psi} = total discharge head, psi. $1 \ H_{ft} \times 0.433 \ H_{psi}$.
L_{pf} = pump head loss due to system piping and fittings, ft. This is rarely more than 10 ft.
L_f = equivalent pump head loss due to filtration, ft.

This usually ≈ 50 ft for sand or permanent media
filters and 90 ft for diatomaceous filters.

L_h = equiv. pump head loss due to heating, ft. If water
is unheated, $L_h = 0$; otherwise L_h rarely >10 ft.

Step 6. Determine the pool's amount of makeup water
flow. When a swimmer enters the pool, a volume of water
equal to the person's immersed volume is displaced
which flows into outlets at the pool's edge; then when
each swimmer leaves the pool the displaced water is re-
plenished from a local water source or by recirculating
the outlet waterflow after purification.

$$Q_m = 0.32 \, B$$

Q_m = pool's rate of makeup waterflow, gpm
B = max. number of bathers using the pool

Step 7. Knowing the capacity of the pool's circulating
pump, compute the effective bed area of the filtration
system. Whether the system is permanent media or diatomaceous earth, its optimal filtration rate is usually
about 2.5 gpm·sf.

$$C_p = 2.5 \, A_f$$

C_p = capacity of pool's circulating pump, gpm
A_f = effective bed area of filtration system, sf

In some pools two identical filters of similar capacity are
installed so one can backwash its filtering media or be
serviced while the other continues to operate. If only
one filter is installed, it usually backwashes late at
night when the pool isn't being used. There are also two
general kinds of filtration systems:

Sand or permanent media: Waterflow rates can be as
high as 20 gpm/sf of bed area, they have a high

dirt-holding capacity, and their backwash rates are high. Rugged, dependable, simple to operate, economical: The "Chevrolet" system.

Diatomaceous earth: Produces a brilliantly clear water, and the open tank allows thorough visual inspection and quick access to filter componentry at all times. Pump horsepowers are smaller; but the system is more complicated, costs more to run, and is 2–3 times larger per 1,000 gal of water filtered: The "Cadillac" system.

Permanent media filters are usually cylindrical and diatomaceous earth filters are usually rectangular. A multiple bar graph showing approximate filter dimensions versus pool water volume appears below.

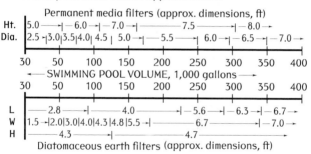

Step 8. Size the pool's backwash sump pump and sump tank. Common sump pump capacities used for backwashing swimming pool filters are 12.5 and 15 gal. The slower pump takes longer to cleanse the filter bed but requires a smaller sump tank.

$$V_s \geq 0.133\, A_f\, C_s$$

V_s = required volume of sump tank, cf
A_f = effective bed area of filtration system, sf
C_s = capacity of sump pump used for backwashing filter system, usually 12.5 or 15 gpm

Step 9. Find the pool's optimal number of inlets from

$$C_p \geq \eta \, C_i$$

C_p = capacity of pool water circulating pump, gpm
η = optimal no. of inlets around pool perimeter.
C_i = optimal discharge capacity of each inlet, gpm.
Each inlet should discharge 10–20 gpm, and they should be equally spaced ≤ 30 ft apart around the pool perimeter.

Regarding pool outlets: each is customarily a single drain located at the lowest point of the pool's floor and is usually sized to drain the pool in 4–12 hr. However, the pool cannot drain faster than its sewer capacity, and its drainage rate is a function of the drain diameter and net opening of its cover plate.

Step 10. Size the pool's disinfecting system. Chlorine is most commonly used, but bromine and ozone are used also. If chlorine, the system drips the chemical into the pool's inlet waterflow to maintain a constant 0.5 ppm of chlorine in the pool water. Thus

$$1,920,000 \, Q_d = \eta \, V_p + 480 \, \eta \, Q_m$$

Q_d = amount of disinfectant required to disinfect pool water, lb/day
η = number of hours per day pool is open, hr
V_p = volume of swimming pool, gal
Q_m = makeup waterflow rate from Step 6, gpm

Step 11. Size the pool's water heater if one is necessary. Unless the pool is an outdoor pool open only during the summer, its incoming water supply is probably heated to the pool water's desired temperature.

$$t\,\mathbf{H}_p \;=\; 4{,}000\,C_p\,(T_i - T_o) + \mathbf{H}_m$$

t = time required to heat total volume of pool water, hr. 48 hr is generally allowed to heat commercial swimming pools.

$\mathbf{H}_p$ = amount of energy required to heat the pool water, Btu/hr

C_p = capacity of pool water circulating pump, gpm

T_i = desired temperature of pool water, °F. Typical indoor pool water temperatures are 75–85° for pleasure swimming, 77-80° for competitive swimming, and 97–104° for whirlpools and spas. 80° is a good average for public pools.

T_o = temperature of local water supply that is heated to pool water's desired temperature, °F.

$\mathbf{H}_m$ = heat migration losses through building envelope while pool is filling, Btu/hr. During the many hours it takes to heat pool water to the desired temperature, some water heat migrates through the pool's floor and walls and into the air above. This escaping heat should be quantified and its hourly loss included in the above formula as $\mathbf{H}_m$.

Climate control system guidelines for indoor pools are:

▸ Optimal indoor pool air temperatures are 75–85° for pleasure swimming, 77–85° for competitive swimming, and 80–85° for whirlpools and spas.
▸ Fresh air requirements = 0.5 cfm/sf of pool and deck area, and ≥ 25 cfm for each occupant.
▸ Supply air circulation volume = 4–8 AC/hr.
▸ Air velocity above deck and diving areas ≤ 25 fpm.

Higher velocities make bathers feel chilly.
▶ Air velocity above pool water ≤ 10 fpm.
▶ Air supply outlets should aim toward the coldest
   envelope surfaces above the pool water to prevent condensation from forming on these surfaces. The largest such surfaces are usually wall
   and ceiling glazing.
▶ Return air grilles for removing warm moist air
   should be located near the top of the room.

Nonwater Plumbing System Design: When
nonwater plumbing conveys petroleums, chemicals, toxic wastes, or environmentally damaging fluids, it requires containment piping, an enclosure of significantly
larger-diameter piping that protects the carrier conduit
from damage and keeps leaks from escaping into sur-

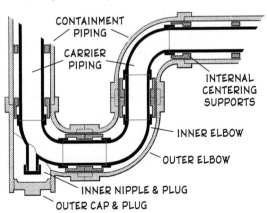

Fig. 8-4. Containment piping details.

rounding media. A few carrier/containment pipe diameter pairings are 2/4, 3/6, 4/8, 6/10, 8/12, 12/18, and 30/42 in. The carrier piping is designed as follows.

Step 1. Find the pipe pressure drop due to flow friction.

$$L \, \Delta P \approx 57 \, P_i - 67 \, P_m - 29 \, H$$

L = effective length of pipe (includes normal number of fittings), ft
ΔP = estim. pipe pressure drop due to flow friction, psi
P_i = initial water pressure, psi
P_m = minimum fixture pressure at highest or farthest outlet, psi
H = head or height of flow, ft

Step 2. Convert the nonwaterflow to equivalent water fixture unit flow.

$$Þ_{fu} \approx 49,000 \, Þ_{gpm} \, \sigma \, \upsilon$$

$Þ_{fu}$ = total equiv. fixture unit flow through pipe, f.u.
$Þ_{gpm}$ = nonfixture unit flow, if any, through pipe, gpm
σ = specific gravity of liquid flowing in pipe
υ = kinematic viscosity of liquid flowing in pipe, from fluid mechanics book or other reference

Step 3. Find the pipe's minimum diameter from Fig. 8-1

Step 4. Convert the liquid's pipe flow from gpm to fps.

$$Þ_{gpm} = 2.45 \, Þ_{fps} \, d^2$$

$Þ_{gpm}$ = volume of liquid or gas flow through pipe, gpm
$Þ_{fps}$ = velocity of liquid or gas flow through pipe, fps
d = clear inside diameter of pipe, in.

Step 5. If the liquid flow velocity exceeds 8 fps, resize the pipe as below.

$$d_r = 0.353 \, d_i \, Þ_{fps}^{0.5}$$

d_r = resized pipe diameter, if necessary, in.
d_i = initial pipe diameter, in.
P_{fps} = theoretical pipe flow velocity, from Step 4, fps.

Pipe Liquid or Gas Flow, cfm vs. fps:

$$3.06 \, P_{cfm} = P_{fps} \, d^2$$

P_{cfm} = volume of liquid or gas flow through pipe, cfm
P_{fps} = velocity of liquid or gas flow through pipe, fps
d = inside diameter of piping, in.

Gas Piping Design, Stored vs. Outlet Volume:

$$14.7 \, V_g = P \, V_c$$

V_g = volume of gas at normal atmospheric pressure, cf
P = pressure of gas when stored in reservoir, psi
V_c = volume of gas cylinder or reservoir, cf

Gas Piping Design, Supply Pipe Diameter:

Step 1. Compute the peak volume of flow in the piping.

$$P = \eta \, F \kappa_d$$

P = peak volume of gas flow in pipe, cfm.
η = number of outlets in system
F = rate of flow at each outlet, cfm
κ_d = diversity factor for systems with multiple outlets, from diversity factor bar graph below:

Number of outlets in system

1	2	3	4	5	6	7	8	9	10	11	12
1.00	0.98	0.93	0.86	0.78	0.70	0.62	0.55	0.49	0.45	0.42	0.40

Diversity factor κ_d

Step 2. Size the supply main.

$$L \, \kappa_m \, \sigma^{0.5} \, Þ^2 \; = \; 120{,}000 \; \Delta P \; d^{\,5}$$

L = length of pipe (includes allowance for normal no. of fittings), ft

κ_m = pipe material coefficient. κ_m = 2.0 for iron or steel, 1.0 for copper or brass.

σ = specific gravity of gas in pipe, from Table 8-5

$Þ$ = peak volume of gas flow in pipe, from Step 1, cfm

ΔP = permissible pressure drop (ppd) in piping, psi. If ΔP is in inches mercury (in. Hg), 1 psi = 2.04 in. Hg.

d = minimum pipe diameter, inside dimension, in. Minimum d = 0.5 in.

TABLE 8-5: PROPERTIES OF COMMON GASES
Values at 60° F. at sea level

GAS	SPEC. GRAVITY	HEATING VALUE
Atmosphere at sea level	1.00	supports combust.
Compressed air	1.00 × atmos. press.	supports combust.
Vacuum	1.00 × atmos. press.	supports combust.
Oxygen (O_2)	1.11	supports combust.
Nitrogen (N_2)	0.97	 0
Carbon dioxide (CO_2)	1.53	 0
Carbon monoxide (CO)	0.97	 0
Hydrogen (H_2)	0.07	275 Btu/ft³
Helium (He_2)	0.14	 0
Ammonia (NH_3)	0.60	 0
Propane (C_3H_3)	1.52	..... 2,370 Btu/ft³
Butane (C_4H_{10})	2.01	..... 2,977 Btu/ft³
Methane (CH_4)	0.55	...... 995 Btu/ft³
Acetylene (C_2H_2)	0.91	..... 1,455 Btu/ft³
Coal gas	≈ 0.55	≈ 450 Btu/ft³
Natural gas (mostly methane)	≈ 0.63	... ≈ 1,000 Btu/ft³
Fuel oil	144,000–150,000 Btu/gal	
Gasoline, kerosene		132,000 Btu/gal

Compressed Air System Design:

Step 1. List all the devices and the number of each that will use the compressed air, locate a convenient air outlet for each device, and list the free compressed air requirement at each outlet in cfm. After laying out the system in plan and elevation, tabulate the length of piping from each compressor to each outlet it serves. This schedule will later list the size of each length of piping plus the airflow rate and air pressure at each outlet.

Step 2. Determine the system load diversity factor for all outlets or devices that will use the compressed air at one time. This is usually estimated by carefully thinking out the frequency, length of time, criticality of use, and portion of maximum possible workload of each device.

Step 3. When selecting the compressor unit, consider its *discharge pressure* and required *capacity*. The discharge pressure should be at least 10 psi greater than the required pressure at any outlet for small systems and as much as 25 psi greater for large systems with long compressor-to-outlet runs. Typical air pressure for compressed air tools = 90 psi.

Step 4. Compute the system's peak demand flow.

$$D_p = 1.1\,\kappa_d\,F\,(1 - 0.000034\,E)$$

D_p = peak demand of compressed air system, cfm.
κ_d = diversity factor, based on feasible ratio of maximum number of outlets used at any one time to total number of outlets.
F = actual fixture flow, fpm.
E = elevation of occupancy above sea level, ft.

Step 5. Size each length of piping.

$$L \, \kappa_m \, \sigma^{0.5} \, \Phi^2 \; = \; 120,000 \, \Delta P \, d^5$$

L = length of piping (includes allowance for normal number of fittings), ft

κ_m = pipe material coefficient. κ_m = 2.0 for iron or steel piping, 1.0 for copper or brass.

σ = specific gravity of gas flowing in pipe, spsi. If air pressure is in actual psi or apsi, $\sigma_{spsi} = (\sigma_{apsi} + 14.7)/14.7$.

Φ = peak volume of gas flow in pipe, fpm

ΔP = permissible pressure drop in piping, psi. If ΔP is in in. mercury (in. Hg), 1 psi = 2.04 in. Hg. ΔP should not $\geq$ 5.0 psi.

d = minimum pipe diameter, inside dimension, in. Minimum d = 0.5 in.

Step 6. Size the compressor.

$$67 \, \mathbb{P} \; = \; \Phi \, P_i \, \{[(P_i - 14.7)/_{14.7}]^{0.29} - 1\}$$

$\mathbb{P}$ = required horsepower of compressor, hp

Φ = peak volume of gas pipe flow in pipe, fpm

P_i = initial pressure in piping, psi. This should $\geq$ 50 psi + ΔP above.

Gas Piping Pressure, Acfm vs. Scfm:

Pressure in psi: $\qquad P_{acfm\text{-}psi} + 14.7 = P_{scfm\text{-}psi}$

Pressure in in. Hg: $\quad P_{acfm\text{-}Hg} + 29.92 = P_{scfm\text{-}Hg}$

$P_{acfm\text{-}psi}$ = actual pressure of air volume (acfm = cubic feet per minute at actual conditions of pressure), 100 psi acfm

$P_{scfm\text{-}psi}$ = standard pressure of air volume (scfm = cubic feet per minute at specified standard conditions of pressure), psi scfm

$P_{acfm\text{-}Hg}$ = actual pressure of air volume, in. Hg
$P_{scfm\text{-}Hg}$ = standard pressure of air volume, in. Hg

Vacuum Air System Design:
Vacuum air systems are commonly designed with an outlet rating of 12 in. Hg, hose diameter of $1\frac{1}{2}$ in, and an air velocity of 3,000–4,500 fpm. The corrosion-resistant piping is usually sized to maintain a vacuum pressure of 10–15 in. Hg at any outlet, which usually requires an operating range of 15–19 in. Hg at the vacuum receiver. Minimum pipe diameter is $\frac{1}{2}$ in, but $\frac{1}{4}$ and $\frac{3}{8}$ in. diameters are OK for outlet stems in small systems. Two or more pumps are usually installed in each system, in which the capacity of each $\approx (\eta - 1)$ pumps ≥ 1.1 peak load. Each system also requires exhaust air outlets, placed where the escaping air won't come into contact with flammables, won't be objectionable, and where its noise isn't annoying. In some vacuum systems *pump-down time* is an important criterion for sizing the compressor(s), which is done as follows:

$$t\,D = V\,\kappa_p$$

t = vacuum air system pump-down time, min
D = pump displacement, cfm
V = volume of vacuum air system including all piping and fittings out to all outlet valves, cf
κ_p = pump-down factor, for single- or multi-stage pumps based on required vacuum pressure of in. Hg from the bar graph below:

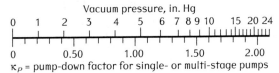

Vacuum pressure, in. Hg

κ_p = pump-down factor for single- or multi-stage pumps

Vacuum Air Pump & Compressor Design:

Step 1. Compute the system's peak demand airflow.

$$Þ = K_d F$$

$Þ$ = peak volume of vacuum airflow in system, cfm
K_d = diversity factor for systems with multiple outlets
F = required vacuum airflow at each outlet, cfm

Step 2. Size the piping.

$$L K_m \sigma^{0.5} Þ^2 = 120,000 \Delta P d^5$$

L = effective length of pipe (including normal number
      of fittings), ft
K_m = pipe material coefficient. $K_m = 2.0$ for iron or
      steel piping, 1.0 for copper or brass.
σ = specific gravity of gas
$Þ$ = peak volume of vacuum airflow in pipe, cfm
ΔP = permissible pressure drop in pipe, psi
d = minimum pipe diameter, inside dimension, in.
      Minimum $d = 0.5$ in.

Step 3. Size the compressor.

$$HP (14.7 - P_v) = 3.22 \, Þ \, \{[^{14.7}\!/(14.7 - P_v)]^{0.29} - 1\}$$

HP = req. horsepower of vacuum air compressor, hp
P_v = maximum vacuum air pressure in pipe, psi
$Þ$ = peak volume of vacuum air flow in pipe, cfm

Pressure Change of Gas in Vertical Piping:

$$\Delta P = 0.0147 \, h \, (1.00 - \sigma)$$

ΔP = pressure increase or decrease of lighter-than-air
      or heavier-than-air gas, psi. If σ of gas > 1.00,
      ΔP is minus.

h = height of travel of lighter-than-air or heavier-than-air gas, ft

σ = specific gravity of gas

Fuel Gas Piping Design: Fuel gas piping branches are typically $\frac{3}{8}$ in. flexible copper tubing for runs to about 80 ft for propane or butane and 50 ft for natural gas. The minimum riser diameter is $\frac{3}{4}$ in. Supply mains are designed as follows:

Step 1. Compute the piping's peak volume of flow.

$$\epsilon = 60 \, Þ \, Q$$

ϵ = rated energy use of appliances served by piping, from product catalogs or other reference, Btu/hr

$Þ$ = peak volume of gas flow in piping, cfm

Q = typical heating value of commercial gas, Btu/cf

Step 2. Size the piping.

$$L \, \kappa_m \, \sigma \, 0.5 \, Þ^2 = 120{,}000 \, \Delta P \, \delta^5$$

L = effective length of pipe (normal no. of fittings), ft

κ_m = pipe material coefficient. κ_m = 2.0 for iron or steel piping, 1.0 for copper or brass.

σ = specific gravity of gas in pipe, from Table 8-5

$Þ$ = volume of gas flow in pipe, from Step 1, 13.1 cfm

ΔP = permissible pressure drop of gas flow, 0.5 in. wg.

δ = minimum pipe diameter, inside dimension, in.

Waste Plumbing, Sanitary Drain Design:

Step 1. If the drain's pitch is not given, determine its optimal pitch by analyzing the plans. Minimum fall = $\frac{3}{8}$ in/ft for $1\frac{1}{2}$ or 2 in. diameter drains and $\frac{1}{4}$ in/LF for larger drains. Here a fall of $\frac{1}{2}$ in/LF is given.

Step 2. Find the drain's diameter.

$$F + 0.08\ W = 10\ d^{2.67}\ \varDelta^{0.5}$$

F = no. of wasteflow fixture units emptying into drain
W = wasteflow rate from nonfixture unit sources only, if any, gal/day. See Table 8-7 for estimated sewage flow rates for various occupancies.
d = minimum pipe diameter, inside dimension, in.
$\varDelta$ = slope of waste drain, in/ft. ½ in. fall/ft = 0.5 in/ft.

Waste Floor Drain Design: A plumbing waste floor drain has a removable inlet grate whose top is mounted flush with the floor, an accessible sediment bucket just below, a gooseneck trap or tailpiece farther below, then the drain, from which extends slightly upward one or more vents. This assembly cannot convey heavy greases or particulates, fecal or organic wastes, or large liquid flows. Other design criteria are:

▶   The floor area being drained must pitch at least ⅛ in/ft down in all directions toward the inlet grate, and the floor area should be rimmed by an

TABLE 8-6: SANITARY DRAIN & VENT DIAMETERS

PLUMBING FIXTURE	Min. dia., in.
Lavatory, drinking fountain, bidet, dental cuspidor	1¼
Bathtub, multiple lavatory, domestic dishwasher or kitchen sink, laundry sink, commercial lavatory (beauty parlor, etc.), surgeon's sink	1½
Domestic kitchen sink w/ food waste grinder & DW, commercial kitchen, comm'l food waste grinder, service sink, shower stall, urinal, floor drain	2
Domestic kitchen sink w/ tray & waste food grinder	2½
Flush valve water closet, sink w/ flushing rim	3
Flush tank water closet, 1 unit, 2; 2 or more units ..	4

TABLE 8-7: ESTIMATED SEWAGE FLOW RATES

OCCUPANCY	gal/day·occupant or other unit
Airports	15/employee + 4/passenger
Apartments	1 BR = 125, 2 BR = 250, 3 BR = 325
Luxury	multiply above × 1.3
Assembly: lecture halls, theaters, auditoriums	3/seat
Carwashes: tunnel, 80/car; handwash	20/5 min cycle
Country clubs, health clubs, gymnasiums	25/locker
Churches, 4/seat; w/ kitchens	7/seat
Dance halls	5/occupant
Day camps	15/camper & staff
Dental offices	750/chair·day
Eateries, 15/occ/meal; w/ cocktail lounge	+3/occ.
Above if on freeway	70/occupant
Factories	25/person·shift not inc. indus. wastes
Above w/ showers, +10/empl.; w/ cafeteria	+5/empl.
Hospitals	150/bed
Hotels: no kitchen, 60/bed; w/ kitchen	70/bed
Laundromats	50/wash cycle or 400/machine/day
Nursing or rest homes	125/bed
Motels, 50/bed; w/ kitchen	60/bed
Offices	15/employee or 0.1/sf floor area
Parks: mobile home	250/space
Residences 1 BR = 150; 2 BR = 300; 3 BR = 400; 4 BR = 475	
Luxury	multiply above × 1.2
Rooming houses	40/guest
Schools: elementary, 15/student; middle & high	20/stud.
Above w/ gym & showers	+15/locker
Above w/ cafeteria	+3/stud.
Above, administrative staff & office	20/employee
Service station, 1st bay = 900; added bays	500/bay
Shopping malls, 15/employee; moviegoers	3/occ.
Stores, 20/employee; w/ public toilets	1/10 ft^2 sales area
Swimming pools w/ bath houses	10/swimmer & staff
Taverns & cocktail lounges	20/occupant
Campground bathhouses 35; w/ built-in baths	50

integral baseboard at least 4 in. high.
▶   The inlet grate must be rust-proof.
▶   The sediment bucket's section area must ≥ 1.5 ×
    the inlet grate's net open area.
▶   The drain must be two pipe sizes larger than the
    tailpiece diameter (select from $1\frac{1}{4}$, $1\frac{1}{2}$, 2, $2\frac{1}{2}$, 3,
    4, 6, 8, and 10 in.).
▶   The drain must pitch from $\frac{1}{4}$ in/LF ($\frac{1}{2}$ in. is better)
    to no more than 6 in/LF down.
▶   Each drain requires a primary vent from the
    basin, a relief vent from just below the trap, and
    relief vents at maximum 100 ft spacing along long
    runs; and the section area of each vent must ≥
    0.5 the section area of the drain piping.

$$\delta = 0.134 \, A^{0.5}$$

δ = minimum diameter of floor drain tailpiece, ? in.
A = area of floorspace to be drained, sf. If this ex-
     ceeds 500 sf, install more than one drain.

Food Waste Grease Separator Design:
Grease separators for many eating occupancies can be
roughly sized as described below:

> Occupancies that serve nonscheduled meals
> to a nonspecific number of occupants:
> $$C_g = 0.09 \, \kappa_A \, \eta \, H \, G \, S$$

> Occupancies that serve scheduled meals
> to a specific number of occupants:
> $$C_g = 0.14 \, M \, G \, S$$

C_g = minimum interior capacity of grease separator, cf.
     $V \geq 100$ cf. Once C_g is known, it is used to deter-
     mine the grease trap's length, width, & height if

rectangular or its diameter & depth if cylindrical.

κ_A = facility access coefficient, depending on principal customer access to the facility. $\kappa_L \approx 1.25$ for freeways and expressways, 1.0 for recreation areas, 0.8 for main highways, 0.5 for lesser roads. κ_L can vary considerably depending on the popularity of the occupancy. For example, a four-star restaurant on a rural country road could have a κ_L of 0.7 while an out-of-favor restaurant on a main highway could have a κ_L of 0.2.

η = number of seats in dining area. If the occupancy is rarely full, a fractional value for η is appropriate. For example, if a cafe has 30 seats and is rarely more than $2/3$ full, $\eta \approx 2/3 \times 30 = 20$.

H = number of hours per day occupancy is open, hr.

M = no. of scheduled meals served per day, 1, 2, or 3.

G = wasteflow rate per seat per hr per meal served, gal. A general value for $G \approx 4.5$ gal.

S = sewage capacity factor, depending on whether grease trap outflow drains into public sewer or onsite leaching field. If public disposal, $S = 1.7$; if onsite disposal, $S = 2.5$.

Generic Grease Separator Design:

Step 1. Determine the capacity of the unit's reservoir.

$$C = 0.19 (14 F + W)$$

C = rated static holding capacity of separator, cf
F = fixture unit flow, if any, emptying into unit
W = peak volume of wasteflow draining into unit, gal/day

Step 2. Size the reservoir. The equation below assumes optimal dimensions of depth ≈ width ≈ 2.3 length.

$$C \approx 2.3 \ d^3$$

C = rated static holding capacity of separator, cf
d = optimal depth of separator, ft

Sump Tank & Ejector Design:
When sanitary drainage occurs below the level of a building's sanitary waste main or public sewer, a pump must be installed to convey the waste upward so it can flow out of the building. If the waste is clearwater or light graywater, a *non-airtight sump* is typically located in a pit that sucks up the drainage. If the waste contains sewage or other smelly or dangerous substances, a *pneumatic ejector* with an airtight receiver must be installed below the building's lowest sanitary waste main. Sizing a pneumatic ejector is a chancy proposition, due to the many variables involved both present and future. Still, the following sequence may be used to estimate one's size.

Step 1. Add up the fixture units located below the sewer main that will discharge into the ejector.

Step 2. Compute the ejector's unit capacity.

$$V = 0.53 \ (F_u + 0.07 \ W)$$

V = required interior volume of ejector, cf
F_u = fixture unit wasteflow draining into ejector, f.u.
W = nonfixture unit wasteflow draining into unit, gal/day

Step 3. Estimate the ejector's height.

$$h \approx 0.08 \ V + 3.75$$

h = estimated total height of ejector, including depth of basin and subdrain invert, ft
V = required interior volume of ejector, cf

Step 4. Determine the unit's required access floor area.

$$A \approx (d + 6)^2$$

A = required access floor area for ejector, sf
d = diameter of ejector, ft

Plumbing Vent Design:

Step 1. Find the total equivalent fixture unit waste flowing in the drainage system served by the vent.

$$W_t \approx F + 0.071\, W$$

W_t = total equiv. fixture unit waste served by vent, f.u.
F = fixture unit waste served by vent, f.u.
W = nonfixture unit waste served by vent, gpm

Step 2. Knowing the sewer diameter, its fixture unit load, and the vent's length, find the vent's diameter from Table 8-8.

Septic Tank Design:

$$C \approx 100 + 33\,(B - 2) + 2.5\,F + 0.2\,W$$

C = interior capacity of septic tank, cf
B = number of bedrooms, if any, in building whose household fixture units drain into septic tank
F = number of plumbing fixture units, if any, draining into tank, f.u.
W = volume of any nonfixture unit waste that drains into tank, gal/day

Leaching Field Design:

Step 1. Find the length of the leaching tiles.

TABLE 8-8: REQUIRED VENT SIZES AND LENGTHS

MINIMUM DIA. OF REQUIRED VENT, IN. — Maximum length of vent, ft

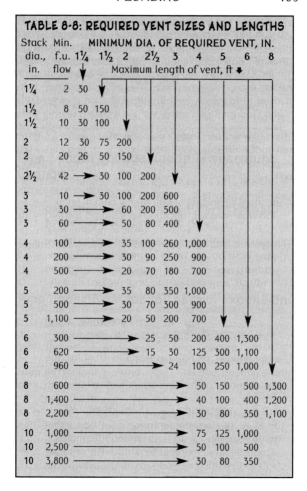

Stack dia., in.	Min. f.u. flow	1¼	1½	2	2½	3	4	5	6	8
1¼	2	30								
1½	8	50	150							
1½	10	30	100							
2	12	30	75	200						
2	20	26	50	150						
2½	42		30	100	200					
3	10		30	100	200	600				
3	30			60	200	500				
3	60			50	80	400				
4	100			35	100	260	1,000			
4	200			30	90	250	900			
4	500			20	70	180	700			
5	200				35	80	350	1,000		
5	500				30	70	300	900		
5	1,100				20	50	200	700		
6	300				25	50	200	400	1,300	
6	620				15	30	125	300	1,100	
6	960					24	100	250	1,000	
8	600						50	150	500	1,300
8	1,400						40	100	400	1,200
8	2,200						30	80	350	1,100
10	1,000							75	125	1,000
10	2,500							50	100	500
10	3,800							30	80	350

$$L \approx 0.57\,w\,(92\,B + 7\,F + 0.6\,W)\,P^{0.39}$$

L = min. length of leaching field drainage tile, LF

w = minimum width of each leaching field trench, ft. Use 3 ft unless otherwise noted.

B = number of bedrooms, if any, whose household fixture units drain into leaching field

F = number of commercial plumbing fixture units of wasteflow, if any, that drain into leaching field

W = volume of any nonfixture wasteflow that drains into leaching field, gal/day

P = perc test result, min/in drop

Step 2. Find the area of the leaching field.

$$A \ge 6\,L$$

A = minimum area of leaching field, sf

L = minimum length of drainage tile, ft

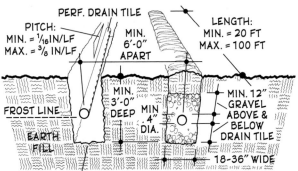

Fig.8-5. Leaching field drain tile details.

Water Reclamation System Design: A gray-water recycling system is designed as follows:

1. Determine the system's *design graywater flow capacity*. Isolate the graywater-producing fixtures, then add up their projected wasteflows or assign an overall unit value per occupant served.
2. Estimate the system's *recycling capacity*: the amount of graywater that can be reused by the occupancy. Isolate the graywater-reusing fixtures or applications, then sum their flow rates.
3. Determine the required water delivery pressure and how it will be generated. Ideally the pressure will be low and can be gravity-generated.
4. Select the methods of filtration (hair, porous baffles, sand, etc.) and how each will be periodically cleaned and maintained.
5. If part of the graywater recycling system is outside the building, draw a plot plan that shows the system's property lines, the building's well location or supply water entry, graywater discharges, piping layouts, topography, slopes, soil types, perc test results, paved areas, etc.

A graywater system for irrigating indoor planting is designed as follows:

$$A = 3 \, \kappa_g \, \eta \, P^{0.39}$$

A = bed area of planters, sf
κ_g = coefficient of graywaterflow per occupant, gal/day. In residential occupancies κ_g usually ≈ 40 gal/day; but this amount should be analyzed carefully for each application.
η = no. of occupants who generate the graywaterflow
P = perc test result of planter bed topsoil, min/in drop

Fire Suppression Systems: Comprehensive fire suppression system design includes (1) identifying the hazards, (2) determining appropriate response, (3) designing the system, (4) protecting the occupants, and (5) protecting the building.

Fire Standpipe System Design:

Standpipe chases: Section width ≈ 2 ft and depth ≈ 2 ft + 1 ft/standpipe.

Firehose racks or cabinets: Typical height = 2'-5" to 3'-7", width = 1'-9" to 2'-11", depth = 8" to 9".

Roof reservoirs and suction tank/upfeed pumps: 3 ft aisle around floor areas of each reservoir.

Fire Standpipe Water Pressure vs. Head:

$$P = 0.433\ H$$

P = water pressure at bottom of pipe, psi
H = head or height of waterflow, ft

Fire Standpipe Diameter:

Step 1. Find the building's number of standpipe zones.

$$Z = |0.00364\ H|$$

Z = required number of standpipe zones, zones
H = height of building, ft

Step 2. Find the required standpipe diameter(s). If $Z \geq$ 1, system is multizone ➜ use 8 in. diameter express riser in all but top zone. If fraction of Z = 0.00–0.36, pipe diameter in top zone = 4 in; if fraction of Z = 0.37–0.54, pipe diameter in top zone = 6 in; if fraction of Z = 0.00–0.36, pipe diameter in top zone = 8 in.

Fire Standpipe Weight:

$$W = H(w + 2 + 0.34\ d^2)$$

W = contained weight of pipe per floor, lb
H = height or length of pipe per floor, ft
w = unit weight of pipe, plf. Thin-walled pipe cannot be used for standpipe plumbing.
d = pipe diameter, in.

Fire Standpipe Expansion Loop Size:

Step 1. Find the lateral length of the expansion loop.

$$Ł \approx 430\ \kappa_t\ L\ (\Delta t + 5)\ d^{0.5}$$

$Ł$ = lateral length of expansion loop, in.
κ_t = coefficient of thermal expansion of piping, in/in.
L = length of piping btwn expansion loops, ft. Max. length for standpipe straight runs = 70 f.
Δt = safe temperature range of riser, °F. Δt = indoor temperature – lowest annual outdoor temp.
d = inside diameter of piping, in.

Step 2. Size the chase required for the expansion loop.

   Length: $b \approx Ł + 1.5\ (d + 2)$
   Height: $h \approx 144\ \kappa_t\ L\ (\Delta t + 5) + 1.5\ (d + 2)$
   Width: $w \approx 1.2\ (5.5\ d + 2)$

b = minimum length or breadth of chase, in.
h = minimum height of chase, in.
w = minimum width of chase, in.
$Ł$ = lateral length of expansion loop, in.
d = inside diameter of piping, in.
κ_t = coeff. of thermal expansion of pipe material, in/in.
L = length of piping between expansion loops, ft
Δt = safe temperature range of riser, °F

Fire Standpipe Reservoir Design:

Step 1. Find the delivery rate of the firehose with the greatest pressure (usually the lowest one).

$$Þ = 119\ \eta\ (25 + 0.433\ H)^{0.5}$$

Þ = rate of hose waterflow at remote outlet, gpm
η = number of hoses in use on each floor
H = head from reservoir base to lowest hose outlet, ft

Step 2. Find the reservoir's required volume of water.

$$V = 4.0\ Þ$$

V = volume of water required for reservoir, cf
Þ = maximum rate of hose waterflow, gpm

Step 3. Size the reservoir.

$$V \approx L\ W\ H$$

V = required volume of water for reservoir, cf
L = optimal length of reservoir, ft
W = optimal width of reservoir, ft
H = optimal height of reservoir, ft

Step 4. Estimate the reservoir's weight when full.

$$w \approx 62.4\ L\ W\ H$$

w = est. weight of reservoir (water only) when full, lb
L = optimal length of reservoir, ft
W = optimal width of reservoir, ft
H = optimal height of reservoir, ft

Fire Sprinkler System Design:
Fig. 8-6 shows a design flow chart for fire sprinkler system design. The method described is known as *pipe schedule design*.

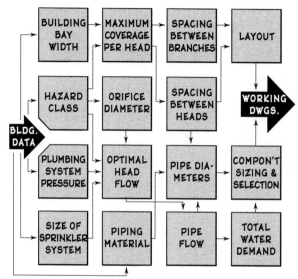

Fig. 8-6. Sprinkler system design flow chart.

Another method, *hydraulic design*, is scientifically meticulous and more detailed but more laborious.

Step 1. Find the occupancy's Hazard Class from below:

Class I, Light Hazard: Residences, schools, offices, most public buildings, museums, theaters including stages, restaurant seating, libraries except large stack areas, and the like.

Class II, Ordinary Hazard: Retail areas, auto parking garages, bakeries, laundries, machine shops, paper mills, restaurant kitchens, wood assembly, warehouses, and the like.

Class III, Extra Hazard: Airplane hangars, factories of combustibles (lumber, textiles, etc.), areas of great heat (metal extruding, die casting, etc.) areas of flammable fluids (paints, oils, etc.), and the like.

Class HS, High-Piled Storage: Warehouses containing combustible items stored more than 15 ft high.

Step 2. Select the type of sprinkler head:

Small orifice: Orifice diameter is $\frac{1}{4}$–$\frac{7}{16}$ in.

Spray: The standard head, orifice diameter is usually $\frac{1}{2}$ or $\frac{17}{32}$ in. and head pressure is 15–60 psi.

Large drop (LD): Orifice diameter is $\frac{5}{8}$ or $\frac{3}{4}$ in, head pressure is 25–95 psi, and maximum number of heads is 20 per rack; used where storage is 15–30 ft high.

Early suppression fast response (ESFR): Orifice diameter is $\frac{3}{4}$ in, head pressure is 50–175 psi, and maximum number of heads is 12 per rack; used in warehouses whose storage is up to 35 ft high.

Water mist: Emits a fine mist instead of a spray.

Step 3. Select the sprinkler head's orientation:

Upright: Heads rise above the pipes and cast spray over horizontal area. Good above suspended ceilings and where hot gases may accumulate.

Pendant: Heads hang down from pipes and cast spray over horizontal area. Good for quenching flames from ordinary combustibles in large open areas.

Sidewall: Heads aim sideways and spray vertical areas.

Multiple spray: Sprinklers spray up and down at the same time. Good where fire hazards exist above and below ceilings.

Step 4. Select the type of sprinkler system:

Wet-pipe: Water is present in all piping; thus an

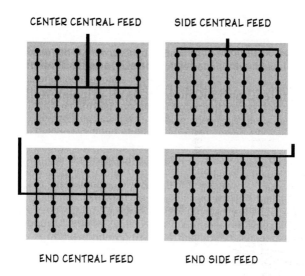

Fig. 8-7. Types of fire sprinkler system layouts.

opened sprinkler head discharges water immediately. Simple, economical, dependable, and fast-operating. NG in areas subject to freezing, where water damage is a concern, or in high-hazard areas.

   Antifreeze: A wet-pipe system whose water supply contains antifreeze to prevent freezing.

   Dry-pipe: Pipes contain a gas which escapes when heads open, then the water follows. Good in areas subject to freezing; but they respond more slowly and require air compressors, heated main controls, and pitched piping that can be drained after use.

   Preaction: A wet-pipe system activated by heat

TABLE 8-9: FIRE SPRINKLER HEAD DESIGN DATA

SPRINKLER HEAD TYPE	SPACING REQUIREMENTS [1] Maximum coverage/head, ft²			
Hazard Class ➡	I	II	III	S
Spray heads, below ceiling	225	130	100	100
Above ceiling, pipe sched. design ..	200	150	105	—
Above ceiling, hydraulic design ...	225	175	120	—
LD heads	—	—	—	130
ESFR heads	—	—	—	100
Space between heads, ft min/max:				
Spray heads	8/15	8/15	6/12	6/12
LD heads	—	—	—	8/12
ESFR heads	—	—	—	8/10
Distance below ceiling, ft: spray heads	1-12 ft for all classes			
LD heads	6-8 ft for all classes			
ESFR heads	6-14 ft for all classes			

OPTIMAL WATERFLOW RANGE PER HEAD

Orifice dia, in.	Hazard Class	Pressure psi, min-norm-max	Flow/head, gpm, min-norm-max
1/4	I	7–15–60	4–6–12
5/16	I	7–15–60	5–8–15
3/8	I	7–15–60	7–11–22
7/16	I	7–15–60	11–17–34
1/2	I	15–25–95	21–29–57
1/2	II	20–30–95	24–32–57
1/2	III	25–35–95	27–34–57
17/32	I	15–25–95	29–41–80
17/32	II	20–30–95	33–45–80
17/32	III	25–35–95	37–49–80
5/8	III	25–50–95	55–80–150
5/8	LD	25–75–95	55–100–150
5/8	ESFR	50–75–95	95–125–190

1. Max. floor area for one sprinkler system riser = 52,000 ft² for Hazard Class I or II, 25,000 ft² for Hazard Class III (pipe schedule design), & 40,000 ft² for Hazard Class III (hydraulic design) or High-piled Storage.

or smoke sensors instead of sprinkler heads.

Deluge: A dry pipe system with open heads; thus when any one sprinkler is activated the whole system area is covered. Some buildings have dry pipe preaction deluge systems.

Foam water: A concentrate mixes with water to produce a foam that discharges through the heads. Good for high-hazard areas where water application is NG; but it creates removal problems afterward.

Flexible stainless steel hose stem: Single feeds made of flexible stainless steel. Good for mounting in exhaust air ducts and where upgrading requires a small number of new heads.

Step 5. Select the type of piping, either *steel* (stronger, but may degrade in areas of high humidity, salty air, or harmful gases) or *copper* (lighter, but more susceptible to damage by high temperatures).

Step 6. Determine the sprinkler head spacing requirements from Table 8-9. First find the maximum coverage per head based on the building's construction and Hazard Class, then determine the most feasible spacing between the heads based on the maximum coverage per head and the building's structural bay dimensions.

Step 7. Determine the sprinkler heads' orifice diameter based on the occupancy's Hazard Class.

Step 8. Knowing the occupation Hazard Class, head orifice diameter, initial pressure of the building's plumbing system, and overall size of the sprinkler system, determine the optimal waterflow range for each head from Table 8-9.

Step 9. Find the diameter of each length of piping in

the system as follows. For large drop (LD) heads steel or copper pipe diameters are 1 in. from outermost head, $1\frac{1}{4}$ in. to nextmost 2 heads, $1\frac{1}{2}$ in. to nextmost 3 heads, 2 in. to nextmost 6 heads, and $2\frac{1}{2}$ in. to maximum 20 heads in each rack. Corresponding diameters for early suppression fast response (ESFR) heads are $1\frac{1}{4}$ in. from outermost head, $1\frac{1}{2}$ in. to nextmost 2 heads, 2 in. to nextmost 4 heads, and $2\frac{1}{2}$ in. to maximum 20 heads in each rack. Each pipe length is sized from the outermost sprinkler head upstream through the branches to the main.

Step 10. Compute the system's total water demand.

$$Ð\,C = Q\,A$$

Ð = req. waterflow for fire sprinkler system riser, gpm
C = area of coverage per sprinkler head, sf
Q = optimal waterflow per sprinkler head, gpm
A = total floor area covered by system riser, sf

Step 11. Lay out in plan the sprinkler water supply system. Each sprinkler head requires a primary and secondary water supply. The primary supply is activated by the building's electric system and is usually a part of the building's general plumbing system. The secondary supply operates if the building's electric system fails and renders the general plumbing system inoperable, in which case an onsite generator activates its controls.

Step 12. Size the secondary water supply reservoir. It may be *gravity feed* (water flows down from a roof or tower reservoir; then each sprinkler head's discharge pressure must be ≥ 25 psi) or *upfeed* (sprinkler head water is pumped upward).

Gravity-feed: $Ð\,t = 30\,V$

Upfeed pump: $Þ \, t \, = \, 77 \, C$

$Þ$ = required waterflow of fire sprinkler system, gpm

t = time duration of water reservoir supply, min. t = 30 min. for Hazard Class I, 60 min. for Hazard Class II, and 90 min. for Hazard Class III.

V = required capacity of gravity-feed reservoir, cf. If system has fewer than 40 heads, V = water demand of four heads.

C = required capacity of upfeed pump reservoir, cf

Fire Sprinkler Floor Drain Design: Fire sprinkler floor drains are constructed similarly as plumbing waste floor drains, which were described on pages 403–405. They are designed as follows:

Step 1. Determine the number of floor drains required per structural bay.

$$\eta \; = \; |0.002 \, A|$$

η = no. of floor drains required in floor area

A = floor area per bay, should be 250–500 sf

Step 2. Find the minimum diameter of each floor drain.

$$\delta \; = \; 1.13 \, (A \, \kappa_a)^{0.5}$$

δ = minimum diameter of each floor drain, in.

A = area of floor drained by each drain outlet

κ_a = drain area factor, 0.050 for Hazard Class I, 0.057 for Hazard Class II, 0.076 for Hazard Class III. Add 0.013 for nonwatertight floor and 0.013 for contents subject to water damage

422 →ß▯I▯▦♀✳✂▯▯♀▯▯

TABLE 9-1: FLEXIBLE CABLE DATA

CABLE TYPE	Group No.	Max. Oper. Temp, °F.
A	–	392
AC ("BX")	–	167
MC (incl. CS & ALS), MI	–	185
NM, NMC ("Romex")	–	167
SIS, TA, TBS	–	194
UF, USE	–	167
RH, RHW	1	167
RHH	1	194
RUH, THW	2	167
T, TW, RUW	2	140
THHN	3	194
THWN	3	167
FEP, PFA, Z	4	194
FEPB	4	392
XHHW	5	194
ZW	5	167

WIRE SIZE	Conductor section area, cmil	Section area incl. insul., in² according to GROUP NO. above				
		1	2	3	4	5
12 AWG	6,530	0.03	0.02	0.01	0.01	—
10 AWG	10,380	0.05	0.02	0.02	0.02	—
8 AWG	16,510	0.09	0.05	0.04	0.03	0.05
6 AWG	26,240	0.12	0.08	0.05	0.07	0.06
4 AWG	41,740	0.16	0.11	0.09	0.10	0.09
2 AWG	66,360	0.21	0.15	0.12	0.13	0.12
1 AWG	83,690	0.27	0.20	0.16	—	0.16
1/0 AWG	105,600	0.31	0.24	0.19	—	0.19
2/0 AWG	133,100	0.36	0.28	0.23	—	0.23
3/0 AWG	167,800	0.42	0.33	0.27	0.25	0.27
4/0 AWG	211,600	0.48	0.39	0.33	—	0.33
250 kcmil	250,000	0.59	0.49	0.40	—	0.40
300 kcmil	300,000	0.68	0.56	0.47	—	0.47
350 kcmil	350,000	0.76	0.63	0.53	—	0.53
400 kcmil	400,000	0.84	0.70	0.59	—	0.60
500 kcmil	500,000	0.98	0.83	0.72	—	0.72

9. ELECTRICAL

Relation Between Amps, Volts, and Watts:

$$W = \Phi A V$$

W = total electric load of circuit or system, kWh
Φ = phase factor, 1.0 for single phase, 1.73 for 3 ph.
A = rate of flow of electric current, amps
V = potential difference of electric current, volts

Initial Estimate of Building Electric Load:

Step 1. Estimate the building's required electric load.

$$\epsilon \approx \kappa_u A$$

ϵ = estimated electric service load of building, watts
κ_u = load use factor, from Table 9-2
A = gross floor area of building, sf

Step 2. Knowing the building service load's total wattage, select its service voltage from Table 9-2

Step 3. Find the building's base ampacity.

$$\epsilon = 1.73\ A\ V$$

ϵ = total electric service load of building, watts

A = base ampacity of electric load, amps
V = voltage of electrical service, volts

Step 4. Find the building's service ampacity by selecting the next value above A from the following standard ampacities for building electrical systems: 60, 100, 200, 400, 600, 800, 1,000, 1,200, 1,600, 2,000, 2,500 amps.

Electric Convenience Circuit Design:

Req. outlets, finished areas: $\eta = 0.083\,P + 0.01\,A$
Req. outlets, unfin. areas: $\eta = 0.05\,P$

TABLE 9-2: ELECTRIC SERVICE LOADS [1]

SERVICE LOAD, kWh or kVA	Type of building	Service voltage
To 12	Small residences, outbuildings	120
12-96	Typical residential, small commercial ...	240
96-900	Typical commercial	208
400-2,000	Large commercial-industrial	480
2,000 + ...	Skyscrapers, corporate offices, other large buildings 2,400, 4,160, 7,200, 13,200, 34,500	

LOAD USAGE Type of building	Est. watts/ft²
Parking garages, unmechanized barns, buildings requiring little electricity	1-2
Residences, apartments, hotels, motels	4
Grammar schools, gyms, retail, museums, churches ...	6
Senior high schools, universities, offices, eateries....	8
Night clubs, hospitals, spaces w/ 24 hr use of elec. ...	10
Factories, industrial laboratories, buildings w/ constantly used large machinery	12-15
Semiconductor fabrication plants	30-50
Data processing & telecommunication centers	100

1. Loads do not include heating and cooling of spaces.

η = required number of convenience outlets in area
P = perimeter of area served by outlets, ft
A = floor area of any part of room more than 8 ft in
      from perimeter, sf

Circuitry load based on no. of outlets: $\diamondsuit = \eta A$

$\diamondsuit$ = electric circuitry load, amps
η = required number of outlets
A = rated amperes per outlet

Electric Lighting Circuit Design:

Lighting load: $\diamondsuit_L V \approx \kappa_L F$
Lighting outlets: $\diamondsuit_L = \eta A$
Lighting system load: $\diamondsuit_L V \approx \kappa_b \eta \epsilon$

$\diamondsuit_L$ = estimated lighting circuitry load of room, space,
      or zone , amps
V = voltage of lighting system, volts
κ_L = occupancy lighting load factor, from Table 9-3
F = net floor area of illuminated space, sf

TABLE 9-3: OCCUPANCY LIGHTING LOADS

OCCUPANCY	Estimated lighting load, Watts/ft^2
Warehouses, storage areas, mech. equip. areas	0.2
Halls, lobbies, stairways, library stacks, garages	0.5
Armories, assembly, recreational, service areas	1.0
Clubs, court rooms, hospitals, hotels, restaurants, other spaces whose ambient lighting levels ≥ 35 fc	1.5
Beauty parlors, residences, schools, stores, other spaces whose ambient lighting levels ≥ 60 fc	2.0
Banks, offices, retail outlets, industrial areas, other spaces whose ambient lighting levels ≥ 90 fc	2.5
Offices and other areas requiring exact work, other spaces whose ambient lighting levels ≥ 150 fc	3.0

η = required number of outlets for lighting

A = rated lighting load for each outlet, amps

κ_b = ballast factor. $\kappa_b \approx 1.0$ if lamp is incandescent or quartz, 1.15 if fluorescent or metal-halide, 1.11 if mercury, 1.18 if sodium.

ϵ = rated electric output of each lamp or fixture, watts

Electric Motor Design, Required Horsepower & Circuitry Load:

Step 1. Find the motor's horsepower based on its initial torque load.

$$T\, \upsilon = 47\, \text{IP}\, \epsilon$$

T = initial torque load of motor, ft-lb

υ = rotational velocity or shaft speed of motor, rpm

IP = required horsepower of motor, hp

ϵ = operational efficiency of motor, %

Step 2. Size the circuit breaker required for the motor.

$$\diamond\, \epsilon\, V = 43{,}100\, \kappa_d\, \Phi\, \text{IP}$$

$\diamond$ = min. circuit breaker size, amps at selected voltage

ϵ = oper. efficiency of motor served by circuit, %

V = peak line voltage of electrical circuit, volts

κ_d = motor duty factor, 1.0 for continuous duty, 1.40 for intermittent duty.

Φ = phase factor, 1.00 if single phase, 1.73 if 3 phase

IP = required horsepower of motor, hp

Electric Motor Design, Energy Savings of Compared Units:

Step 1. Compute annual operating cost difference between new efficient motors and old replaced ones.

$$\Delta_{ac} = 0.009 \, ¢ \, \eta \, \kappa_c \, \epsilon \, t \, (100/\epsilon_o - 100/\epsilon_n)$$

Δ_{ac} = annual operating cost difference between old and new motors, \$/yr

$¢$ = unit cost of electricity, ¢/kWh

η = number of compared units

κ_c = power conversion factor. κ_c = 0.746 if power unit is hp, 1.00 if kVA, 0.001 if watts.

ϵ = rated electrical power of each unit, hp or watts

t = operating time that the compared units run, hr

ϵ_o = operational efficiency of old unit(s), %

ϵ_n = operational efficiency of new unit(s), %

TABLE 9-4: ELECTRIC MOTOR SPECIFICATIONS [1]

	SE (STD EFFIC.) MOTORS			PE (PREM EFFIC.) MOTORS		
HP	Efficiency %	Size L×W×H	Wt. lb	Efficiency %	Size L×W×H	Wt. lb
1	72.1	11×9×7	38	82.5	11×9×7	31
2	76.1	13×11×9	58	84.0	12×9×7	37
3	78.5	14×11×9	73	86.5	13×11×9	51
5	80.3	15×11×9	82	87.5	15×11×9	93
7.5	83.3	17×14×11	160	88.5	18×14×11	160
10	84.7	18×14×11	200	89.5	20×14×11	200
15	86.6	21×18×13	280	91.0	21×18×13	280
20	87.8	23×18×13	324	91.0	23×18×13	324
25	88.8	24×20×15	356	91.7	24×20×15	404
30	89.4	25×20×15	376	92.4	25×20×15	456
40	90.4	26×22×16	490	93.0	26×22×16	560
50	91.1	28×22×16	531	93.0	28×22×16	614
60	91.6	28×25×18	733	93.6	28×25×18	716
75	92.2	30×25×18	790	94.1	30×25×18	766
100	92.8	33×25×20	957	94.1	45×33×22	1,850
125	93.2	35×25×20	1,063	94.5	45×33×22	1,850
150	93.4	38×33×23	1,200	95.0	48×33×22	1,850
200	93.6	40×33×23	1,420	95.0	48×33×22	2,250

1. Average estimates for common 1,800 rpm open motors.

Step 2. Compute the energy payback span of the compared units.

$$E_p \Delta_{ac} \approx \eta \, (\$_{in} - \$_{io})$$

E_p = energy payback span for compared units, yr
Δ_{ac} = annual operating cost difference between old and new units, \$/yr
η = number of compared units
$\$_{in}$ = initial cost of new unit(s)
$\$_{io}$ = initial cost of old unit(s)

This formula may be used to compare the annual energy savings for any new versus old component (lamps, heaters, added insulation, etc.).

Electric Motor Design, Required Cooling Airflow:

Step 1. Determine the amount of heat produced by the operating electric motor.

$$H \, \varepsilon = 2,545 \, HP \, (100 - \varepsilon)$$

H = heat produced by motor, Btu/hr
ε = operational efficiency of motor, %
HP = rated horsepower of electric motor, HP

Step 2. Compute the cooling airflow required to remove the heat produced by the motor.

$$C = 108 \, Q \, (t_m - t_i)$$

C = cooling load required to remove heat produced by continuously operating motor, Btu/hr
Q = incoming cooling airflow required to remove unwanted heat, cfm
t_m = rated temperature of motor, °F
t_i = desired temperature of air around motor, °F

Electric Fan Design, Required Horsepower & Circuitry Load:

Step 1. Compute the fan motor's required horsepower.

$$75 \; \text{H} \, \varepsilon \, (1 - 0.000034 \, E) \; = \; f \, \rho \, (0.00057 \, \nu)^2$$

H = required horsepower of motor, hp
ε = operational efficiency of motor, %
E = site elevation above sea level, ft
f = fan airflow capacity, actual or required, cfm
ρ = static resistance of airflow, in. wg. If static resistance is in psi, $\rho_{iwg} = 0.068 \, \rho_{psi}$.
ν = rotational velocity or shaft speed of fan, rpm

Step 2. Size the circuit breaker required for the motor.

$$\diamond \, \varepsilon \, V \; = \; 43{,}100 \, \kappa_d \, \phi \, \text{H}$$

$\diamond$ = min. circuit breaker size, amps at selected voltage
ε = efficiency of motor served by circuit breaker, %
V = selected peak line voltage, volts
κ_d = motor duty factor, 1.25 for continuous duty, 1.40 for intermittent duty
ϕ = phase factor, 1.00 if single phase, 1.73 if 3 phase
H = required horsepower of motor, hp

Electric Conductor Cable Design:

Amperage is given: $\quad C \, V \, \Delta V \; = \; 200 \, \Omega \, \phi \, A \, L$
Wattage is given: $\quad C \, V^2 \, \Delta V \; = \; 200 \, \Omega \, \phi \, \omega \, L$

C = section area of conductor, circular mils. From Table 9-1 select an AWG or kcmil wire size whose conductor section $\geq C$.
V = voltage of circuit, volts
ΔV = voltage drop through length of conductor, %.

Maximum ΔV = 5%.

Ω = resistance of conductor material, ohms/cmil-ft.
   Ω = 10.7 for copper, 17.7 for aluminum.
Φ = phase factor, 1.00 for single phase, 1.73 for 3 ph.
A = ampacity of circuit, 200 amps
ω = wattage of circuit, watts
L = length of conductor, ft

Electric Conductor Junction Box Design:

AWG wire size	14	12	10	8	6
Min. volume per wire in box, in³	5.0	6.0	7.0	8.0	10.0

Electric Busway Chase Design:

$$A \approx 0.007\, \eta\, [(w_b + 10)\,(d_b + 6)]^{1.1}$$

A = section area of busway chase or shaft, sf
η = number of busways in chase
w_b = width of each busway, in.
d_b = depth or height of each busway, in.

Electric Rigid Conduit Enclosure Design:

Conduit size: $0.31\, \eta\, \delta^2 \geq \eta_1 A_1 + \ldots + \eta_Z A_Z$

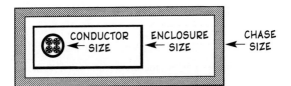

Fig. 9-1. Relation between electrical
conductor, enclosure, and chase.

η = minimum number of conduits required, units
δ = diameter of conduits, in.
η_1 = number of first type of cables to be carried
A_1 = section area of first type of cable, in^2
η_2 = number of second type of cables to be carried
A_2 = section area of second type of cable, in^2

Conduit chase width: $w \approx \eta_w (d + 1) + 15$
Conduit chase height: $h \approx \eta_h (d + 3) + 13$

w = estimated width of chase, in. Minimum w = 16 in.
η_w = no. of conduits arranged across width of chase
h = estimated height of chase, in. Min. h = 16 in.
η_h = no. of conduits arranged through height of
        chase. If diameters vary, use max. dia. in row.
d = diameter of conduits, in.

Electric Pull Box Design:

Straight pull boxes: conductors leave box through
side opposite the side they entered.

$$L \geq 8\, \delta_{max} \qquad\qquad W \geq 6\, \delta_{max}$$

U-pull boxes: conductors leave box through the same
side they entered.

$$L \geq 9\, \delta_{max} \qquad\qquad W \geq 6\, \delta_{max}$$

Angle pull boxes: conductors leave box through a side
adjacent to the one they entered.

$$L \geq 6\, \delta_{max} + S \qquad W \geq 6\, \delta_{max} + S \qquad A \geq 6\, \delta_{max}$$

Depth of any pull box: $D \geq 2\, \delta_{max}$

δ_{max} = diameter of largest conduit entering box, in.
L = min. interior clear length of long side of box, in.
W = min. interior clear width of short side of box, in.
A = minimum diagonal distance between conduits en-

tering in adjacent walls of box, in.

S = sum of all less-than-maximum-diameter conduits entering the box, in.

D = depth of any pull box, in. $D \geq 2 \times$ diameter of largest conduit entering or leaving box.

Electric Wireway Enclosure Design:

$$0.20\, A_t \geq \eta_1 A_1 + \dots + \eta_z A_z$$

A_t = total minimum section area of wireway, in². Solve for A_t, then choose next-largest-size section from $2\frac{1}{2} \times 2\frac{1}{2}$ in. = 6.25 in², $4 \times 4 = 16$ in², $6 \times 6 = 36$ in², $8 \times 8 = 64$ in², or $12 \times 12 = 144$ in².

η_1 = number of 1st cable to be carried
A_1 = section area of 1st cable to be carried, in²
η_2 = number of 2nd cable to be conveyed
A_2 = section area of 2nd cable to be carried, in²

Electric Cable Tray Enclosure Design:

Tray width: $W \approx 5\,(\eta_1 A_1 + \dots + \eta_z A_z)$
Tray height: $H \approx 6$ in. unless otherwise specified

W = min. width of tray, in. $W = 6, 12, 18, 24, 30, 36$ in.
η_1 = number of first type of conductor in tray
A_1 = section area of first type of conductor in tray, in²

Chase width: $W \approx 22 + w$
Chase height: $H \approx 18 + h + 18\,(S - 1)$

W = estimated width of chase or shaft, in.
w = width of tray, in.
H = est. height of chase or shaft, in². 12 in. clear must be between trays and lowest part of ceiling.
h = height of each tray, in.
S = number of stacked trays in system

Electric Manhole Design: Draw elevations of the banks of conduits in each wall of the manhole, then note the number of columns and rows in each bank.

Manhole length: $L \geq \delta (\eta_{tot} + \eta_{out}) + \delta (c_e + c_x + r_e + r_x)$
Manhole width: $W \geq \delta (\eta_{in} + \eta_{out}) + \delta (c_e + r_e)$

L = minimum length of rect. manhole, in. $L \geq 96$ in.
W = minimum width of rect. manhole, in. $W \geq 90$ in.
δ = largest diameter of all conduits in manhole, in.
η_{tot} = total number of conduits entering manhole
η_{out} = largest no. of conduits exiting one wall of manhole
η_{in} = largest number of conduits entering one wall
c_e = no. of columns in largest bank of entering conduits
c_x = no. of columns in largest bank of exiting conduits
r_e = no. of rows in largest bank of entering conduits
r_x = no. of rows in largest bank of exiting conduits

Transformer Design, Optimal Capacity:

$$833\ \varepsilon = V A$$

ε = optimal power capacity or nameplate rating of transformer, from Table 9-5, kVA
V = voltage of transformer service load, volts
A = amperage of transformer service load, amps

Transformer Design, Amps vs. Volts:

Step 1. Find the transformer's primary amperage.

$$1,000\ \varepsilon = \Phi\ V_p A_p$$

ε = power capacity of transformer, kVA
Φ = phase factor, 1.00 if single phase, 1.73 if 3 phase
V_p = primary voltage of transformer, volts
A_p = primary amperage of transformer, amps

Step 2. Find the transformer's secondary amperage.

$$971 \, \epsilon \;=\; \Phi \, V_s \, A_s$$

ϵ = power capacity of transformer, kVA
Φ = phase factor, from Step 1
V_s = secondary voltage of transformer, volts
A_s = secondary amperage of transformer, amps

Transformer Design, Required Floor Area:

$$A \;\geq\; (w + 5)(d + 3.5) \;\geq\; 30 \text{ sf}$$

A = req. floor area for wall-mounted transformer, sf
w = width of transformer unit, ft
d = front-to-back depth of transformer unit, ft

TABLE 9-5: TRANSFORMER SPECIFICATIONS [1]

CAPACITY, kVA	Size h w d, ft.	← Approximate weight [2] → Type 1	Type 2	Type 3	Type 4
10	1.25 × 0.83 × 1.00	165	180	200	230
15	2.25 × 1.67 × 1.33	220	240	260	300
25	2.50 × 1.67 × 1.67	245	280	310	400
50	3.00 × 1.67 × 1.67	350	400	450	600
75	3.50 × 2.50 × 2.00	475	600	700	900
100	4.00 × 2.67 × 2.50	650	720	1,000	1,200
150	4.00 × 3.00 × 2.50	800	1,100	1,100	1,500
225	4.20 × 3.33 × 2.67	1,030	1,300	1,450	2,100
300	4.67 × 4.00 × 3.00	1,450	1,800	2,000	3,000
500	5.00 × 4.67 × 3.00	2,100	2,550	3,100	4,400

1. Dimensions & weights in this table are averages and do not apply to variable-voltage transformers.
2. Type 1 = dry type ventilated transformers w/ aluminum windings; Type 2 = Dry type ventilated units w/ copper windings; Type 3 = Energy-saving, nonlinear, control power, or shielded isolated units; Type 4 = non-ventilated, liquid-filled, or cast coil units.

Onsite Electric Generator Design, Required Engine Airflow:

Step 1. Determine the internal-combustion engine's carburetion and radiator airflow requirements from

$$A \approx 156 \, \Omega$$

A = internal combustion engine's carburetion and air-flow requirements, cfm
Ω = generating capacity of genset, kW or kVA

Step 2. Find the engine room's maximum cooling load.

$$\mathbf{C} \approx A\,(t_o - t_i) + 2{,}400 \, \Omega$$

$\mathbf{C}$ = maximum cooling load of room in which genset is operating, Btu/hr
A = airflow requirements of engine, cfm
t_o = summer design temperature for occupancy, °F
t_i = desired indoor temperature of occupancy, °F
Ω = generating capacity of genset, kW or kVA

Onsite Electric Generator Design, Engine Fuel Tank Capacity:

Step 1. Find the capacity of the unit's primary fuel tank.

$$C \approx 48 \, \eta \, \kappa_{HP} \, \kappa_F \, \kappa_E \, \Omega$$

C = optimal capacity of engine fuel tank, gal
η = number of days between fuel delivery
κ_{HP} = kilowatt-to-horsepower conversion factor.
κ_F = fuel consumption factor. Internal-combustion engines typically use about 0.047 gal/hr per engine HP.
κ_E = engine load factor. Internal-combustion engines typically run at about 85% of capacity.
Ω = generating capacity of genset, kW or kVA

Step 2. Find the capacity of the unit's day tank. This is usually located near the engine and holds enough fuel to operate it for 4–8 hr at full load.

$$C_d \approx \eta \, \kappa_{IP} \, \kappa_F \, \Omega$$

C_d = optimal capacity of engine's day tank, gal
η = number of hours of engine operation supplied by day tank, hr

κ_{IP}, κ_F, and Ω are as previously defined.

Electric Generation from Natural Sources:

The equations below are used to estimate the optimal size of small electric generators for use in homes and small businesses during natural energy usage or power outages.

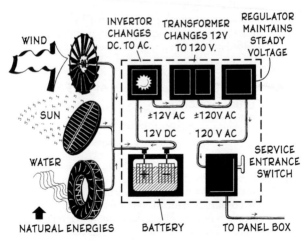

Fig. 9-2. Onsite generation of electricity.

Average daily load: $\$ \approx 0.30 \, ¢ \, \epsilon_a$

$\$$ = dollar amount of monthly electric bill, $\$$
$¢$ = local unit cost of electricity, cents/kWh
ϵ_a = aver. daily electric load of occupancy, kWh/day

Critical daily load: $\epsilon_c \approx 1.5 \, \eta + 2$

ϵ_c = critical daily electric load of occupancy: energy
required to operate essential electric appliances
run by onsite generation systems, kWh
η = no. of occupants using the generated electricity

This equation may be used to estimate the optimal size of a
small generator for use in homes and small businesses dur-
ing power outages.

Wind Electric Power System Design:

Step 1. Compute the generating system's electric pow-
er potential. The formula below is for a system whose me-
chanical/electrical subcomponentry is 70 % efficient.

$$5{,}900 \, \Omega \approx \delta^2 v^3$$

Ω = electric power potential of prop-driven wind gen-
erator, watts
δ = propeller diameter, ft
v = average onsite wind velocity, mph

Step 2. Compare the system's power potential with the
occupancy's critical daily electric load.

$$\Omega \approx 42 \, \epsilon_c$$

Ω = electric power potential of wind generator, watts
ϵ_c = critical daily elec. load of occupancy, kWh/day

Step 3. Estimate the cost of installing the wind generator, its tower, and battery storage system, then compare this total cost with the system's potential energy savings according to the payback span formula below:

$$\$ \approx S\,E_p$$

$\$$ = total cost of installation, dollars
S = annual energy savings due to installation, dollars
E_p = estimated energy payback span, years

Water Electric Power System Design:

Step 1. Compute the system's electric power potential.

$$660\ \Omega \approx H\,\mathcal{E}\,V$$

Ω = electric power potential of water generator, kWh
H = head or vertical distance of waterflow between its crest and striking of turbine, ft
$\mathcal{E}$ = efficiency of generating system, equals efficiency of each separate component of system multiplied together, %
V = volume of waterflow that strikes turbine, cfs

Step 2. Compare the occupancy's daily critical electric load with the system's electric power potential.

$$\mathcal{E}_c \leq 24\ \Omega$$

$\mathcal{E}_c$ = critical daily electric load of occupancy, kWh/day
Ω = electric power potential of water generator, kWh

Photovoltaic Electric System Design:

$$100\ \mathcal{E}_c \approx \Phi\,\kappa_c\,\kappa_u\,\Omega\,A\,\rho^{0.7}\,(1 + 0.000014\ E)$$

$\mathcal{E}_c$ = critical electric load of occupancy, watts
Φ = incident clear-day insolation on a surface per-

pendicular to sunrays at location of PV array

κ_c = cloudiness coefficient: site's average percentage of sunshine received ÷ 100

κ_u = umbra fraction: portion of collector surface that is shaded during the day

Ω = generating efficiency of photovoltaic cells, %

A = required area of photocell panels, sf

ρ = ratio of days of energy collected to days of energy used. ρ must ≥ 1.0.

E = elevation of site above sea level, ft

Electric Battery Storage Design:

Step 1. Find the required capacity of the battery storage system.

$$C \approx 800 \, \varepsilon_c \, \rho \, (100/\kappa_g)^{1.6}$$

C = required storage capacity of batteries, watts

ε_c = critical daily elec. load of occupancy, kWh/day

ρ = ratio of days of energy collected to days of energy used

κ_g = generation factor: average percent of time system generates energy during desirable climatic conditions. $\kappa_g \approx 75\%$ for wind generation, 95% for water generation, and percent of average local sunshine for solar generation.

Step 2. Compute the number of batteries required for the system.

$$C = \omega \, \eta$$

C = required storage capacity of batteries, watts

ω = unit storage capacity of each battery, watts

η = minimum number of batteries required, units

TABLE 10-1: LIGHT DEPRECIATION FACTORS [1]
(Interpolate for intermediate values)

DEPRECIATION DUE TO VOLTAGE FLUC. (±5 VAC)	δ_v
No appreciable fluc. ... 1.00	F 0.97
HID (w/ ballast) 0.98	MV, MH, I, Q 0.87

DEPRECIATION DUE TO LAMP POSITION	δ_p
I, vertical, base up 1.00	I, hor or vert, base down 0.96
F, hor.; HID, ver 1.00	HID, 40-90° from ver ... 0.91

DEPRECIATION DURING LAMP LIFE (2,500 hr/yr)	δ_n
S, 1 year 0.99	F, 1 year 0.92
Q, 8 months 0.98	F, 3 years 0.89
S, 3 years 0.96	MH, 1 year 0.88
MV, 1 year; I, 3 months 0.95	MH, 3 years 0.75

DEPRECIATION DUE TO LUMINAIRE TEMP. INCREASE	δ_t
Open or vented luminaire 1.00	1 Q, 1 F, sealed ... 0.95
2 F, sealed lum. w/ r.a.d.[2] 0.99	2 I, sealed 0.94
1 HID, sealed 0.98	2 F, sealed 0.93
3 F, sealed w/ r.a.d. 0.98	3 F, sealed 0.91
4 F, sealed w/ r.a.d. 0.97	4 F, sealed 0.88

DEPRECIATION DUE TO LUMINAIRE DIRT ACCUM.	δ_d
Direct illumination 0.96	Semi-indirect illum.. 0.88
Semi-direct illumin. ... 0.93	Indirect illumin. 0.86
Direct-indirect illum... 0.91	

DEPRECIATION DUE TO ROOM AIR DIRT	δ_a
Very clean: modern offices away from production	0.96
Clean: offices in old buildings; light assembly	0.93
Medium: construction offices, light industrial	0.89
Dirty: industrial operations making moderate dust	0.84
Very dirty: industrial oper. making visible dust ...	0.76

DEPRECIATION DURING LENGTH OF SERVICE CYCLE	δ_m
1 year service cycle ... 1.00	2 year service cycle 0.91
1½ year service cycle 0.93	3 year service cycle 0.85

1. I = incand., Q = quartz, F = fluor., HID = high-intensity discharge, MV = mercury, MH = metal halide, S = sodium.
2. r.a.d. = return air ducting.

10. ILLUMINATION

Basic Lighting Formula:

$$\diamond \; \lambda_\eta \; \beta \; U \;_L\!\Delta \; \mho \; R \; \Theta \cos \angle \; = \; (\Phi - \mathbb{D}) \; D^2$$

$\diamond$ = rated output of light source, lm
λ_η = light source near-field factor, 0.0–1.0
β = ray or beam concentration factor, 0.0–1.0
U = luminaire coefficient of utilization, 0.0–1.0
$_L\!\Delta$ = light depreciation factor, 0.0–1.0
$\mho$ = room coefficient of utilization, 0.0–1.0
R = visual task reflectance, 0.0–1.0
Θ = occupancy factor, 0.0–1.0
$\angle$ = angle of incidence of light ray to task plane, 0–90°
Φ = required illumination level of visual task, fc
$\mathbb{D}$ = amount of daylighting arriving at visual task, fc
D = distance between light source and visual task, ft

Near vs. Far Field:

Step 1. Find the light source dimensional ratios $D/_L$ and $D/_W$ as described below:

D = distance between light source and visual task, ft
L = length of light source, ft
W = width of light source, ft

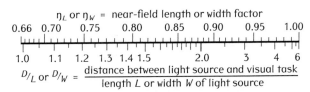

Fig. 10-1. Near-field adjustment bar graph.

TABLE 10-2: RAY CONCENTRATION FACTORS
(Interpolate for intermediate values)

CONCENTRATION due to portion of enclosure	ρ_e
Full-sphere (aperture angle ≈ 330°)	1.0
0.33 enclosed (aperture angle ≈ 240°)	1.2
0.50 enclosed (aperture angle ≈ 180°)	1.4
0.67 enclosed (aperture angle ≈ 120°; 60° cutoff) ..	1.7
0.75 enclosed (aperture angle ≈ 90°; 45° cutoff) ...	2.0
"Flood" lamp beam spread ≈ 30°	3.6
"Spot" lamp beam spread ≈ 15°	5.2
"Pencil" lamp beam spread ≈ 9°	6.8

CONCENTRATION due to reflector contour	ρ_c
Box, pyramid, cylinder, hyperbolic, 'gable', asymmetric shapes; also plenums, coves, valences, coffers, soffits, cornices, etc.	1.00
Circle or ellipse (one direction) × trough	1.05
Scoop, parabola (one direction) × trough, circle or ellipse (two directions)	1.10
Parabola (two directions), Fresnel or conc. lens ...	1.20
Constrictions (return edges, pinholes, etc.)	ignore

CONCENTRATION due to reflector finish	ρ_f
Mirror finish: glass, stainless steel, etc	0.93
Spun or satin aluminum, satin brass, etc.	0.88
White baked enamel, matte, semi-gloss, glossy	0.83
Black, flat black, coilex baffle, etc.	0.55
Other material acting as reflector .. use reflectance value

Step 2. Determine if the light source is *point, line,* or *area* as follows:

$D_{/L}$ and $D_{/W} \geq 6$ .... light source is *point*

Only $D_{/L} \leq 6$ .... light source is *line*

$D_{/L}$ and $D_{/W} \leq 6$ .... light source is *area*

Step 3. Find the light source's near-field factor from

$$\lambda_\eta = \eta_L\, s_L\, \eta_W\, s_W$$

λ_η = light source near-field factor. For point light sources, $\lambda_\eta = 1$.

η_L = near-field length factor

s_L = light source length factor

η_W = near-field width factor

s_W = light source width factor

If $D_{/L} \leq 1$, $\eta_L = 0.66$ and $s_L = D$

If $D_{/L} > 1 < 6$, find η_L from Fig. 10-1 and $s_L = L$

If $D_{/L} \geq 6$, η_L and $s_L = 1.00$

If $D_{/W} \leq 1.00$, $\eta_W = 0.66$ and $s_W = D$

If $D_{/W} > 1 < 6$, find η_W from Fig. 10-1 and $s_W = W$

If $D_{/W} \geq 6$, $\eta_W = 1.00$ and $s_W = 1.00$

Ray Concentration: $ß \approx \rho_e\, \rho_c\, \rho_f$

$ß$ = total ray or beam concentration factor

ρ_e = ray concentration due to portion of lamp's spherical output that is enclosed

ρ_c = ray concentration due to contour of enclosure

ρ_f = ray concentration due to finish of enclosure

Luminaire Coefficient of Utilization:

$$\Phi = \diamond\, \mho$$

Φ = net rated output of luminaire, lm

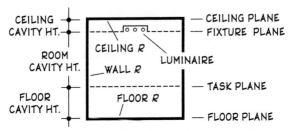

Fig. 10-2. Zonal cavity ℧ calculation details.

TABLE 10-3: LUMINAIRE COEFFS. OF UTILIZATION

DESCRIPTION OF LUMINAIRES	Luminaire ℧
Bare I lamp; R40 flood w/o shielding, light pipes ...	1.00
2 × 235° reflector lamps in open strip unit	0.98
Single row F lamp cove w/o reflector	0.93
Fiber optic end-dedicated extrusion, per LF	0.90
1 or 2 F lamps in open strip unit	0.88
R flood w/ spec. reflector, 45° cutoff	0.85
Phosphor-coated HID lamp w/ high bay reflector ...	0.81
Pendant diffusing sphere w/ any lamp, globe lights	0.80
High-output F lamp in suspended unit w/ lens below	0.78
Clear HID lamp w/ high bay vented reflector	0.77
Surface-mounted F lamp w/ wraparound lens	0.75
Clear HID uplight or downlight w/ prismatic lens	0.73
I downlight in circular reflector w/ enclosed lens ...	0.71
2 F lamp unit w/ prismatic wraparound	0.70
Recessed baffled downlight w/ 5½ in. dia. opening	0.68
Uniform ceiling illumination w/ diffusing plastic lens	0.65
4 F lamp troffer w/ flat lens or dropped diffuser	0.61
F lamp in batwing fixture w/ lateral louvers	0.60
EAR 38 downlight w/ 3 in. dia. aperture	0.54
4 F lamp troffer w/ 45° plastic louvers	0.50
4 F lamp troffer w/ 45° white metal louvers	0.46
AR 38 downlight w/ 2 in. dia. aperture	0.43

◇ = rated output of light source in luminaire, lm
ʊ = luminaire coeff. of utilization, from Table 10-3

Light Depreciation: $_L\Delta \approx \delta_v \delta_p \delta_n \delta_t \delta_d \delta_a \delta_m$

$_L\Delta$ = total light depreciation factor (see Table 10-1)
δ_v = light depreciation due to voltage fluctuation
δ_p = light depreciation due to lamp position
δ_n = light depreciation during lamp life
δ_t = light deprec. due to luminaire temp. increase
δ_d = light deprec. due to luminaire dirt accumulation
δ_a = light depreciation due to room air dirt
δ_m = light depreciation due to length of service cycle

Room Coefficient of Utilization:

Step 1. Compute the room's average reflectance r_a by listing each wall, ceiling, and floor surface, finding the area a and reflectance r of each surface, multiplying each $a \times r$, then dividing the total by the room's surface area.

Step 2. Compute the room's coefficient of utilization.

$$\upsilon \approx 1.13 \left[R\,W\,L/10\;H\,(W+L) \right]^{0.34}$$

ʊ = coefficient of utilization of illuminated room, space, or zone
R = average reflectance of room, space, or zone
W = average width of room's zonal cavity, ft
L = average breadth or length of zonal cavity, ft
H = average height of zonal cavity = room ht – ceiling cavity ht. – floor cavity ht, ft.

Surface or Task Reflectance: $L = \Phi R$

L = luminance of room surface or visual task, fL

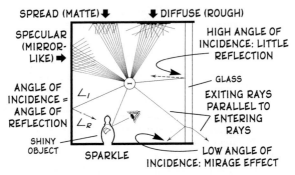

Fig. 10-3. Types of reflectance.

TABLE 10-4: COEFFICIENTS OF REFLECTANCE

SURFACE	R	SURFACE	R
Primary hues: red	0.24	Orange	0.35
Yellow	0.69	Green	0.28
Blue	0.23	Violet	0.14
Other hues: sky blue	0.45	Light gray	0.58
Medium gray	0.20	Dark gray	0.11
Maroon, cobalt blue	0.08	Black ink	0.05
Brown, grocery bag	0.25	White paper	0.82
Pastels	0.60–0.80	White plaster	0.91
Other Surfaces: Pine	0.34	Maple	0.21
Light oak	0.32	Dark oak	0.13
Slate	0.08	Granite	0.40
Brick, dark red	0.13	Brick, light buff	0.48
Concrete	0.42	Asphalt, old	0.18
Stainless steel	0.60	Aluminum	0.55
Vegetation, average	0.15	Grass, dark	0.10
Snow, new	0.78	Snow, old	0.64
Mirror	0.85	Light source	1.00
Clear pane, night, or no illumination outside			0.09

Φ = incident light upon room surface or visual task, fc

R = reflectance of room surface or visual task

Occupancy Factors: $\Theta \approx \kappa_d \kappa_e \kappa_f \kappa_p \left(40/\kappa_a\right)^{0.85}$

Θ = total occupancy factor

κ_d = duration factor, ranges from 1.0 for short visual tasks to 0.85 for tasks of day-long duration

κ_e = error factor, from 1.00 (task errors have no serious consequences) to 0.85 (task errors have very serious consequences)

κ_f = fenestration factor

κ_p = protective lens factor, ranges from 1.0 to 0.85 unless work standards require a lower figure

κ_a = occupants' age, yrs. Below age 40, $\kappa_a = 40$.

Lighting Contrast: $L_n = \Phi_t R_t / \Phi_s R_s$

L_n = restful illuminance ratio. Typical task/surround illuminance ratios are given in Table 10-6.

Φ_t = incident light upon visual task, fc

R_t = reflectance of visual task

Φ_s = incident light upon surround or background, fc

R_s = reflectance of surround, from Table 10-4

Daylighting: $\diamondsuit \theta \tau \lambda_\eta {}_L \Delta (1 + 0.5 \kappa_G) \approx \Phi D^2$

$\diamondsuit$ = output of natural light source. If $\diamondsuit$ is *point*, $\diamondsuit_P$ = fc; if $\diamondsuit$ is *line*, $\diamondsuit_L$ = fc/LF; if $\diamondsuit$ is *area*, $\diamondsuit_A$ = fc/sf.

θ = obstructions (foliage, buildings, terrain, etc.) in front of opening. θ = sin (angle formed by top of obstructions and surface of glazing) × (1 − solid-to-opening ratio of any screen over opening).

τ = transmittance of glazing, from Table 10-7

λ_η = light source near-field factor (see pp. 441–443)

$_L\Delta$ = light depreciation factor, from Table 10-1
κ_G = ground reflectance factor, from Table 7-9
Φ = incident light upon visual task, fc
D = distance between light source and visual task, ft

Comparative Cost of Light Sources:

$$100 \, \$_i = L \, (\cent - 0.001 \, \epsilon \, W)$$

$\$_i$ = initial cost of each light source, dollars
L = rated life of each light source, hr

TABLE 10-5: VISUAL TASK ILLUMINATION LEVELS	
AREA OR TASK	Illuminance, fc
Surgical or emergency operating rooms	2,000
Exacting inspection at frequent intervals	1,000
Low-contrast inspection, fine machine work	750
Fine inspection, autopsy rooms	500
TV studios, precise assembly, bacterial lab work	300
Merchandise showcases, medical examination	200
Drafting, accounting, fine layout work, tailoring	150
Private offices, cataloguing, theater stages	100
Classrooms, cashier areas, general office	75
General industrial, major entrances, conf. rooms	50
Service area breakdown, elevators, rest rooms, dressing, bathing, cafeterias, signage	30
Machine rooms, recreational, eating	20
Hallways and lobbies, warehouses, record storage ..	15
Service entrances, night lights, intimate dining	10
Garages, stockrooms, dance halls, drop-off areas, mechanical equipment rooms, ambient residential ...	7.5
Emergency exits, video viewing, bin storage	5
Hospital corridors at night, basements	3
Pediatric nurseries, theater seating dur. performance	2
Inactive storage, candle flame 1 ft away	1
Dormitory areas at night, watching movies	0.2

¢ = total initial plus lifetime operating cost of each
    light source, ¢/hr
€ = unit cost of local electric power, ¢/kWh
W = wattages of light sources that have equal out-
    puts, watts

Energy Cost of Light Sources:

$$\$ \approx 0.00001\, \omega\, ¢\, L$$

$\$$ = cost of energy consumed during lamp's life, dollars
ω = wattage of lamp, watts
¢ = local cost of electric power, ¢/kWh
L = rated lamp life, hr

Energy Efficiency of Light Sources:

$$H \approx 0.034\, \eta\, W\, Q$$

H = heating energy load of lighting system, Btu/hr
η = number of lamps in lighting system
W = wattage of each lamp, watts

TABLE 10-6: RESTFUL ILLUMINATION RATIOS

CONTRAST: Task area/Surround area	Restful range
General task/surround, "figure/ground"	3:1–20:1
Task/light background	2:1–8:1
Task/dark background	3:1–15:1
Light source (luminaire or opening)/surround	2:1–30:1
Video terminal display/surround	4:1–8:1
Uniform lighting, lightest/darkest area	≈ 3:1
Highlighting, featured object/surround	3:1–10:1
Perceived twice as bright	≈ 10:1
Low theatrical effect	≈ 5:1
High theatrical effect ≈ 15:1; Dramatic effect	≈ 25:1
Maximum ratio of bright white/dull black	30:1

Q = lamp heat losses: percentage of ballast, infrared, and conduction/convection heat emitted from each lamp, from manufacturers' catalogs

Programmed Lighting Controls Design:

Step 1. Divide the plan into zones of similar daylighting and task illumination levels.

Step 2. Find the annual maximum and minimum daylighting for each zone. The annual maximum determines the lowest range of controls while the annual minimum is subtracted from the task lighting requirements to determine the maximum artificial lighting requirements.

Step 3. Compute the zone's theoretical maximum task illumination.

$$\Phi - \mathbb{D}_{min} \approx \phi_{max\ L}\Delta\ \Theta$$

Φ = required infant task illumination, fc
$\mathbb{D}_{min}$ = annual min. daylighting level at visual task, fc
ϕ_{max} = theoretical max. visual task lighting level, fc
$_L\Delta$ = light depreciation factor
Θ = occupancy factor

Step 4. Compute the zone's theoretical minimum task illumination.

$$\Phi - \mathbb{D}_{max} \approx \phi_{min}$$

Φ = required infant task illumination, fc
$\mathbb{D}_{max}$ = annual max. daylighting level at visual task, fc
ϕ_{min} = theoretical minimum visual task illumination level, fc. ϕ_{min} must ≥ 0.

Subsequent Steps. The Æ designer, knowing the lighting loads for each zone, determines the required number of fixtures; then the manufacturer designs the programmed controls.

Design of Illuminated Vertical Surfaces:

Step 1. If the illumination is a line light source ($D_{/L} < 6$) or area light source ($D_{/L} < 6$ and $D_{/W} < 6$), compute its near-field factor as described on pages 441-443.

Step 2. Compute the net illumination arriving at the vertical visual task.

Point light sources w/ beamspread designations:
$$\diamondsuit_< U\ _L\Delta\ \Theta \approx 12.6\ \Phi\ D^2$$

Other point light sources: $\diamondsuit_P\ ß\ U\ _L\Delta\ \Theta \approx \Phi\ D^2$

Line light sources: $\diamondsuit_L\ \lambda_\eta\ ß\ U\ _L\Delta\ \Theta \approx L\ \Phi\ D^2$

Area light sources: $\diamondsuit_A\ \lambda_\eta\ ß\ U\ _L\Delta\ \Theta \approx A\ \Phi\ D^2$

$\diamondsuit_<$ = output of point light source with beamspread designation, CBCP

$\diamondsuit_P$ = output of light source with no beamspread designation, lm

$\diamondsuit_L$ = output of line light source, lm

$\diamondsuit_A$ = output of area light source, lm

U = luminaire coefficient of utilization or transmittance of glazing (from Table 10-7)

$_L\Delta$ = light depreciation factor

Θ = occupancy factor

Φ = net illumination arriving at visual task, fc

D = distance between light source and visual task, ft

$ß$ = ray or beam concentration factor

λ_η = light source near-field factor, from Step 1, ft

L = length of line light source, ft

A = facing area of area light source, sf

Step 3. Compute the actual illumination of the vertical visual task.
$$\Phi_v\ D = \Phi\ D_h$$

Φ_v = actual illumination of vertical visual task, lm
D = axial distance from light source to visual task, ft
Φ = net illumination arriving at visual task, lm
D_h = horiz. distance from light source to visual task, ft

Optimal Floor Area per Light Fixture:

$$\diamond \, \eta \, ß \, U \, {}_L\!\Delta \, \mho \, \Theta \approx A \, \Phi$$

$\diamond$ = rated output per lamp, lm.
η = number of lamps per luminaire
$ß$ = ray or beam concentration factor
U = luminaire coefficient of utilization or
   transmittance of glazing
${}_L\Delta$ = light depreciation factor
$\mho$ = coefficient of utilization of room, space, or zone
Θ = occupancy factor
A = optimal coverage area for one fixture, sf
Φ = infant task illumination, fc

Optimal Number of Fixtures in Ceiling Area:

$$\diamond \, \eta \, L \, ß \, U \, {}_L\!\Delta \, \mho \, \Theta = A \, \Phi$$

$\diamond$ = rated output per lamp, lm
η = number of lamps per luminaire
L = number of luminaires in room, bay, or zone
$ß$ = ray or beam concentration factor
U = luminaire coefficient of utilization from Table
   10-3 or transmittance of glazing from Table 10-7
${}_L\Delta$ = light depreciation factor
$\mho$ = coefficient of utilization of room, space, or zone
Θ = occupancy factor
A = Area of illuminated space, sf
Φ = required infant task illumination, fc

Spacing Criteria: Spacing criteria or *SC* is a luminaire's ratio of maximum horizontal spacing to its height
above the visual task.

$$S = RH$$

S = maximum spacing of luminaires, ft
R = spacing criteria of luminaires. *R* should ≈ 1.4.
H = height of luminaires above visual task, ft

Lighting Environments: A lighting environment is
a specific light/space/task scenario: it may have a natural or artificial light source, and it is the basic 3-D tool
for creating satisfactory lighting indoors.

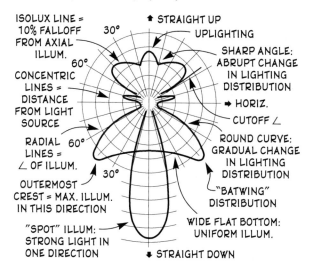

Fig. 10-4. Reading a light fixture's isolux lines.

Lighting Envir. Design, Canopies & Soffits:

Step 1. Find the near-field factor of this usually area light source as described in Fig. 10-1 on page 442.

Step 2. Find the light source's required output from

$$\diamond_A \lambda_\eta \, \text{ß} \, U \,_L\Delta \, \Theta \approx A \, \Phi \, D^2$$

$\diamond_A$ = required total output of area light source, lm
λ_η = light source near-field factor, from Step 1
ß = ray or beam concentration factor
U = luminaire coefficient of utilization from Table 10-3 or transmittance of glazing from Table 10-7
$_L\Delta$ = light depreciation factor
Θ = occupancy factor
A = facing area of area light source, sf
Φ = required infant task illumination, fc
D = distance between light source and task plane, ft

Step 3. Select the light source(s) from light intensity tables or catalogs.

Lighting Envir. Design, Ceiling Systems:

$$\diamond \eta \, L \, \text{ß} \, U \, \Delta \, \textit{U} \, \Theta \approx \Phi \, A$$

$\diamond$ = rated output of lamp, lm
η = number of lamps in each luminaire
L = number of luminaires in room, space, or zone
ß = ray or beam concentration factor
U = luminaire coefficient of utilization
Δ = light depreciation factor
$\textit{U}$ = coefficient of utilization of room, bay, or zone
Θ = occupancy factor
Φ = required infant task illumination, fc
A = ceiling area of room, bay, or zone, sf

Lighting Environment Design, Coffers:

A coffer is a recessed ceiling panel that contains one or more lighting fixtures. A skylight is typically a coffer lighting environment.

Step 1. Find the near-field factor of this usually area light source as described in Fig. 10-1 on page 442.

Step 2. Find the light source's required output from

$$\diamondsuit_A \, \lambda_\eta \, \text{ß} \, U \, {}_L\Delta \, \Theta \approx A \, \Phi \, D^2$$

$\diamondsuit_A$ = required output of area light source lm
λ_η = light source near-field factor, from Step 1
ß = ray or beam concentration factor
U = luminaire coefficient of utilization or transmittance of glazing
${}_L\Delta$ = light depreciation factor
Θ = occupancy factor
A = facing area of area light source, sf
Φ = required infant task illumination, fc
D = distance between light source and task plane, ft

TABLE 10-7: COEFFICIENTS OF TRANSMITTANCE

TYPE OF GLAZING	Transmittance τ
Clear glass or plastic lens	0.95
¼ in. single pane glass: clear	0.88
¼ in. thermopane glass: clear	0.78
¼ in. plastic: clear, 0.80-0.92; Milky plexiglas	0.50
Opal glass, 0.35; Glass block	0.60-0.80
Insect screen .... multiply glass t by 0.7	
Tissue paper, veils, lampshades, parchments	≈ 0.60
Lamp diffusers: frosted glass, white plastic	≈ 0.70
Clear water .... 0.90 per 2 in. depth measured ∥ rays	

Step 3. Select the light source(s) from light intensity tables or catalogs.

Lighting Environment Design, Cornices:

A cornice is a projection that contains a row of concealed lamps that brightens areas below.

Step 1. As this is a *line* light source ($D/L < 6$), compute its near-field factor as described in Fig. 10-1.

Step 2. Find the light source's required output from

$$\diamondsuit_L \, \lambda_n \, \text{ß} \, U \, _L\Delta \, \Theta \approx \Phi \, D^2$$

$\diamondsuit_L$ = required unit output of line light source, lm/LF
λ_n = light source near-field factor, from Step 1
ß = ray or beam concentration factor
U = luminaire coefficient of utilization
$_L\Delta$ = light depreciation factor
Θ = occupancy factor
Φ = required infant task illumination, fc
D = distance between light source and visual task, ft

Step 3. Select the light source(s) from light intensity tables or catalogs.

Lighting Environment Design, Coves:

Step 1. If the ceiling is square or nearly so, assume that approximately one-quarter of the light arrives from each side. Then, knowing the ceiling's dimensions, find the near-field factor of this normally line light source from Fig. 10-1 on page 442.

Step 2. Find the light source's required output from

$$\diamondsuit_L \, \lambda_n \, \text{ß} \, U \, _L\Delta \, \Theta \approx \Phi \, D^2$$

$\Diamond_L$ = required unit output of line light source, lm/LF of perimeter

λ_η = light source near-field factor, from Step 1

ß = ray or beam concentration factor

U = luminaire coefficient of utilization or transmittance of glazing

$_L\Delta$ = light depreciation factor

Θ = occupancy factor

Φ = required infant task illumination, fc

D = distance between light source and visual task, ft

Step 3. Select the light source(s) from light intensity tables or catalogs.

Lighting Environment Design, Fiber Optics:

$$\Diamond_i \kappa_f \kappa_b \approx 10.8\ \Phi\ D^2\ \delta^2\ \tau^L$$

$\Diamond_i$ = required initial output of illuminator lamp, CBCP

κ_f = filter factor: transmissivity of any filters between illuminator and fiber. τ for filters of certain colors are as follows: clear = 0.9; orange = 0.6; pink, yellow, light blue = 0.80; red or dark blue = 0.3; green, violet, medium brown = 0.4 . If more than 1 filter, sum the κ_fs. If no filters, κ_f = 1.0.

κ_b = beamspread factor, based on end fitting and material of optic fiber, from bar graph below:

Glass κ_b	0.060	0.040	0.020	0.010	0.008
Beamspread	20°	30°	40°	50°	60°	70°
Acrylic κ_b	0.090	0.060	0.030	0.020	0.013

Fiber optic end fitting factor bar graph.

Φ = required visual task illumination, fc

D = distance between end fitting and visual task, ft

δ = diameter of FO cable core, in. If core is many thin fibers with a tail size, $\delta = 0.0433$ (tail size no.)$^{0.5}$; maximum tail size = 400. If core is solid glass or acrylic, δ = actual diameter. Glass diameter = 0.002–0.50 in, acrylic diameter = 0.010–0.50 in.

τ = transmissivity of FO cable. $\tau = 0.976$ for acrylic, 0.93 for glass.

L = length of FO cable between illuminator and end fitting, ft

Lighting Envir. Design, Fixed Luminaires:

A fixed luminaire is the generic "light fixture". It is usually a small lamp that provides general illumination.

Step 1. Find the light source's ray concentration factor from

$$ß \approx \rho_e \, \rho_c \, \rho_f$$

$ß$ = ray or beam concentration factor

ρ_e = ray concentration due to portion of lamp's spherical output that is enclosed

ρ_c = ray concentration due to enclosure contour

ρ_f = ray concentration due to enclosure finish

Step 2. Find the light source's required output from

$$\diamond \, ß \, U \, {}_L\Delta \, \Theta \approx \Phi \, D^2$$

$\diamond$ = rated output of point light source, lm. If this value includes luminaire τ, U below = 1.0.

$ß$ = ray concentration factor

U = luminaire coefficient of utilization

${}_L\Delta$ = light depreciation factor

Θ = occupancy factor
Φ = infant task illumination, fc, from Table 10-5
D = distance between light source and visual task, ft

Lighting Envir. Design, Floods & Spots:

Floodlights and spotlights have fairly well-defined beamspreads that range from about 4° to 134°. Generally if the lamp's beamspread is less than 20° it is categorized as *narrow*, if it is from 20 to 35° it is *medium*, and if it is 35° or more it is *wide*. The cone of light radiating from each lamp also has a *central axis* (center of the cone of light where its candlepower is greatest), *pattern* (shape of light the beam casts), *cutoffs* (the cone's "edge" of light where its axial candlepower has diminished to 10 percent of axial output), and a *throw* (length of the central axis at where the axial candlepower has weakened to 10 percent of initial output).

Relation between beamspread & throw: $\beta_w \approx T \sin \angle$

β_w = width of beamspread, ft
T = length or throw of beamspread, ft
$\angle$ = angle of beamspread to task plane, °

    Full design: $\diamondsuit_{<} U_L\Delta\, \Theta \approx 12.6\, \Phi\, D^2$

$\diamondsuit_<$ = output of light source with beamspread designation, CBCP. Compute this value, then select the light source(s) from light intensity tables or catalogs. If this value includes luminaire coefficient of utilization, U below = 1.00.
U = luminaire coefficient of utilization
$_L\Delta$ = light depreciation factor
Θ = occupancy factor
Φ = required infant task plane illumination, fc
D = distance between light source and visual task, ft

Lighting Environment Design, Light Pipes:

A light pipe is a large linear lamp that provides uniform low-glare light, creates no heat buildup in the illuminated area, and has no wiring or connectors near the emitted light and thus can be immersed in water.

Step 1. Find the light source's required output from

$$0.66 \diamond \text{ß} \, \mho \, \Theta \approx \Phi \, D$$

$\diamond$ = req. unit output of light pipe installation, lm/LF

ß = ray or beam concentration factor. ß = 1.00 if fixture's emitting sector is 240°, 1.57 if 180°, 1.64 if 120°, and 2.25 if 90°.

$\mho$ = room coefficient of illumination or reflectance of surface around the light source

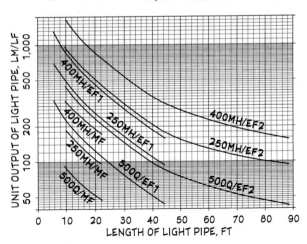

Fig. 10-5. Light pipe locator graph.

Θ = occupancy factor
Φ = required infant task illumination, fc
D = distance between light source and visual task, ft

Step 2. Find the type of unit and its maximum length in the light pipe locator graph in Fig. 10-5. The standard notation for the lamps in this graph is as follows: the first numbers (250, 400, 500) indicate the lamp wattage, the letters MH (metal halide) or Q (quartz) indicate the type of lamp, and EF1 (lamp on one end) or EF2 (lamps on both ends) indicate the fixture's number of end fittings.

Lighting Envir. Design, Light Ribbons:

A light ribbon is a surface illumination that is only $\frac{1}{50}$ in. thick, $\frac{5}{16}$ to $22\frac{1}{2}$ in. wide, and up to 1,500 ft long. It can be as bright as 50 fL, generates no heat, and can withstand temperatures from –40 to 250° F.

> **Required wattage:** $W = 425\,\kappa_b A$
> **Required amperage:** $\diamond = 1.93\,\kappa_b A$

W = req. wattage of light ribbon area circuitry, watts
$\diamond$ = required amperage of area circuitry, amps
κ_b = brightness factor, based on lighting level of system. κ_b for 8 fL system = 0.0004, 17 fL = 0.0006, 25 fL = 0.0008, 25 fL = 0.0012, 50 fL = 0.0016.
A = surface area of installation, in^2

Lighting Envir. Design, Plug-in Buses:

A plug-in bus is a row of ceiling-mounted luminaires that contain usually fluorescent lamps that can be quickly disassembled and relocated.

Step 1. Find the near-field factor of this usually area light source as described in Fig. 10-1 on page 442.

Step 2. Find the light source's required output from

$$\Diamond_L \, \lambda_\eta \, \text{ß} \, U \, {}_L\Delta \, \Theta \, \approx \, \Phi \, D^2$$

$\Diamond_L$ = required unit output of line light source, lm/LF
λ_η = light source near-field factor
ß = ray or beam concentration factor
U = luminaire coefficient of utilization
${}_L\Delta$ = light depreciation factor
Θ = occupancy factor
Φ = required infant task illumination, fc
D = distance between light source and visual task, ft

Step 3. Select the light source(s) from light intensity tables or catalogs.

Lighting Envir. Design, Portable Luminaires:
This usually point light source typically has a reflector or translucent shade and is mounted on a pedestal, then the fixture is located near a visual task. Its output is usually determined by socket selection of its lamp and adjustment of the fixture after it is installed.

Lighting Environment Design, Sconces:
A sconce is a small wall-mounted lamp that is shielded with a translucent or opaque diffuser that eliminates frontal glare and directs the lamp's light against the surface behind it.

Step 1. Determine the ray concentration factor of this usually partly enclosed point light source from

$$\text{ß} \, \approx \, \rho_e \, \rho_c \, \rho_f$$

ß = ray or beam concentration factor
ρ_e = ray concentration due to portion of lamp's spher-

ical output that is enclosed

ρ_c = ray conc. due to contour of reflective enclosure

ρ_f = ray conc. due to finish of reflective enclosure

Step 2. Find the light source's required output from

$$\diamond \; \text{ß} \; U \, _L\Delta \; \Theta \; \approx \; \Phi \, D^2$$

$\diamond$ = required output of point light source, lm. If this value includes luminaire CU, U below = 1.0.

ß = ray or beam concentration factor

U = luminaire coefficient of utilization

$_L\Delta$ = light depreciation factor

Θ = occupancy factor

Φ = infant task illumination, fc

D = distance between light source and visual task, ft

Step 3. Select the light source(s) from light intensity tables or manufacturers' catalogs.

Lighting Environment Design, Valences:

A valence is a combination of cove and cornice lighting whose usually line light source has a concealing face-board that sends the light into spaces above and below.

Step 1. Find the the uplighting's near-field factor as described in Fig. 10-1 on page 442.

Step 2. Find the light source's required output from

$$\diamond_{vu} \, \lambda_\eta \; \text{ß} \; U \, _L\Delta \; \Theta \; \approx \; \Phi \, D_u^{\,2}$$

$\diamond_{vu}$ = required unit output for valence uplighting

λ_η = light source near-field factor, from Step 2

ß = ray or beam concentration factor

U = luminaire coefficient of utilization

$_L\Delta$ = light depreciation factor

Θ = occupancy factor
Φ = req. infant task illumination for uplighting, fc
D_u = distance between light source & visual task above light source, ft

Step 3. Find the downlighting's near-field factor as described in Fig. 10-1 on page 442.

Step 4. Find the light source's required output from

$$\diamond_{vd} \lambda_\eta \, \text{ß} \, U \, _L\Delta \, \Theta \approx \Phi \, D_d{}^2$$

$\diamond_{vd}$ = required unit output for valence downlighting
λ_η = light source near-field factor
ß = ray or beam concentration factor
U = luminaire coefficient of utilization
$_L\Delta$ = light depreciation factor
Θ = occupancy factor
Φ = req. infant task illumination for downlighting, fc
D_d = distance between light source and visual task below light source, ft

Step 5. Find the valence's total required output from

$$\diamond_t \approx \diamond_u + \diamond_d$$

$\diamond_t$ = total required unit output for valence, lm/LF
$\diamond_u$ = req. unit output for valence uplighting, lm/LF
$\diamond_d$ = req. unit output for valence downlighting, lm/LF

Step 6. Position the valence faceboard so its top and bottom openings create the required lighting levels.

    Uplighting angle: $\angle_t \diamond_{vu} \approx \angle_u (\diamond_{vu} + \diamond_{vd})$
    Downlighting angle: $\angle_t \diamond_{vd} \approx \angle_d (\diamond_{vu} + \diamond_{vd})$

$\angle_t$ = total of two angles subtended by uplighting and downlighting openings behind faceboard.

$\diamond_{vu}$ = unit output for valence uplighting, lm/LF
$\diamond_{vd}$ = unit output for valence downlighting, lm/LF
$\angle_u$ = optimal angle subtended by upper opening of faceboard, °
$\angle_d$ = optimal angle subtended by lower opening of faceboard, °

Step 3. Select the light source(s) from light intensity tables or catalogs.

Outdoor Lighting Systems: Outdoor lighting differs from indoor lighting as follows:

▸   Lack of enclosing interior surfaces usually requires more precise aiming of luminaires. Optimal angle between light axis and task plane ≈ 35° and the angle between light axis and observer's line of view ≥ 15°.

▸   Contrast, which is usually more prominent at night anyway, is often more important.

TABLE 10-8: OUTDOOR NIGHT LIGHTING LEVELS		
	ILLUMINANCE, fc	
AREA OR TASK PLANE	Bright surround	Dark surround
White or very light	15	8
Light gray, buff, water	20	12
Medium gray, tan brick, sandstone	30	15
Dark, red brick, brownstone	50	25
Sidewalks, residential streets		1
General parking, outdoor landscaping		2
Parking for evening attractions, security lighting around buildings		3–5
Entrance gates, ramps, stairs, bikeways		5–8
Building entries, terraces, general recreation		10–15
Gate houses, major building entrances		20–25

▸ Lamps should generally be concealed to avoid
glare and add mystery to their effect.
▸ Weather extremes and the need for vandal resistance often require fixtures to have special connections and stronger housings.
▸ Lighting is usually related to utilitarian, recre-
ational, and aesthetic needs more than econom-
ics; thus occupancy factors usually equal 1.00.
▸ Heat emittance problems are usually nonexistent.

Landmark Outdoor Lighting Design:
Landmark lighting is the illumination of facades, monu-
ments, and other prominent outdoor objects at night.

Step 1. Find the distance between the light source and
visual task depending on given data.

> **Vertical distance given:** $V = D \sin \angle$
> **Horizontal distance given:** $H = D \cos \angle$
> **Both V and H given:** $D = (V^2 + H^2)^{0.5}$

V = vertical distance from lamp(s) to visual task, ft
H = horiz. distance from lamp(s) to visual task, ft
D = axial distance from lamp(s) to visual task, ft
$\angle$ = incident angle of lamp axis to visual task, °

Step 2. Compute the light source's required output.

$$ \diamondsuit_< U_L \Delta\, \Theta \approx 12.6\, \Phi\, D^2 $$

$\diamondsuit_<$ = output of light source with beamspread designation, CBCP. Lighting loads of clustered lamps are
additive if their centerbeams align.
U = luminaire coefficient of utilization
$_L\Delta$ = light depreciation factor
Θ = occupancy factor. For outdoor lighting, Θ

typically = 1.00.

Φ = required infant task illumination, fc

D = distance between light source and visual task, ft

Landscape Outdoor Lighting Design:

Step 1. On a plan of the landscaping locate the prominent foliage and other features to be highlighted, the viewers' points or paths of observation, and the optimal locations for the luminaires.

Step 2. Note the distances between the light sources and illuminated areas as well as the beamspreads for their optimal illumination.

Step 3. Compute the output for each luminaire from

> **R, PAR & MR lamps:** $\diamond_< \beta\, U_L\Delta \approx 12.6\,\Phi\, D^2$
> **All other lamps:** $\diamond_n \beta\, U_L\Delta \approx \Phi\, D^2$

$\diamond_<$ = output of R, PAR, or MR lamp w/ beamspread designation, CBCP.

$\diamond_n$ = output of any lamp that has no beamspread designation, lm

β = ray or beam concentration factor. For floods and spots, β = 1.

U = luminaire coefficient of utilization

$_L\Delta$ = light depreciation factor

Φ = required infant task illumination, fc

D = distance between light source and visual task, ft

Note: Security, parking, and arena lighting are designed similarly as is landscape lighting. However, instead of performing the calculations in Step 3, an Æ designer often uses manufacturers' catalogs to select fixtures with the optimal outputs and beamspreads.

TABLE 11-1: ACOUSTIC STC RATINGS OF WALLS

WALL CONSTRUCTION	STC Rating [1]
2 × 4 wood studs 16" o.c., 32; batt insul. in voids	36
3½" metal studs 16" o.c., 38; batt insul. in voids	45
2 × 4 staggered studs on 6" plate, 42; " " " "	47
Double 2 × 4 wood studs 16" o.c. on double plates	44
4" batt insul. in voids, 56; 10" insul. in voids	59
½" fiberboard between studs	+ 9
Add to any above: + 2 × ½" drywall 1S or ⅝" 2S	+ 2
Resilient channels under drywall 1S, + 5; 2S	+ 8
Masonry or reinf. concrete, 6", 47; each extra 2" t	+ 3
Brick, 4", 41; each extra 2" thick	+ 4
Concrete block, 4" lightweight, 36; each extra 2" t	+ 5
Concrete block, 4" standard, 38; each extra 2" t	+ 5
½" drywall on rigid furs 1S, + 4; 2S	+ 7
Batts in furring cavities 1S, + 3; 2S	+ 5
Plaster on lath on rigid furs 1S, + 6; 2S	+ 10
Plaster on resilient mounts 24" o.c. 1S, + 10; 2S	+ 15
Sand added to cores of any block	+ 3
Double masonry walls w/ 4" airspace btwn withes	+ 15
Add to any masonry: plaster 1S, + 2; 2S	+ 4
Lead, ¹⁄₁₆" thick, 34; Steel, 18 gauge sheet	30
Doors: 1½" hollow core wood, unsealed	19
Gasketed or sealed all around	26
1¾" solid core wood, unsealed	21
Gasketed or sealed all around	29
1¾" hollow metal, unsealed	22
Gasketed or sealed all around	30
2½" acoustical, unsealed	26
Gasketed or sealed all around	38
Windows: ⅛" fixed pane, 21; ¼" plate	26
1" thermopane, 32; ⁹⁄₃₂" laminated glass	36
Operable wood sash w/ ⅛" or ¼" pane:	
Unsealed, 25; sealed all around	28
3½" glass block	40

1. STC variations of 2 dB are slight, 5 dB are noticeable, 10 dB are dramatic.

11. ACOUSTICS

Property of Sound, Velocity:

$$v_t = v_o [1 + (T - 32)/491]^{0.5}$$

v_t = speed of sound through selected medium at given temperature, fps

v_o = speed of sound through selected medium at 32° F (0° C), fps. Sound velocities through several media at 32° F are as follows:

Medium	Velocity, fps	Medium	Velocity, fps
Air	1,087	Water	4,450
Glass or steel	15,600	Pine, dry	3,560
Oak, dry	5,350	Brick or conc.	11,500

T = temperature of selected medium, °F

Property of Sound, Frequency: $v = \lambda f$

v = speed of airborne sound wave, fps
λ = length of airborne sound wave, ft
f = frequency of airborne sound wave, Hz

Property of Sound, Intensity:

$$dB = S - 0.7 - 20 \log D$$

cB = sound intensity level at distance D from source, cB
S = sound intensity level at source, cB
D = distance between sound source and receiver, ft

Property of Sound, Adding Intensities:

$$cB = 10 \log (10^{0.1 \, cB_1} + 10^{0.1 \, cB_2} + ... + 10^{0.1 \, cB_Z})$$

cB = total intensity of all sounds at receiver, cB
cB_1 = sound intensity level of loudest sound, cB
cB_2 = sound intensity level of 2nd loudest sound, cB
cB_Z = sound intensity level of softest sound, etc., cB

When combining sound sources, their powers should be nearly the same; otherwise the contributions of the weaker sources are negligible.

Property of Sound, Relative Intensities:

Step 1. Compute the sound's loudness at a distance from its source.

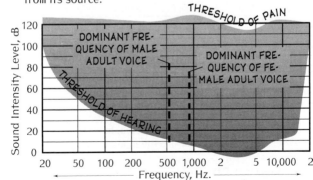

Fig. 11-1. Sound frequency vs. intensity.

$$\text{dB}_n - \text{dB}_f = 20 \log (D_f/D_n)$$

dB_n = sound intensity level at near listener, dB
dB_f = sound intensity level at far listener, dB
D_f = far distance from sound source, ft
D_n = near distance from sound source, ft

Step 2. Compute the distance at which the sound is reduced to the level of human speech.

$$\text{dB}_n - \text{dB}_f = 20 \log (D_f/D_n)$$

dB_n = sound intensity level at near listener, dB
dB_f = sound intensity level at far listener, dB
D_f = far distance from sound source, ft
D_n = near distance from sound source, ft

Note: Over long distances sound intensity decreases as air humidity increases, and this difference is more pronounced at higher frequencies.

Property of Sound, Diffuse Noise:

Step 1. Find the occupancy's diffuse noise level from

$$\text{dB}_L \approx \text{dB}_1 + \log (\eta_1 \times 10^{0.1\ dB1} + ... + \eta_z \times 10^{0.1\ dBz})$$

dB_L = diffuse noise level at listener, dB
dB_1 = sound intensity level of loudest sound, dB
η_1 = number of units of loudest sound
dB_2 = sound intensity level of 2nd loudest sound, dB
η_2 = number of units of 2nd loudest sound
dB_3 = sound intensity level of 3rd loudest sound, dB
η_3 = number of units of 3rd loudest sound
dB_4 = sound intensity level of 4th loudest sound, dB
η_4 = number of units of 4th loudest sound
dB_z = sound intensity level of least loudest sound, dB
η_z = number of units of least loudest sound

Step 2. From the OSHA permissible noise levels listed below, determine if the sound level found in Step 1 is safe for occupants for the duration of time they are exposed to the sound.

Slow-response sound level (dB) vs. safe toler. time (hr)

dB	hr or less	dB	hr or less	dB	hr or less
90	...... 8.0	92	...... 6.0	95	...... 4.0
97	...... 3.0	100	...... 2.0	102	...... 1.5
105	...... 1.0	110	... 30 min	115	... 15 min

Note: Noise levels as low as 75–80 dB may contribute to physical and mental disorders for some people.

Loudness of Airborne Sound:

$$dB = S + 10 \log [Q/(12.6\ D^2) + 4\ ^{(1-\alpha)}/_{\alpha\ A}]$$

dB = loudness of sound at listener, dB
S = loudness of sound at source, dB. If a loudspeaker's nameplate rating is in watts, convert to dB. If more than one speaker is used, find their total power from the first equation on page 470.
Q = directivity factor: a ratio that is often included in equipment specifications, or it may be found for any directional source from Fig. 11-2
D = distance between sound source and listener, ft
α = sound absorption coeff. of all enclosing surfaces
A = surface area of enclosing surfaces, sf

Intensity of Electrically Produced Sound:

$$10 \log E = dB - 119.32 + 20 \log D$$

E = acoustic power level of electric amplifier, watts
dB = sound intensity level at listener, dB
D = distance between sound source and listener, ft

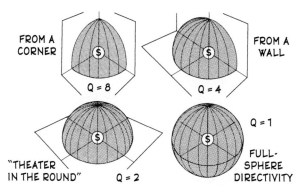

Fig. 11-2. Sound source directivity factors.

Sound Amplification Design:

$$dB = S - 0.7 - 20 \log D$$

dB = req. sound intensity level at max. distance from
source, dB. In listening environments the propa-
gated sound, whether amplified or not, should remain at least 25 dB above background noise levels.
S = intensity level of amplified sound at its source, dB
D = soundpath length from source to farthest seat, ft

Sound Reverberation in Enclosed Spaces:

Step 1. Find the space's reverberation time.

$$\alpha R = 0.049 V$$

α = total sound absorp. of enclosing surfaces, sabins
R = reverb. time of space where sound originates, sec
V = volume of space in which sound originates, cf

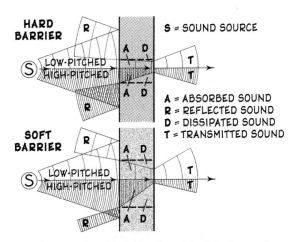

Fig. 11-3. Barrier behavior of incident sound.

TABLE 11-2: SOUND REVERBERATION TIMES

OCCUPANCY	Optimal reverberation time, sec.
Office, home, hospital patient room	0.3–0.5
Broadcast and recording studios	0.4–0.6
Laboratory, hotel lobby, elementary classroom	0.5–0.8
Lecture and conference rooms, cinema	0.6–1.3
Movie theater, restaurant, museum, fine retail	0.8–1.2
Musical comedy, operetta, theatrical production	1.1–1.5
Semi-classical concerts, dances, chorals	1.1–1.8
Recital, chamber music, contemporary orchestra	1.3–1.8
Community church nave	1.3–2.2
Auditorium, gymnasium, ballroom, opera hall	1.4–1.8
Symphony concert, secular choral	1.7–2.1
Cathedral nave, liturgical w/ orchestra, organ	1.9–3.4
Sports arenas, convention halls, large assembly	minimal

Step 2. Compare the space's actual reverberation time with its optimal reverberation time.

$$R_L \leq R \leq R_U$$

R_L = lower limit of desired reverb. time for space
R = actual reverberation time of space, sec
R_U = upper limit of desirable reverb. time for space, sec

Step 3. If the space's reverberation time is too low, select enclosing surfaces with lower absorption coefficients; if too high, select higher coefficients.

Sound Absorption in Enclosed Spaces:

$$\alpha_t \approx \alpha_1 A_1 + \alpha_2 A_2 + \alpha_3 A_3 + \ldots + \alpha_Z A_Z$$

α_t = total absorption of sound by the space, sabins
α_1 = coefficient of sound absorption for 1st enclosing surface. For human conversation, $\alpha \approx 1,000$ Hz.
A_1 = area of 1st enclosing surface, sf
α_2 = coeff. of sound abs. for 2nd enclosing surface
A_2 = area of 2nd surface, sf
α_3 = coeff. of sound abs. for 3rd enclosing surface
A_3 = area of 3rd enclosing surface, sf
α_Z = coeff. of sound abs. for final enclosing surface
A_Z = area of final enclosing surface, sf

Sound Transmission Class:

$$S_{TC} = S - \text{dB}$$

S_{TC} = net STC rating of acoustic barrier construction, from Table 11-1 or 11-3, dB
S = sound intensity level on source side of barrier construction, dB
dB = sound intensity level on destination side of barrier construction, dB

TABLE 11-3: STC & IIC RATINGS OF FLOORS

FLOOR CONSTRUCTION	STC[1]	IIC[1]
Hdwd fin. fl. on plywd on joists, drywall below	37	34
Add to above: w/w carpet on pad, light pile	+ 1	+ 20
Medium pile, + 2 & + 22; Deep pile	+ 3	+ 25
Linol. fin. fl., 0 & + 5; ¼" cork tile fin. fl.	0	+ 10
Fin. fl. on resilient damping	+ 7	+ 2
Fin. fl. on floating sleepers on resil. dmpg	+ 10	+ 8
Batts btwn sleepers or under resil. dmpg	+ 3	+ 1
Resilient channels btwn joists & clg below	+ 10	+ 8
Above w/ 4 in. insulated batts in joist voids	+ 3	+ 7
Plaster on lath ceiling below	+ 2	+ 2
2" concrete on metal deck, 38 & 29; 4" conc.	41	34
4" concrete slab, 41 & 34; 6" slab	46	34
8" precast cellular concrete slab	53	36
Add to any above, wall/wall carpet on pad:		
Light pile, + 4 & + 20; Deep pile	+ 6	+ 30
Linoleum fin. fl., 0 & + 4; ¼" cork tile fin. fl.	0	+ 12
Wood floor on floating sleepers on slab	+ 7	+ 15
Above on resilient damping	+ 12	+ 20
Concrete topping on 1" fiberglass mat or =	+ 10	+ 15
Batts btwn sleepers or under resil. damping	+ 3	+ 1
Modular raised fl. or access fl. panel system	+ 8	+ 5
Fin. ceiling to furring, shallow airspace	+ 7	+ 0
Suspended ceiling w/ deep airspace	+ 7	+ 4
Above on resil. runners or hangers	+ 12	+ 8
Plaster or paint on underside of slab	+ 2	+ 0

IMPACT NOISE LEVELS

Activity	Typical IIC, dB	Activity	Typical IIC, dB
Man's rubber heels	68	Table shoved into wall	77
Foot tapping to music	70	Slamming S/C door	80
Small dropped object	73	Large dropped object	80
Jumping 200 lb adult	83	Woman's spiked heels	85
Woman's 2 in. broad heels	77	Water hammer	94

1. STC variations of 2 dB are slight, 5 dB are noticeable, 10 dB are dramatic.

Acoustic Barrier Construction Design:

$$S_{TC} \approx B + 0.5 \, B \, (^T/_B - 1)$$

S_{TC} = effective STC rating of acoustic barrier const., dB
B = STC rating of portion of barrier construction
with highest STC rating, dB
T = total STC rating of all individual materials or assemblies in barrier construction, dB

Note: For below-average comfort requirements, subtract 4 dB from above values. For above-average comfort requirements, add 3 dB.

Impact Isolation Class:

$$I_{IC} = I_s - I_r - M$$

I_{IC} = required IIC rating of acoustic barrier const., dB
I_s = sound level of impact noise in source space, 85 dB
I_r = tolerable impact noise level in reception space, dB
M = masking level of background noise in reception
space, dB

Step 2. Select an adequate barrier construction for the above sound level.

$$I_{IC} \approx B + 0.5 \, B \, (^T/_B - 1)$$

I_{IC} = effective IIC rating of acoustic barrier const., dB
B = IIC rating of portion of barrier construction w/
highest IIC rating, dB, from Table 11-3
T = total IIC rating of barrier construction, dB

Loudness Limits:
A crucial aspect of acoustic design is the decibel difference between the loudness of generated sounds and the tolerance of received sounds in two adjacent spaces, or *loudness limit*.

TABLE 11-4: LOUDNESS LIMITS OF INTERIOR SPACES

ARCHITECTURAL SPACE OR AREA	Loudness Limits, dB	
	Generation	Reception
Athletic, indoor, amateur & semi-pro	85	50
Auditoriums, churches, courtrooms	82	35
Dressing and rehearsal rooms	74	30
Locker rooms, general offstage	77	40
Set design and offstage areas	83	60
Bars, night clubs, cafeterias	80	50
Concert halls, opera houses	90	35
Circulation areas: halls, stairs, elevators	72	70
Exhibit areas: art galleries, museums	59	36
Hospitals: examination, treatment	80	33
Industrial: service, shipping	78	64
Fabrication, rough and finish	82	60
Kitchens, commercial (res. ≈ 74 and 52)	76	55
Living, dining, and TV areas, residential	77	52
Libraries: reading and study areas	54	32
Catalog areas, copying, checkout	68	50
Lobbies: hotels, banks, post offices	73	60
Mechanical equipment areas	85	70
Museums, fine restaurants	70	35
Music practice areas: choral & orchestral	83	33
Offices, private, managerial	72	33
Semi-private	73	38
Conference rooms, small lecture areas	77	36
Open spaces & reception areas	75	62
Rest rooms, public & private, service areas	73	32
Restaurants	73	55
Retail: shops, discount merchandise	76	54
Boutiques, jewelry stores	72	49
Schools: classrooms, labs, seminars	78	40
Indoor recreation, eating	80	70
Sleeping: separate hotel, motel, hospital	72	28
Bedrooms in suites, houses, apts	72	30
Storage areas, closets	48	58
Studios: broadcast, music recording	76	25

Step 1. List the loudness limits for generation and reception in the two adjacent spaces from Table 11-4. An example is shown below.

Space	Loudness Limit, dB.	
	Generation	Reception
Living, residential	77	 52
Sleeping: separate apts	72	 28

Step 2. Find the barrier construction's STC rating.

$$S_{TC} = \ell_G - \ell_R - 10 \log (A/\alpha)$$

S_{TC} = required STC rating of acoustic barrier const., dB

ℓ_G = loudness limit of louder sound entering barrier construction: highest of four numbers listed in Step 1, dB

ℓ_R = loudness limit of softer sound leaving barrier construction: lowest of four numbers listed in Step 1, dB

A = surface area of barrier construction, sf

α = sound absorption of enclosing surfaces of two adjacent spaces, sabins

Masking of Unwanted Sound:

$$S_{TC} \approx 10 + S_B - I_R - M - 10 \log (A/\alpha)$$

S_{TC} = required STC rating of masked acoustic barrier construction, dB

S_B = STC rating of barrier const. minus masking, dB

I_R = minimum tolerance threshold of sound reception (loudness limit) from adjacent spaces, dB, from Table 11-4

M = masking level of background sound, dB

A = surface area of barrier construction, sf

α = sound absorption of enclosing surfaces of reception space, sabins

Sound Leakage through Openings in Otherwise Solid Construction:

Step 2. Find the actual open area in the construction.

$$A_o = L_1 w_1 + L_2 w_2 + ... + L_z w_z$$

A_o = leakage area of openings (door & window seams, vents, etc.) in acoustic barrier construction, in^2
L_1 = length of 1st seam around opening, in.
w_1 = width of 1st seam around opening, in.
L_2 = length of 2nd seam around opening, in.
w_2 = width of 2nd seam around opening, in.
L_z = length of final seam around opening, in.
w_z = width of final seam around opening, in.

Step 2. Find the percentage of open area in the construction.

$$\% A_s = 100 A_o$$

$\%$ = percentage of open area in barrier const., in^2
A_s = total surface area of barrier construction, in^2
A_o = total open area in barrier construction, in^2

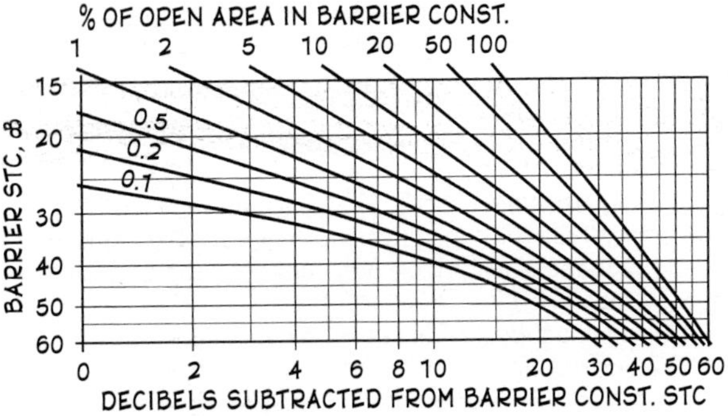

Fig. 11-4. Sound leakage graph.

Step 3. From Fig. 11-4 find the number of ꭰB to be sub-tracted from the barrier construction's STC rating.

Isolation Efficiency of Resilient Mounts for Noise-Producing Machinery:
An average 30 percent of commercial building budgets is spent on mechanical and electrical equipment that makes noise. Operation of these components can turn an otherwise well-designed occupancy into a chaos of vibrations, rumblings, hammerings, buzzes, and whistles. Numerous methods of reducing such unwanted noise are shown in Fig. 11-5. The spring isolators, or resilient mounts, in this drawing are designed as follows.

Step 1. Find the minimum isolation efficiency of the noise-producing machinery as follows:

$$\mathcal{L}_R \, \mathcal{E} \approx 80 \, \mathcal{L}_R + 52 \, (\eta \, \kappa_B)^{0.5}$$

$\mathcal{L}_R$ = loudness limit of sound reception from adjacent spaces, ꭰB, from Table 11-4

$\mathcal{E}$ = isolation efficiency of resilient mount(s), %. $\mathcal{E} \approx$ 85% for single ground-floor unit next to noncritical occupancies to 98.5% for several upper-floor units next to critical occupancies.

η = number of machines within enclosed area

κ_B = barrier factor. $\kappa_B = 1$ if occupied spaces are above ceiling over sound source, 2 if any spaces are behind any adjacent wall up to four walls, and 4 if any spaces exist below floor. Add 12 if other sound sources are within occupied space.

Step 2. Find the typical isolation efficiency of the noise-producing machinery from the data below and compare this value with $\mathcal{E}$ found in Step 1; then use the larger value in subsequent analysis.

Typical Isolation Efficiencies of HVAC Components

Equipment	Isolation efficiency, %
Condensers, fan-coil units, 80; cooling towers	85
Packaged air conditioners, 90; centrifugal compr.	98
Recip. compr: to 15 ℍP = 85, to 60 ℍP = 90, to 150 ℍP =	95
Centrifugal fans: to 200 rpm	90–95
200–350 rpm if fan diameter ≤ 48 in.	70
200–350 rpm if fan diameter ≥ 48 in.	70–80
350–800 rpm	70–90
Absorption units, steam generators, centrifugal pumps, piping, large ducting	95

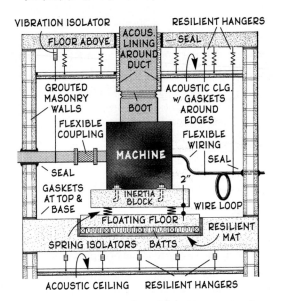

Fig. 11-5. Methods of isolating mechanical noise.

Step 3. Find the resilient mount's desired stroke or static deflection from the formula below.

$$\Delta_m \, \mathcal{E} \, S^2 \; = \; 181{,}000{,}000$$

Δ_m = optimal stroke of resilient mount, in.

$\mathcal{E}$ = isolation efficiency of resilient mount(s), %

S = operating speed of motor or machinery on resilient mount, rpm. If the mount supports more than one machine whose rpms are different, use the lowest rpm.

Step 4. Knowing Δ_b, the maximum deflection of the structure that supports the noise-producing machinery due to its total load, compare Δ_b with the mount's static deflection Δ_m as found in Step 3 according to the formula $0.10 \, \Delta_m \; \leq \; \Delta_b$. If this relation is not satisfied, use $0.10 \, \Delta_b$ in subsequent analysis.

Step 5. From manufacturer's specifications or catalog, select a resilient mount based on its required static deflection and its range of load.

Outdoor Sound Design:

$$N_R \; \approx \; 10 \log (h^2/d) + 10 \log f - 17$$

N_R = noise reduction due to outdoor acoustic barrier construction, dB

h = height of acoustic barrier construction, ft

d = distance from acoustic barrier construction to source or receiver, whichever is less, ft

f = dominant frequency of generated sound, Hz

Note: An outdoor sound barrier reduces sound transmission by an added 3 dB for every octave the dominant frequency increases.

TABLE 12-1: BUILDING OCCUPANCY LOADS

OCCUPANCY	Net area per occ., ft²	Grossing factor, ft²
Apartments	250	1.3
Assembly areas w/o individual seats	7	2.5
Assembly areas w/ individual seats	11	2.3
Standing room areas	5	1.5
Theater stage apron (min. 6 × 28 ft):	250	8
Theater lobbies & other public areas	10	1.2
Ticket booths, each	30	1.8
Dance floors, 12 & 1.5: Gyms & ice rinks	50	1.4
Locker rooms: locker areas	35	1.6
Showers and toilets	25	1.6
Trainer areas, first aid, towel service	10	1.6
Conference & meeting rooms	15	2.0
Taverns and bars, 18 & 1.3; Night clubs	25	1.3
Food service: luncheonettes: seating	12	1.3
Cafeterias, seating	14	1.5
Restaurants: seating	24	1.5
Food serving & disposal areas	6	1.4
Kitchen & food storage areas	8	1.5
Hotels & motels: Lobby areas	10	1.4
Private areas	120	1.4
Hospitals, per bed unit: infirmary areas	125	1.6
Diagnostic and treatment	50	1.5
Industrial: fabrication, storage	200	1.4
Laboratories, educational & industrial	140	1.5
Libraries: open reading rooms, per user	35	1.5
Museums: exhibit areas, per max. visitors	15	1.2
Exhibit preparation	20% of exhibit area	
Offices: private, management	150	1.3
Semiprivate & open, nonmanagement	120	1.3
Retail: ground floor	30	1.4
Upper floors, 50 & 1.2; Basement	20	1.3
Schools: pre-elem., day-care centers	45	1.9
Small classrooms, seminar rooms	20	1.6
Large classrooms	15	1.6

12. DESIGN

Catchments: $C \approx A U I$

C = total catchment or economic potential, \$/yr
A = no. of units in catchment. A may be acreage or square miles determined by halving the distance to similar facilities in every direction, or the number of economic or social entities in a district.
U = number of occupancy units in each area unit
I = potential per occupancy unit

Market Potential: $M U \approx C - F U$

M = unit market potential. This is usually the feasible floor area of the occupancy, sf
U = output per unit area, annual sales/sf
C = total catchment or market potential, \$/yr
F = floor area of competing facilities, if any, sf

Market Penetration Rate:

$$M_P \approx \frac{100\,\eta_u}{\dfrac{N_u\,O_r\,P_i\,N_f}{U_f - N_u\,(1 - O_r)} + \dfrac{N_u}{A_L} + \dfrac{N_n}{t}}$$

M_p = market penetration rate, %
η_u = number of units planned
N_u = number of units in catchment
O_r = occupancy rate of existing units, fraction of unity
P_i = projected annual population increase, %/100
N_f = fraction of newcomers desiring similar units
U_f = fraction of pop. living in similar units as planned
A_l = average lifespan of existing units
N_n = number of similar units presently being planned or built in area
t = average planning & construction time for units

Access Roads, Roadway Design:

$$\kappa_s \approx d_t \kappa_t + d_b \kappa_b + d_{sb} \kappa_{sb}$$

κ_s = strength coefficient of road construction based

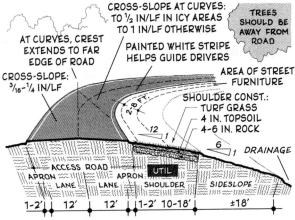

CROSS-SLOPE AT CURVES:
TO ½ IN/LF IN ICY AREAS
TO 1 IN/LF OTHERWISE

TREES SHOULD BE AWAY FROM ROAD

AT CURVES, CREST EXTENDS TO FAR EDGE OF ROAD

PAINTED WHITE STRIPE HELPS GUIDE DRIVERS

CROSS-SLOPE: 3/16–¼ IN/LF

AREA OF STREET FURNITURE

2–8 FT.

SHOULDER CONST.:
TURF GRASS
4 IN. TOPSOIL
4–6 IN. ROCK

12 1

6 1 DRAINAGE

ACCESS ROAD
APRON LANE APRON LANE UTIL SHOULDER SIDESLOPE

1–2' 12' 12' 1–2' 10–18' ±18'

Fig. 12-1. Roadway profile.

on type & speed of traffic flow, from below:

Type of access road use	κ_s
Tract house driveway	1.20
Custom residential driveway	1.40
Employee or res. parking, 10 mph auto travel	1.80
Entries, exits, 20 mph auto travel	2.10
Service yards, 10 mph large truck travel	2.40
Two-lane road for 30–40 mph auto travel	2.90

d_t = depth of road topping, in.
κ_t = layer coefficient for road topping, from next page
d_b = depth of road base, in.
κ_b = layer coefficient for road base, from next page
d_{sb} = depth of road sub-base, in.
κ_{sb} = layer coeff. for road sub-base, from next page

TABLE 12-2: ACCESS ROAD DATA

VEHICULAR SPECIFICATIONS			Dimension, ft
Typical turning radii for vehicles (to outer curb):			
Passenger cars, small trucks (typ. wheelbase = 11 ft)			24
Single-unit trucks, buses (typ. wheelbase = 20 ft)			42
Semitrailer trucks (typical wheelbase = 40 ft)			40
Larger trailer trucks (typical wheelbase = 45 ft)			45

SURFACE GEOMETRY REQUIREMENTS	Design speed, mph			
	10	20	30	40
Roadway lane width, ft	11	12	12	12
Parking lane width, ft	—	8–10	8–10	8–10
Maximum grade, ° slope	12	10	7	5
Min. horizontal curve radius, ft	50	125	273	508
Min. horizontal curve arc, °	17	13.5	9.5	7
Max. horizontal curve arc, °	180	75	32	12.5
Min. vertical crown curve radius, ft	950	2,150	4,250	7,160
Min. stopping sight distance, ft	50	125	200	275
Min. passing sight distance, ft	300	700	1,100	1,500
Min. roadside clear width, ft	12	16	20	25

Layer coeff. κ_t, κ_b, κ_{sb}	Layer coeff. κ_t, κ_b, κ_{sb}
Low-stability road mix, 0.20; Sandy clay 0.10	
High-stability plant mix, 0.44; Sandy gravel .. 0.11	
Sand asphalt, 0.40; 1.5 in. dia. gravel 0.07	
Sand, 0.05; 3–4 in. dia. crushed stone 0.14	

Access Roads, Length vs. Incline:

Step 1. Find the horizontal length of a road whose incline decreases uniformly either from a lower elevation A to zero at its crown or from its crown down to A.

$$E = L_h \, \Delta$$

E = change in elevation of road from pt. A to crown, %
L_h = horiz. length of road from pt. A to crown, ft
Δ = rate of change of uniformly decreasing slope of incline from elevation A to crown, ft/LF

Step 2. Find the incline's elevation at its crown.

$$E_c = E_b + L_A \, \Delta$$

E_c = elevation of uniformly decreasing incline at its crown, ft ASL
E_b = elevation at base of incline at elevation A, ft ASL
    L_A and Δ are as previously defined.

Parking Area Design:

Area, sf: $A = 300 \, S + 400 \, C$
Area, acres: $43{,}560 \, A = 300 \, S + 400 \, C$

A = area of parking, sf or acres
S = number of cars served by street access
C = number of cars served by inner access roads

Sidewalk Design: $W \approx 3 + F + V + 0.0025\,P$

W = optimal width of sidewalk, ft. $W \geq 3$ ft if private
     walk, 5 ft if park & suburban walk, 8 ft if city walk

F = street furniture corridor for any lamp posts, util-
     ity poles, trash bins, mailboxes, etc. located
     along street side of walk, ft. $F \geq 2$ ft.

V = viewing corridor for any store windows, building
     entrances, and other interactive elements along
     outer side of walk, ft. $V \geq 1.5$ ft.

P = maximum projected pedestrian flow, people/hr

Signage Design:

> **Approaching pedestrians:** $H \geq 0.035\,D$
> **Approaching vehicles:**
> $$0.10\,v + 0.004\,v^2 \approx H \geq 0.035\,D$$

H = required height of upper/lower-case lettering to
     be read from a certain distance, in. If highway
     signage contains more than 6 words, multiply H
     by 1.5 for every 6 added words a motorist must
     read to interpret the message.

D = distance between signage and viewer, ft

v = initial velocity of motorist, mph. 1 mph = 1.47 fps.

TABLE 12-3: DESIRABLE PARKING RATIOS

BUILDING TYPE SERVED	Pkg area/gross floor area
Apartments, condominiums	0.4 to 0.7
Assembly halls, churches, theaters	1.4 to 1.9
Hotels and motels: served primarily by autos	1.0 to 1.4
Served primarily by other transportation	0.2 to 0.6
Offices: served primarily by autos	0.9 to 1.1
Served primarily by mass transit	0.3 to 0.6
Shopping centers	2.0 to 2.3

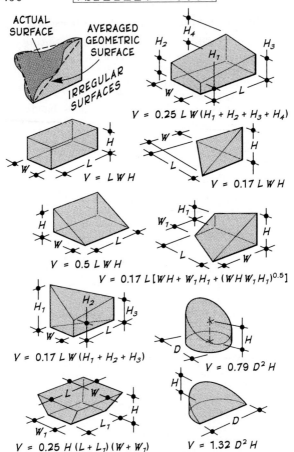

Fig. 12-2. Excavation volume formulas.

ACTUAL SURFACE

AVERAGED GEOMETRIC SURFACE

IRREGULAR SURFACES

$$V = 0.25\,L\,W\,(H_1 + H_2 + H_3 + H_4)$$

$$V = L\,W\,H$$

$$V = 0.17\,L\,W\,H$$

$$V = 0.5\,L\,W\,H$$

$$V = 0.17\,L\,[W\,H + W_1\,H_1 + (W\,H\,W_1\,H_1)^{0.5}]$$

$$V = 0.17\,L\,W\,(H_1 + H_2 + H_3)$$

$$V = 0.79\,D^2\,H$$

$$V = 0.25\,H\,(L + L_1)\,(W + W_1)$$

$$V = 1.32\,D^2\,H$$

Excavation Cuts & Fills: Fig. 12-2 gives formulas for finding excavation and other geometric volumes.

Slope and Ramp Design:

      Required grade of slope: $L \varDelta = 100\ h$
      Required length of ramp: $L = 12\ h + 5\ |0.2\ h|$

L = horiz. length of slope or ramp (incl. landings), ft
$\varDelta$ = uniform grade of slope or ramp, from Table 12-4, %
h = total height btwn start & end of slope or ramp, ft

Length of Curved Ramp or Incline:

Step 1. Find the incline's circumferential length.

$$100\ h = \varDelta\ (L - 12)$$

h = height between ends of ramp, ft
$\varDelta$ = uniform grade of ramp, from Table 12-4, %
L = circumference (horizontal projection) of curved ramp along inside curb, ft

Step 2. Find the radius of the ramp at its inside curb.

$$L = 6.28\ R\ C$$

L = circumference of curved ramp, ft
R = radius of curved ramp to inside curb, ft
C = circle fraction of ramp, fraction of whole. If ramp inscribes arc of $A°$, $C = {}^A/_{360} = 0.00278\ A$.

Staircase Design, Risers & Treads:

Number of risers in a flight: $H \approx 7\ \eta$
Optimal tread width: $R\ T \approx 74$
Optimal riser height: $2.7\ R \approx 24 - [(T - 8)\ (T - 2)]^{0.5}$

TABLE 12-4: SLOPE & RAMP SPECIFICATIONS
ALLOWABLE GRADES

TYPE OF SURFACE	Allow. grade, %
Appears level to the eye; also sidewalks	0–4
Pedestrian ramps, 4-8.33; side incline	4–16.7
Pkg areas: Roofed approaches: curved 1-12; str	1–20
Unroofed access ramps: curved, 1-6; straight	1–10
Driveways: dry, 1-12; wet, 1-10; icy	1–4
Roads: little or no winter ice, 0-12; w/ winter ice	0–8
Grassy recreation areas	1–3
Slopes, gentle grades suitable for construction	4–10
Slopes: grassy, 1-25; w/ ground cover	0–50
Ground sloping away from buildings	2–50
Drainage areas: unpaved or large paved	min. 1.0
Small paved	min. 0.3
Drainage ditches and culverts	2–10
Sewers, dia.: 4-8", 2–15; 8-12"; 0.6–7; 12"+	0.4–4

REQUIRED DIMENSIONS

DIMENSION	Requirement
Pedestrian walks & ramps, maximum slope (Δ)	1:12
Maximum L, ft: Δ = 1:16–1:20, 40; Δ = 1:12–1:16	30
Landings required at top & bottom if $\Delta \geq$ 1:16	
Minimum clear W: up to 10 occupants	2'-6"
Up to 50 occupants, 3'-0"; 50 occ. or more	3'-8"
Aisles in fixed assembly seating, maximum slope	1:5
Landings: min. W, 5'-0"; min. L top & bottom	6'-0"
Minimum lengths of any intermediate landings	5'-0"
Maximum vertical distance btwn any 2 landings	5'-0"
Door swings cannot reduce any minimum landing dimension by more than 3½"	
Handrails, minimum projection from walls	3½"
Minimum space between inside of rail & wall	1½"
Required thickness	1¼ to 2"
Req. height of ₵ above ramp surface	2'-10" to 3'-2"
Handrails req. on both sides if $\Delta \geq$ 1:16 & L $\geq$ 6'-0"	
Surfaces must be rough or non-slip ($\kappa_{fric} \geq$ 0.6)	

H = floor-to-floor height of staircase steps, in.
η = optimal number of risers in staircase, units
R = optimal height of each riser, in. $5.75 \le R \le 8$ in.
T = optimal width of each tread, in. $T \ge 10.0$ in.

Staircase Design, Total Length:

Step 1. Find the number of risers in the staircase.

If straight run:	$H = R\eta$
If equal segmental flights:	$H = R\eta S$
If horseshoe staircase:	$H = R\eta S + 4R$

H = floor-to-floor height of staircase, in.

TABLE 12-5: COMFORTABLE STAIRCASE DIMENSIONS

STAIRCASE COMPONENT	Dimension, in.
Treads: straight run, private stairs up to 10 occ.	11 min.
All public stairs	12 min.
Winding or spiral runs ... 10" min. 12" from narrow end	
Risers: straight runs, all occupancies	$5\frac{3}{4}$–8
Max. diff. btwn largest & smallest rise or run	$\frac{3}{8}$"
Width, minimum clear: private stairs to 10 occ.	30"
All public stairs: < 50 occ., 36; ≥ 50 occ.	44"
Landings: minimum length (L)...... width of stairs to 48"	
Minimum width (W)	≥ stair width
Maximum vertical distance between landings	12'-0"
Door swing cannot reduce landing less than 0.5 W	
Handrails: maximum projection from walls	$3\frac{1}{2}$"
Minimum space between inside of rail & wall	$1\frac{1}{2}$"
Required thickness	$1\frac{1}{4}$ to 2"
Required height above step nosings ... 2'-6" to 2'-10"	
Public stairs up to 88 in. wide require rails both sides	
Wider public stairs req. inner rail every horiz. 88 in.	
Trim, maximum projection from wall	$1\frac{1}{2}$"
Headroom, min. vertical clear above step nosings	6'-8"
Nosings, public ... must be rough or non-slip ($\kappa_{fric} \ge 0.6$)	

R = height of each riser, in. R may need to be adjusted after finding η, then if the tread width T is known, $70 \leq TR \leq 77$. If not, adjust R or T.

η = no. of risers. If not a whole number, make η the next larger or smaller integer then recompute R.

S = no. of equal segments if staircase is in halves, thirds, etc. with landings btwn segments, units

Step 2. Find the length of the staircase, not including any landings.

$$L = T(\eta - 1)$$

L = horizontal length of staircase or segment, in.

T = width of tread, in. 70 must $\leq TR \leq 77$. If not OK, adjust R or T.

η = number of risers in staircase

Escalator Design: There are eight common escalator designs, as described below:

Width & step speed	Capacity	Tread size	Min. landing area
24 in. at 90 fpm	3,500 pers/hr	16 × 16 in.	6 sf
24 in. at 120 fpm	4,400 pers/hr	16 × 16 in.	9 sf
32 in. at 90 fpm	5,000 pers/hr	16 × 24 in.	8 sf
32 in. at 120 fpm	6,250 pers/hr	16 × 24 in.	12 sf
36 in. at 90 fpm	5,750 pers/hr	16 × 28 in.	8 sf
36 in. at 120 fpm	7,200 pers/hr	16 × 28 in.	12 sf
48 in. at 90 fpm	8,000 pers/hr	16 × 40 in.	8 sf
48 in. at 120 fpm	10,000 pers/hr	16 × 40 in.	12 sf

Moving Walk and Ramp Design:

$$\varepsilon \, \textit{HP} \approx 0.01\, C\, (0.00345\, L + 0.4) + 0.0013\, L\, w + 0.6$$

ε = efficiency of moving walk or ramp, usually ≈ 80%

$\textit{HP}$ = horsepower required to operate walk or ramp through horizontal length L, $\textit{HP}$

C = capacity of moving walk or ramp, total live and dead loads, tons/hr
L = horizontal length of moving walk or ramp, ft
w = width of walk or ramp, ft

Elevators, General Design:

Cab area: $\quad 226\ E\ C \approx \kappa_c\ \eta\ A$

E = number of elevators, units
C = estimated optimal area of elevator cab, sf
κ_c = elevator capacity factor, from Table 12-6
η = number of floors in building
A = net area of each floor, sf

Cab depth: $\quad d \approx 0.84\ C^{0.5}$
Cab width: $\quad w \approx 1.18\ C^{0.5}$
Shaft depth: $\quad d_s \approx d + 33$
Shaft width: $\quad w_s \approx w + 24$

d = estimated depth of cab, ft
w = estimated width of cab, ft
C = area of elevator cab, sf
d_s = inside depth of elevator shaft, in.
w_s = inside width of elevator shaft, in.

Cab velocity: $\quad \nu \approx 1.6\ H + 350$

ν = optimal velocity of elevator, fpm. During peak hours an elevator typically has a net velocity of about one-quarter its optimal velocity due to the numerous stops it makes.
H = height of building, ft

Lobby area, main landing: $\quad F\Theta = 5\ \kappa_c\ A\ \eta$
Lobby area, minor landings: $\quad F\Theta = 5\ \kappa_c\ A$

F = minimum floor area of lobby or landing, sf

TABLE 12-6: ELEVATOR SPECIFICATIONS [1]

TYPE OF ELEVATOR (STANDARD RECTANGULAR CABS)

DIMENSION	PASSENGER Trac.	Hyd.	SERVICE (Trac. or Hyd.)	DUMB-WAITER
Capacity, lb....	1,200-4,000+ ea.		2,500-20,000	to 500
Design live load, psf ...	120	120	varies	—
Design area/per, ft^2	2	2	2	—
Velocity, ft/min	to 400+	100 max.	50-200	45-100
Cab width (W), in.				
Cap. ≤ 2,000 lb ..	54 min.	54 min.	—	24-42
Cap. ≥ 2,000 lb ..	68 min.	68 min.	60-144	—
Opening width, in. ..	36-48	42-54	W - 4	W - 4
Shaft width, in.	W + 22	W + 24	W + 20	W + 14
Gate depth, in.	20 typ.	20 typ.	18 typ.	14 typ.
Cab depth (D)^2	51+	52-66	84+	30-36
Shaft depth, in.^{2}....	D + 33	D + 15	D + 15	D + 19
Cab height (H), in.	100 typ.	100 typ.	94 min.	30-48
Opening height, in. ...	84	84	84 min.	H + 2
Max. rise, ft	300 [3]	60	300	30
Penthouse ht, ft	34-36	12	24	14
Pit depth, ft	11-13	4 [4]	6	2.5

ELEVATOR CAPACITY FACTOR

BUILDING TYPE	κ_c	BUILDING TYPE	κ_c
Offices, single-purpose occupancy			0.33
Offices, diverse occupancy			0.22
Apartments, condominiums			0.15
Hotels, motels, ...			0.38
Hospitals			0.12
Parking garages, retail facilities			0.16

1. Specifications are for standard cabs. Custom cabs may have any dimensions.
2. Deeper if cab travel exceeds 400 ft/min.
3. Maximum rise for gearless elevators is unlimited.
4. This does not include the depth of the boring for the plunger.

Θ = occupancy load of floor area served, from Table 12-1, sf/occ.
κ_c = elevator capacity factor, from Table 12-6
A = net area of each floor served by elevator, sf
η = number of floors served by elevator

Traction Elevator Design:
A traction elevator's machine room, penthouse, shafts, pits, and landings are all major spatial components in the parent building and usually comprise more than 10 percent of its cost.

Penthouse floor area: $A_P = 2\,A_S$

A_P = approximate floor area of an elevator's penthouse and adjacent machine room, sf
A_S = floor area of elevator shaft(s) served by penthouse and machine room, sf

Elevator sheave diameter: $\delta_S = 40\,\delta_R$

δ_S = minimum diameter of elevator sheave, in. Maximum diameter is usually limited by cab's maximum velocity and horizontal distance between cab $\cent$ and counterweight $\cent$.
δ_R = diameter of cables that support the cab, in.

Motor speed: $3.82\,\upsilon_c = \delta\,\upsilon_m$

υ_c = maximum velocity of elevator cab, fpm.
δ = diameter of elevator sheave, in.
υ_m = maximum velocity of elevator motor, rpm.

Bucket Elevator Design:
A bucket elevator is much like an escalator with buckets instead of steps: the buckets revolve around a lower and higher drum from which they continually raise a collected load from a lower to a higher level.

Height of travel: $\varepsilon\ HP \approx 0.2\ C\ H$
Length of Travel:
$\varepsilon\ HP \approx 0.01\ C\ (0.00345\ L + 0.4) + 0.0013\ L\ w + 0.6$

ε = efficiency of bucket elevator or conveyer belt machinery, usually about 80%
HP = horsepower required to operate elevator through length of travel (height H or hor. distance L), HP.
C = capacity of elevator or belt: total live and dead load the unit is assumed to carry when its buckets are 60% full, tons/hr
H = height of travel: vertical distance btwn highest and lowest points of the buckets' centroids as they rotate around the upper and lower drums, ft
L = length (horiz. projection) of height of travel, ft
w = width of elevator or belt, ft. w is usually relevant only when the load path is a gentle incline.

Occupancy Loads: A building occupancy's floor areas are defined in several ways. *General Areas* are lobbies, hallways, elevators, stairs, rest rooms, service and mechanical areas, chimneys, shafts, and interior walls measured to the inner faces of exterior walls. *Net Areas* include occupied floorspaces and related storage measured from the outer faces of walls enclosing general areas to the inner faces of exterior walls. *Gross Area* = Net Area + General Area + exterior wall thickness. *Grossing Factor* (also known as *Floor Space Index* or *FSI*) is the ratio of usable space to total space, which equals (Net Area + General Area) ÷ Net Area. Also useful is *Building Efficiency*, which equals 100 percent × net floor area/gross floor area. The grossing factors in Table 12-1 do not consider vertical circulation: these values are slightly less for one-story buildings and slightly more for elevatored buildings.

> **Grossing factor:** $\kappa_g A_{net} = A_{net} + A_{gro}$
> **Building efficiency:** $\varepsilon A_{gro} = 100 A_{net}$
> **Net floor area:** $A_{net} = A_1 + A_2 + ... + A_Z$

κ_g = grossing factor of building or occupancy
A_{net} = net floor area of building or occupancy, sf
A_{gro} = gross floor area of building or occupancy, sf
ε = efficiency of building or occupancy, %
$A_1, A_2, ... A_Z$ = optimal net floor area of each space
      based on its occupancy, from Table 12-1

> **Optimal floor area:** $A = \kappa \, \Theta \, F \kappa_v$

A = optimal floor area of occupancy, sf
κ = grossing factor of occupancy, from Table 12-1
Θ = occupancy load, no. of people
F = optimal floor area per occ., from Table 12-1, sf
κ_v = vertical circulation factor. If area is one floor,
    $\kappa_v \approx 0.9$; if two or three floors, $\kappa_v \approx 1.0$; if build-
    ing has elevators, $\kappa_v \approx 1.1$ to 1.3 (value increas-
    es as number of floors increase).

Seating Capacity of Assembly Area:

$$A \approx 6 \, (\eta^{0.5} + 4)^2$$

A = floorspace required for listening area, sf
η = number of seats in listening area

Waste Handling Area Design:

$$A \approx 7 \, \eta + 50$$

A = estimated floor area of waste handling area, sf
η = number of occupants supplying waste

Opening Areas in Buildings:

Doors, residential entry: At least 6'-8" high, 3'-0" to 4'-0" wide, open at least 90°, 2'-8" clear width when fully open, any added leaves are 2'-0"–4'-0" wide.

Doors, commercial entry: Width (ft) ≥ occupancy load ÷ 50, must contain a minimum 200 in^2 transparent viewing area or have an adjacent sidelight.

> **Windows, total glazing area:** $A_u \geq 0.10 \, A_f$
> **Windows, openable glazing area:** $A_o \geq 0.05 \, A_f$

A_u = min. area of unobstructed glazing excl. frame, sf
A_f = floor area served by glazing, sf
A_o = min. area of openable glass including frame, sf

> **Attic vent areas:** $A_v \geq 0.0067 \, A_f$
> **Crawlspace vent areas:** $A_v \geq 0.02 \, P$

A_v = minimum net free open area of vents, sf
A_f = floor area served by vents, sf
P = perimeter length of foundation wall, ft

Plan Geometry:

Square or rectangle. This module is typically a checkerboard grid whose lines are equally spaced.

Hexagon. When circular areas of uniform size are close-packed in a plane, their most efficient arrangement is a hexagonal grid. This organic fact was not lost on Frank Lloyd Wright, as evidenced by his beautiful hexagonal plans for the Hanna House in California and Palmer House in Michigan.

Octagon. This geometry combines the construction simplicity of the square and the movement fluidity of the curve. One may dimension any part of an octagon by using the numerical ratios in Fig. 12-3. Some of

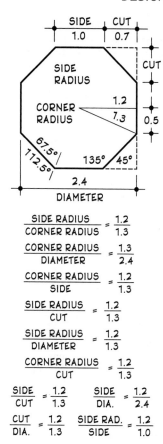

$$\frac{\text{SIDE RADIUS}}{\text{CORNER RADIUS}} = \frac{1.2}{1.3}$$

$$\frac{\text{CORNER RADIUS}}{\text{DIAMETER}} = \frac{1.3}{2.4}$$

$$\frac{\text{CORNER RADIUS}}{\text{SIDE}} = \frac{1.2}{1.3}$$

$$\frac{\text{SIDE RADIUS}}{\text{CUT}} = \frac{1.2}{1.3}$$

$$\frac{\text{SIDE RADIUS}}{\text{DIAMETER}} = \frac{1.2}{1.3}$$

$$\frac{\text{CORNER RADIUS}}{\text{CUT}} = \frac{1.2}{1.3}$$

$$\frac{\text{SIDE}}{\text{CUT}} = \frac{1.2}{1.3} \qquad \frac{\text{SIDE}}{\text{DIA.}} = \frac{1.2}{2.4}$$

$$\frac{\text{CUT}}{\text{DIA.}} = \frac{1.2}{1.3} \qquad \frac{\text{SIDE RAD.}}{\text{SIDE}} = \frac{1.2}{1.0}$$

Fig. 12-3. Geometry of the octagon.

these ratios are inaccurate by less than 1.0 percent, which is negligible in perception and construction.

Golden Section. In 1948 Le Corbusier invented *Le Modulor*, a series of "divine ratio" numbers based on "well-shaped human bodies" 72 in. tall which he used to design buildings that were comfortable and beautiful. In order that these European-invented numbers may be more compatible with American building practice, this author added to Le Modulor's RED and BLUE columns PINK and PURPLE columns to create the *Modified Modular* which appears in Table 12-7 on the next page.

TABLE 12-7: THE MODIFIED MODULAR

MODULAR DIMENSIONS, BASED ON HT. OF 72 IN.

PINK	RED	BLUE	PURPLE
		1, 2, 3, 5	
	4	8	18
14	6.5 (6)	13	30
24	10.5 (10)	21 (20)	48
38	17 (16)	34	78
62	27.5 (28)	55 (54)	
100	44.5 (44)	89 (88)	
	72	144	

MODULAR UNIT OR ACTIVITY   Aver. adult dimension, in

Heights: door/window header, 78; coffee table 13
  Window sill or low wall by standing adult ..... 48 or 55
  Window sill or low wall by seated adult 34, 44, 48
  Closet rod or coat hook, 62; wall storage ... up to 78
  Shoulder-high partition , 55, 62; full open wall ... 78
  Countertop: 34, 38; Table: 28, 30, Seat or chair 17
  Eye level above floor: stdng. adult, 62; std. adult 44
Widths and reaches: aisle width: resi: 38, 44; comm'l 62
  Width of adult: 24 at shldrs, 21 at thighs, 17 at knees
  Standing frontal reach, body to shelf 24
  Seated frontal reach: normal 17, extended or leaning 24
  From back of seated adult to edge of table 17
  Leg room, i.e. btwn edge of sofa & coffee table 13, 17
Horizontal areas: Counter task area for one (on desk,
    table, vanity, workbench, etc) .... 17 × 27
  Access area along sides or back of above .. 10, 14, 17
  Stg area: stool, 13 dia; chair, 17 × 17; sofa .. 24 × 24
  Bed size: single .... (38 or 44) × (72 or 78)
    Double .... (54 or 62) × (72 or 78)
  Area of toilet compartment .... 30 × 54
  Area of bathroom sink compartment .... (30 or 38) × 48
Clearances: toes under cabinets .... 3 H, 5 W, 4 D
  Knees under counters .... 24 H, 27 W, 13 D

A. USEFUL FORMULAS

Exponential Relations:

$$a^m a^n = a^{m+n} \qquad a^m/a^n = a^{m-n}$$
$$a^p a^q/a^r = a^{p+q-r} \qquad (a^m)^n = a^{mn}$$
$$1/a^m = a^{-m} \qquad (a\,b)^m = a^m b^m$$

Quadratic Equation:

$$x = \frac{-b \pm (b^2 - 4\,a\,c)^{0.5}}{2\,a} \quad \begin{array}{l} \text{when } a\,x^2 + b\,x + c = 0 \\ \text{and } a \neq 0 \end{array}$$

Logarithms: A logarithm is the inverse of an exponential. Thus $x = a^y$ becomes $y = \log_a x$. Any positive number except 1 can be the base of a logarithmic function, but the two most common are 10 and e (= 2.71828). A logarithm has a *characteristic* (its integer portion) and a *mantissa* (its decimal portion). The characteristic describes what power of 10 the mantissa is taken to, and the mantissa describes the logarithm's value between 1 and 10. Thus in the logarithm 2.345, 2. indicates that the mantissa is multiplied by 10 to the 2nd power and .345 indicates that the logarithm's value between 1 and 10 is 2.213; thus $\log_{10} 2.345 = 10^2 \times 2.213 = 221.3$.

$$\log (xy) = \log x + \log y \qquad \log_{10} e = 0.4343$$
$$\log (x/y) = \log x - \log y \qquad \log_e 10 = 2.3026$$

To find a number's common logarithm: $\log_{10} A = B$
To change $\log_{10}$ to $\log_e$: $2.3026 \times \log_{10} = \log_e$

Angles: If an angle is less than 90°, it is *acute*; if 90° it is *right*; if more than 90° it is *obtuse*; if 180° it is a *straight line*. If two angles differ by 360°, they are *congruent*, which is indicated by the sign ≅ (e.g. 30° ≅ 390°).

All Triangles: A triangle is a polygon with three sides and three angles. If none of a triangle's sides are equal it is *scalene*; if two sides are equal it is *isosceles*; if all three sides are equal it is *equilateral*. If one of a triangle's three angles is 90° it is a *right* triangle; if one angle is greater than 90° it is an *obtuse* triangle; if all angles are less than 90° it is an *acute* triangle. The branch of mathematics that is concerned with solving triangles is trigonometry.

Any Triangle:

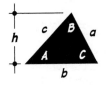

$$\sin 2\angle = 2 \sin \angle \cos \angle$$
$$\cos 2\angle = \cos^2 \angle - \sin^2 \angle$$
$$a/\sin A = b/\sin B = c/\sin C$$
$$a^2 = b^2 + c^2 - 2bc \cos A$$
$$\sin (A + B) = \sin A \cos B + \cos A \sin B$$
$$\sin (A - B) = \sin A \cos B - \cos A \sin B$$
$$\cos (A + B) = \cos A \cos B - \sin A \sin B$$
$$\cos (A - B) = \cos A \cos B + \sin A \sin B$$
$$\text{Area} = 0.5\, bh = 0.5\, a\,(c^2 - a^2)^{0.5} = 0.5\, b\,(c^2 - b^2)^{0.5}$$
$$= 0.25\,[(a + b + c)\,(- a + b + c)\,(a - b + c)\,(a + b - c)]^{0.5}$$

Right-Angle Triangles:

sine or sin $\angle$ = OPP/HYP = Q and Q is ≤ 1.00
cosine or cos $\angle$ = ADJ/HYP = Q and Q is ≤ 1.00
tangent or tan $\angle$ = OPP/ADJ = Q is 0 to ∞
cosecant or csc $\angle$ = 1/sin $\angle$ = Q is ≥ 1.00
secant or sec $\angle$ = 1/cos $\angle$ = Q and Q is ≥ 1.00
cotangent or cot $\angle$ = 1/tan $\angle$ = Q is 0 to ∞

$$\tan^2 \angle + 1 = \sec^2 \angle \qquad \sin^2 \angle + \cos^2 \angle = 1$$
$$\cot^2 \angle + 1 = \csc^2 \angle \qquad A^2 + B^2 = C^2$$

$\angle$ = value of angle, °
OPP = side opposite angle $\angle$
ADJ = side adjacent angle $\angle$
HYP = hypotenuse

HYP: C
OPP: B
ADJ: A

Equilateral Triangles:

$a = b = c$
All three angles = 60°.
Height: $h = 0.866\ a$
Area: $\underline{A} = 0.433\ a^2$

Isosceles Triangles:

side a = side b
angle A = angle B.
Height: $h = (a^2 + 0.5\ c^2)^{0.5}$
Area: $\underline{A} = 0.5\ c\ h$
$= 0.5\ a \sin A$
$C = 2 \sin^{-1} (0.5\ ^c/_a)$

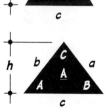

Four-Sided Figures (Quadrilaterals): If a
four-sided figure has equal sides and 90° angles, it is a
square. If it has equal sides and no 90° angles, it is a

rhombus. If its angles are 90° and its adjacent sides are unequal, it is a *rectangle*. If its adjacent sides are unequal and it has no 90° angles, it is a *rhomboid* or *parallelogram*. If two opposite sides of the figure are parallel, it is a *trapezoid*; if the two remaining sides equal each other, the figure is an *isosceles trapezoid*.

Squares:

Area .... $A = s^2 = 0.5\,d^2$
Perimeter ..... $P = 4\,s$
Length of diagonal $d = 1.414\,s$
$\quad d = 1.414\,\underline{A}^{0.5} = 0.354\,P$
Length of side
$s = 0.707\,d = \underline{A}^{0.5} = 0.250\,P$

Rectangles:

Area .... $\underline{A} = b\,h$
Perimeter ..... $P = 2\,(b + h)$
Length of diag. $d = (b^2 + h^2)^{0.5}$
Length of base $b = (d^2 - h^2)^{0.5}$
Height .... $h = (d^2 - b^2)^{0.5}$

Parallelograms:

Altitude ... $h = r \sin \alpha$
Area ...... $\underline{A} = r\,s\,\sin \alpha$
Perimeter $P = 2\,(r + s)$
Length of long diagonal
$D = (r^2 + s^2 - 2\,r\,s\,\cos \beta)^{0.5}$
Length of short diagonal
$d = (r^2 + s^2 - 2\,r\,s\,\cos \alpha)^{0.5}$

Trapezoids:

Area of trapezoid
  $\underline{A}$ = 0.5 h (B + b)
Length of a shorter side
  r = $(h^2 + n^2)^{0.5}$
Length of a longer side
  s = $(h^2 + m^2)^{0.5}$

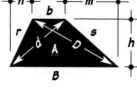

Length of shorter diagonal ... d = $[h^2 + (b + n)^2]^{0.5}$
Length of longer diagonal ... D = $[h^2 + (b + m)^2]^{0.5}$

Any $\angle$ cos $\angle$ = $\dfrac{(s_{1st\ side})^2 + (s_{2nd\ side})^2 - (d_{opp.\ diag.})^2}{2\,(s_{1st\ side})\,(s_{2nd\ side})}$

h = height of trapezoid
B = length of base of trapezoid
b = length of cap of trapezoid

Regular Polygons: A regular polygon is a planar figure with the same number of equal sides and equal angles. A three-sided regular polygon is an *equilateral triangle*, a four-sided one is a *square*, and a five-sided one is a *pentagon*. Others are:

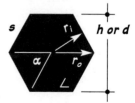

  6 sides = *hexagon*
  7 sides = *heptagon*
  8 sides = *octagon*
  9 sides = *nonagon*
  10 sides = *decagon*
  12 sides = *duodecagon*

Parts of regular polygons are:

Side (s) = the equal edges that form a polygon's
    perimeter; their number defines the polygon.
Vertex = an angle formed by two adjacent sides.

Base = the side on which the polygon stands.

Altitude or *height* (*h*) = the perpendicular distance from its base to its highest corner or edge.

Diagonal = a straight line joining any two nonadjacent angles.

Outer radius (*R*) = distance from the polygon's center to any corner.

Inner radius (*r*) = distance from its center to the center of any side.

Interior angle (*α*) = the inside of an outer corner angle formed by two adjacent sides.

Central angle (θ) = an angle formed by two radii extending to two adjacent corners.

Inscribed polygon = a regular polygon drawn inside a circle so its corners coincide with the circle's circumference.

Circumscribed polygon = a regular polygon drawn outside a circle so the centers of its sides coincide with the circle's circumference.

Perimeter of regular polygon .... $P = s\,n$

Central angle .... $\angle = 360/n$

Length of outer radius .... $r_o = s/2 \sin(180/n)$

Length of inner radius .... $r_i = s/2 \tan(180/n)$

Interior $\angle$ between two sides ..... $\angle = 180(1 - 2/n)$

Area .... $A = n\,r_i^2 \tan(180/n)$

s = length of each side of regular polygon
n = number of sides in regular polygon
α = angle formed by 2 radii to 2 adj. outer corners, °
r_o = length of outer radius (radius to corner)
r_i = length of inner radius (radius to center of side)
$\angle$ = inner angle formed by two adjacent sides, °
A = area of regular polygon, in^2

Circles: A circle is a locus of points (circumference) equidistant (radius) from a fixed point (center). A small part of a circle's radius is an *arc*, an area bounded by an arc and its end radii is a *sector*, and an area bounded by an arc and a chord is a *segment*.

Equation of circle (center at $x = 0$, $y = 0$) $r^2 = x^2 + y^2$

Area of circle .... $A = 0.785\ \delta^2$

Circumference of circle .... $c = 3.14\ \delta$

Length of chord $e = \delta \sin 0.5 \angle = \delta \sin (14.32\ \widehat{a}/\delta)$

Height of segment .... $h = \delta (0.5 - \cos 0.5 \angle)$

Area of segment $A_{seg} = 0.00873\ r^2 \angle - (r - r\cos 0.5 \angle)^2$

Area of sector ... $A_{sec} = 0.00873\ r^2 \angle$

Length of arc ... $\widehat{a} = 0.00873\ \delta \angle$

δ = diameter of circle
h = height of segment
$\angle$ = central angle subtended by arc, chord, segment, or sector of circle, °

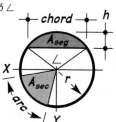

Ellipses: An ellipse is a locus of points placed so the sum of their distances from two fixed points, or foci, is a constant.

Equation of ellipse (center at $x = 0$, $y = 0$):

$$\frac{x^2}{a^2} + \frac{y^2}{b^2} = 1$$

Area of ellipse: $A = 3.14\ a\ b$

Circum.: $c = 4.44\ (a^2 + b^2)^{0.5}$

a = length of major axis
b = length of minor axis

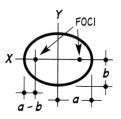

Rectangular Solids: A rectangular solid is a six-sided geometric figure whose every side is a rectangle. Thus the six sides together have 4 "*X*" edges, 4 "*Y*" edges, and 4 "*Z*" edges; and the four edges in each orthogonal direction are equal and parallel to each other. At any corner the angle formed by the three orthogonal planes is a *trihedral angle*; wherein the planes' point of intersection is the angle's *vertex*, the planes' intersecting faces are the angle's *edges*, the angle between any two adjacent edges is a *face angle*, and the angle between two intersecting faces is a *dihedral angle*. This nomenclature is the same for any geometric solid whose surface is made of planar faces. A trihedral angle is also a three-faced polyhedral angle, while a four-faced polyhedral angle is a *tetrahedral angle*; a five-faced one is a *pentahedral angle*, and so on.

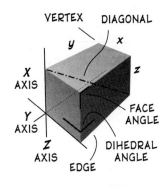

Surface area .... $A = 2(xy + xz + yz)$
Volume .... $V = xyz$
Diagonal .... $d = (x^2 + y^2 + z^2)^{0.5}$

x = length of side that is parallel to *X*-axis
y = length of side that is parallel to *Y*-axis
x = length of side that is parallel to *Z*-axis
d = length of diagonal

Pyramids: A pyramid has a polygonal base with a line extending from each corner to a common apex above. In a regular pyramid the base is a regular polygon and the apex is directly above its center. A three-sided pyramid is a triangular pyramid; and a four-sided one may be square, rhombic, rectangular, or parallelogramic. If a plane parallel to a pyramid's base passes between its base and its apex, the lower figure is a *frustum of a pyramid.*

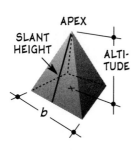

Total surface area of regular pyramid:

$$A = 0.50\ n\,r^2 \sin (360/n) + 0.50\ s\,n\,b$$

Volume of regular pyramid:

$$V = 0.167\ h\,n\,r^2 \sin (360/n)$$

Total surface area of frustum of regular pyramid:

$$A_f = 0.50\ s\ (\text{lower base perimeter} + \text{upper base perimeter}) + 0.50\ (B_l + B_u)$$

Volume of frustum of regular pyramid:

$$V_f = 0.333\ h\,[B_l + B_u + (B_l\,B_u)^{0.5}]$$

n = number of sides in base of regular pyramid
r = radius of base: length from center to each corner
s = slant height of each lateral face: distance from center of face's base to pyramid's apex
b = length of side of base
B_l = area of lower base [= $0.5\ n\,r^2 \sin (360/n)$] of frustum of pyramid
B_u = area of upper base of frustum of pyramid

Cylinders:

Cylinders: A cylinder is generated by a straight line that traces a closed curve of any shape that lies between two parallel end planes or bases. The resulting form may be as tall and thin as a metal rod, or as short and wide as a manhole cover. If the curve is a circle the figure is a *circular cylinder*; if its sides are perpendicular to the planes it is a *right cylinder*; and if the sides extend at an angle between the end planes the figure is an *oblique cylinder*. In a circular right cylinder, the circle's axis extends through the cylinder's center; then the axis' length and the circle's radius define the solid. The area of the side is the cylinder's *lateral area*, the sums of the two base areas is its *base area*, and the sums of the lateral and base areas are its *total area*. A cylinder may also be cut lengthwise to form a trough or tunnel shape.

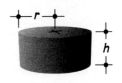

Lateral surface area of circ. cylinder ... $S = 6.28\, r\, h$

Total surface area of circ. cylinder $A = 6.28\, r\,(r + h)$

Volume of circular cylinder .... $V = 3.14\, r^2\, h$

r = radius of base of circular cylinder

h = height of cylinder: perpendicular distance between end planes